taste of home

healthy
cooking

2009
annual
recipes

2009 Healthy Cooking Annual Recipes

©2009 Reiman Media Group, Inc.
5400 S. 60th St., Greendale WI 53129

International Standard Book Number (10):
0-89821-637-0

International Standard Book Number (13):
978-0-89821-637-0

International Standard Serial Number: 1944-7736

Printed in U.S.A.

Cover Photography
Photographers: Jim Wieland, Dan Roberts
Food Stylists: Kaitlyn Besasie, Diane Armstrong
Set Stylist: Dee Dee Jacq

Pictured on Front Cover:
Rustic Italian Tortellini Soup (p. 37); Caramel Toffee Ice Cream Pie (p. 235); Special Radicchio-Spinach Salad (p. 57) and Chicken Artichoke Pasta (p. 101).

Pictured on Back Cover:
Chutney Turkey Burgers (p. 269); Corn & Pepper Orzo (p. 66); Pumpkin Oat Bran Muffins (p. 195) and Tortellini with Salmon-Ricotta Sauce (p. 166).

For other Taste of Home books and products, visit:
ShopTasteofHome.com

Editor in Chief
Catherine Cassidy

Vice President & Executive Editor/Books
Heidi Reuter Lloyd

Creative Director
Ardyth Cope

Food Director
Diane Werner

Senior Editor/Books
Mark Hagen

Editor/Healthy Cooking
Mary Spencer

Art Director
Gretchen Trautman

Content Production Supervisor
Julie Wagner

Design Layout Artists
Nancy Novak, Kathleen Bump

Proofreader
Linne Bruskewitz

Recipe Asset Systems
Coleen Martin, Sue A. Jurack

Premedia Supervisor
Scott Berger

Recipe Testing & Editing
Taste of Home Test Kitchen

Food Photography
Taste of Home Photo Studio

Editorial Assistant
Barb Czysz

Chief Marketing Officer
Lisa Karpinski

Vice President/Book Marketing
Dan Fink

Creative Director/Creative Marketing
Jim Palmen

The Reader's Digest Association, Inc.
President and Chief Executive Officer
Mary G. Berner

President, RDA Food & Entertaining
Suzanne M. Grimes

President, Consumer Marketing
Dawn Zier

Featuring recipes for everything from snacks to desserts and from weekday breakfasts to weekend dinner parties, this brand-new cookbook promises to keep you on the path of healthy eating for years to come.

Contents

Eating right is a breeze with the incredible variety of recipes in this new cookbook.
Not only have we kept the best of "Light & Tasty Annual Recipes,"
but we've added plenty of extras to help you plan your family's menus.

Welcome to the debut edition of *Healthy Cooking Annual Recipes*, a colorful cookbook that was created for you and readers of the former *Light & Tasty* magazine.

When we asked how to make *Light & Tasty* better, you said you wanted to eat and live healthier. Your suggestions prompted us to transform the magazine into *Taste of Home Healthy Cooking*. This cookbook is a compilation of a year's worth of recipes, informational nuggets and kitchen tips to help you reach your overall health goals. We even rounded out the book by adding several bonus recipes that didn't appear in *Healthy Cooking*.

After all, eating right isn't just about counting the calories in the food you eat. It's about getting the nutrients and energy you need each day, plus getting enough variety to avoid boredom and feeling truly satisfied with what you eat.

In other words, if it's a weeknight meal, quick and easy is OK, but if it's a special occasion, the food has to be special, too—in addition to good for you. No problem. Just turn to our chapter called "Celebrate" and you'll find dozens of recipes, menus and food ideas for holidays and other gatherings.

And, finally, we know there will be days when you'll crave something sweet. Eating a cookie or brownie shouldn't derail your healthy eating plan. So, flip to the "Treat Yourself" chapter for all of the satisfaction and none of the guilt. You'll be happy with the tasty tidbit and yourself.

This cookbook meets every culinary need you'll face while living a healthy lifestyle. Just take a look inside. You'll find:

• More makeover recipes than ever before, from appetizers all the way through desserts.

• Easy-to-spot icons that highlight recipes that are particularly low in fat, sodium or even carbohydrates.

• A meatless icon to help with meal planning when looking to cut back a bit on meat.

• Recipes that address food allergies and ways to accommodate them.

• Family-friendly menus and inspiring stories in the chapter "My Healthy Life."

• An entire chapter devoted to incredible dishes that are table-ready in just half an hour.

• Entrees, side dishes and sweets that are sized right for a pair in the "Table for Two" chapter.

• Dozens of hints for lightening up your tried-and-true family favorites at home.

• 489 sensational recipes in all, perfect for any day and any occasion.

We hope you enjoy this refreshing collection of recipes, menus and hints as much as we've enjoyed bringing it to you. In addition, we hope this new cookbook inspires you to bring a little healthy cooking into your kitchen each and every day.

Peggy Woodward, RD

Food Editor, *Healthy Cooking*

Nutrition Facts Nuggets

Nutritional Guidelines

Every recipe in *Healthy Cooking Annual Recipes* fits the lifestyle of health-conscious cooks. The recipes represent a variety of foods that will fit into any meal plan that is within the standards of the USDA's "My Pyramid Plan" for moderately active adults (see box below). The target nutritional content of recipes, on a per serving basis, is:

- 400 calories (or less)
- 12 grams of fat (or less)
- 1,000 mg sodium (or less)
- 100 mg cholesterol (or less)

How We Calculated the Nutrition Facts

- Whenever a choice of ingredients is given in a recipe (such as 1/3 cup of sour cream or plain yogurt), the first ingredient listed is always the one calculated in the Nutrition Facts.
- When a range is given for an ingredient (such as 2 to 3 teaspoons), we calculate the first amount given.
- Only the amount of marinade absorbed during preparation is calculated.
- Garnishes listed in recipes are generally included in our calculations.

Diabetic Exchanges

All recipes in this book have been reviewed by a Registered Dietitian. Diabetic Exchanges are assigned to recipes in accordance with guidelines from the American Diabetic and American Dietetic Associations. The majority of recipes in *Healthy Cooking Annual Recipes* are suitable for diabetics.

Special Diet Indicators

To help those on restricted diets easily find dishes to suit their needs, we clearly indicate recipes that are low in carbohydrates, fat or sodium or those that contain no meat. You'll find these colored special diet indicators after the recipe title where appropriate:

F One serving contains 3 grams or less of fat

S One serving contains 140 milligrams or less of sodium

C One serving contains 15 grams or less of carbohydrates

M Appetizers, salads, savory breads, side dishes and entrees that contain no meat

---

Your Serving Size Guide

This list is a general guide for healthy eating for most adults.

Grains
1 bread slice, pancake or waffle
Half of an average bagel (the size of a hockey puck)
1 cup dry cereal
1/2 cup cooked cereal, rice or pasta

Vegetables
1 cup raw leafy greens
1/2 cup of any chopped vegetable, raw or cooked
6-ounce glass of vegetable juice
1 small potato

Fruits
1 medium piece of fruit
1/2 cup sliced fruit
6-ounce glass of orange juice or any 100% fruit juice

Dairy
8-ounce container of yogurt
1/2 cup cottage cheese
1-1/2 ounces cheese (size of two dominoes)
8-ounce glass of milk

Meat and Beans
3 ounces cooked lean meat, poultry or fish (size of a deck of cards)
2 tablespoons peanut butter
1/2 cup beans

Daily Nutrition Guide

	Women 25–50	Women over 50	Men over 24
Calories	2,200	1,900	2,900
Fat	73 g or less	63 g or less	96 g or less
Saturated Fat	24 g or less	21 g or less	32 g or less
Cholesterol	300 mg or less	300 mg or less	300 mg or less
Sodium	2,400 mg or less	2,400 mg or less	2,400 mg or less
Carbohydrates	335 g	283 g	446 g
Fiber	20–30 g	20–30 g	20–30 g
Protein	50 g	50 g or less	63 g

This chart is only a guide. Calorie requirements vary, depending on age, weight, height and amount of activity. Children's dietary needs vary as they grow.

MAKEOVER GREEN OLIVE TAPENADE

MINI APPLE STRUDELS

MINI RASPBERRY MOUSSE PARFAITS

Starters & Snacks

Cheers to good food...and good health! Watching what you eat doesn't mean passing up appetizer buffets altogether. You can feel free to enjoy the party with this delicious selection of savory hors d' oeuvres and refreshing beverages.

Mini Raspberry Mousse Parfaits [S]

PREP: 30 min. + chilling **YIELD:** 4 servings

HEALTHY COOKING TEST KITCHEN

Sweet, tart and delicious, this elegant recipe is the perfect finish to a special meal. Better still, the parfaits can be made ahead for easy entertaining.

1-3/4	cups fresh or frozen unsweetened raspberries, thawed
3	Tbsp. sugar
2	tsp. cornstarch
2	tsp. orange juice
1-1/3	cups whipped topping
1/3	cup cubed angel food cake (1/2-in. cubes)

1. Press raspberries through a strainer and discard seeds and pulp. In a small saucepan, combine sugar and cornstarch; stir in raspberry puree. Bring to a boil; cook and stir for 2 minutes or until thickened. Refrigerate until chilled.

2. Divide raspberry mixture in half. Stir orange juice into one portion; set aside. Place remaining mixture in a small bowl; fold in whipped topping.

3. Divide angel food cake among four small cocktail glasses or dessert dishes. Layer each with a scant tablespoon of reserved raspberry-orange mixture and 1/3 cup creamy mixture. Refrigerate until serving.

Nutrition Facts: 1 parfait equals 143 calories, 4 g fat (4 g saturated fat), 0 cholesterol, 29 mg sodium, 24 g carbohydrate, 1 g fiber, 1 g protein. **Diabetic Exchanges:** 1 starch, 1 fat, 1/2 fruit.

Creamy Cucumber Yogurt Dip [C] [M]

PREP: 15 min. + chilling **YIELD:** 1-3/4 cups

DONNA ROBERTS • SHUMWAY, ILLINOIS

Everything about this dip is good. It's not only lower in fat and low-calorie, it's also fast to prepare and fantastic to eat.

1	carton (8 oz.) reduced-fat plain yogurt
4	oz. reduced-fat cream cheese
1/2	cup chopped seeded peeled cucumber
1-1/2	tsp. finely chopped onion
1-1/2	tsp. snipped fresh dill or 1/2 tsp. dill weed
1	tsp. lemon juice
1	tsp. grated lemon peel
1	garlic clove, minced
1/4	tsp. salt
1/4	tsp. pepper

Assorted fresh vegetables

1. In a small bowl, combine yogurt and cream cheese. Stir in the cucumber, onion, dill, lemon juice, peel, garlic, salt and pepper.

2. Cover and refrigerate until chilled. Serve with the vegetables.

Nutrition Facts: 1/4 cup (calculated without vegetables) equals 63 calories, 4 g fat (3 g saturated fat), 13 mg cholesterol, 176 mg sodium, 3 g carbohydrate, trace fiber, 4 g protein. **Diabetic Exchange:** 1 fat.

Makeover Green Olive Tapenade [C]

PREP/TOTAL TIME: 10 min. **YIELD:** 1-3/4 cups

TERESA SPENCER • OCONOMOWOC, WISCONSIN

This quick-to-fix recipe offers an excellent way to create a fancy and full-flavored appetizer. It's perfect with wine and other drinks. Best of all, I can enjoy all the olives in the Tapenade without guilt.

2	Tbsp. olive oil
1	Tbsp. water
1	Tbsp. lemon juice
2	anchovy fillets
1	garlic clove, peeled
1/4	tsp. pepper

Dash sugar

2	cups pimiento-stuffed olives
14	slices French bread (1/2 in. thick), toasted

1. In a food processor, combine the first seven ingredients; cover and process until smooth.

2. Add olives; cover and pulse until coarsely chopped. Serve with toasted French bread.

Nutrition Facts: 2 tablespoons tapenade with 1 slice bread equals 87 calories, 6 g fat (trace saturated fat), trace cholesterol, 501 mg sodium, 8 g carbohydrate, trace fiber, 1 g protein.

Baked Potato Pizza

PREP: 25 min. **BAKE:** 25 min. **YIELD:** 12 pieces

CHARLOTTE GEHLE • BROWNSTOWN, MICHIGAN

I wanted to re-create a light version of a restaurant pizza my friends and I used to get all the time in college. Here's what I came up with!

- 3 medium potatoes, peeled and cut into 1/8-in. slices
- 1 loaf (1 lb.) frozen pizza dough, thawed
- 3 Tbsp. reduced-fat butter
- 4 garlic cloves, minced
- 1/4 tsp. salt
- 1/4 tsp. pepper
- 1 cup (4 oz.) shredded part-skim mozzarella cheese
- 1/4 cup shredded Parmigiano-Reggiano cheese
- 6 turkey bacon strips, cooked and crumbled
- 2 green onions, chopped
- 2 Tbsp. minced chives

Reduced-fat sour cream, optional

1. Place the potato slices in a small saucepan and cover with water. Bring to a boil. Reduce the heat; cover and simmer for 15 minutes or until tender. Drain and pat slices dry.

2. Unroll dough onto a 14-in. pizza pan coated with cooking spray; flatten dough and build up edges slightly. In a microwave-safe bowl, melt butter with garlic; brush over dough.

3. Arrange potato slices in a single layer over dough; sprinkle with salt and pepper. Top with cheeses. Bake at 400° for 22-28 minutes or until crust is golden and cheese is melted.

4. Sprinkle with bacon, onions and chives. Serve with sour cream if desired.

Editor's Note: This recipe was tested with Land O'Lakes light stick butter.

Nutrition Facts: 2 pieces (calculated without sour cream) equals 359 calories, 11 g fat (5 g saturated fat), 36 mg cholesterol, 799 mg sodium, 48 g carbohydrate, 1 g fiber, 14 g protein.

Mexican Hot Chocolate S

PREP/TOTAL TIME: 15 min. **YIELD:** 6 servings

PATRICIA NIEH • PORTOLA VALLEY, CALIFORNIA

My entire family will enjoy this festive drink. Cinnamon sticks give it a great flavor kids will love.

- 4 cups fat-free milk
- 3 cinnamon sticks (3 in.)
- 5 oz. 53% cacao dark baking chocolate, coarsely chopped
- 1 tsp. vanilla extract

Additional cinnamon sticks, optional

1. In a large saucepan, heat the milk and cinnamon sticks over medium heat until bubbles form around the sides of the pan. Discard the cinnamon. Whisk in the chocolate until smooth.

2. Remove from the heat; stir in the vanilla. Serve in mugs with additional cinnamon sticks if desired.

Nutrition Facts: 3/4 cup equals 177 calories, 9 g fat (5 g saturated fat), 3 mg cholesterol, 85 mg sodium, 21 g carbohydrate, 2 g fiber, 7 g protein.

Shrimp Bites F S C

PREP/TOTAL TIME: 25 min. **YIELD:** 2-1/2 dozen

ROBERT LOGAN • CLAYTON, CALIFORNIA

Living near the coast, I have a real advantage when it comes to getting fresh seafood. This recipe is special because it is light and so simple to make!

- 6 oz. reduced-fat cream cheese
- 2 Tbsp. fat-free sour cream
- 2 Tbsp. minced fresh parsley
- 2 tsp. dried minced onion
- 1/2 tsp. Worcestershire sauce
- 1/4 tsp. seafood seasoning
- 1 cup finely chopped cooked peeled shrimp
- 1/2 cup shredded part-skim mozzarella cheese
- 2 pkg. (2.1 oz. *each*) frozen miniature phyllo tart shells

1. In a small bowl, beat the cream cheese with the sour cream until well blended. Add the parsley, onion, Worcestershire sauce and seafood seasoning; mix well. Stir in shrimp and mozzarella cheese.

2. Spoon the filling into the phyllo tart shells. Place on an ungreased baking sheet. Bake at 350° for 8-12 minutes or until the shells are lightly browned. Serve warm or cold.

Nutrition Facts: 1 appetizer equals 48 calories, 3 g fat (1 g saturated fat), 16 mg cholesterol, 63 mg sodium, 3 g carbohydrate, trace fiber, 3 g protein.

BAKED POTATO PIZZA

GREEK BRUSCHETTA

SPINACH BACON TARTLETS

SHRIMP BITES

Greek Bruschetta F S C M

PREP/TOTAL TIME: 30 min. **YIELD:** 4 dozen

JOY SHIND • SMYRNA, TENNESSEE

The summer-fresh taste of these Mediterranean-flavored bites will have guests going back for seconds. But they can do so without guilt because this terrific starter is so healthful. They add festive color to any party table.

3	plum tomatoes, finely chopped
1	cup water-packed artichoke hearts, rinsed, drained and chopped
1/2	cup shredded part-skim mozzarella cheese
1/2	cup crumbled feta cheese
3	Tbsp. thinly sliced fresh basil leaves
1	Tbsp. olive oil
2	garlic cloves, minced
48	slices French bread baguette (1/4 in. thick)

1. In a small bowl, combine the first seven ingredients.

2. Place bread slices on ungreased baking sheets. Broil 3-4 in. from the heat for 1-2 minutes or until golden brown. With a slotted spoon, top each slice with about 1 tablespoon tomato mixture.

Nutrition Facts: 1 appetizer equals 26 calories, 1 g fat (trace saturated fat), 1 mg cholesterol, 62 mg sodium, 4 g carbohydrate, trace fiber, 1 g protein.

Spinach Bacon Tartlets F S C

PREP: 25 min. **BAKE:** 15 min. **YIELD:** 2-1/2 dozen

LINDA EVANCOE-COBLE • LEOLA, PENNSYLVANIA

These delicious appetizers make a lovely presentation and yes, real men WILL eat quiche...especially these mini versions!

1	pkg. (8 oz.) reduced-fat cream cheese
1	egg white
1/2	cup frozen chopped spinach, thawed and squeezed dry
3	Tbsp. chopped green onions (white part only)
1	tsp. salt-free seasoning blend
1/4	tsp. ground nutmeg
2	pkg. (2.1 oz. *each*) frozen miniature phyllo tart shells
3	turkey bacon strips, diced and cooked

1. In a small bowl, beat the first six ingredients until blended. Spoon the filling into tart shells. Place on an ungreased baking sheet.

2. Bake at 350° for 10 minutes. Sprinkle with bacon; bake 2-5 minutes longer or until filling is set and shells are lightly browned. Serve warm.

Nutrition Facts: 1 tartlet equals 46 calories, 3 g fat (1 g saturated fat), 7 mg cholesterol, 63 mg sodium, 3 g carbohydrate, trace fiber, 2 g protein.

Crispy Baked Wontons F S C

PREP: 30 min. **BAKE:** 10 min. **YIELD:** about 4 dozen

BRIANNA SHADE • BEAVERTON, OREGON

These quick wontons are great for an afternoon snack or with a soothing soup on a cold day. While they make ideal appetizers, try them as a side dish with Asian entrees.

- 1/2 lb. ground pork
- 1/2 lb. extra-lean ground turkey
- 1 small onion, chopped
- 1 can (8 oz.) sliced water chestnuts, drained and chopped
- 1/3 cup reduced-sodium soy sauce
- 1/4 cup egg substitute
- 1-1/2 tsp. ground ginger
- 1 pkg. (12 oz.) wonton wrappers

Cooking spray

Sweet-and-sour sauce, optional

1. In a large skillet, cook the pork, turkey and onion over medium heat until meat is no longer pink; drain. Transfer to a large bowl. Stir in the water chestnuts, soy sauce, egg substitute and ginger.

2. Position a wonton wrapper with one point toward you. (Keep remaining wrappers covered with a damp paper towel until ready to use.) Place 2 heaping teaspoons of filling in the center of wrapper. Fold bottom corner over filling; fold sides toward center over filling. Roll toward the remaining point. Moisten top corner with water; press to seal. Repeat with remaining wrappers and filling.

3. Place on baking sheets coated with cooking spray; lightly coat wontons with additional cooking spray. Bake at 400° for 10-12 minutes or until golden brown, turning once. Serve warm with sweet-and-sour sauce if desired.

Nutrition Facts: 1 wonton (calculated without sweet-and-sour sauce) equals 38 calories, 1 g fat (trace saturated fat), 5 mg cholesterol, 103 mg sodium, 5 g carbohydrate, trace fiber, 3 g protein.

Hot Spiced Green Tea F S C

PREP/TOTAL TIME: 15 min. **YIELD:** 4 servings

HEALTHY COOKING TEST KITCHEN

With ginger, lemon and honey, this balanced tea is ideal for any time of day or occasion. You'll agree this aromatic drink smells just as wonderful as it tastes.

2 cinnamon sticks (3 in.)
4 individual green tea bags
1/2 tsp. minced fresh gingerroot
1/2 tsp. grated lemon peel
4 cardamom seeds, crushed
4 cups boiling water
2 Tbsp. honey

1. In a large bowl, combine the first five ingredients. Add boiling water. Cover and steep for 5-6 minutes. Strain, discarding tea bags and spices. Stir honey into tea. Serve immediately.

Nutrition Facts: 1 cup equals 33 calories, trace fat (0 saturated fat), 0 cholesterol, trace sodium, 9 g carbohydrate, trace fiber, trace protein. **Diabetic Exchange:** 1/2 starch.

Chicken Skewers with Cool Avocado Sauce F S C

PREP: 25 min. + marinating **GRILL:** 10 min.
YIELD: 16 skewers (3/4 cup sauce)

VERONICA CALLAGHAN • GLASTONBURY, CONNECTICUT

I'm always looking for lighter recipes to take on tailgate outings. This one is quick and easy to marinate and take along.

1 lb. boneless skinless chicken breasts
1/2 cup lime juice
1 Tbsp. balsamic vinegar
2 tsp. minced chipotle pepper in adobo sauce
1/2 tsp. salt
SAUCE:
1 medium ripe avocado, peeled and pitted
1/2 cup fat-free sour cream
2 Tbsp. minced fresh cilantro
2 tsp. lime juice
1 tsp. grated lime peel
1/4 tsp. salt

1. Flatten chicken to 1/4-in. thickness; cut lengthwise into sixteen 1-in.-wide strips. In a large resealable plastic bag, combine the lime juice, vinegar, chipotle pepper and salt; add the chicken. Seal bag and turn to coat; refrigerate for 30 minutes.

2. Meanwhile, for the sauce, place remaining ingredients in a food processor; cover and process until blended. Transfer to a serving bowl; cover and refrigerate until serving.

3. Drain chicken and discard marinade. Thread onto 16 metal or soaked wooden skewers. Coat grill rack with cooking spray before starting the grill. Grill, covered, over medium heat for 4-6 minutes on each side or until no longer pink. Serve with sauce.

Nutrition Facts: 1 skewer with about 2 teaspoons sauce equals 59 calories, 3 g fat (trace saturated fat), 17 mg cholesterol, 74 mg sodium, 3 g carbohydrate, 1 g fiber, 6 g protein. **Diabetic Exchanges:** 1 very lean meat, 1/2 fat.

For a fun change-of-pace try the **Chicken Skewers** on a roll for lunch or even dinner. The exotic sandwiches are terrific topped with lettuce leaves, sliced tomato and the Cool Avocado Sauce as a condiment.

CHICKEN SKEWERS WITH COOL AVOCADO SAUCE

HOT SPICED GREEN TEA

Artichoke Bread M

PREP: 30 min. + cooling
BAKE: 15 min. **YIELD:** 1 loaf (12 slices)

SHERRY CAMPBELL • ST. AMANT, LOUISIANA

A creamy, rich artichoke spread tops these warm, crusty bites that folks just love. You won't find a much quicker and more delicious appetizer or last-minute side!

- 1 tube (11 oz.) refrigerated crusty French loaf
- 1 can (14 oz.) water-packed artichoke hearts, drained and chopped
- 1/2 cup seasoned bread crumbs
- 1/3 cup grated Parmesan cheese
- 1/3 cup reduced-fat mayonnaise
- 2 garlic cloves, minced
- 1 cup (4 oz.) shredded part-skim mozzarella cheese

1. Bake loaf according to package directions; cool. Cut bread in half lengthwise; place on an ungreased baking sheet.

2. In a small bowl, combine the artichokes, bread crumbs, Parmesan cheese, mayonnaise and garlic; spread evenly over cut sides of bread. Sprinkle with mozzarella cheese.

3. Bake at 350° for 15-20 minutes or until the cheese is melted. Slice and serve warm.

Nutrition Facts: 1 slice equals 151 calories, 5 g fat (2 g saturated fat), 10 mg cholesterol, 456 mg sodium, 18 g carbohydrate, 1 g fiber, 7 g protein. **Diabetic Exchanges:** 1 starch, 1 fat.

ARTICHOKE BREAD

Sangria F S C

PREP/TOTAL TIME: 10 min. **YIELD:** 9 servings

HEALTHY COOKING TEST KITCHEN

What a thirst-quenching, elegant beverage for summer parties! Filled with frozen fruit, this fresh blend is a snap to put together. Serve over ice if desired.

- 1 bottle (750 milliliters) red Zinfandel or other dry red wine
- 2 cups diet lemon-lime soda
- 1/2 cup orange juice
- 1-1/2 Tbsp. sugar
- 1 cup *each* frozen unsweetened blueberries, raspberries and sliced peaches

Ice cubes, optional

1. In a pitcher, stir the wine, soda, orange juice and sugar until sugar is dissolved.

2. Add the frozen fruit. Serve over ice if desired.

Nutrition Facts: 3/4 cup equals 104 calories, trace fat (trace saturated fat), 0 cholesterol, 9 mg sodium, 11 g carbohydrate, 1 g fiber, 1 g protein.

Cranberry Jalapeno Cheese Spread F S C M

PREP: 25 min. + cooling **YIELD:** 2 cups

DIANE NEMITZ • LUDINGTON, MICHIGAN

This easy spread is based on several different spreads I've tasted before. I love the sweet and spicy flavors!

- 1 cup dried cranberries
- 1/2 cup packed brown sugar
- 1/2 cup orange juice
- 4 tsp. chopped seeded jalapeno pepper
- 1 Tbsp. lemon juice
- 1 tsp. grated orange peel
- 1/4 tsp. Chinese five-spice powder
- 1 pkg. (8 oz.) reduced-fat cream cheese

Assorted crackers

SANGRIA

1. In a small saucepan, combine the first seven ingredients. Bring to a boil. Reduce heat; simmer, uncovered, for 10 minutes or until thickened. Remove from the heat; cool completely.

2. In a large bowl, beat the cream cheese until fluffy. Beat in cranberry mixture until blended. Serve with assorted crackers.

Editor's Note: When cutting hot peppers, disposable gloves are recommended. Avoid touching your face.

Nutrition Facts: 2 tablespoons (calculated without crackers) equals 88 calories, 3 g fat (2 g saturated fat), 10 mg cholesterol, 63 mg sodium, 14 g carbohydrate, trace fiber, 2 g protein. **Diabetic Exchanges:** 1 starch, 1/2 fat.

Mini Apple Strudels F S

PREP: 30 min. **BAKE:** 20 min. **YIELD:** 6 servings

HEALTHY COOKING TEST KITCHEN

Crisp phyllo dough surrounds tender apple slices in this clever play on strudel. Walnuts and cinnamon enhance the traditional apple pie flavor.

1-1/2	cups chopped peeled tart apples
2	Tbsp. plus 2 tsp. sugar
2	Tbsp. chopped walnuts
1	Tbsp. all-purpose flour
1/4	tsp. ground cinnamon
6	sheets phyllo dough (14 in. x 9 in.)

Butter-flavored cooking spray
Confectioners' sugar, optional

1. In a small bowl, combine the apples, sugar, walnuts, flour and cinnamon. Set aside.

2. Place one sheet of phyllo dough on a work surface (keep remaining dough covered with plastic wrap and a damp towel to prevent it from drying out). Spray with butter-flavored spray.

3. Fold in half widthwise; spray again with butter-flavored spray. Spoon a scant 1/3 cup filling onto phyllo about 2 in. from a short side. Fold side and edges over filling and roll up. Place seam side down on a baking sheet coated with cooking spray. Repeat.

4. With a sharp knife, cut diagonal slits in tops of strudels. Spray strudels with butter-flavored spray. Bake at 350° for 20-22 minutes or until golden brown. Sprinkle with confectioners' sugar if desired.

Nutrition Facts: 1 strudel equals 100 calories, 3 g fat (trace saturated fat), 0 cholesterol, 45 mg sodium, 17 g carbohydrate, 1 g fiber, 2 g protein. **Diabetic Exchanges:** 1/2 starch, 1/2 fruit, 1/2 fat.

It's easy to mix up the flavors in **Mini Apple Strudels.** Toss a handful of fresh cranberries into the apple mixture or stir in tablespoon or two of cherry pie filling. You can also replace the apples with chopped pears.

GOAT CHEESE, PEAR & ONION PIZZA

MINI POLENTA PIZZAS

Goat Cheese, Pear & Onion Pizza M

PREP: 30 min. **BAKE:** 10 min. **YIELD:** 12 slices

RADELLE KNAPPENBERGER • OVIEDO, FLORIDA

My husband and I developed this recipe several years ago. It's always a hit! You can always vary the toppings, herbs and seasonings to fit your family's tastes.

3	cups thinly sliced red onions
3	tsp. olive oil, *divided*
2	garlic cloves, minced
1	prebaked thin Italian bread shell crust (10 oz.)
2	medium pears, peeled and sliced
3/4	cup shredded part-skim mozzarella cheese
1/3	cup goat cheese
8	fresh basil leaves, thinly sliced
1	tsp. dried oregano
1/4	tsp. pepper

1. In a large nonstick skillet coated with cooking spray, saute onions in 2 teaspoons oil until tender. Add garlic; saute 2-3 minutes longer. Place crust on an ungreased 12-in. pizza pan; spread with onion mixture to within 1 in. of edges.

2. In the same skillet, saute pears in remaining oil until tender. Arrange over onion mixture. Sprinkle with cheeses.

3. Bake at 450° for 10-12 minutes or until edges are lightly browned. Sprinkle with basil, oregano and pepper.

Nutrition Facts: 1 slice equals 154 calories, 6 g fat (2 g saturated fat), 9 mg cholesterol, 204 mg sodium, 20 g carbohydrate, 2 g fiber, 6 g protein.

Mini Polenta Pizzas F C M

PREP/TOTAL TIME: 30 min. **YIELD:** 2 dozen

LILLIAN JULOW • GAINESVILLE, FLORIDA

These tasty pizza bites are special enough for any fancy gathering you might host.

2	tubes (1 lb. *each*) polenta
1/2	cup grated Parmesan cheese
12	oil-packed sun-dried tomatoes, halved
1/4	cup prepared pesto

1. Cut polenta into 24 slices; place on ungreased baking sheets. Sprinkle with half of the cheese. Top each with a tomato half and 1/2 teaspoon pesto; sprinkle with remaining cheese.

2. Bake the mini pizzas at 450° for 7-10 minutes or until cheese is melted.

Nutrition Facts: 1 mini pizza equals 57 calories, 2 g fat (1 g saturated fat), 2 mg cholesterol, 182 mg sodium, 8 g carbohydrate, 1 g fiber, 2 g protein. **Diabetic Exchanges:** 1/2 starch, 1/2 fat.

Autumn Pecans S C

PREP: 20 min. **BAKE:** 15 min. **YIELD:** 5 cups

TARI AMBLER • SHOREWOOD, ILLINOIS

I usually make at least two batches of these nuts at a time and package them in containers to give as gifts. Though high in fat, nuts are also high in heart-healthy monounsaturated fat. Pecans contain vitamin E, magnesium and fiber, too.

> 2 Tbsp. sugar
> 1 tsp. pumpkin pie spice
> 1/2 tsp. salt
> 1/2 tsp. ground ginger
> 2 Tbsp. water
> 2 Tbsp. honey
> 2 tsp. canola oil
> 1-1/4 lbs. pecan halves (about 5 cups)

1. Combine the sugar, pie spice, salt and ginger; set aside. In a Dutch oven, bring the water, honey and oil to a boil. Add pecans; cook and stir until all of the liquid is evaporated, about 1 minute. Immediately sprinkle with reserved sugar mixture; toss to coat.

2. Transfer to an ungreased 15-in. x 10-in. baking sheet. Bake at 325° for 15-20 minutes or until browned, stirring twice. Cool on a wire rack. Store in an airtight container.

Nutrition Facts: 1/4 cup equals 202 calories, 20 g fat (2 g saturated fat), 0 cholesterol, 59 mg sodium, 7 g carbohydrate, 3 g fiber, 2 g protein.

Chunky Tomato Salsa F C M

PREP: 45 min. **COOK:** 1-1/4 hours + chilling
YIELD: 4 cups

CAROL CARPENTER • JANSEN, NEBRASKA

Our college-age daughter, two of her friends and a nephew ate a quart of this salsa with chips in one sitting. They loved it so much that they each took a quart home with them. So be sure to make lots!

> 3-1/2 cups peeled chopped tomatoes (about 4 large)
> 1 large green pepper, chopped
> 1 medium onion, chopped
> 1 serrano pepper, seeded and chopped
> 1 jalapeno pepper, seeded and chopped
> 1 Tbsp. sugar
> 2-1/4 tsp. salt
> 1 garlic clove, minced
> 3/4 tsp. ground cumin
> 1 can (6 oz.) tomato paste
> 1/4 cup white vinegar
> 2 Tbsp. lemon juice
> Baked tortilla chip scoops

1. In a large saucepan, combine the first nine ingredients. Stir in the tomato paste, vinegar and lemon juice. Bring to a boil. Reduce heat; simmer, uncovered, for 1 hour, stirring frequently.

2. Cool to room temperature. Cover and refrigerate until chilled. Serve with chips.

Editor's Note: When cutting hot peppers, disposable gloves are recommended. Avoid touching your face.

Nutrition Facts: 1/4 cup (calculated without chips) equals 28 calories, trace fat (trace saturated fat), 0 cholesterol, 344 mg sodium, 6 g carbohydrate, 1 g fiber, 1 g protein.
Diabetic Exchange: 1 vegetable.

CHUNKY TOMATO SALSA

AUTUMN PECANS

Ginger-Glazed Grilled Honeydew F S

PREP/TOTAL TIME: 25 min. **YIELD:** 6 servings

JACQUI CORREA • LANDING, NEW JERSEY

If you've never grilled fruit before, you're in for a real treat! Feel free to try this unique recipe with pineapple chunks or thick cubes of cantaloupe.

1/4	cup peach preserves
1	Tbsp. lemon juice
1	Tbsp. chopped candied or crystallized ginger
2	tsp. grated lemon peel
1/8	tsp. ground cloves
1	medium honeydew, cut into 2-in. cubes

1. In a small bowl, combine the first five ingredients. Thread honeydew onto six metal or soaked wooden skewers; brush with half of the glaze.

2. Coat grill rack with cooking spray before starting the grill. Grill honeydew, covered, over medium-high heat for 2-3 minutes on each side or just until melon begins to soften and brown, basting frequently with remaining glaze.

Nutrition Facts: 1 skewer equals 101 calories, trace fat (trace saturated fat), 0 cholesterol, 18 mg sodium, 26 g carbohydrate, 1 g fiber, 1 g protein. **Diabetic Exchanges:** 1 fruit, 1/2 starch.

Chili con Queso Dip F C M

PREP/TOTAL TIME: 25 min. **YIELD:** 3 cups

SARAH MOHRMAN • FORT WAYNE, INDIANA

This cheesy dip never lets on that it only contains a couple of fat grams per serving. Chilies and garlic kick up the flavor, making it a real crowd-pleaser. You can even serve it with celery or carrot sticks for an even healthier spin. What a great way to change up a typical veggie tray!

1	can (14-1/2 oz.) no-salt-added diced tomatoes
1	can (10 oz.) diced tomatoes and green chilies
1	small onion, chopped
2	garlic cloves, minced
1	tsp. olive oil
1	pkg. (8 oz.) fat-free cream cheese, cubed
6	oz. reduced-fat process cheese (Velveeta), cubed
1	tsp. chili powder
2	Tbsp. minced fresh cilantro

Baked tortilla chip scoops

1. Pour both cans of tomatoes into a colander over a small bowl; drain, reserving 1/3 cup liquid. Discard remaining liquid or save for another use.

2. In a large skillet, saute onion and garlic in oil until tender. Stir in cream cheese until melted. Add the tomatoes, process cheese, chili powder and reserved liquid. Cook and stir over low heat until cheese is melted. Stir in cilantro.

3. Transfer to a small slow cooker or chafing dish; keep warm. Serve with the tortilla chips.

Nutrition Facts: 1/4 cup (calculated without chips) equals 66 calories, 2 g fat (1 g saturated fat), 7 mg cholesterol, 411 mg sodium, 6 g carbohydrate, 1 g fiber, 6 g protein. **Diabetic Exchanges:** 1/2 starch, 1/2 fat.

Mini Neapolitan Baked Alaskas F S

PREP: 30 min. **BROIL:** 5 min. **YIELD:** 4 servings

HEALTHY COOKING TEST KITCHEN

Surprise—there's ice cream inside! With fancy looks and decadent flavor, this recipe's a real showstopper. Kids and adults will love this scaled-down classic.

4	foil muffin liners
4	chocolate wafers
1	cup reduced-fat strawberry ice cream
3	egg whites
6	Tbsp. sugar
1/8	tsp. cream of tartar
1/2	tsp. vanilla extract

1. Flatten muffin liners; place on a baking sheet. Place a wafer on each. Scoop 1/4 cup of ice cream onto each wafer; freeze.

GINGER-GLAZED GRILLED HONEYDEW

CHILI CON QUESO DIP

2. Meanwhile, in a small heavy saucepan, combine the egg whites, sugar and cream of tartar; beat on low speed with a portable mixer for 1 minute. Continue beating over low heat until mixture reaches 160°, about 12 minutes. Remove from the heat; add vanilla. Beat until stiff peaks form and sugar is dissolved, about 4 minutes.

3. Remove baking sheet from the freezer; immediately spread the meringue over ice cream, sealing to edges of wafers. Broil 4-6 in. from the heat for 1-2 minutes or until meringues are lightly browned. Serve immediately.

Nutrition Facts: 1 serving equals 163 calories, 2 g fat (1 g saturated fat), 8 mg cholesterol, 99 mg sodium, 32 g carbohydrate, trace fiber, 5 g protein. **Diabetic Exchange:** 2 starch.

Zucchini Salsa F C M

PREP: 35 min. **COOK:** 45 min. + chilling
YIELD: 7 cups

CHERYL JACOBSEN • WARBURG, ALBERTA

I received this recipe through a friend at a weight-loss group. I make at least eight batches every year. It's truly a hit with family and friends!

- 5 cups shredded zucchini (about 5 medium)
- 4 medium tomatoes, peeled, seeded and chopped
- 2 medium onions, chopped
- 2 medium green peppers, chopped
- 1 small sweet red pepper, chopped
- 1/2 cup packed brown sugar
- 1 jalapeno pepper, seeded and finely chopped
- 1 cup white vinegar
- 1 can (8 oz.) tomato sauce
- 2 Tbsp. tomato paste
- 3 garlic cloves, minced
- 3 tsp. ground mustard
- 2-1/4 tsp. salt
- 3/4 tsp. crushed red pepper flakes
- 1/2 tsp. garlic powder
- 1/2 tsp. *each* ground cumin, nutmeg and turmeric
- 1/2 tsp. pepper

1. In a Dutch oven, combine all ingredients. Bring to a boil. Reduce heat; simmer, uncovered, for 40-50 minutes or until thickened, stirring occasionally.

2. Cool to room temperature. Cover and refrigerate until chilled. Serve with your favorite snack chips or grilled meats.

Editor's Note: When cutting hot peppers, disposable gloves are recommended. Avoid touching your face.

Nutrition Facts: 1/4 cup equals 35 calories, trace fat (trace saturated fat), 0 cholesterol, 233 mg sodium, 8 g carbohydrate, 1 g fiber, 1 g protein. **Diabetic Exchange:** 1/2 starch.

WATERMELON SALSA

Watermelon Salsa F S C M

PREP: 20 min. + chilling **YIELD:** 3 cups

CAROLYN BUTTERFIELD • LAKE STEVENS, WASHINGTON

I entered this recipe at our local fair, and it took first place! This is one of my favorites because all of the ingredients (except for the lime juice) came directly from my garden and my beehives.

2	cups seeded finely chopped watermelon
1/2	cup finely chopped peeled cucumber
1/4	cup finely chopped red onion
1/4	cup finely chopped sweet red pepper
1	jalapeno pepper, seeded and minced
1/4	cup minced fresh cilantro
1	Tbsp. minced fresh basil
1	Tbsp. minced fresh mint
2	Tbsp. honey
1	tsp. lime juice

Baked tortilla chip scoops

1. In a large bowl, combine the melon, cucumber, onion, peppers and herbs. Drizzle with honey and lime juice; gently toss to coat.

2. Refrigerate for at least 1 hour. Serve with chips.

Editor's Note: When cutting hot peppers, disposable gloves are recommended. Avoid touching your face.

Nutrition Facts: 1/4 cup (calculated without chips) equals 22 calories, trace fat (trace saturated fat), 0 cholesterol, 1 mg sodium, 6 g carbohydrate, trace fiber, trace protein. **Diabetic Exchange:** 1/2 starch.

Green Tea Frappes F S

PREP/TOTAL TIME: 20 min. **YIELD:** 4 servings

HEALTHY COOKING TEST KITCHEN

This delicious frappe captures the flavor of green tea with a hint of sweetness. You'll love the tasty drink at get-togethers or as part of a relaxing family brunch.

3	individual green tea bags
1	cup boiling water
1-1/2	cups ice cubes
3/4	cup fat-free sweetened condensed milk
1/2	cup fat-free milk

1. Place the tea bags in a small bowl; add boiling water. Let stand for 15 minutes or until lukewarm.

2. Discard tea bags. Pour tea into a blender; add the remaining ingredients. Cover and process for 30-45 seconds or until smooth. Pour into chilled glasses; serve immediately.

Nutrition Facts: 3/4 cup equals 174 calories, trace fat (trace saturated fat), 4 mg cholesterol, 77 mg sodium, 37 g carbohydrate, 0 fiber, 6 g protein.

Makeover Mini Bacon Quiches F S C

PREP/TOTAL TIME: 30 min. **YIELD:** 2-1/2 dozen

JULIE HIEGGELKE • GRAYSLAKE, ILLINOIS

I wanted to lighten up one of my favorite appetizer recipes, but I didn't want to lose any bacon flavor. The "Healthy Cooking" Test Kitchen showed me how with this recipe.

1	egg, lightly beaten
1/2	lb. sliced bacon, cooked and crumbled
1/2	cup reduced-fat ricotta cheese
1/2	cup shredded part-skim mozzarella cheese
1/2	cup shredded reduced-fat cheddar cheese
1	small onion, finely chopped
1/4	tsp. garlic powder

Dash cayenne pepper
Dash pepper

2	pkg. (2.1 oz. *each*) frozen miniature phyllo tart shells

1. In a small bowl, combine the first nine ingredients. Place tart shells on an ungreased baking sheet; fill each with 2 teaspoons mixture.

2. Bake at 350° for 8-10 minutes or until filling is set and shells are lightly browned. Serve warm.

Nutrition Facts: 1 appetizer equals 54 calories, 3 g fat (1 g saturated fat), 13 mg cholesterol, 77 mg sodium, 3 g carbohydrate, trace fiber, 3 g protein.

Golden Fruit Punch F S

PREP: 10 min. + freezing
YIELD: 21 servings (4 quarts)

CINDY STEFFEN • CEDARBURG, WISCONSIN

This is a refreshing punch that isn't as sweet as most. My family loves the tart wake-me-up flavor. Plus, it won't stain carpeting the way a red punch would!

4	maraschino cherries
1	medium navel orange, thinly sliced
1	small lemon, thinly sliced
1	small lime, thinly sliced
1	can (12 oz.) frozen lemonade concentrate, thawed
1	can (12 oz.) frozen limeade concentrate, thawed
1	can (12 oz.) frozen pineapple-orange juice concentrate, thawed
2	liters diet ginger ale, chilled

1. Arrange fruit in a 5-cup ring mold; add 3/4 cup water. Freeze until solid. Add enough water to fill mold; freeze until solid.

2. Just before serving, in a punch bowl, combine juice concentrates with 2 cups water. Stir in ginger ale. Unmold ice ring by wrapping the bottom of the mold in a hot, damp dishcloth. Invert onto a baking sheet; place fruit side up in punch bowl.

Nutrition Facts: 3/4 cup equals 96 calories, trace fat (trace saturated fat), 0 cholesterol, 22 mg sodium, 24 g carbohydrate, trace fiber, trace protein. **Diabetic Exchanges:** 1 starch, 1/2 fruit.

GOLDEN FRUIT PUNCH

MAKEOVER MINI BACON QUICHES

Pear Cheesecake Pizza

PREP: 30 min. + rising
BAKE: 20 min. **YIELD:** 12 servings

CAROL MEAD • LOS ALAMOS, NEW MEXICO

Classic autumn tastes steal the show in this kid-friendly treat. With a from-scratch crust and a hint of citrus, it's wonderful for adults, too!

1	pkg. (1/4 oz.) active dry yeast
1/4	cup warm water (110° to 115°)
1/3	cup warm fat-free milk (110° to 115°)
3	Tbsp. butter, softened
2	Tbsp. sugar
1/2	tsp. salt
1-3/4 to 2	cups all-purpose flour

TOPPING:

3	oz. reduced-fat cream cheese, softened
1/3	cup packed brown sugar
1	egg, lightly beaten
1	Tbsp. orange juice
1	tsp. grated orange peel
3	medium pears, peeled and sliced

SAUCE:

1/2	cup packed brown sugar
1/4	cup reduced-fat sour cream
4-1/2	tsp. butter

1. In a large bowl, dissolve the yeast in warm water. Add the milk, butter, sugar, salt and 1 cup flour. Beat until smooth. Stir in enough remaining flour to form a soft dough. Turn onto a lightly floured surface; knead the dough until smooth and elastic, about 6-8 minutes. Place in a bowl coated with cooking spray, turning once to coat the top. Cover and let rise until doubled, about 30 minutes.

2. Punch dough down. Roll into a 15-in. circle. Transfer to a 14-in. pizza pan coated with cooking spray; build up edges slightly. Cover and let rest for 10 minutes.

3. In a small bowl, beat the cream cheese and brown sugar until smooth. Beat in the egg, orange juice and peel just until blended. Spread over the crust; top with pears. Bake at 375° for 20-25 minutes or until the crust is lightly browned and cream cheese topping is set.

4. In a small saucepan, bring the brown sugar, sour cream and butter to a boil. Reduce heat; cook and stir until sauce is smooth, about 2 minutes. Drizzle over top of pizza. Serve warm.

Nutrition Facts: 1 slice equals 229 calories, 7 g fat (4 g saturated fat), 36 mg cholesterol, 190 mg sodium, 38 g carbohydrate, 2 g fiber, 4 g protein.

Salmon Salad-Stuffed Endive Leaves ⒻⓈⒸ

PREP/TOTAL TIME: 15 min. **YIELD:** 14 appetizers

MELISSA CARAFA • BROOMALL, PENNSYLVANIA

Salmon is the filling for this elegant and vibrant appetizer. It's quick to prepare and can even be made ahead of time.

1	salmon fillet (6 oz.), cooked and flaked
1/4	cup tartar sauce
2	tsp. capers
1	tsp. snipped fresh dill
1/4	tsp. lemon-pepper seasoning
1	head Belgian endive (about 5 oz.), separated into leaves

Additional snipped fresh dill, optional

1. In a small bowl, combine the salmon, tartar sauce, capers, dill and lemon-pepper. Spoon about 2 teaspoonfuls onto each endive leaf.

2. Garnish with additional dill if desired. Refrigerate until serving.

Nutrition Facts: 1 appetizer equals 42 calories, 3 g fat (trace saturated fat), 9 mg cholesterol, 60 mg sodium, 2 g carbohydrate, 1 g fiber, 3 g protein. **Diabetic Exchange:** 1/2 fat.

Spicy Shrimp Salsa ⒻⓈⒸ

PREP/TOTAL TIME: 15 min. **YIELD:** 2 cups

MARY RELYEA • CANASTOTA, NEW YORK

Radishes add a wonderful crunch to this colorful salsa that's also great over grilled fish. There's just enough jalapeno to give it flavor without too much heat.

1/2	lb. cooked shrimp, peeled, deveined and chopped
1	large tomato, chopped
1/4	cup finely chopped onion
3	radishes, chopped
1/4	cup minced fresh cilantro
2	Tbsp. lime juice
1-1/2	tsp. finely chopped seeded jalapeno pepper
1/4	tsp. salt

Baked tortilla chip scoops

1. In a small bowl, combine the first eight ingredients.

2. Refrigerate until serving. Serve with chips.

Editor's Note: When cutting hot peppers, disposable gloves are recommended. Avoid touching your face.

SALMON SALAD-STUFFED ENDIVE LEAVES

Nutrition Facts: 1/4 cup (calculated without chips) equals 38 calories, 1 g fat (trace saturated fat), 43 mg cholesterol, 119 mg sodium, 2 g carbohydrate, trace fiber, 6 g protein. **Diabetic Exchange:** 1 very lean meat.

Guacamole for the Gang S C M

PREP: 20 min. + chilling **YIELD:** 3 cups

CHRISTINE SCHENHER • YPSILANTI, MICHIGAN

Serve guacamole that's fresh, flavorful and lower in fat! I make this popular dip for get-togethers, and it's always a hit. It's delicious year-round and a great way to use up extra produce during the summer months!

1/2	cup reduced-fat plain yogurt
1/2	cup fat-free sour cream
2	medium ripe avocados, peeled and pitted, *divided*
2	plum tomatoes, chopped
1	small onion, chopped
2	jalapeno peppers, seeded and chopped
1	Tbsp. minced fresh cilantro
1/2	tsp. salt
2	Tbsp. lime juice

Baked tortilla chip scoops

1. Line a strainer with four layers of cheesecloth or one coffee filter and place over a bowl. Place yogurt in prepared strainer; cover yogurt with edges of cheesecloth. Refrigerate for 8 hours or overnight.

2. Remove yogurt from cheesecloth and discard liquid from bowl. In a small bowl, beat the yogurt, sour cream and one avocado until blended. Stir in the tomatoes, onion, jalapenos, cilantro and salt. In another bowl, mash remaining avocado with lime juice; stir into guacamole. Serve with tortilla chips.

Editor's Note: When cutting or seeding hot peppers, use rubber or plastic gloves to protect your hands. Avoid touching your face.

Nutrition Facts: 1/4 cup (calculated without chips) equals 75 calories, 5 g fat (1 g saturated fat), 2 mg cholesterol, 118 mg sodium, 6 g carbohydrate, 2 g fiber, 2 g protein. **Diabetic Exchanges:** 1 fat, 1/2 starch.

Don't have time to strain the yogurt for Guacamole for the Gang? Beat the clock by purchasing a container of reduced-fat Greek yogurt, which is pre-strained.

BERRY 'N' SMOKED TURKEY TWIRLS

Berry 'n' Smoked Turkey Twirls F S C

PREP: 25 min. + chilling   **YIELD:** 40 appetizers

PATRICIA HARMON • BADEN, PENNSYLVANIA

Here's a new twist on a traditional appetizer that's just bursting with low-fat flavor. Best of all, the twirls can be assembled ahead of time for convenience.

>   1 pkg. (8 oz.) reduced-fat cream cheese
>   1 cup shredded reduced-fat Mexican cheese blend
> 1/4 lb. thinly sliced deli smoked turkey, finely chopped
>   2 Tbsp. chopped dried cranberries
>   2 Tbsp. chopped pimiento-stuffed olives
>   2 Tbsp. salsa
> 3/4 tsp. chili powder
>   4 flour tortillas (10 in.)

1. In a small bowl, beat cream cheese until smooth. Stir in the cheese blend, turkey, cranberries, olives, salsa and chili powder. Spread 1/2 cup mixture over each tortilla; roll up tightly. Wrap in plastic wrap and refrigerate for 2 hours or until firm.

2. Unwrap and cut into scant 1-in. slices. Serve chilled or place 1 in. apart on a baking sheet coated with cooking spray. Bake at 400° for 5-7 minutes or until heated through.

Nutrition Facts: 1 appetizer equals 49 calories, 2 g fat (1 g saturated fat), 7 mg cholesterol, 117 mg sodium, 4 g carbohydrate, 1 g fiber, 3 g protein.

Spiced Pecans S C

PREP/TOTAL TIME: 30 min.   **YIELD:** 5 cups

AUDREY STEWART • FOREST HILL, MARYLAND

My mother makes these, and they're fantastic. If you arrive at her house late, there might not be any left! The nuts are a perfect hostess gift.

>   1 egg white
>   1 lb. pecan halves
> Sugar substitute equivalent to 1/2 cup sugar
>   3 tsp. ground cinnamon
> 1/2 tsp. salt

1. In a large bowl, beat the egg white until frothy. Add pecans; stir gently to coat. Combine the sugar substitute, cinnamon and salt; add to the nut mixture and stir gently to coat.

2. Spread into a 15-in. x 10-in. baking pan coated with cooking spray. Bake, uncovered, at 325° for 20 minutes or until lightly browned, stirring once. Cool completely. Store in an airtight container.

Nutrition Facts: 1/4 cup equals 161 calories, 16 g fat (1 g saturated fat), 0 cholesterol, 62 mg sodium, 4 g carbohydrate, 2 g fiber, 2 g protein.

Fun-on-the-Run Snack Mix **M**

PREP/TOTAL TIME: 5 min. **YIELD:** 8 cups

CARRIE HUBBARD • BUENA VISTA, COLORADO

My kids love this and have no idea they're eating cranberries. It's a great healthy snack. Pack up a few bags for long car rides or mix up a batch for slumber parties.

- 2 cups Wheat Chex
- 2 cups miniature fish-shaped crackers
- 2 cups pretzel sticks
- 1 cup salted peanuts
- 1 cup dried cranberries

1. In a large bowl, combine the cereal, crackers, pretzels, peanuts and cranberries.

2. Store in an airtight container.

Nutrition Facts: 1/2 cup equals 143 calories, 6 g fat (1 g saturated fat), 0 cholesterol, 207 mg sodium, 20 g carbohydrate, 2 g fiber, 4 g protein. **Diabetic Exchanges:** 1 starch, 1 fat.

Paradise Granola **S**

PREP: 20 min. **BAKE:** 20 min. + cooling
YIELD: 7 cups

ROBYN LARABEE • LUCKNOW, ONTARIO

Even our 4-year-old, who isn't fond of dried fruit, enjoys this granola. It's lower in fat, full of fiber and just plain delicious! Try it with milk in the mornings.

- 2 cups old-fashioned oats
- 1/2 cup flaked coconut
- 1/2 cup toasted wheat germ
- 1/4 cup oat bran
- 1/4 cup sunflower kernels
- 1/4 cup slivered almonds
- 1/4 cup chopped pecans
- 2 Tbsp. sesame seeds
- 1/4 cup honey
- 2 Tbsp. canola oil
- 2 Tbsp. grated orange peel
- 1 tsp. vanilla extract
- 1/2 tsp. salt
- 1 cup dried cranberries
- 3/4 cup chopped dates
- 1/2 cup chopped dried figs
- 1/2 cup chopped dried apricots
- 3 Tbsp. raisins

1. In a large bowl, combine the first eight ingredients. In a small bowl, whisk the honey, oil, orange peel, vanilla and salt; pour over oat mixture and mix well. Spread evenly into an ungreased 15-in. x 10-in. baking pan.

2. Bake at 350° for 20-25 minutes or until golden brown, stirring once. Cool completely on a wire rack. Stir in dried fruits. Store in an airtight container.

Nutrition Facts: 1/4 cup equals 132 calories, 5 g fat (1 g saturated fat), 0 cholesterol, 57 mg sodium, 23 g carbohydrate, 3 g fiber, 3 g protein. **Diabetic Exchanges:** 1 starch, 1/2 fruit, 1/2 fat.

FUN-ON-THE-RUN SNACK MIX

PARADISE GRANOLA

SPICED PECANS

Gluten-Free Snack Mix [S]

PREP: 15 min. **BAKE:** 10 min. + cooling
YIELD: 10 cups

HEALTHY COOKING TEST KITCHEN

This crunchy, on-the-go snack makes a great treat at any time of day. Kids will love the sweet, cinnamon flavor and the chance to eat with their hands!

8	cups popped popcorn
2	cups Koala Crisp cereal
1	pkg. (5 oz.) dried cherries
1/3	cup butter, cubed
1/3	cup honey
1/2	tsp. ground cinnamon

1. In a large ungreased roasting pan, combine the popcorn, cereal and cherries. In a small saucepan, melt butter. Add honey and cinnamon; cook and stir until heated through. Pour over popcorn mixture and toss to coat.

2. Bake at 325° for 15 minutes, stirring every 5 minutes. Cool completely. Store in airtight containers.

Editor's Note: Ingredient formulas and production facilities vary among brands. If you're concerned that your brand may contain gluten, contact the company.

Nutrition Facts: 1/2 cup equals 110 calories, 5 g fat (2 g saturated fat), 8 mg cholesterol, 89 mg sodium, 16 g carbohydrate, 1 g fiber, 1 g protein. **Diabetic Exchanges:** 1 starch, 1 fat.

GLUTEN-FREE SNACK MIX

Warm Spinach Dip [F] [C] [M]

PREP/TOTAL TIME: 20 min. **YIELD:** 2 cups

DEBBIE MARRONE • WARNER ROBINS, GEORGIA

I created this version of a hot spinach dip after my husband and five kids raved about a similar appetizer at one of our favorite restaurants. It's great with tortilla chips or bagel chips.

1	pkg. (10 oz.) frozen chopped spinach, thawed and squeezed dry
4	oz. fat-free cream cheese
1/2	cup shredded reduced-fat cheddar cheese
1/2	cup reduced-fat sour cream
1	Tbsp. spicy brown mustard
1	tsp. minced garlic
3/4	tsp. hot pepper sauce
1/4	tsp. salt

Assorted fresh vegetables

1. In a large saucepan, combine the first eight ingredients. Bring to a boil over medium heat.

2. Reduce heat; simmer, uncovered, for 7-8 minutes or until cheese is melted, stirring occasionally. Serve warm with vegetables.

Nutrition Facts: 1/4 cup (calculated without vegetables) equals 64 calories, 3 g fat (2 g saturated fat), 11 mg cholesterol, 259 mg sodium, 4 g carbohydrate, 1 g fiber, 6 g protein.

Walnut Oat Brownies

PREP: 15 min. **BAKE:** 25 min. + cooling **YIELD:** 1 dozen

MARILYN YATES • ROANOKE, VIRGINIA

Oatmeal and wheat germ add a nutritious touch to these fudgy brownies. The recipe seems too good to be true, but these brownies really taste great.

1/3	cup quick-cooking oats
1/3	cup nonfat dry milk powder
1/4	cup toasted wheat germ
1/4	cup packed brown sugar
2	Tbsp. sugar
1/2	tsp. baking powder
1/4	tsp. salt
6	squares (1 oz. *each*) semisweet chocolate
1/4	cup butter
1/2	cup egg substitute
1/4	cup chopped walnuts
1	tsp. vanilla extract

Confectioners' sugar, optional

1. In a large bowl, combine the first seven ingredients. In a microwave-safe bowl, melt chocolate and butter; cool slightly. Stir in the egg substitute, walnuts and vanilla. Stir into the dry ingredients.

2. Pour into an 8-in. square baking dish coated with cooking spray. Bake at 350° for 25-30 minutes or until a toothpick inserted near the center comes out clean. Cool on a wire rack. Dust with confectioners' sugar if desired. Cut into bars.

Nutrition Facts: 1 brownie equals 180 calories, 10 g fat (5 g saturated fat), 11 mg cholesterol, 145 mg sodium, 19 g carbohydrate, 2 g fiber, 5 g protein. **Diabetic Exchanges:** 2 fat, 1 starch.

Tangy Black Bean Salsa F C M

PREP: 20 min. + chilling **YIELD:** 4-2/3 cups

ANN YARBER • WASHINGTON, OKLAHOMA

Some folks describe my salsa as "healthy for you and full of flavor." The colorful, tangy combination of beans, vegetables and spices is a hit with family and friends.

1	can (15 oz.) black beans, rinsed and drained
1	large tomato, seeded and chopped
1	medium cucumber, seeded and chopped
1	medium red onion, chopped
1	small sweet yellow pepper, chopped
6	radishes, chopped
1	jalapeno pepper, seeded and chopped
2	Tbsp. minced fresh parsley
3	Tbsp. red wine vinegar
3	Tbsp. olive oil
1/2	tsp. salt
1/2	tsp. garlic powder
1/2	tsp. ground cumin
1/4	tsp. pepper

Baked tortilla chip scoops

1. In a large bowl, combine the beans, tomato, cucumber, onion, yellow pepper, radishes, jalapeno and parsley. In a small bowl, whisk the vinegar, oil and seasonings. Pour over bean mixture and toss to coat.

2. Cover and refrigerate for at least 1 hour. Serve with the tortilla chips.

Editor's Note: When cutting hot peppers, disposable gloves are recommended. Avoid touching your face.

Nutrition Facts: 1/3 cup (calculated without chips) equals 63 calories, 3 g fat (trace saturated fat), 0 cholesterol, 144 mg sodium, 7 g carbohydrate, 2 g fiber, 2 g protein. **Diabetic Exchanges:** 1/2 starch, 1/2 fat.

Blended Fruit Chiller F C

PREP: 10 min. + chilling **YIELD:** 6 servings

KIRSTEN GUNDERSON • OTTAWA, ONTARIO

This smoothie is great any time of the day. I especially like to serve it when my kids are in a finicky mood. Try it as a replacement for dessert.

3	cups (24 oz.) fat-free plain yogurt
1	cup unsweetened pineapple juice, chilled
1	cup fresh or frozen unsweetened strawberries
1	medium ripe banana, sliced
1/2	cup fresh or canned unsweetened pineapple chunks
3	Tbsp. honey
1	tsp. vanilla extract

1. Place half of each ingredient in a blender; cover and process until blended. Repeat.

2. Pour into chilled glasses; serve immediately.

Nutrition Facts: 1 cup equals 143 calories, trace fat (trace saturated fat), 3 mg cholesterol, 69 mg sodium, 34 g carbohydrate, 2 g fiber, 6 g protein. **Diabetic Exchanges:** 2 fruit, 1/2 fat-free milk.

Chocolate Fruit Dip S C

PREP: 10 min. + chilling
COOK: 5 min. + cooling **YIELD:** 1 cup

ABIGAIL SIMS • TERRELL, TEXAS

This dip offers an excellent way to add kid appeal to fresh fruit and makes an ideal after-school snack.

- 1-1/2 cups plain yogurt
- 2 Tbsp. fat-free milk
- 10 miniature marshmallows
- 2 Tbsp. semisweet chocolate chips
- Assorted fresh fruits

1. Line a strainer with four layers of cheesecloth or one coffee filter and place over a bowl. Place yogurt in prepared strainer; cover yogurt with edges of cheesecloth. Refrigerate for 8 hours or overnight.

2. In a small heavy saucepan, combine the milk, marshmallows and chocolate chips. Cook and stir until chips are melted and mixture is smooth. Transfer to a small bowl; cool to room temperature.

3. Remove yogurt from cheesecloth and discard liquid from bowl. Gradually stir yogurt into milk mixture. Refrigerate until serving. Serve with fruit.

Nutrition Facts: 1/4 cup (calculated without fruit) equals 88 calories, 5 g fat (3 g saturated fat), 12 mg cholesterol, 47 mg sodium, 9 g carbohydrate, trace fiber, 4 g protein. **Diabetic Exchanges:** 1 fat, 1/2 starch.

Crab-Stuffed Marinated Mushrooms F C

PREP: 15 min. + marinating
BAKE: 20 min. **YIELD:** 20 appetizers

SHIRLEY DOYEN • YORBA LINDA, CALIFORNIA

This recipe was given to me by a friend, and I've made it many times. It's easy, quick to put together and always well liked. Who'd guess it's lower in fat, too? These are the only stuffed mushrooms I've had where the mushrooms are seasoned before being cooked.

- 20 large fresh mushrooms
- 1 cup fat-free Italian salad dressing
- 1 egg, lightly beaten
- 1-1/2 cups canned crabmeat, drained, flaked and cartilage removed
- 3/4 cup soft bread crumbs
- 1/4 cup reduced-fat mayonnaise
- 1/4 cup finely chopped onion
- 1 Tbsp. lemon juice

1. Remove mushroom stems; discard or save for another use. Place mushroom caps in a large resealable plastic bag; add Italian dressing. Seal bag and turn to coat; refrigerate for 8 hours or overnight.

2. In a small bowl, combine the egg, crab, bread crumbs, mayonnaise, onion and lemon juice. Drain and discard the marinade; stuff mushroom caps with the crab mixture.

3. Place in a 15-in. x 10-in. baking pan coated with cooking spray. Bake at 375° for 20-25 minutes or until stuffing is lightly browned.

Nutrition Facts: 1 stuffed mushroom equals 40 calories, 2 g fat (trace saturated fat), 21 mg cholesterol, 174 mg sodium, 3 g carbohydrate, trace fiber, 3 g protein. **Diabetic Exchange:** 1/2 lean meat.

Mediterranean Pockets

PREP: 20 min. **BAKE:** 15 min. **YIELD:** 1 dozen

TINA SCARPACI • CHANDLER, ARIZONA

These tasty appetizers feature lean meat wrapped in reduced-fat crescent rolls. The filling has low-calorie, nutritious veggies and feta cheese, which is lower in fat and calories than many other cheeses.

1/3	lb. lean ground turkey
1	small garlic clove, minced
1/3	cup crumbled feta cheese
1/4	cup frozen peas, thawed
1/4	cup chopped roasted sweet red pepper
1	green onion, chopped
2	Tbsp. minced fresh parsley
1-1/2	tsp. lemon juice
1/2	tsp. grated lemon peel
1/2	tsp. dried oregano
1/4	tsp. salt
1/4	tsp. pepper
2	tubes (8 oz. *each*) refrigerated reduced-fat crescent rolls

1. In a large nonstick skillet coated with cooking spray, cook turkey and garlic over medium heat until meat is no longer pink; drain.

2. Remove from the heat. Stir in the cheese, peas, red pepper, onion, parsley, lemon juice and peel, oregano, salt and pepper.

3. Unroll crescent dough into two rectangles; seal seams and perforations. Cut each rectangle into six squares. Place 2 tablespoons turkey mixture in the center of each square. Fold dough over filling to form a triangle and seal edges.

4. Place on an ungreased baking sheet. Bake at 375° for 12-14 minutes or until golden brown.

Nutrition Facts: 1 appetizer equals 167 calories, 8 g fat (2 g saturated fat), 12 mg cholesterol, 424 mg sodium, 17 g carbohydrate, trace fiber, 6 g protein.

Trail Mix Clusters Ⓕ Ⓒ

PREP: 25 min. + chilling **YIELD:** 4 dozen

ALINA NIEMI • HONOLULU, HAWAII

These delicious treats make wonderful gifts, and although they look and taste like they came from an expensive chocolate shop, they couldn't be more guilt-free. Bet you can't eat just one!

2	cups (12 oz.) semisweet chocolate chips
1/2	cup unsalted sunflower kernels
1/2	cup salted pumpkin seeds or pepitas
1/2	cup coarsely chopped cashews
1/2	cup coarsely chopped pecans
1/4	cup flaked coconut
1/4	cup finely chopped dried apricots
1/4	cup dried cranberries
1/4	cup dried cherries *or* blueberries

1. In a large microwave-safe bowl, melt chocolate chips; stir until smooth. Stir in the remaining ingredients.

2. Drop by tablespoonfuls onto waxed paper-lined baking sheets. Refrigerate until firm. Store in the refrigerator.

Nutrition Facts: 1 piece equals 79 calories, 6 g fat (2 g saturated fat), 0 cholesterol, 26 mg sodium, 8 g carbohydrate, 1 g fiber, 2 g protein. **Diabetic Exchanges:** 1 fat, 1/2 starch.

> Feel free to adjust the recipe for **Trail Mix Clusters** to fit your family's tastes. Swap out the cashews or pecans for walnuts or almonds. Replace some of the dried fruit with raisins or banana chips. Instead of the flaked coconut, consider using crisp rice cereal. You can also add milk or dark chocolate to the semisweet mixture.

TRAIL MIX CLUSTERS

TASTY TORTILLA SOUP

EASY BEEF BARLEY SOUP

FULLY LOADED CHILI

Soups

Few foods chase the chill and satisfy hunger like soup. Loaded with veggies, beans and lean meats, soup is also a no-fuss fit with healthy eating goals, making this chapter one you'll gladly turn to time and again. Ladle out some comfort tonight.

Fully Loaded Chili

PREP: 20 min. **COOK:** 40 min.
YIELD: 8 servings (2 quarts)

CYNTHIA BACA • CRANBERRY TOWNSHIP, PENNSYLVANIA

With lean ground beef, four types of beans and lots of seasonings and toppings, this chili is truly "loaded." But those aren't the only heavyweights here; every serving provides a hefty 26 g protein and 11 g fiber.

1	lb. lean ground beef
1	medium onion, chopped
1	medium green pepper, chopped
1-3/4	cups water
2	cans (8 oz. *each*) tomato sauce
1	can (16 oz.) kidney beans, rinsed and drained
1	can (15-1/2 oz.) great northern beans, rinsed and drained
1	can (15 oz.) garbanzo beans *or* chickpeas, rinsed and drained
1	can (15 oz.) black beans, rinsed and drained
1	Tbsp. baking cocoa
2	tsp. Louisiana-style hot sauce
1/2	tsp. pepper
1/2	tsp. chili powder
1/4	tsp. garlic powder
1/8	tsp. cayenne pepper

GARNISHES:
1/2	cup reduced-fat sour cream
1/2	cup crushed baked tortilla chip scoops
1/2	cup shredded reduced-fat cheddar cheese

1. In a Dutch oven over medium heat, cook the beef, onion and pepper until meat is no longer pink; drain.

2. Stir in the water, tomato sauce, beans, cocoa, hot sauce and seasonings. Bring to a boil. Reduce heat; cover and simmer for 30 minutes. Garnish each serving with 1 tablespoon each of sour cream, crushed chips and cheese.

Nutrition Facts: 1 cup equals 351 calories, 9 g fat (4 g saturated fat), 38 mg cholesterol, 762 mg sodium, 42 g carbohydrate, 11 g fiber, 26 g protein. **Diabetic Exchanges:** 2-1/2 starch, 2 lean meat, 1 vegetable, 1/2 fat.

Black Bean Soup 🅼

PREP: 20 min. **COOK:** 25 min.
YIELD: 8 servings (2 quarts)

ANGEE OWENS • LUFKIN, TEXAS

This is an awesome main dish soup that's light and meatless, too. You could add lean beef or chicken for a simple variation.

3	cans (15 oz. *each*) black beans, rinsed and drained, *divided*
3	celery ribs with leaves, chopped
1	large onion, chopped
1	medium sweet red pepper, chopped
1	jalapeno pepper, seeded and chopped
4	garlic cloves, minced
2	Tbsp. olive oil
2	cans (14-1/2 oz. *each*) reduced-sodium chicken broth *or* vegetable broth
1	can (14-1/2 oz.) diced tomatoes with green peppers and onions, undrained
3	tsp. ground cumin
1-1/2	tsp. ground coriander
1	tsp. Louisiana-style hot sauce
1/4	tsp. pepper
1	bay leaf
1	tsp. lime juice
1/2	cup reduced-fat sour cream
1/4	cup chopped green onions

1. In a small bowl, mash one can black beans; set aside. In a Dutch oven, saute the celery, onion, red pepper, jalapeno and garlic in oil until tender. Stir in the broth, tomatoes, cumin, coriander, hot sauce, pepper, bay leaf, remaining beans and reserved mashed beans.

2. Bring to a boil. Reduce heat; cover and simmer for 15 minutes. Discard bay leaf. Stir in lime juice. Garnish each serving with 1 tablespoon sour cream and 1-1/2 teaspoons green onion.

Editor's Note: When cutting hot peppers, disposable gloves are recommended. Avoid touching your face.

Nutrition Facts: 1 cup equals 222 calories, 5 g fat (1 g saturated fat), 5 mg cholesterol, 779 mg sodium, 32 g carbohydrate, 9 g fiber, 11 g protein. **Diabetic Exchanges:** 2 starch, 1 very lean meat, 1 vegetable, 1 fat.

Makeover Hash Brown Soup

PREP: 15 min. **COOK:** 6 hours
YIELD: 8 servings

JUDITH WEBB • BLUE SPRINGS, MISSOURI

My niece served this once, and I loved it. I was pleased that "Healthy Cooking" skimmed away 420 calories for this version.

- 2   green onions, chopped
- 2   tsp. canola oil
- 1   pkg. (28 oz.) frozen O'Brien hash brown potatoes, thawed
- 2   cups 2% milk
- 1   can (10-3/4 oz.) reduced-fat reduced-sodium condensed cream of chicken soup, undiluted
- 6   turkey bacon strips, diced and cooked
- 1/2   cup shredded cheddar cheese

1. In a small skillet, saute onions in oil until tender. In a 5-qt. slow cooker, combine the potatoes, milk, soup and onion mixture. Cover and cook on low for 6-7 hours or until heated through. Top each serving with 2 tablespoons bacon and 1 tablespoon cheese.

Nutrition Facts: 3/4 cup equals 206 calories, 9 g fat (4 g saturated fat), 26 mg cholesterol, 520 mg sodium, 24 g carbohydrate, 2 g fiber, 8 g protein.

Herbed Tomato Soup F M

PREP/TOTAL TIME: 30 min. **YIELD:** 4 servings

HEALTHY COOKING TEST KITCHEN

No one will ever guess that a soup this smooth and creamy could be healthy! Our home economists combined wonderful herb flavors to create this keeper.

- 1   can (14-1/2 oz.) diced tomatoes, undrained
- 2   Tbsp. minced fresh parsley
- 1   Tbsp. finely chopped onion
- 3/4   tsp. dried basil
- 1/2   tsp. salt
- 1/8   tsp. pepper
- 1/4   cup tomato paste
- 3/4   cup nonfat dry milk powder
- 3   Tbsp. all-purpose flour
- 2   cups 2% milk

1. In a large saucepan, combine the first six ingredients; bring to a boil. Reduce heat; simmer, uncovered, for 10 minutes.

2. Stir in tomato paste until blended. In a small bowl, combine milk powder and flour; stir in milk until smooth. Gradually stir into soup. Cook and stir until thickened and heated through.

Nutrition Facts: 1 cup equals 201 calories, 3 g fat (2 g saturated fat), 14 mg cholesterol, 621 mg sodium, 31 g carbohydrate, 3 g fiber, 14 g protein. **Diabetic Exchanges:** 2 vegetable, 1 starch, 1 fat-free milk.

White Bean Soup

PREP: 20 min. + soaking
COOK: 2 hours **YIELD:** 11 servings (1-3/4 quarts)

ELIZABETH WAGNER • CLIO, MICHIGAN

I turned to this hearty recipe after my husband had open-heart surgery. We love it. I often serve it with salad and bread.

- 1/2   lb. dried baby lima beans
- 1/2   lb. dried great northern beans
- 2   lbs. boneless skinless chicken breasts, cubed

1 tsp. salt, *divided*
2 Tbsp. canola oil, *divided*
1 large onion, chopped
3 medium carrots, sliced
2 celery ribs, thinly sliced
1 garlic clove, minced
4 cups reduced-sodium chicken broth
2 cups water
1/2 tsp. pepper
1/4 cup minced fresh parsley

1. Sort beans and rinse with cold water. Place in a Dutch oven; add water to cover by 2 in. Bring to a boil; boil for 2 minutes. Remove from the heat; cover and let stand for 1-4 hours or until beans are softened.

2. Drain and rinse beans, discarding liquid; set beans aside. Sprinkle chicken with 1/2 teaspoon salt. In the same pan, saute chicken in 1 tablespoon oil until no longer pink. Drain and set aside. Saute onion in remaining oil until tender. Add the carrots, celery and garlic; saute 2 minutes longer.

3. Stir in the broth, water, pepper, beans and chicken; bring to a boil. Reduce heat; cover and simmer for 1-3/4 to 2-1/4 hours or until beans are tender. Stir in parsley and remaining salt.

Nutrition Facts: 1 cup equals 270 calories, 5 g fat (1 g saturated fat), 46 mg cholesterol, 499 mg sodium, 30 g carbohydrate, 9 g fiber, 27 g protein. **Diabetic Exchanges:** 2 starch, 2 very lean meat, 1/2 fat.

Two-Bean Chili F M

PREP: 40 min. **COOK:** 8 hours
YIELD: 6 servings (2 quarts)

RONALD JOHNSON • ELMHURST, ILLINOIS

The first time I had this chili, at a Super Bowl party, I was on my second bowl before I realized it had no meat. Chock-full of ingredients and flavor, it's hard to believe this one's low-fat.

1/2 lb. sliced fresh mushrooms
1 large green pepper, chopped
1 large sweet red pepper, chopped
2 celery ribs, chopped
1 medium onion, chopped

1 jalapeno pepper, seeded and chopped
1 Tbsp. olive oil
4 garlic cloves, minced
2 tsp. ground cumin
1 tsp. dried oregano
1 can (28 oz.) diced tomatoes, undrained
1 can (16 oz.) red beans, rinsed and drained
1 can (15 oz.) black beans, rinsed and drained
1 large carrot, chopped
1/2 cup water
1/2 cup barbecue sauce
1/4 cup chili powder
1 tsp. Liquid Smoke, optional

OPTIONAL TOPPINGS: Reduced-fat sour cream, hot pepper sauce, shredded cheddar cheese, chopped onion *and/or* crushed baked tortilla chip scoops

1. In a large skillet over medium heat, cook and stir the mushrooms, peppers, celery, onion and jalapeno in oil until onion is lightly browned. Add garlic, cumin and oregano; cook and stir 2 minutes longer. Transfer to a 5-qt. slow cooker. Stir in tomatoes, beans, carrot, water, barbecue sauce, chili powder and Liquid Smoke if desired.

2. Cover and cook on low for 8 hours or until vegetables are tender. Serve with optional toppings if desired.

Editor's Note: When cutting hot peppers, disposable gloves are recommended. Avoid touching your face.

Nutrition Facts: 1-1/3 cups (calculated without optional toppings) equals 185 calories, 3 g fat (trace saturated fat), 0 cholesterol, 702 mg sodium, 32 g carbohydrate, 10 g fiber, 9 g protein.

TWO-BEAN CHILI

WHITE BEAN SOUP

Italian-Style Lentil Soup F

PREP: 15 min. **COOK:** 40 min. **YIELD:** 6 servings

RACHEL KELLER • ROAN4OKE, VIRGINIA

I like to serve lentils often because they're inexpensive and nutritious. I sometimes add them to my homemade spaghetti sauce which I serve over noodles.

2	medium onions, chopped
2	celery ribs, thinly sliced
1	medium carrot, chopped
2	tsp. olive oil
5-1/4	cups water
1	cup dried lentils, rinsed
1/4	cup minced fresh parsley
1	Tbsp. reduced-sodium beef bouillon granules
1/2	tsp. pepper
1	can (6 oz.) tomato paste
2	Tbsp. white vinegar
2	tsp. brown sugar
1/2	tsp. salt
2	Tbsp. shredded Parmesan cheese

1. In a large saucepan coated with cooking spray, saute the onions, celery and carrot in oil until almost tender. Stir in the water, lentils, parsley, bouillon and pepper. Bring to a boil. Reduce heat; cover and simmer for 20-25 minutes or until lentils are tender, stirring occasionally.

2. Stir in the tomato paste, vinegar, brown sugar and salt; heat through. Sprinkle each serving with cheese.

Nutrition Facts: 1 cup equals 122 calories, 2 g fat (1 g saturated fat), 1 mg cholesterol, 420 mg sodium, 21 g carbohydrate, 6 g fiber, 6 g protein. **Diabetic Exchanges:** 2 vegetable, 1 starch.

"Apres-Ski" Soup F C

PREP/TOTAL TIME: 30 min. **YIELD:** 6 servings

NANCY HAMLIN • LITTLETON, COLORADO

"Apres-ski," French for "after skiing," refers to the social time directly after getting off the slopes, and this microwave soup is perfect for the occasion. Chock-full of healthy veggies, it'll warm you to your toes!

1	Tbsp. butter
1-1/4	cups cubed acorn squash
1	carrot, thinly sliced
1	medium leek (white portion only), thinly sliced
3	cans (14-1/2 oz. *each*) reduced-sodium chicken broth
1	small zucchini, halved and sliced
1/2	cup uncooked elbow macaroni
1	bay leaf
1/2	tsp. dried basil
1/4	tsp. dried thyme
1/8	tsp. salt
1/8	tsp. pepper

1. Place butter in a 3-qt. microwave-safe bowl; microwave on high for 20-30 seconds or until melted. Add the squash, carrot and leek; stir to coat. Cover and cook on high for 6 minutes.

2. Stir in the remaining ingredients; cover and cook on high for 12-14 minutes or until vegetables and macaroni are tender, stirring twice. Discard bay leaf.

Editor's Note: This recipe was tested in a 1,100-watt microwave.

Nutrition Facts: 1 cup equals 92 calories, 2 g fat (1 g saturated fat), 5 mg cholesterol, 594 mg sodium, 15 g carbohydrate, 3 g fiber, 4 g protein. **Diabetic Exchanges:** 1 vegetable, 1/2 starch, 1/2 fat.

Spiced Butternut Squash Soup F

PREP: 50 min. **COOK:** 25 min.
YIELD: 12 servings (3 quarts)

JULIE HESSION • LAS VEGAS, NEVADA

I like making this recipe year-round, but it's best in the fall and winter months when butternut squash is in season.

ITALIAN-STYLE LENTIL SOUP

SPICED BUTTERNUT SQUASH SOUP

2 medium butternut squash (about 3 lbs. *each*)
2 large onions, sliced
1 Tbsp. olive oil
1 Tbsp. butter
2 cinnamon sticks (3 in.)
2 Tbsp. brown sugar
1 Tbsp. minced fresh gingerroot
2 garlic cloves, minced
3 cans (14-1/2 oz. *each*) reduced-sodium chicken broth
2-1/4 cups water
1-1/4 tsp. salt
1 Tbsp. minced fresh parsley

1. Cut squash in half; discard the seeds. Place squash cut side down in a 15-in. x 10-in. x 1-in. baking pan coated with cooking spray. Bake at 400° for 40-50 minutes or until tender. Cool slightly; scoop out the pulp and set aside.

2. In a Dutch oven over medium heat, cook and stir onions in oil and butter for 2 minutes. Add the cinnamon, brown sugar, ginger and garlic; cook 2 minutes longer or until onions are tender. Stir in the broth, water, salt and reserved squash. Bring to a boil. Reduce heat; cover and simmer for 10 minutes.

3. Cool soup slightly. Discard cinnamon. In a blender, process soup in batches until smooth. Return all to the pan and heat through. Sprinkle each serving with parsley.

Nutrition Facts: 1 cup equals 133 calories, 2 g fat (1 g saturated fat), 3 mg cholesterol, 596 mg sodium, 28 g carbohydrate, 7 g fiber, 4 g protein. **Diabetic Exchanges:** 2 starch, 1/2 fat.

Southwest Bean Soup F

PREP: 15 min. **COOK:** 30 min.
YIELD: 13 servings (2-1/4 quarts)

MARIANNE BROWN • GLENDALE, ARIZONA

I've given this recipe to members of my weight-loss group, and they've said it's out of this world!

1 large onion, chopped
1 medium green pepper, chopped
3 garlic cloves, minced
3 cans (14-1/2 oz. *each*) reduced-sodium beef broth
2 cans (15 oz. *each*) black beans, rinsed and drained
1 can (28 oz.) diced tomatoes, undrained
2 cans (4 oz. *each*) chopped green chilies
1 cup frozen corn
1-1/2 tsp. chili powder
1 tsp. ground cumin
1/2 cup minced fresh cilantro

1. In a large nonstick saucepan coated with cooking spray, cook and stir the onion, green pepper and garlic over medium heat until almost tender.

2. Stir in the broth, beans, tomatoes, chilies, corn, chili powder and cumin. Bring to a boil. Reduce heat; cover and simmer for 20 minutes. Stir in cilantro.

Nutrition Facts: 1 cup equals 95 calories, trace fat (trace saturated fat), 2 mg cholesterol, 459 mg sodium, 18 g carbohydrate, 5 g fiber, 5 g protein. **Diabetic Exchanges:** 1 starch, 1 vegetable.

WINTER HARVEST VEGETABLE SOUP

Winter Harvest Vegetable Soup F M

PREP: 25 min. **COOK:** 50 min. **YIELD:** 12 servings (3 quarts)

BARBARA MARAKOWSKI • LOYSVILLE, PENNSYLVANIA

Root vegetables blend with savory spices and apples in this wonderful soup. A friend gave me the recipe after my husband's cardiac surgery, and now it's our favorite.

  3 medium carrots, halved and thinly sliced
3/4 cup chopped celery
  1 medium onion, chopped
  2 green onions, thinly sliced
  1 garlic clove, minced
  1 Tbsp. butter
  1 Tbsp. olive oil
  7 cups reduced-sodium chicken broth *or* vegetable broth
  3 cups cubed peeled potatoes
  2 cups cubed peeled butternut squash
  2 large tart apples, peeled and chopped
  2 medium turnips, peeled and chopped
  2 parsnips, peeled and sliced
  1 bay leaf
1/2 tsp. dried basil
1/4 tsp. dried thyme
1/4 tsp. pepper
Additional thinly sliced green onions, optional

1. In a Dutch oven over medium heat, cook and stir the carrots, celery, onions and garlic in butter and oil until tender.

2. Add the broth, potatoes, squash, apples, turnips, parsnips and bay leaf. Bring to a boil. Reduce heat; simmer, uncovered, for 20 minutes.

3. Stir in the basil, thyme and pepper; simmer 15 minutes longer or until vegetables are tender. Discard bay leaf before serving. Garnish with additional green onions if desired.

Nutrition Facts: 1 cup equals 134 calories, 2 g fat (1 g saturated fat), 3 mg cholesterol, 404 mg sodium, 27 g carbohydrate, 5 g fiber, 4 g protein. **Diabetic Exchanges:** 1-1/2 starch, 1 vegetable.

Spicy Three-Bean Chili F M

PREP: 20 min. **COOK:** 30 min.
YIELD: 8 servings (2-1/2 quarts)

MELISSA MENDEZ • GILBERT, MINNESOTA

Even my meat-loving family devours this chunky meatless chili. Since it's more fun to eat with your hands, we scoop it up with chips! Don't let the ingredient list fool you. It's so fast and simple to make. Try it and see.

  1 medium green pepper, chopped
  1 medium sweet yellow pepper, chopped
  1 jalapeno pepper, seeded and chopped
  1 medium onion, chopped
  3 garlic cloves, minced
  1 Tbsp. olive oil
  2 cans (14-1/2 oz. *each*) diced tomatoes with mild green chilies, undrained
  1 can (10 oz.) diced tomatoes and green chilies, undrained
  1 can (16 oz.) kidney beans, rinsed and drained
  1 can (15 oz.) black beans, rinsed and drained

1 cup vegetable broth
1 tsp. chili powder
3/4 tsp. ground cumin
1/2 tsp. cayenne pepper
1 can (16 oz.) spicy fat-free refried beans
1/3 cup shredded reduced-fat cheddar cheese
1/3 cup thinly sliced green onions

1. In a Dutch oven coated with cooking spray, saute the peppers, onion and garlic in oil until tender. Stir in the tomatoes, kidney beans, black beans, broth, chili powder, cumin and cayenne. Bring to a boil. Reduce heat; simmer, uncovered, for 10 minutes.

2. Stir in refried beans; simmer 10 minutes longer. Garnish each serving with 2 teaspoons each of cheese and green onions.

Editor's Note: When cutting or seeding hot peppers, use rubber or plastic gloves to protect your hands. Avoid touching your face.

Nutrition Facts: 1-1/4 cups equals 201 calories, 3 g fat (1 g saturated fat), 3 mg cholesterol, 803 mg sodium, 34 g carbohydrate, 8 g fiber, 10 g protein. **Diabetic Exchanges:** 2 starch, 1 very lean meat, 1 vegetable.

Italian Dinner Soup

PREP: 20 min. **COOK:** 1-1/4 hours
YIELD: 7 servings (about 2-1/2 quarts)

JOAN WINTERLE • CENTER BARNSTEAD, NEW HAMPSHIRE

My husband takes soup or stew to work for lunch daily. He requests this hearty dish nearly every time I ask him what I should make him.

1 lb. boneless skinless chicken breasts, cubed
1 medium green pepper, chopped
1 medium sweet red pepper, chopped
1 medium onion, chopped
1 celery rib, thinly sliced
1 small carrot, thinly sliced
1 garlic clove, minced
4 cups water
1 can (28 oz.) Italian crushed tomatoes
1 can (14-1/2 oz.) reduced-sodium chicken broth
3 Tbsp. grated Parmesan cheese
1 tsp. Italian seasoning
1/2 tsp. crushed red pepper flakes
1/4 tsp. salt
1/4 tsp. pepper
1 cup uncooked elbow macaroni
7 Tbsp. shredded part-skim mozzarella cheese

1. In a nonstick Dutch oven coated with cooking spray, cook the chicken over medium heat until no longer pink. Remove and keep warm.

2. Add the peppers, onion, celery, carrot and garlic to the pan; cook and stir until crisp-tender. Add the chicken, water, tomatoes, broth, Parmesan cheese and seasonings. Bring to a boil. Reduce heat; simmer, uncovered, for 40 minutes.

3. Stir in macaroni; cook 20 minutes longer or until macaroni is tender. Sprinkle each serving with mozzarella cheese.

Nutrition Facts: 1-1/2 cups equals 203 calories, 4 g fat (2 g saturated fat), 42 mg cholesterol, 707 mg sodium, 22 g carbohydrate, 3 g fiber, 20 g protein. **Diabetic Exchanges:** 2 very lean meat, 1-1/2 starch.

Yellow Pepper Soup

PREP: 20 min. **COOK:** 40 min. **YIELD:** 5 servings

EDWARD GRIFFITHS • STOWE, VERMONT

Enjoy a robust cup of soup that's flavored with the mild and sweet taste of yellow peppers. Garlic and minced chives are a lovely addition.

2-1/2 cups water
3 large sweet yellow peppers, chopped
1 large potato, chopped
1 large onion, chopped
3 garlic cloves, minced
1-1/2 tsp. sugar
3/4 tsp. salt
1/4 tsp. pepper
1 Tbsp. butter
1 Tbsp. olive oil
1 Tbsp. minced chives

1. In a large saucepan, combine the first eight ingredients. Bring to a boil. Reduce heat; cover and simmer for 30 minutes or until vegetables are tender. Cool slightly.

2. In a blender, process soup in batches until smooth. Return to the pan. Add butter and oil; cook and stir until heated through and butter is melted (do not boil). Sprinkle with chives.

Nutrition Facts: 1 cup equals 152 calories, 5 g fat (2 g saturated fat), 6 mg cholesterol, 385 mg sodium, 25 g carbohydrate, 3 g fiber, 3 g protein. **Diabetic Exchanges:** 2 vegetable, 1 starch, 1 fat.

SPICY THREE-BEAN CHILI

Curried Chicken Corn Chowder

PREP: 15 min. **COOK:** 30 min.
YIELD: 9 servings (2-1/4 quarts)

KENDRA DOSS • SMITHVILLE, MISSOURI

This recipe is close to one my mom used to make for us kids when the weather turned cold. Her's called for heavy cream, but I came up with a slimmer version that I think is pretty true to the original.

2	medium onions, chopped
2	celery ribs, chopped
1	Tbsp. butter
3	cans (14-1/2 oz. *each*) reduced-sodium chicken broth
5	cups frozen corn
2	tsp. curry powder
1/4	tsp. salt
1/4	tsp. pepper

Dash cayenne pepper

1/2	cup all-purpose flour
1/2	cup 2% milk
3	cups cubed cooked chicken breast
1/3	cup minced fresh cilantro

1. In a Dutch oven, saute onions and celery in butter until tender. Stir in the broth, corn, curry, salt, pepper and cayenne. Bring to a boil. Reduce heat; cover and simmer for 15 minutes.

2. In a small bowl, whisk flour and milk until smooth. Whisk into the pan. Bring to a boil; cook and stir for 2 minutes or until thickened. Add chicken and cilantro; heat through.

Nutrition Facts: 1 cup equals 221 calories, 4 g fat (1 g saturated fat), 40 mg cholesterol, 517 mg sodium, 29 g carbohydrate, 3 g fiber, 20 g protein. **Diabetic Exchanges:** 2 starch, 2 very lean meat.

New England Clam Chowder

PREP: 20 min. **COOK:** 35 min. **YIELD:** 5 servings

SANDY LARSON • PORT ANGELES, WASHINGTON

In the Pacific Northwest, we dig our own razor clams, and I grind them for this light and creamy chowder. Razor clams aren't available everywhere, but canned clams are also perfectly acceptable.

4	center-cut bacon strips
2	celery ribs, chopped
1	large onion, chopped
1	garlic clove, minced
3	small potatoes, peeled and cubed
1	cup water
1	bottle (8 oz.) clam juice
3	tsp. reduced-sodium chicken bouillon granules
1/4	tsp. white pepper
1/4	tsp. dried thyme
1/3	cup all-purpose flour
2	cups fat-free half-and-half, *divided*
2	cans (6-1/2 oz. *each*) chopped clams, undrained

1. In a Dutch oven, cook bacon over medium heat until crisp. Remove to paper towels to drain; set aside. Saute the celery, onion and garlic in the drippings until tender. Stir in the potatoes, water, clam juice, bouillon, pepper and thyme. Bring to a boil. Reduce heat; simmer, uncovered, for 15-20 minutes or until potatoes are tender.

2. In a small bowl, combine flour and 1 cup half-and-half until smooth. Gradually stir into soup. Bring to a boil; cook and stir for 1-2 minutes or until thickened.

3. Stir in clams and remaining half-and-half; heat through (do not boil). Crumble the reserved bacon; sprinkle over each serving.

Nutrition Facts: 1-1/3 cups equals 260 calories, 4 g fat (1 g saturated fat), 22 mg cholesterol, 788 mg sodium, 39 g carbohydrate, 3 g fiber, 13 g protein. **Diabetic Exchanges:** 2-1/2 starch, 1 lean meat.

NEW ENGLAND CLAM CHOWDER

CURRIED CHICKEN CORN CHOWDER

RUSTIC ITALIAN TORTELLINI SOUP

Rustic Italian Tortellini Soup

PREP: 20 min. **COOK:** 20 min. **YIELD:** 6 servings (2 quarts)

TRACY FASNACHT • IRWIN, PENNSYLVANIA

This is my favorite soup recipe. It's quick to fix on a busy night.

3	Italian turkey sausage links (4 oz. *each*), casings removed
1	medium onion, chopped
6	garlic cloves, minced
2	cans (14-1/2 oz. *each*) reduced-sodium chicken broth
1-3/4	cups water
1	can (14-1/2 oz.) diced tomatoes, undrained
1	pkg. (9 oz.) refrigerated cheese tortellini
1	pkg. (6 oz.) fresh baby spinach, coarsely chopped
2-1/4	tsp. minced fresh basil *or* 3/4 tsp. dried basil
1/4	tsp. pepper

Dash crushed red pepper flakes

Shredded Parmesan cheese, optional

1. Crumble sausage into a Dutch oven; add onion. Cook and stir over medium heat until meat is no longer pink. Add garlic; cook and stir 2 minutes longer. Add the broth, water and tomatoes. Bring to a boil.

2. Stir in tortellini; return to a boil. Reduce heat; simmer, uncovered, for 5-8 minutes or until tortellini are tender, stirring occasionally. Add the spinach, basil, pepper and pepper flakes; cook 2-3 minutes longer or until spinach is wilted. Serve with cheese if desired.

Nutrition Facts: 1-1/3 cups (calculated without cheese) equals 203 calories, 8 g fat (2 g saturated fat), 40 mg cholesterol, 878 mg sodium, 18 g carbohydrate, 3 g fiber, 16 g protein.

Broccoli Soup c

PREP: 15 min. **COOK:** 25 min. **YIELD:** 5 servings

LORRAINE ELLINGSON • STRATHMORE, ALBERTA

This makes a great comfort meal on a cold day. Feel free to adjust the amount of Dijon mustard, cumin or nutmeg when stirring up a batch for your family.

1	large onion, chopped
1	garlic clove, minced
1	Tbsp. butter
2	cups water
1	can (10-1/2 oz.) condensed chicken broth, undiluted
3	medium carrots, thinly sliced
1	tsp. Dijon mustard
1/4	tsp. ground cumin
1/4	tsp. ground nutmeg
1	bunch broccoli (about 1-1/2 lbs.)
5	Tbsp. reduced-fat sour cream

1. In a large saucepan, saute onion and garlic in butter until tender. Add the water, broth, carrots, mustard, cumin and nutmeg. Bring to a boil. Reduce heat; cover and simmer for 10 minutes.

2. Meanwhile, peel broccoli stalks and cut into 1/4-in. slices. Coarsely chop florets. Add to onion mixture; cover and simmer for 8-10 minutes or until vegetables are tender. Cool slightly.

3. In a blender, cover and process soup in batches until smooth. Return all to the pan and heat through. Dollop each serving with sour cream.

Nutrition Facts: 1 cup equals 123 calories, 5 g fat (3 g saturated fat), 12 mg cholesterol, 478 mg sodium, 5 g carbohydrate, 5 g fiber, 8 g protein. **Diabetic Exchanges:** 2 vegetable, 1 fat.

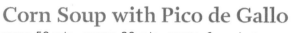

Corn Soup with Pico de Gallo

PREP: 50 min. **COOK:** 20 min. **YIELD:** 6 servings

ELAINE SWEET • DALLAS, TEXAS

My son loves the way the kitchen smells when this soup is cooking. He comes into the kitchen and fans the aroma into his face, and I know he is happy.

3	corn tortillas (6 in.), cut into 1-in. strips
4	medium ears sweet corn, husks removed
1/2	tsp. canola oil
1/2	tsp. *each* salt, pepper and paprika
1	medium red onion, chopped
1	bacon strip, chopped
6	garlic cloves, minced
1/4	cup all-purpose flour
3	cups reduced-sodium chicken broth
1	cup fat-free milk
1	can (4 oz.) chopped green chilies
1	tsp. ground cumin
1	tsp. dried oregano
1/2	cup minced fresh cilantro
1/4	cup lime juice

PICO DE GALLO:

2	plum tomatoes, chopped
1	medium ripe avocado, peeled and chopped
1	small serrano pepper, seeded and chopped
1	garlic clove, minced
1/4	tsp. salt
1/4	tsp. pepper

1. Place tortilla strips on a baking sheet coated with cooking spray; bake strips at 350° for 8-10 minutes or until crisp.

2. Coat grill rack with cooking spray before starting the grill. Rub corn with oil; sprinkle with seasonings. Grill, covered, over medium heat for 10-12 minutes or until tender, turning frequently. Cool slightly; cut corn from cobs and set aside.

3. In a saucepan, saute onion, bacon and garlic for 5 minutes. Stir in flour until blended; gradually add broth. Bring to a boil; cook and stir for 2 minutes or until thickened. Add corn, milk, chilies, cumin and oregano; heat through. Remove from heat; stir in cilantro and lime juice.

4. Combine pico de gallo ingredients. Serve with soup and tortilla strips.

Editor's Note: When cutting hot peppers, disposable gloves are recommended. Avoid touching your face.

Nutrition Facts: 3/4 cup soup with 1/4 cup pico de gallo and 3 tortilla strips equals 217 calories, 8 g fat (1 g saturated fat), 3 mg cholesterol, 740 mg sodium, 33 g carbohydrate, 6 g fiber, 8 g protein. **Diabetic Exchanges:** 2 starch, 1-1/2 fat.

Satisfying Lentil Soup F M

PREP: 20 min. **COOK:** 65 min.
YIELD: 10 servings (2-1/2 quarts)

EDNA HOFFMAN • HEBRON, INDIANA

This heart-healthy soup packs 15 g of fiber into each serving. Believe me—you'll want seconds!

4	medium carrots, chopped
2	celery ribs, chopped
1	large onion, chopped
2	Tbsp. olive oil
1	Tbsp. minced fresh gingerroot
2	tsp. curry powder
2	garlic cloves, minced
3/4	tsp. ground cumin
3/4	tsp. ground coriander
5	cups water
2	cans (14-1/2 oz. *each*) reduced-sodium chicken broth *or* vegetable broth
1	pkg. (16 oz.) dry lentils

2 Tbsp. minced fresh cilantro
3/4 tsp. salt
Dash pepper

1. In a Dutch oven, saute the carrots, celery and onion in oil until tender. Add the ginger, curry, garlic, cumin and coriander; cook and stir 1 minute longer.

2. Add the water, broth and lentils; bring to a boil. Reduce heat; cover and simmer for 50-55 minutes or until the lentils are tender. Stir in the cilantro, salt and pepper.

Nutrition Facts: 1 cup equals 203 calories, 3 g fat (trace saturated fat), 0 cholesterol, 415 mg sodium, 31 g carbohydrate, 15 g fiber, 14 g protein. **Diabetic Exchanges:** 1-1/2 starch, 1 vegetable, 1 fat.

Farmer's Delight Chili

PREP: 10 min. + standing **COOK:** 1-1/4 hours
YIELD: 6 servings (2-1/4 quarts)

IOLA EGLE • BELLA VISTA, ARKANSAS

Bulgur and kidney beans bring plenty of fill-you-up fiber to this flavorful chili. Feel free to toss in whatever veggies you happen to have on hand for extra flavor.

    1 cup bulgur
    1 cup boiling water
    1 lb. lean ground beef
    1 large onion, chopped
    1 medium green pepper, chopped
    2 cans (14-1/2 oz. *each*) reduced-sodium beef broth
    1 can (16 oz.) kidney beans, rinsed and drained
    1 can (14-1/2 oz.) diced tomatoes, undrained
    1 can (8 oz.) tomato sauce
  1/2 cup water
    1 Tbsp. chili powder
  1/4 tsp. salt
  1/8 tsp. white pepper
  1/8 tsp. cayenne pepper

1. Place bulgur in a small bowl; stir in boiling water. Cover and let stand for 30 minutes or until most of the liquid is absorbed.

2. In a Dutch oven, cook the beef, onion and green pepper over medium heat until meat is no longer pink; drain. Stir in the broth, beans, tomatoes, tomato sauce, water and seasonings.

3. Drain bulgur; stir into chili and bring to a boil. Reduce heat; cover and simmer for 1 hour.

Nutrition Facts: 1-1/2 cups equals 308 calories, 6 g fat (2 g saturated fat), 40 mg cholesterol, 799 mg sodium, 39 g carbohydrate, 10 g fiber, 25 g protein. **Diabetic Exchanges:** 2 starch, 2 lean meat, 2 vegetable.

Makeover Creamy Seafood Soup

PREP/TOTAL TIME: 30 min. **YIELD:** 6 servings

MILDRED FASIG • STEPHENS CITY, VIRGINIA

I've learned that cutting fat and calories doesn't always mean giving up the dishes you enjoy. We love seafood soup, but needed this lighter version to fit with my health goals.

  1/2 lb. uncooked medium shrimp, peeled and deveined
  1/2 lb. bay scallops
    2 Tbsp. butter, *divided*
    2 celery ribs, thinly sliced
    1 medium sweet red pepper, finely chopped
    1 medium onion, finely chopped
  1/4 cup all-purpose flour
    2 cups fat-free milk
    2 cups half-and-half cream
  1/4 cup sherry *or* reduced-sodium chicken broth
    1 Tbsp. minced fresh thyme *or* 1 tsp. dried thyme
  1/2 tsp. salt
  1/4 tsp. cayenne pepper
  1/8 tsp. ground nutmeg

1. In a Dutch oven, saute shrimp and scallops in 1 tablespoon butter until shrimp turn pink. Remove and set aside.

2. In the same pan, saute the celery, red pepper and onion in remaining butter until tender. Sprinkle with flour; stir until blended. Gradually stir in the remaining ingredients. Bring to a boil; cook and stir for 2 minutes or until thickened. Return seafood to the pan; heat through.

Nutrition Facts: 1 cup equals 274 calories, 13 g fat (8 g saturated fat), 120 mg cholesterol, 436 mg sodium, 16 g carbohydrate, 1 g fiber, 19 g protein.

Bay scallops are a key ingredient in Makeover Creamy Seafood Soup. When purchasing scallops, keep in mind that there are two varieties. Bay scallops are small and slightly sweet. They are a bit more expensive than sea scallops. Sea scallops are larger (about 1–1/2 inches in diameter, roughly 30 to a pound) and more common.

MAKEOVER CREAMY SEAFOOD SOUP

Tasty Tortilla Soup

PREP: 20 min. **COOK:** 40 min. **YIELD:** 7 servings

JENNIFER GILES • DES MOINES, IOWA

I got this terrific recipe from a friend. There's a restaurant in our town that serves a fabulous tortilla soup. I've been told that this version rivals theirs.

1	large onion, chopped
2	green onions, thinly sliced
2	Tbsp. butter
4	garlic cloves, minced
2	Tbsp. all-purpose flour
4-1/2	cups reduced-sodium chicken broth
2	cans (14-1/2 oz. *each*) no-salt-added diced tomatoes, undrained
1	can (8 oz.) no-salt-added tomato sauce
1	can (4 oz.) chopped green chilies
1	Tbsp. minced fresh oregano *or* 1 tsp. dried oregano
2	tsp. ground cumin
1/4	tsp. pepper
3	cups cubed cooked chicken breast
2	Tbsp. minced fresh cilantro
1-1/3	cups crushed baked tortilla chip scoops
7	Tbsp. shredded reduced-fat cheddar cheese

1. In a Dutch oven, saute onion and green onions in butter until tender. Add garlic; saute 2 minutes longer.

2. Stir in flour until blended; gradually add broth. Stir in the tomatoes, tomato sauce, chilies, oregano, cumin and pepper. Bring to a boil. Reduce heat; cover and simmer for 20 minutes. Add chicken and cilantro; heat through.

3. For each serving, place 2 tablespoons chips in a soup bowl. Top with 1-1/2 cups soup. Garnish each serving with 1 tablespoon each of cheese and chips.

Nutrition Facts: 1 serving equals 256 calories, 8 g fat (4 g saturated fat), 60 mg cholesterol, 654 mg sodium, 23 g carbohydrate, 4 g fiber, 24 g protein. **Diabetic Exchanges:** 3 very lean meat, 2 vegetable, 1 starch, 1/2 fat.

TASTY TORTILLA SOUP

Rich 'n' Savory Tomato Soup

PREP: 15 min. **COOK:** 40 min. **YIELD:** 4 servings

CINDY REYNOLDS • DECATUR, ILLINOIS

This has to be the best tomato soup recipe ever! I serve it, or variations of it, at least once a week due to popular demand. It's often the first course for company.

1	large onion, chopped
8	fresh baby carrots, sliced
1	Tbsp. olive oil
2	Tbsp. all-purpose flour
1	can (14-1/2 oz.) reduced-sodium chicken broth
1	can (28 oz.) diced tomatoes, undrained
1/2	tsp. sugar
1/8	tsp. pepper
Dash salt	
1/2	cup refrigerated nondairy creamer
1/4	tsp. vanilla extract
2	Tbsp. minced fresh basil

1. In a large saucepan, saute onion and carrots in oil until tender. Stir in flour until blended; gradually add broth. Stir in the tomatoes, sugar, pepper and salt. Bring to a boil. Reduce heat; cover and simmer for 30 minutes. Cool slightly.

2. Transfer to a blender. Cover and process until smooth. Return to the pan; stir in creamer and vanilla. Heat through (do not boil). Garnish with basil.

Nutrition Facts: 3/4 cup equals 151 calories, 6 g fat (1 g saturated fat), 0 cholesterol, 615 mg sodium, 22 g carbohydrate, 4 g fiber, 4 g protein. **Diabetic Exchanges:** 1-1/2 starch, 1/2 fat.

Easy Beef Barley Soup

PREP: 15 min. **COOK:** 55 min. **YIELD:** 4 servings

CAROLE LANTHIER • COURTICE, ONTARIO

This soup is really easy and takes very little time to put together. Serve it for lunch or supper with some fresh homemade bread.

1/2	lb. lean ground beef
2	large fresh mushrooms, sliced
1	celery rib, chopped
1	small onion, chopped

EASY BEEF BARLEY SOUP

MAKEOVER BAKED POTATO SOUP

2 tsp. all-purpose flour

3 cans (14-1/2 oz. *each*) reduced-sodium beef broth

2 medium carrots, sliced

1 large potato, peeled and cubed

1/2 tsp. pepper

1/8 tsp. salt

1/3 cup medium pearl barley

1 can (5 oz.) evaporated milk

2 Tbsp. tomato paste

1. In a Dutch oven over medium heat, cook and stir the beef, mushrooms, celery and onion until meat is no longer pink; drain. Stir in flour until blended; gradually add broth. Stir in the carrots, potato, pepper and salt. Bring to a boil. Stir in barley.

2. Reduce heat; cover and simmer for 45-50 minutes or until barley is tender. Whisk in milk and tomato paste; heat through.

Nutrition Facts: 1-3/4 cups equals 317 calories, 7 g fat (3 g saturated fat), 45 mg cholesterol, 753 mg sodium, 42 g carbohydrate, 6 g fiber, 21 g protein. **Diabetic Exchanges:** 2-1/2 starch, 2 lean meat, 1 vegetable.

Makeover Baked Potato Soup

PREP: 30 min. **COOK:** 20 min.
YIELD: 8 servings (2 quarts)

JUDY TYLER • BOSSIER CITY, LOUISIANA

We adore baked potato soup, but with my husband's high cholesterol, we didn't enjoy it much. This version changed that!

3 medium potatoes

5 bacon strips, diced

1 medium onion, chopped

1/4 cup plus 3 Tbsp. all-purpose flour, *divided*

6 cups reduced-sodium chicken broth

1/4 cup minced fresh parsley

2 garlic cloves, minced

1-1/2 tsp. dried basil

1/4 tsp. salt

1/4 tsp. pepper

1/2 to 1-1/2 tsp. hot pepper sauce

2 cups milk

1/2 cup shredded sharp cheddar cheese

1/4 cup chopped green onions (white portion only)

Additional parsley, cheese, green onions and crumbled cooked bacon, optional

1. Scrub and pierce potatoes; place on a microwave-safe plate. Microwave, uncovered, on high for 8-12 minutes or until tender, turning once.

2. Meanwhile, in a large saucepan, cook bacon over medium heat until crisp. Using a slotted spoon, remove to paper towels.

3. In the drippings, saute onion until tender. Stir in 1/4 cup flour; cook and stir for 5-7 minutes or until golden brown. Gradually stir in broth. Add the parsley, garlic, basil, salt, pepper and hot pepper sauce. Bring to a boil; cook and stir for 2 minutes or until thickened.

4. In a small bowl, whisk the remaining flour with milk until smooth; add to the pan. Bring to a boil; cook and stir for 2 minutes or until slightly thickened.

5. Peel and cube potatoes; add to soup. Add bacon. Cook and stir until heated through. Add cheese and green onions; stir just until cheese is melted. Garnish with additional parsley, cheese, green onions and bacon if desired.

Editor's Note: This recipe was tested in a 1,100-watt microwave.

Nutrition Facts: 1 cup (calculated without optional toppings) equals 235 calories, 12 g fat (6 g saturated fat), 25 mg cholesterol, 720 mg sodium, 22 g carbohydrate, 2 g fiber, 9 g protein.

BROWN RICE SALAD

POTATO SALAD

BISTRO TURKEY SANDWICHES

Salads & Sandwiches

It's no surprise that a heart-smart cookbook includes refreshing salads, but most cooks wouldn't expect to find creamy potato salads or piled-high sandwiches! Page through this colorful chapter and you'll be amazed at what's in store.

Bistro Turkey Sandwiches

PREP/TOTAL TIME: 30 min. **YIELD:** 6 servings

VERONICA CALLAGHAN • GLASTONBURY, CONNECTICUT

Sweet and savory flavors come together in this healthful sandwich. It's great for busy weeknights.

- 1 small red onion, thinly sliced
- 4 tsp. brown sugar, *divided*
- 1 Tbsp. olive oil
- 1/4 tsp. salt
- 1/8 tsp. cayenne pepper
- 1/4 cup Dijon mustard
- 1 Tbsp. apple cider *or* unsweetened apple juice
- 6 wheat sandwich buns, split
- 6 Bibb *or* Boston lettuce leaves
- 1 medium pear, peeled and thinly sliced
- 1 lb. cooked turkey breast, thinly sliced
- 1/4 cup loosely packed basil leaves
- 6 Tbsp. crumbled Gorgonzola cheese

1. In a small skillet over medium heat, cook onion and 1 teaspoon brown sugar in oil for 8-10 minutes or until golden brown, stirring frequently. Stir in salt and cayenne.

2. Combine the mustard, apple cider and remaining brown sugar; spread over bun bottoms. Layer with lettuce, pear, turkey, basil and cheese. Top with caramelized onion. Replace tops.

Nutrition Facts: 1 sandwich equals 346 calories, 8 g fat (3 g saturated fat), 71 mg cholesterol, 708 mg sodium, 35 g carbohydrate, 4 g fiber, 31 g protein. **Diabetic Exchanges:** 3 very lean meat, 2 starch, 1 fat.

Potato Salad **F** **M**

PREP: 30 min. + chilling **YIELD:** 6 servings

DOROTHY BAYES • SARDIS, OHIO

I made my Potato Salad when I worked at a small hospital. It was served in the cafeteria to patients who were on diabetic, heart-healthy and regular diets.

- 4 cups cubed peeled potatoes
- 1 celery rib, thinly sliced
- 1/3 cup finely chopped onion
- 1/3 cup sweet pickle relish
- 3/4 cup fat-free mayonnaise
- 1 tsp. ground mustard
- 1/2 tsp. salt
- 1/4 tsp. celery seed
- 1/8 tsp. pepper
- 2 hard-cooked eggs, sliced
- 1/8 tsp. paprika

1. Place potatoes in a large saucepan and cover with water. Bring to a boil. Reduce heat; cover and simmer for 10-15 minutes or until tender. Drain and cool to room temperature.

2. In a large bowl, combine the potatoes, celery, onion and relish. In a small bowl, combine the mayonnaise, mustard, salt, celery seed and pepper. Pour over potato mixture and toss to coat. Cover and refrigerate until chilled. Top with eggs and sprinkle with paprika.

Nutrition Facts: 3/4 cup equals 163 calories, 3 g fat (1 g saturated fat), 74 mg cholesterol, 582 mg sodium, 31 g carbohydrate, 3 g fiber, 4 g protein. **Diabetic Exchanges:** 2 starch, 1/2 fat.

Brown Rice Salad **F** **M**

PREP: 10 min. + chilling **YIELD:** 6 servings

ROSEMARIE BUSH • BURLINGTON, NORTH CAROLINA

Bottled salad dressing gives just the right amount of punch to this cold rice-and-beans salad. It's perfect for warm summer picnics and casual get-togethers.

- 2 cups cooked brown rice, cooled
- 1 can (16 oz.) kidney beans, rinsed and drained
- 2 celery ribs with leaves, chopped
- 1 medium red onion, chopped
- 2 garlic cloves, minced
- 4-1/2 tsp. minced fresh parsley *or* 1-1/2 tsp. dried parsley flakes
- 1/4 tsp. salt
- 1/4 tsp. pepper
- 1/2 cup fat-free Italian salad dressing

1. In a large bowl, combine the first eight ingredients. Add salad dressing; toss to coat.

2. Cover and refrigerate until chilled.

Nutrition Facts: 2/3 cup equals 162 calories, 1 g fat (trace saturated fat), 1 mg cholesterol, 522 mg sodium, 32 g carbohydrate, 6 g fiber, 7 g protein. **Diabetic Exchange:** 2 starch.

Fennel Waldorf Salad C M

PREP/TOTAL TIME: 25 min. **YIELD:** 4 servings

DONNA NOEL • GRAY, MAINE

The old standby Waldorf salad is simply too good to let slip away! Here's a new slant featuring fresh fennel. Try Braeburn apples for fresh, crisp flavor.

1-1/2	cups sliced fennel bulb
1-1/2	cups sliced apples
3	Tbsp. fat-free mayonnaise
1-1/2	tsp. fat-free milk
1-1/2	tsp. grated onion
1/8	tsp. salt
1/3	cup chopped pecans, toasted

1. In a large bowl, combine fennel and apples. In a small bowl, whisk the mayonnaise, milk, onion and salt.

2. Pour over fennel mixture and toss to coat. Just before serving, stir in pecans.

Nutrition Facts: 3/4 cup equals 112 calories, 8 g fat (1 g saturated fat), 1 mg cholesterol, 172 mg sodium, 12 g carbohydrate, 3 g fiber, 1 g protein. **Diabetic Exchanges:** 1-1/2 fat, 1 vegetable, 1/2 fruit.

Apple Cranberry Delight F S

PREP/TOTAL TIME: 25 min. + chilling **YIELD:** 6 servings

BEVERLY KOESTER • APPLETON, WISCONSIN

My husband and I went to a cranberry festival, and I came home with 5 pounds of berries! Luckily, they freeze well and taste great in this four-item dish.

1-1/2	cups fresh or frozen cranberries
1-3/4	cups unsweetened apple juice, *divided*
1	pkg. (.3 oz.) sugar-free cranberry gelatin
2	cups chopped peeled Golden Delicious apples

1. In a small saucepan, combine cranberries and 1 cup apple juice. Bring to a boil. Reduce heat; cover and simmer for 10-15 minutes or until the berries pop. Stir in gelatin until dissolved. Remove from the heat; stir in apples and remaining apple juice.

2. Pour into a 4-cup mold coated with cooking spray. Refrigerate for 4 hours or until firm. Unmold onto a serving plate.

Nutrition Facts: 1/2 cup equals 70 calories, trace fat (trace saturated fat), 0 cholesterol, 42 mg sodium, 16 g carbohydrate, 2 g fiber, 1 g protein. **Diabetic Exchange:** 1 fruit.

Greek Chicken Sandwiches

PREP/TOTAL TIME: 25 min. **YIELD:** 4 servings

TOM WOLF • TIGARD, OREGON

My wife and I ate sandwiches similar to these at a restaurant and enjoyed them. But they weren't nearly as flavorful as this quick and zesty recipe I came up with!

- 1 lb. boneless skinless chicken breasts, cut into 1-in. cubes
- 1/3 cup fat-free Caesar salad dressing
- 1/4 cup crumbled feta cheese
- 1/4 cup pitted Greek olives, finely chopped
- 1/4 tsp. garlic powder
- 4 pita breads (6 in.), halved
- 8 lettuce leaves
- 1 medium tomato, sliced
- 1 small onion, sliced

1. In a large nonstick skillet coated with cooking spray, cook and stir chicken over medium heat until no longer pink. Add the dressing, cheese, olives and garlic powder; heat through.

2. Line pita halves with lettuce, tomato and onion; add about 1/3 cup chicken mixture to each.

Nutrition Facts: 2 filled pita halves equals 381 calories, 7 g fat (2 g saturated fat), 66 mg cholesterol, 832 mg sodium, 47 g carbohydrate, 3 g fiber, 31 g protein.

Italian Beef Sandwiches

PREP: 20 min. **COOK:** 5 hours **YIELD:** 12 servings

TROY PARKOS • VERONA, WISCONSIN

With a little kick and plenty of tender meat and juices, these filling sandwiches eat like a meal! If you have calories to spare, add a slice of provolone for a real treat.

- 1 boneless beef chuck roast (3 lbs.)
- 1 tsp. Italian seasoning
- 1/4 tsp. cayenne pepper
- 1/4 tsp. pepper
- 1/4 cup water
- 1 jar (16 oz.) sliced pepperoncinis, undrained
- 1 medium sweet red pepper, julienned
- 1 medium green pepper, julienned
- 1 garlic clove, minced
- 1 envelope reduced-sodium onion soup mix
- 2 Tbsp. Worcestershire sauce
- 2 loaves (1 lb. *each*) Italian bread, halved lengthwise

1. Cut roast in half; place in a 5-qt. slow cooker. Sprinkle with Italian seasoning, cayenne and pepper. Add water. Cover and cook on high for 4 hours or until the meat is tender.

2. Remove roast; shred meat with two forks and return to the slow cooker. In a large bowl, combine the pepperoncinis, peppers, garlic, soup mix and Worcestershire sauce; pour over meat. Cover and cook on high for 1 hour or until the peppers are tender.

3. Spoon beef mixture over the bottom halves of the bread; replace the bread tops. Cut each loaf into six sandwiches.

Nutrition Facts: 1 sandwich equals 428 calories, 14 g fat (5 g saturated fat), 74 mg cholesterol, 661 mg sodium, 43 g carbohydrate, 3 g fiber, 29 g protein.

> If you would like to cut additional calories from the **Italian Beef Sandwiches** serve them open-faced with one piece of bread for each. You'll save 102 calories, and you'll need only one loaf of Italian bread.

APPLE CRANBERRY DELIGHT

GREEK CHICKEN SANDWICHES

Pineapple-Papaya Slaw S C M

PREP: 20 min. + chilling **YIELD:** 8 servings

HEALTHY COOKING TEST KITCHEN

This is no ordinary, boring slaw! Guests will rave over the summery dish, bursting with flavor from fresh fruit, cilantro and red bell pepper, for days!

1/2	cup unsweetened pineapple juice
1/4	cup olive oil
2	Tbsp. lime juice
2	Tbsp. minced fresh cilantro
1/2	tsp. ground cumin
1/4	tsp. salt
6	cups shredded cabbage
1-1/2	cups cubed fresh pineapple
1-1/2	cups chopped peeled papaya
1	small sweet red pepper, chopped

1. In a jar with a tight-fitting lid, combine the pineapple juice, oil, lime juice, cilantro, cumin and salt; shake well.

2. In a large bowl, combine the cabbage, pineapple, papaya and pepper. Drizzle with dressing and toss to coat. Cover and refrigerate for at least 2 hours. Stir just before serving.

Nutrition Facts: 1 cup equals 110 calories, 7 g fat (1 g saturated fat), 0 cholesterol, 85 mg sodium, 12 g carbohydrate, 2 g fiber, 1 g protein.

Makeover Creamy Cucumber Salad C M

PREP: 15 min. + chilling **YIELD:** 12 servings

JEAN PATTERSON • WEST ALLIS, WISCONSIN

After joining a weight-loss program, I knew I had to trim down my favorite recipes, and this was one of them. Replacing some of the mayonnaise with yogurt made all the difference.

9	cups thinly sliced peeled cucumbers
8	green onions, thinly sliced
1/4	tsp. onion salt
1/4	tsp. garlic salt
1/4	tsp. pepper
1/2	cup plain yogurt
1/2	cup reduced-fat mayonnaise
1/4	cup sugar
1/4	cup evaporated milk
1/4	cup cider vinegar
2	drops hot pepper sauce

1. In a large bowl, combine the first five ingredients.

2. In a small bowl, combine the remaining ingredients; pour over cucumber mixture and toss to coat. Cover and refrigerate for at least 4 hours.

Nutrition Facts: 3/4 cup equals 87 calories, 4 g fat (1 g saturated fat), 6 mg cholesterol, 167 mg sodium, 11 g carbohydrate, 2 g fiber, 2 g protein. **Diabetic Exchanges:** 1 vegetable, 1 fat.

Can't find papaya for **Pineapple-Papaya Slaw?** Use mango in the salsa instead. And, to shave a few minutes off the kitchen clock, remember to pick up a package of shredded cabbage rather than shredding it yourself.

PINEAPPLE-PAPAYA SLAW

MAKEOVER CREAMY CUCUMBER SALAD

Grilled Veggie Sandwiches With Cilantro Pesto M

PREP: 20 min. + standing
GRILL: 10 min. **YIELD:** 4 servings

CAROLYN PHENICIE • TITUSVILLE, PENNSYLVANIA

I ate a sandwich similar to this one while vacationing in Sedona, Arizona, and I fell in love with it. When I returned home, I developed this recipe; it tastes just like the original.

2/3	cup packed fresh cilantro sprigs
1/4	cup packed fresh parsley sprigs
2	Tbsp. grated Parmesan cheese
2	garlic cloves, peeled
2	Tbsp. water
1	Tbsp. pine nuts
1	Tbsp. olive oil

Cooking spray

2	large sweet red peppers
4	slices eggplant (1/2 in. thick)
1/2	tsp. salt
1/4	tsp. pepper
1/2	cup shredded part-skim mozzarella cheese
4	hard rolls, split

1. For the Cilantro Pesto, place the cilantro, parsley, Parmesan cheese and garlic in a small food processor; cover and pulse mixture until chopped. Add water and pine nuts; cover and process until blended. While processing, gradually add the oil in a steady stream. Set aside.

2. Coat grill rack with cooking spray before starting the grill. Grill peppers over medium heat for 10-15 minutes or until the skins blister, turning frequently. Immediately place peppers in a large bowl; cover and let stand for 15-20 minutes. Peel off and discard charred skin. Halve and seed peppers; set aside.

3. Lightly coat eggplant on both sides with cooking spray; sprinkle with salt and pepper. Grill, covered, over medium heat for 3-5 minutes on each side or until tender.

4. Top each eggplant slice with a pepper half; sprinkle with mozzarella cheese. Grill, covered, for 2-3 minutes or until cheese is melted.

5. Spread each roll with 1 tablespoon reserved pesto; top each with an eggplant stack. Replace roll tops.

Nutrition Facts: 1 sandwich equals 290 calories, 10 g fat (3 g saturated fat), 10 mg cholesterol, 717 mg sodium, 39 g carbohydrate, 5 g fiber, 12 g protein. **Diabetic Exchanges:** 2 starch, 1 lean meat, 1 vegetable, 1 fat.

California Chicken Wraps

PREP/TOTAL TIME: 15 min. **YIELD:** 4 servings

DONNA MUNCH • EL PASO, TEXAS

Hummus and feta cheese give these wraps unbeatable flavor. The whole wheat tortillas offer a nice change of pace. Hummus is a great alternative to mayonnaise; try it on your favorite sandwich today!

1/3	cup prepared hummus
4	whole wheat tortillas (8 in.)
2	cups cubed cooked chicken breast
1/4	cup chopped roasted sweet red peppers
1/4	cup crumbled feta cheese
1/4	cup thinly sliced fresh basil leaves

> Look for hummus in the specialty, refrigerated cases near the deli department of most large grocery stores. And when assembling **California Chicken Wraps**, consider using spinach tortillas instead.

1. Spread the hummus over the tortillas.

2. Top with chicken, peppers, cheese and basil. Roll up.

Nutrition Facts: 1 wrap equals 300 calories, 8 g fat (2 g saturated fat), 58 mg cholesterol, 408 mg sodium, 26 g carbohydrate, 3 g fiber, 27 g protein. **Diabetic Exchanges:** 3 very lean meat, 2 starch, 1/2 fat.

Italian Green Bean Salad F S M

PREP: 20 min. **COOK:** 15 min. **YIELD:** 9 servings

KATHY KITTELL • LENEXA, KANSAS

Basil and sweet red pepper lend bright flavor to this festive green bean salad. You'll love the crunch pine nuts provide!

1-1/2	lbs. fresh green beans, trimmed
1/2	cup fresh basil leaves, thinly sliced
1/2	cup thinly sliced roasted sweet red peppers
3	Tbsp. pine nuts, toasted
2	Tbsp. plus 1-1/2 tsp. olive oil
1	Tbsp. lemon juice
1/4	tsp. garlic powder
1/4	tsp. pepper
1/8	tsp. salt

Additional fresh basil leaves, optional

1. Place beans in a large saucepan and cover with water. Bring to a boil. Cook, uncovered, for 8-10 minutes or until crisp-tender. Drain and immediately place in ice water. Drain and pat dry.

2. Transfer to a salad bowl; add the basil, peppers and pine nuts. In a small bowl, whisk the oil, lemon juice, garlic powder, pepper and salt. Drizzle over bean mixture and toss to coat. Garnish with additional basil if desired.

Nutrition Facts: 3/4 cup equals 76 calories, 5 g fat (1 g saturated fat), 0 cholesterol, 87 mg sodium, 6 g carbohydrate, 2 g fiber, 2 g protein. **Diabetic Exchanges:** 1 vegetable, 1 fat.

Carrot Radish Salad M

PREP/TOTAL TIME: 15 min. **YIELD:** 4 servings

CAROLE RESNICK • CLEVELAND, OHIO

This salad always brings bright spring colors to any meal. It blends a trio of nutritious ingredients with a truly refreshing, homemade lime dressing.

- 3 cups shredded carrots
- 7 radishes, sliced and cut into strips
- 1/4 cup raisins

LIME VINAIGRETTE:
- 2 Tbsp. lime juice
- 2 Tbsp. olive oil
- 1/2 tsp. sugar
- 1/2 tsp. salt
- 1/2 tsp. grated lime peel
- 1/4 tsp. pepper

Lettuce leaves, optional

1. In a small bowl, combine the carrots, radishes and raisins. In a jar with a tight-fitting lid, combine vinaigrette ingredients; shake well.

2. Drizzle over carrot mixture and toss to coat. Serve in a lettuce-lined bowl if desired.

Nutrition Facts: 3/4 cup equals 124 calories, 7 g fat (1 g saturated fat), 0 cholesterol, 356 mg sodium, 16 g carbohydrate, 3 g fiber, 1 g protein. **Diabetic Exchanges:** 1-1/2 fat, 1 vegetable, 1/2 fruit.

Orange Cream Fruit Salad F M

PREP: 15 min. + chilling **YIELD:** 9 servings

SHEILA EGGERT • ELGIN, ILLINOIS

My son calls this great-tasting fruit salad "awesome," and it was an instant hit with my family. I love that it's virtually fat-free and a favorite at brunches.

- 1-1/2 cups cold fat-free milk
- 1 pkg. (1 oz.) sugar-free instant vanilla pudding mix
- 1/3 cup orange juice concentrate
- 3/4 cup fat-free plain yogurt
- 1 can (20 oz.) unsweetened pineapple chunks, drained
- 1 can (11 oz.) mandarin oranges, drained
- 1-1/2 cups frozen unsweetened peach slices, thawed and chopped
- 2 medium apples, peeled and cubed
- 2 medium firm bananas, cut into 1/4-in. slices

Kiwifruit wedges, optional

1. In a large mixing bowl, beat the milk, pudding mix and orange juice concentrate on low speed for 2 minutes. Stir in yogurt. Fold in the pineapple, oranges, peaches and apples. Cover and refrigerate for 2 hours.

2. Just before serving, fold in bananas. Garnish with kiwi if desired.

Nutrition Facts: 1 cup equals 163 calories, 1 g fat (trace saturated fat), 2 mg cholesterol, 170 mg sodium, 37 g carbohydrate, 3 g fiber, 4 g protein. **Diabetic Exchanges:** 2 fruit, 1/2 starch.

ORANGE CREAM FRUIT SALAD

CARROT RADISH SALAD

Corn & Black Bean Salad M

PREP: 15 min. + chilling **YIELD:** 8 servings

KRISTA FRANK • RHODODENDRON, OREGON

All ages will love this colorful salad. Try it with summer entrees, or serve it as a salsa!

- 1 can (15-1/4 oz.) whole kernel corn, drained
- 1 can (15 oz.) black beans, rinsed and drained
- 2 large tomatoes, finely chopped
- 1 large red onion, finely chopped
- 1/4 cup minced fresh cilantro
- 2 garlic cloves, minced

DRESSING:
- 2 Tbsp. sugar
- 2 Tbsp. white vinegar
- 2 Tbsp. canola oil
- 1-1/2 tsp. lime juice
- 1/4 tsp. salt
- 1/4 tsp. ground cumin
- 1/4 tsp. pepper

1. In a large bowl, combine the first six ingredients. In a small bowl, whisk the dressing ingredients; pour over the corn mixture and toss to coat.

2. Cover and refrigerate for at least 1 hour. Stir before serving. Serve with a slotted spoon.

Nutrition Facts: 2/3 cup equals 142 calories, 4 g fat (trace saturated fat), 0 cholesterol, 326 mg sodium, 21 g carbohydrate, 4 g fiber, 4 g protein. **Diabetic Exchanges:** 1 starch, 1 vegetable, 1 fat.

Simon's Famous Tuna Salad

PREP/TOTAL TIME: 15 min. **YIELD:** 5 servings

SIMON SEITZ • HIGHLAND, NEW YORK

This nicely seasoned tuna salad makes for a no-fuss, satisfying lunch. Crunchy carrots give it a tasty twist you'll love.

- 3 cans (6 oz. *each*) light water-packed tuna, drained and flaked
- 3/4 cup fat-free mayonnaise
- 1/4 cup chopped celery
- 1/4 cup chopped carrot
- 1/2 tsp. onion powder
- 1/2 tsp. garlic powder
- 1/4 tsp. dill weed
- 10 slices whole wheat bread, toasted
- 5 lettuce leaves

1. In a small bowl, combine the first seven ingredients.

2. For each sandwich, layer a slice of toast with a lettuce leaf and 1/2 cup tuna salad. Top with a second slice of toast.

Nutrition Facts: 1 sandwich equals 289 calories, 4 g fat (1 g saturated fat), 34 mg cholesterol, 907 mg sodium, 29 g carbohydrate, 5 g fiber, 34 g protein.

Quinoa Salad M

PREP: 30 min. + chilling **YIELD:** 8 servings

SONYA FOX • PEYTON, COLORADO

This fresh-tasting salad combines the sweetness of raisins and jicama with super-healthy quinoa.

- 1 cup quinoa, rinsed
- 2 cups water
- 1 medium jicama, peeled and chopped
- 1 celery rib, chopped
- 1/2 cup raisins
- 3 Tbsp. olive oil
- 2 Tbsp. lemon juice
- 1/2 tsp. salt
- 1/4 tsp. ground cinnamon

CORN & BLACK BEAN SALAD

SIMON'S FAMOUS TUNA SALAD

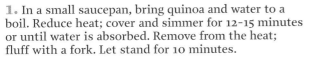

1. In a small saucepan, bring quinoa and water to a boil. Reduce heat; cover and simmer for 12-15 minutes or until water is absorbed. Remove from the heat; fluff with a fork. Let stand for 10 minutes.

2. In a large bowl, combine the quinoa, jicama, celery and raisins. In a small bowl, whisk the oil, lemon juice, salt and cinnamon. Pour over the quinoa mixture and toss to coat. Cover and refrigerate for at least 1 hour.

Nutrition Facts: 3/4 cup equals 185 calories, 6 g fat (1 g saturated fat), 0 cholesterol, 161 mg sodium, 30 g carbohydrate, 6 g fiber, 4 g protein. **Diabetic Exchanges:** 1 starch, 1 vegetable, 1 fat, 1/2 fruit.

Fruited Turkey Wraps

PREP/TOTAL TIME: 15 min. **YIELD:** 4 servings

LISA RENSHAW • KANSAS CITY, MISSOURI

You just know this pretty wrap is going to be great and so good for you! It's packed with lean protein, fruit and veggies and bundled in whole-grain goodness!

 1/2 cup fat-free mayonnaise
 1 Tbsp. orange juice
 1 tsp. grated orange peel
 3/4 tsp. curry powder
 4 whole wheat tortillas (8 in.)

 2 cups finely shredded Chinese *or* napa cabbage
 1/2 cup thinly sliced red onion
 1 can (11 oz.) mandarin oranges, drained
 2/3 cup dried cranberries
 1/2 lb. thinly sliced deli smoked turkey

1. Combine the mayonnaise, orange juice, peel and curry; spread over tortillas.

2. Top with cabbage, onion, oranges, cranberries and turkey. Roll up.

Nutrition Facts: 1 wrap equals 332 calories, 5 g fat (trace saturated fat), 23 mg cholesterol, 845 mg sodium, 54 g carbohydrate, 5 g fiber, 17 g protein.

When packing **Fruited Turkey Wraps** for lunch, put a frozen ice pack in a resealable plastic bag, and set it at the bottom of your brown bag. This keeps lunches cold and dry. Delicate items such as bags of pretzels should go at the top of the lunch bag so they're not crushed.

Havarti Turkey Hero

PREP/TOTAL TIME: 15 min. **YIELD:** 8 servings

AGNES WARD • STRATFORD, ONTARIO

Everyone likes the combination of chutney and chopped peanuts in this sandwich. I like to make this when I have company in the afternoon, or at night after a game of cards.

1/3	cup mango chutney
2	Tbsp. reduced-fat mayonnaise
2	Tbsp. chopped unsalted peanuts

Dash cayenne pepper

1	loaf (1 lb.) French bread, halved lengthwise
3/4	lb. thinly sliced deli turkey
6	lettuce leaves
2	oz. thinly sliced Havarti cheese
1	medium Red Delicious apple, cored and cut into thin rings

1. In a small bowl, combine the chutney, mayonnaise, peanuts and cayenne; spread evenly over the cut side of bread bottom.

2. Layer with turkey, lettuce, cheese and apple. Replace bread top. Cut into eight slices.

Nutrition Facts: 1 slice equals 302 calories, 7 g fat (2 g saturated fat), 27 mg cholesterol, 973 mg sodium, 45 g carbohydrate, 2 g fiber, 16 g protein. **Diabetic Exchanges:** 3 starch, 1 lean meat, 1/2 fat.

Summer Corn Salad Ⓜ

PREP: 20 min. + standing **YIELD:** 4 servings

PRISCILLA YEE • CONCORD, CALIFORNIA

This beautiful salad truly captures the summer season. It's chock-full of fresh veggies and basil, and feta cheese gives it a savory flavor the whole family will love. Double or triple the recipe for potlucks.

1	Tbsp. lime juice
1/4	tsp. salt
1/4	tsp. hot pepper sauce
5	tsp. olive oil, *divided*
1-1/2	cups fresh or frozen corn, thawed
1-1/2	cups cherry tomatoes, halved
1/2	cup finely chopped cucumber
1/4	cup finely chopped red onion
2	Tbsp. minced fresh basil *or* 2 tsp. dried basil
1/4	cup crumbled feta cheese

1. In a small bowl, whisk the lime juice, salt, pepper sauce and 4 teaspoons oil; set aside.

2. In a large skillet, saute corn in remaining oil until tender. Transfer to a salad bowl; add the tomatoes, cucumber, onion and basil. Drizzle with dressing and toss to coat. Let stand for 10 minutes before serving or refrigerate until chilled. Sprinkle with cheese just before serving.

Nutrition Facts: 3/4 cup equals 136 calories, 8 g fat (2 g saturated fat), 4 mg cholesterol, 231 mg sodium, 16 g carbohydrate, 3 g fiber, 4 g protein. **Diabetic Exchanges:** 1-1/2 fat, 1 starch.

Turkey Sloppy Joes

PREP: 20 min. **COOK:** 4 hours **YIELD:** 10 servings

LISA ANN DINUNZIO • VINELAND, NEW JERSEY

Slow simmering is key to getting all the flavor in these mildly sweet sloppy joes. This recipe is a keeper and sure to be a family favorite!

> 2 lbs. lean ground turkey
> 1 medium onion, finely chopped
> 1 small green pepper, chopped
> 2 cans (8 oz. *each*) no-salt-added tomato sauce
> 1 cup water
> 2 envelopes sloppy joe mix
> 1 Tbsp. brown sugar
> 10 hamburger buns, split

1. In a large nonstick skillet coated with cooking spray, cook the turkey, onion and pepper over medium heat until meat is no longer pink; drain. Transfer to a 3-qt. slow cooker.

2. Stir in the tomato sauce, water, sloppy joe mix and brown sugar. Cover and cook on low for 4-5 hours or until flavors are blended. Spoon 1/2 cup onto each bun.

Nutrition Facts: 1 sandwich equals 304 calories, 9 g fat (3 g saturated fat), 72 mg cholesterol, 870 mg sodium, 33 g carbohydrate, 2 g fiber, 20 g protein.

Makeover Family-Recipe Salad Dressing `C`

PREP/TOTAL TIME: 15 min. **YIELD:** 1-1/4 cups

CONNIE PETTERSEN • AITKIN, MINNESOTA

The "Healthy Cooking" team lightened-up this wonderful recipe from my mother-in-law. Try it and see! It's fantastic on green salads but just as good in macaroni salads.

> 1/4 cup water
> 1/4 cup ketchup
> 2 Tbsp. white vinegar
> 2 Tbsp. canola oil
> 1 small onion, cut into wedges
> 1/2 cup reduced-fat mayonnaise
> Sugar substitute equivalent to 5 tsp. sugar
> 1 tsp. dried parsley flakes
> 1/2 tsp. salt-free seasoning blend
> 1/2 tsp. paprika
> 1 small garlic clove, peeled
> 1/4 tsp. ground mustard
> 1/4 tsp. celery seed

1. In a blender, combine all ingredients; cover and process until blended. Transfer to a small pitcher or bowl. Refrigerate until serving.

Editor's Note: This recipe was tested with Splenda No Calorie Sweetener.

Nutrition Facts: 2 tablespoons equals 76 calories, 7 g fat (1 g saturated fat), 4 mg cholesterol, 167 mg sodium, 4 g carbohydrate, trace fiber, trace protein.

To decrease the fat in **Makeover Family-Recipe Salad Dressing,** the original amount of oil was reduced and water was added to keep the original recipes's volume and consistency.

SUMMER CORN SALAD

TURKEY SLOPPY JOES

Cranberry Medley **F** **S**

PREP: 15 min. COOK: 15 min. + chilling YIELD: 6 cups

GLORIA WIECH • FRONTENAC, MINNESOTA

I saw a chutney recipe that used sugar, oil and other flavors I didn't care for, so I made this combination with sugar substitute and eliminated the oil. Now it's a family favorite.

- 1 pkg. (12 oz.) fresh or frozen cranberries, thawed
- 2 cups chopped peeled tart apples
- 1 large navel orange, peeled, sectioned, and finely chopped

Sugar substitute equivalent to 2/3 cup sugar

- 1/3 cup chopped dried apricots
- 1/3 cup golden raisins
- 3 Tbsp. cider vinegar
- 3 Tbsp. orange juice

1. In a large saucepan, combine all ingredients. Cook, uncovered, over medium heat until the berries pop, about 15 minutes, stirring occasionally.

2. Transfer to a small bowl; cover and refrigerate until chilled.

Nutrition Facts: 1/2 cup equals 63 calories, trace fat (trace saturated fat), 0 cholesterol, 4 mg sodium, 16 g carbohydrate, 3 g fiber, 1 g protein. **Diabetic Exchange:** 1 fruit.

Texas Barley Salad **M**

PREP: 30 min. + chilling YIELD: 5 servings

MARILYN SONNENBERG • EDMONTON, ALBERTA

I got this recipe from a cook in Mexico while I was there on a mission trip. I've been making it ever since.

- 1 cup reduced-sodium chicken broth *or* vegetable broth
- 1/2 cup quick-cooking barley
- 1 medium tomato, seeded and chopped
- 3/4 cup frozen corn, thawed
- 1/2 cup chopped sweet red pepper
- 1/4 cup chopped seeded peeled cucumber
- 2 green onions, thinly sliced
- 2 Tbsp. canola oil
- 4 tsp. cider vinegar
- 1 garlic clove, minced
- 1/4 tsp. salt
- 1/4 tsp. pepper
- 1/4 tsp. ground cumin
- 1/4 tsp. chili powder

1. In a small saucepan, bring the broth to a boil. Stir in the barley. Reduce heat; cover and simmer for 10-12 minutes or until tender. Cool.

2. In a large bowl, combine the tomato, corn, red pepper, cucumber, onions and barley. In a small bowl, whisk the remaining ingredients. Pour over barley mixture and toss to coat. Cover and refrigerate for at least 1 hour.

Nutrition Facts: 3/4 cup equals 155 calories, 6 g fat (1 g saturated fat), 0 cholesterol, 251 mg sodium, 22 g carbohydrate, 5 g fiber, 4 g protein. **Diabetic Exchanges:** 1-1/2 starch, 1 fat.

Fettuccine Slaw **M**

PREP: 25 min. + chilling YIELD: 14 servings

MARY TALLMAN • ARBOR VITAE, WISCONSIN

Fettuccine is the base of this fresh, filling picnic salad. Healthy veggies give it a delightful crunch that'll keep you coming back for more.

- 8 ounces uncooked fettuccine
- 3 cups finely chopped cabbage
- 4 celery ribs, sliced
- 2 cups thinly sliced cucumbers
- 2 cups shredded carrots
- 1 cup (8 oz.) reduced-fat plain yogurt
- 1/2 cup reduced-fat mayonnaise
- 2 Tbsp. white vinegar
- 1 tsp. sugar
- 1/2 tsp. salt
- 1/2 tsp. ground mustard
- 1/4 tsp. white pepper

TEXAS BARLEY SALAD

CRANBERRY MEDLEY

PIZZA ROLL-UP

1. Break fettuccine into thirds. Cook according to package directions; drain and rinse in cold water.

2. In a large bowl, combine the fettuccine, cabbage, celery, cucumbers and carrots. In a small bowl, combine the remaining ingredients. Pour over fettuccine mixture and toss to coat. Refrigerate until chilled.

Nutrition Facts: 3/4 cup equals 112 calories, 4 g fat (1 g saturated fat), 4 mg cholesterol, 188 mg sodium, 17 g carbohydrate, 2 g fiber, 4 g protein. **Diabetic Exchanges:** 1 starch, 1 vegetable, 1/2 fat.

Pizza Roll-Up

PREP: 15 min. **BAKE:** 25 min. **YIELD:** 6 servings

JAN CHRISTOFFERSON • EAGLE RIVER, WISCONSIN

I live in the northwoods, and this is a great, hearty dish for brunch, lunch or dinner. It's also tasty made with ground turkey or Italian sausage instead of ground beef.

1/2 pound lean ground beef
  1 tube (13.8 oz.) refrigerated pizza crust
  1 pkg. (10 oz.) frozen chopped spinach, thawed and squeezed dry
  1 jar (7 oz.) roasted sweet red peppers, drained and sliced

  1 cup (4 oz.) shredded part-skim mozzarella cheese
1/2 tsp. onion powder
1/2 tsp. pepper
1/2 cup loosely packed basil leaves
Cooking spray
  1 Tbsp. grated Parmesan cheese
  1 can (8 oz.) pizza sauce, warmed

1. In a small nonstick skillet, cook beef over medium heat until no longer pink; drain.

2. Unroll dough into one long rectangle; top with spinach, beef, roasted peppers and mozzarella cheese. Sprinkle with onion powder and pepper. Top with basil.

3. Roll up jelly-roll style, starting with a short side; tuck ends under and pinch seam to seal. Place roll-up on a baking sheet coated with cooking spray; spritz top and sides with additional cooking spray. Sprinkle with Parmesan cheese.

4. Bake at 375° for 25-30 minutes or until golden brown. Let stand for 5 minutes. Cut into scant 1-in. slices. Serve with pizza sauce.

Nutrition Facts: 2 slices with 2 tablespoons pizza sauce equals 316 calories, 8 g fat (3 g saturated fat), 30 mg cholesterol, 824 mg sodium, 37 g carbohydrate, 3 g fiber, 20 g protein.

Mediterranean Salad Sandwiches M

PREP/TOTAL TIME: 30 min. **YIELD:** 4 servings

CANDICE GARCIA • WINTER HAVEN, FLORIDA

These filling, fresh-tasting sandwiches are like a refreshing summer salad. Add iced tea and sorbet for dessert, and call it an easy supper!

2	Tbsp. olive oil, *divided*
1	garlic clove, minced
1/4	tsp. salt
4	large portobello mushrooms, stems removed
2	cups spring mix salad greens
1	medium tomato, chopped
1/2	cup chopped roasted sweet red peppers
1/4	cup crumbled reduced-fat feta cheese
2	Tbsp. chopped pitted Greek olives
1	Tbsp. red wine vinegar
1/2	tsp. dried oregano
4	slices sourdough bread, toasted and halved

1. In a small bowl, combine 1 tablespoon oil, garlic and salt; brush over mushrooms.

2. Coat grill rack with cooking spray before starting the grill. Grill mushrooms, covered, over medium heat for 6-8 minutes on each side or until tender.

3. In a large bowl, combine the salad greens, tomato, peppers, cheese and olives. In a small bowl, whisk the vinegar, oregano and remaining oil. Drizzle over salad mixture; toss to coat. Layer each of four half slices of toast with a mushroom and 3/4 cup salad mixture; top with remaining toast.

Nutrition Facts: 1 serving equals 225 calories, 9 g fat (2 g saturated fat), 3 mg cholesterol, 495 mg sodium, 26 g carbohydrate, 3 g fiber, 8 g protein. **Diabetic Exchanges:** 2 vegetable, 2 fat, 1 starch.

Asian Broccoli Salad C M

PREP: 20 min. + chilling **YIELD:** 4 servings

FLORENCE HENDRICKSON • ALBUQUERQUE, NEW MEXICO

This nutritious recipe is my favorite potluck contribution. I lightened it up, and I think it's tastier than the original!

4	cups fresh broccoli florets
2	Tbsp. reduced-sodium soy sauce
1	Tbsp. balsamic vinegar
2	garlic cloves, minced

Sugar substitute equivalent to 2 tsp. sugar

1/4	tsp. pepper
1	Tbsp. olive oil
1	jar (4 oz.) diced pimientos, drained
2	Tbsp. slivered almonds, toasted

1. Place broccoli in a steamer basket; place in a large saucepan over 1 in. of water. Bring to a boil; cover and steam for 4-7 minutes or until crisp-tender. Rinse in cold water; drain. Transfer to a large bowl; cover and refrigerate until chilled.

2. In a small bowl, combine the soy sauce, vinegar, garlic, sugar substitute and pepper. Whisk in the oil. Let stand for 30 minutes to allow flavors to blend.

3. Add pimientos and almonds to the broccoli; drizzle with dressing and toss to coat.

Editor's Note: This recipe was tested with Splenda No Calorie Sweetener.

Nutrition Facts: 1 cup equals 87 calories, 5 g fat (1 g saturated fat), 0 cholesterol, 327 mg sodium, 8 g carbohydrate, 3 g fiber, 4 g protein. **Diabetic Exchanges:** 1 vegetable, 1 fat.

Special Radicchio-Spinach Salad S C M

PREP/TOTAL TIME: 20 min. **YIELD:** 12 servings

ROXANNE CHAN • ALBANY, CALIFORNIA

Almost too pretty to eat, this colorful salad combines mint, chipotle pepper and a little bit of honey for a delightful sweet-spicy combination.

6	cups fresh baby spinach
1	head radicchio, torn
2	cups fresh raspberries
1/2	cup raisins
1/4	cup pine nuts, toasted
1/4	cup finely chopped red onion
1/4	cup minced fresh mint
3	Tbsp. lime juice
2	Tbsp. olive oil
2	tsp. honey
1-1/2	to 3 tsp. chopped chipotle pepper in adobo sauce
1/4	tsp. salt
1/2	cup crumbled feta cheese

1. In a large salad bowl, combine the first seven ingredients. In a small saucepan, combine the lime juice, oil, honey, chipotle pepper and salt.

2. Cook and stir until blended and heated through. Immediately pour over salad; toss to coat. Sprinkle with feta cheese.

Nutrition Facts: 3/4 cup equals 92 calories, 5 g fat (1 g saturated fat), 3 mg cholesterol, 117 mg sodium, 11 g carbohydrate, 3 g fiber, 3 g protein. **Diabetic Exchanges:** 1 vegetable, 1 fat, 1/2 fruit.

Hawaiian Fruit Salad F S M

PREP/TOTAL TIME: 30 min. **YIELD:** 14 servings

PAT HABIGER • SPEARVILLE, KANSAS

This salad says summer because it's so light and colorful. The banana dressing really tops it off. It's great alongside grilled items and summer fare.

3-1/2	cups cubed fresh pineapple
3	cups honeydew balls
1-1/2	cups cantaloupe balls
1	medium mango, peeled and cubed
1	cup green grapes
1	cup halved fresh strawberries
1	kiwifruit, peeled, quartered and sliced

BANANA DRESSING:
2	small bananas, cut into 1-in. pieces
1	cup (8 oz.) reduced-fat sour cream
1/4	cup packed brown sugar
1-1/2	tsp. lemon juice

1. In a large bowl, combine the first seven ingredients. In a food processor, combine the bananas, sour cream, brown sugar and lemon juice.

2. Cover and process until smooth. Serve with fruit.

Nutrition Facts: 3/4 cup fruit with 2 tablespoons dressing equals 112 calories, 2 g fat (1 g saturated fat), 6 mg cholesterol, 21 mg sodium, 24 g carbohydrate, 2 g fiber, 2 g protein. **Diabetic Exchanges:** 1-1/2 fruit, 1/2 fat.

HAWAIIAN FRUIT SALAD

SPECIAL RADICCHIO-SPINACH SALAD

SOUTHWESTERN BAKED BEANS

GO FOR THE GRAINS CASSEROLE

WARM GARLICKY GRAPE TOMATOES

Side Dishes & Sauces

Nothing rounds out a menu like a savory side dish. Hearty potatoes, buttery noodles and wild rice delights are just some of the all-time favorites that make meals complete. Turn to this chapter when you need a side for any occasion.

Warm Garlicky Grape Tomatoes F C M

PREP/TOTAL TIME: 30 min. **YIELD:** 4 servings

ROSE GULLEDGE • CROFTON, MARYLAND

This is one of our favorite quick ways to use up a bumper crop of grape tomatoes (or to remedy an overzealous tomato shopper)! This is wonderful over slices of rustic sourdough bread or as a side dish for grilled chicken, pork and steak. I often serve leftovers as a filling in omelets.

    2   cups grape tomatoes
    3   garlic cloves, minced
1-1/2   tsp. minced fresh basil
  1/2   tsp. salt-free garlic seasoning blend
  1/4   tsp. salt
  1/8   tsp. pepper
    1   tsp. olive oil, *divided*
  1/4   cup soft whole wheat bread crumbs
  1/4   cup crumbled feta cheese

1. In a small bowl, combine the tomatoes, garlic, basil, seasoning blend, salt and pepper. Add 1/2 teaspoon oil; toss to coat. Transfer to a 3-cup baking dish coated with cooking spray.

2. Bake at 425° for 15 minutes. Combine bread crumbs and remaining oil; sprinkle over the top. Sprinkle with cheese. Bake 5-10 minutes longer or until cheese is softened and tomatoes are tender.

Nutrition Facts: 1/2 cup equals 64 calories, 3 g fat (1 g saturated fat), 4 mg cholesterol, 259 mg sodium, 8 g carbohydrate, 2 g fiber, 3 g protein. **Diabetic Exchanges:** 1 vegetable, 1/2 fat.

Go for the Grains Casserole M

PREP: 25 min. **BAKE:** 55 min. **YIELD:** 10 servings

MELANIE BLAIR • WARSAW, INDIANA

This casserole is hearty and delicious. A friend gave me the recipe, and it was love at first bite. This colorful side has "good for you" written all over it.

    5   medium carrots, thinly sliced
    2   cups frozen corn, thawed
    1   medium onion, diced
    1   cup quick-cooking barley
  1/2   cup bulgur

  1/3   cup minced fresh parsley
    1   tsp. salt
  1/2   tsp. pepper
    3   cups vegetable broth
    1   can (15 oz.) black beans, rinsed and drained
1-1/2   cups (6 oz.) shredded reduced-fat cheddar cheese

1. In a large bowl, combine the carrots, corn, onion, barley, bulgur, parsley, salt and pepper. Stir in broth and beans. Transfer to a 13-in. x 9-in. baking dish coated with cooking spray.

2. Cover and bake at 350° for 50-55 minutes or until grains are tender, stirring once. Sprinkle with cheese. Bake, uncovered, 3-5 minutes longer or until cheese is melted.

Nutrition Facts: 3/4 cup equals 226 calories, 5 g fat (3 g saturated fat), 12 mg cholesterol, 741 mg sodium, 38 g carbohydrate, 8 g fiber, 12 g protein. **Diabetic Exchanges:** 2 starch, 1 lean meat, 1 vegetable.

Julienned Summer Vegetable Medley F C M

PREP/TOTAL TIME: 30 min. **YIELD:** 6 servings

CHARLENE CHAMBERS • ORMOND BEACH, FLORIDA

I tried this at a famous resort and loved it, so I wrote down what I thought the ingredients were and repeated the recipe at home. Luckily, I nailed it! It's a great low-fat use of fresh veggies.

    3   medium carrots, julienned
    1   medium red onion, halved and thinly sliced
    2   tsp. canola oil
    2   medium yellow summer squash, julienned
    2   medium zucchini, julienned
  1/2   tsp. salt
  1/4   tsp. garlic powder
  1/4   tsp. pepper

1. In a large nonstick skillet, saute carrots and onion in oil for 2 minutes.

2. Add remaining ingredients; saute 5-7 minutes longer or until crisp-tender.

Nutrition Facts: 3/4 cup equals 55 calories, 2 g fat (trace saturated fat), 0 cholesterol, 226 mg sodium, 9 g carbohydrate, 3 g fiber, 2 g protein. **Diabetic Exchange:** 2 vegetable.

ELEGANT VEGETABLE CASSEROLE

Elegant Vegetable Casserole

PREP: 1 hour **BAKE:** 50 min.
YIELD: 14 servings (1 cup each)

VIRGINIA ANTHONY • JACKSONVILLE, FLORIDA

Please everyone at the table with this innovative and space-saving recipe. Three traditional sides line up to create a tasty, eye-appealing dish.

PARSNIP POTATOES:
- 2 lbs. potatoes, peeled and cubed (about 4 medium)
- 4 medium parsnips, peeled and cubed
- 1 carton (8 oz.) reduced-fat sour cream
- 3 Tbsp. fat-free milk
- 1 tsp. salt

SQUASH:
- 1 medium butternut squash (about 3 lbs.), peeled and cubed
- 1/2 tsp. salt
- 1/4 tsp. ground nutmeg

SPINACH:
- 2 eggs
- 1 Tbsp. fat-free milk
- 1/4 tsp. salt
- 2 pkg. (10 oz. *each*) frozen chopped spinach, thawed and squeezed dry
- 1-1/2 cups (6 oz.) shredded reduced-fat Swiss cheese
- 3/4 cup soft bread crumbs
- 1 small onion, grated

1. Place potatoes and parsnips in a large saucepan; cover with water and bring to a boil. Reduce heat; cover and simmer for 15-20 minutes or until tender. Drain. Mash with sour cream, milk and salt; set aside.

2. Place squash in another large saucepan and cover with water. Bring to a boil. Reduce heat; cover and simmer for 15-20 minutes or until tender. Drain. Mash with salt and nutmeg; set aside.

3. In a small bowl, whisk the eggs, milk and salt. Stir in the spinach, cheese, bread crumbs and onion.

4. Place half of parsnip potatoes at one end of a 13-in. x 9-in. baking dish coated with cooking spray. Add squash to dish, forming a stripe. Repeat with spinach. Place remaining parsnip potatoes at opposite end of dish. (Dish will be full.)

5. Cover and bake at 350° for 45-55 minutes or until a meat thermometer inserted in the spinach reads 160°.

Nutrition Facts: 1 cup equals 183 calories, 3 g fat (2 g saturated fat), 40 mg cholesterol, 410 mg sodium, 31 g carbohydrate, 6 g fiber, 10 g protein. **Diabetic Exchanges:** 2 starch, 1/2 fat.

Cranberry Applesauce F S

PREP: 15 min. **COOK:** 20 min. **YIELD:** 4 cups

PEGGY SPITLER • BUCYRUS, OHIO

This is simple to make and so refreshing. The zippy flavor makes it a nice change of pace from regular applesauce.

- 5 medium Gala apples, peeled and cubed
- 1 cup fresh *or* frozen cranberries
- 1/3 cup water
- 5 Tbsp. sugar
- 1 tsp. grated orange peel

1. In a large saucepan, combine the apples, cranberries, water and sugar. Bring to a boil. Reduce heat; cover and simmer for 15-20 minutes or until apples are tender and the berries pop, stirring occasionally. Remove from the heat; stir in orange peel. Mash until sauce is desired consistency. Serve warm or cold.

Nutrition Facts: 1/2 cup equals 75 calories, trace fat (trace saturated fat), 0 cholesterol, trace sodium, 20 g carbohydrate, 2 g fiber, trace protein. **Diabetic Exchanges:** 1 fruit, 1/2 starch.

Double-Stuffed Potatoes M

PREP: 1-1/4 hours **BAKE:** 20 min. **YIELD:** 14 servings

HEALTHY COOKING TEST KITCHEN

Baked potatoes and sweet potatoes are stuffed with a tasty mixture of pears, brown sugar and cinnamon in this delicious, crowd-pleasing recipe.

4	medium baking potatoes
3	medium sweet potatoes
2	medium pears, peeled and cubed
5	Tbsp. butter, cubed
1/2	cup fat-free milk
1	egg, lightly beaten
1	tsp. salt
1/4	tsp. pepper
1/4	tsp. ground cinnamon
1/2	cup packed brown sugar

1. Scrub and pierce the baking and sweet potatoes. Bake at 400° for 50-55 minutes or until tender. Meanwhile, place pears in a large saucepan and cover with water. Bring to a boil. Reduce heat; cover and cook for 15-20 minutes or until tender. Drain and set aside.

2. Cool potatoes slightly; cut each in half lengthwise. Scoop out the pulp, leaving thin shells. In a bowl, mash the pulp with butter. Stir in the milk, egg, salt, pepper, cinnamon and reserved pears.

3. Spoon mixture into potato shells. Sprinkle with brown sugar. Place on a baking sheet. Bake, uncovered, at 400° for 20-25 minutes or until a thermometer reads 160°.

Nutrition Facts: 1 stuffed potato half equals 182 calories, 5 g fat (3 g saturated fat), 26 mg cholesterol, 218 mg sodium, 34 g carbohydrate, 3 g fiber, 3 g protein. **Diabetic Exchanges:** 2 starch, 1 fat.

Brown & Wild Rice Medley M

PREP: 20 min. **COOK:** 30 min. **YIELD:** 8 servings

SHARON FLEMING • BOGOTA, COLOMBIA

This savory delight starts with a simple boxed mix. It's a quick dish that goes with just about anything.

1	pkg. (6.7 oz.) mushroom-flavored brown and wild rice mix
1	large onion, chopped
1	cup cut fresh green beans (1/2-in. pieces)
1	Tbsp. olive oil
1	cup sliced fresh mushrooms
2	medium carrots, shredded
1/4	cup chopped sweet red pepper
1/4	cup slivered almonds, toasted

1. In a large saucepan, cook rice mix according to package directions, omitting butter.

2. Meanwhile, in a large nonstick skillet, saute onion and green beans in oil for 2 minutes. Add the mushrooms, carrots and pepper; saute 3-5 minutes longer or until vegetables are tender. Add vegetables and almonds to cooked rice; stir until blended.

Nutrition Facts: 3/4 cup equals 135 calories, 4 g fat (trace saturated fat), 0 cholesterol, 325 mg sodium, 23 g carbohydrate, 2 g fiber, 4 g protein. **Diabetic Exchanges:** 1 starch, 1 vegetable, 1/2 fat.

The easy recipe for **Brown & Wild Rice Medley** is so versatile because you can add whatever vegetables you want. Toss in some frozen peas for extra color.

DOUBLE-STUFFED POTATOES

BROWN & WILD RICE MEDLEY

Balsamic-Glazed Onions & Garlic S C

PREP: 30 min. **BAKE:** 55 min. **YIELD:** 6 servings

LILLIAN JULOW • GAINESVILLE, FLORIDA

Balsamic vinegar and a hint of garlic give these pearl onions great taste. It's an ideal side dish for steak or grilled chicken.

2	large whole garlic bulbs
1	lb. fresh pearl onions
1	Tbsp. olive oil
1	Tbsp. butter, melted
1/4	cup balsamic vinegar
2	tsp. honey
1/4	tsp. salt
1/8	tsp. pepper

1. In a Dutch oven, bring 6 cups water to a boil. Remove papery outer skin from garlic; separate into cloves. Boil garlic and onions for 3 minutes; drain and rinse in cold water. Cool. Peel garlic and onions; place in a 1-1/2-qt. baking dish coated with cooking spray. Add oil and butter and toss to coat.

2. Combine the vinegar, honey, salt and pepper. Pour over onion mixture and stir to coat.

3. Cover and bake at 350° for 30 minutes. Uncover and stir. Bake, uncovered, 25-30 minutes longer or until garlic and onions are tender and sauce is slightly thickened, stirring every 10 minutes.

Nutrition Facts: 1/2 cup equals 95 calories, 4 g fat (1 g saturated fat), 5 mg cholesterol, 73 mg sodium, 14 g carbohydrate, 2 g fiber, 2 g protein. **Diabetic Exchanges:** 2 vegetable, 1 fat.

Sweet Pepper Wild Rice Salad M

PREP: 20 min. **COOK:** 1 hour **YIELD:** 8 servings

SHERRYL LUDLOW • ROLLA, MISSOURI

I really enjoy this wild rice salad that's packed with healthy and refreshing flavors in every bite.

1/2	cup uncooked wild rice
1	can (14-1/2 oz.) reduced-sodium chicken broth or vegetable broth, *divided*
1-1/4	cups water, *divided*
3/4	cup uncooked long grain rice
1	medium sweet red pepper, chopped
1	medium sweet yellow pepper, chopped
1	medium zucchini, chopped
2	Tbsp. olive oil, *divided*
4	green onions, chopped
1/2	tsp. salt
1/4	tsp. pepper
2	Tbsp. lemon juice

1. In a small saucepan, combine the wild rice, 1 cup broth and 1/2 cup water. Bring to a boil. Reduce heat; cover and simmer for 50-60 minutes or until rice is tender.

2. Meanwhile, in a large saucepan, combine the long grain rice and remaining broth and water. Bring to a boil. Reduce heat; cover and simmer for 15-18 minutes or until rice is tender.

3. In a large nonstick skillet, saute the peppers and zucchini in 1 tablespoon oil for 3 minutes. Add onions; saute 1-2 minutes longer or until vegetables are tender. Transfer to a large bowl.

4. Drain wild rice if necessary; stir into vegetable mixture. Stir in white rice. Sprinkle with salt and pepper. Drizzle with lemon juice and remaining oil; toss to coat. Serve warm or at room temperature.

Nutrition Facts: 3/4 cup equals 154 calories, 4 g fat (1 g saturated fat), 0 cholesterol, 287 mg sodium, 26 g carbohydrate, 2 g fiber, 4 g protein. **Diabetic Exchanges:** 1-1/2 starch, 1 fat.

SWEET PEPPER WILD RICE SALAD

CREAMY FETTUCCINE

Creamy Fettuccine

PREP/TOTAL TIME: 30 min. **YIELD:** 6 servings

DONNA MOSHER • AUGUSTA, MONTANA

Try this creamy and comforting side dish with a wide variety of entrees. It's fast and so tasty. It's great with salmon!

8	oz. uncooked fettuccine
3	Tbsp. olive oil
1	Tbsp. all-purpose flour
1	can (12 oz.) fat-free evaporated milk
2	green onions, chopped
2	Tbsp. minced fresh basil *or* 2 tsp. dried basil
1/4	tsp. salt
1/4	tsp. garlic powder
1/4	tsp. grated lemon peel
1/8	tsp. pepper
1/3	cup grated Parmesan cheese

Additional grated Parmesan cheese and minced fresh basil, optional

1. Cook fettuccine according to package directions; drain. Add oil; toss to coat.

2. In a large saucepan, combine flour and milk until smooth. Stir in the onions, basil, salt, garlic powder, lemon peel and pepper. Bring to a boil; cook and stir for 2 minutes or until slightly thickened. Remove from the heat; stir in cheese until blended. Pour over fettuccine and toss to coat. Sprinkle with additional cheese and basil if desired.

Nutrition Facts: 1/2 cup (calculated without additional cheese) equals 261 calories, 9 g fat (2 g saturated fat), 6 mg cholesterol, 259 mg sodium, 34 g carbohydrate, 2 g fiber, 12 g protein.

Couscous with Feta 'n' Tomatoes

PREP/TOTAL TIME: 20 min. **YIELD:** 6 servings

JOSEPHINE PIRO • EASTON, PENNSYLVANIA

This light and lovely side dish features tangy flavors mellowed by easy-to-cook couscous. It really comes together in a snap. Add some cooked and sliced chicken for a dinner.

1	cup boiling water
1/2	cup sun-dried tomatoes (not packed in oil)
1	can (14-1/2 oz.) vegetable broth
1-1/4	cups uncooked couscous
1/2	cup crumbled feta cheese
1/4	cup minced fresh parsley
1-1/2	tsp. minced fresh oregano *or* 1/2 tsp. dried oregano
3	tsp. lemon juice
1	tsp. water
1	tsp. olive oil

1. In a small bowl, pour boiling water over tomatoes; let stand for 5 minutes. Meanwhile, in a small saucepan, bring broth to a boil. Stir in couscous. Remove from the heat; let stand, covered, for 5 minutes or until broth is absorbed.

2. Drain and chop tomatoes; add to couscous. Gently stir in the remaining ingredients. Serve warm or chilled.

Nutrition Facts: 3/4 cup equals 187 calories, 3 g fat (1 g saturated fat), 5 mg cholesterol, 481 mg sodium, 33 g carbohydrate, 3 g fiber, 8 g protein. **Diabetic Exchanges:** 2 starch, 1/2 fat.

Baked Southern Grits M

PREP: 20 min. **BAKE:** 30 min. **YIELD:** 8 servings

KAREN MAU • JACKSBORO, TENNESSEE

This dish turns a Southern favorite into a tasty lighter dish with a jalapeno kick and a rich texture.

4	cups water
1	cup quick-cooking grits
4	egg whites
2	eggs
1-1/2	cups (6 oz.) shredded reduced-fat cheddar cheese
1/2	cup fat-free milk
1	to 2 jalapeno peppers, seeded and chopped
1/2	tsp. garlic salt
1/4	tsp. white pepper
4	green onions, chopped, *divided*

1. In a large saucepan, bring water to a boil. Add grits; cook and stir over medium heat for 5 minutes or until thickened. Remove from the heat.

2. In a small bowl, whisk egg whites and eggs. Stir a small amount of hot grits into eggs; return all to the pan, stirring constantly. Stir in the cheese, milk, jalapenos, garlic salt, pepper and half of the onions.

3. Transfer to a 2-qt. baking dish coated with cooking spray. Bake, uncovered, at 350° for 30-35 minutes or until golden brown. Sprinkle with the remaining onions.

Editor's Note: When cutting or seeding hot peppers, use rubber or plastic gloves to protect your hands. Avoid touching your face.

Nutrition Facts: 3/4 cup equals 158 calories, 6 g fat (3 g saturated fat), 68 mg cholesterol, 300 mg sodium, 17 g carbohydrate, 1 g fiber, 11 g protein. **Diabetic Exchanges:** 1 starch, 1 lean meat, 1/2 fat.

Savory Brussels Sprouts
F S C M

PREP/TOTAL TIME: 30 min. **YIELD:** 4 servings

PAULA MICHAUD • WATERBURY, CONNECTICUT

A simple mustard sauce makes these brussels sprouts different than most other recipes out there. A hint of celery seed adds a nice touch, but you could also experiment with a little bit of nutmeg if you'd like.

1	lb. fresh brussels sprouts

DIJON MUSTARD SAUCE:

1/2	cup fat-free plain yogurt
1	Tbsp. reduced-fat mayonnaise
1-1/2	tsp. Dijon mustard
1/4	tsp. celery seed

1. Cut an "X" in the core of each brussels sprout. Place in a steamer basket; place in a large saucepan over 1 in. of water. Bring to a boil; cover and steam for 8-11 minutes or until tender.

2. Meanwhile, in a small saucepan, combine the yogurt, mayonnaise, mustard and celery seed. Cook and stir just until heated through. Serve with brussels sprouts.

Nutrition Facts: 3/4 cup brussels sprouts with 2 tablespoons sauce equals 76 calories, 2 g fat (trace saturated fat), 2 mg cholesterol, 120 mg sodium, 13 g carbohydrate, 4 g fiber, 5 g protein. **Diabetic Exchange:** 2 vegetable.

Spiced Pear Chutney [F] [S]

PREP: 20 min. **COOK:** 45 min. **YIELD:** 1-3/4 cups

MARIE TOWNSEND • SALEM, OREGON

Try flavorful chutney on meat or poultry instead of heavy gravy. This simple, healthy recipe features 3 grams of fiber in every serving, thanks mostly to the pears.

1	small onion, chopped
1	garlic clove, minced
2/3	cup cider vinegar
1/4	cup packed brown sugar
1/4	cup chopped dates
1-1/2	tsp. mustard seed
1	tsp. ground ginger
1/4	tsp. salt
1/4	tsp. ground coriander
3	cups chopped peeled ripe pears

1. In a small saucepan coated with cooking spray, cook and stir the onion and garlic over medium heat for 2 minutes. Stir in the vinegar, brown sugar, dates and seasonings.

2. Bring to a boil. Reduce heat; carefully stir in pears. Cook, uncovered, over low heat for 40-50 minutes or until pears are tender and mixture achieves desired thickness.

Nutrition Facts: 1/4 cup equals 99 calories, 1 g fat (trace saturated fat), 0 cholesterol, 88 mg sodium, 25 g carbohydrate, 3 g fiber, 1 g protein. **Diabetic Exchanges:** 1 fruit, 1/2 starch.

Red Cabbage with Apples [F] [S]

PREP/TOTAL TIME: 30 min. **YIELD:** 4 servings

MICHELLE DOUGHERTY • LEWISTON, IDAHO

Looking for a delicious, lower-in-sodium alternative to sauerkraut to serve with pork entrees? Try this colorful side dish with the slightly sweet flavor of apples.

3	cups shredded red cabbage
1	medium apple, peeled and thinly sliced
1	small onion, halved and sliced
2	Tbsp. water
2	Tbsp. apple juice concentrate
1/2	tsp. chicken bouillon granules
1/4	tsp. salt
1/4	tsp. caraway seeds
1	Tbsp. red wine vinegar

1. In a large saucepan, combine the first eight ingredients. Bring to a boil.

2. Reduce heat; cover and simmer for 10-15 minutes or until cabbage is tender. Stir in vinegar.

Nutrition Facts: 1/2 cup equals 62 calories, trace fat (trace saturated fat), trace cholesterol, 261 mg sodium, 15 g carbohydrate, 2 g fiber, 1 g protein. **Diabetic Exchanges:** 1 vegetable, 1/2 fruit.

Acorn Squash with Peaches [S] [M]

PREP: 15 min. **BAKE:** 55 min. **YIELD:** 4 servings

MARY LOUISE FASH • WALTERBORO, SOUTH CAROLINA

Here's a dish that's sure to win over those who say they don't like squash. I enjoy it alongside chicken entrees.

2	small acorn squash
1/4	tsp. salt
1/8	tsp. pepper
1-1/4	cups frozen unsweetened peach slices, thawed
2	Tbsp. brown sugar
1	tsp. lemon juice
4	tsp. butter
1	Tbsp. minced fresh parsley, optional

1. Cut squash in half; remove seeds. Place cut side up in a 13-in. x 9-in. baking dish coated with cooking spray. Sprinkle with salt and pepper.

2. Place the peaches, brown sugar and lemon juice in a food processor. Cover and process until blended. Spoon over squash; dot with butter. Cover and bake at 350° for 55-65 minutes or until tender. Sprinkle with parsley if desired.

Nutrition Facts: 1/2 squash equals 173 calories, 4 g fat (2 g saturated fat), 10 mg cholesterol, 110 mg sodium, 36 g carbohydrate, 4 g fiber, 2 g protein.

ACORN SQUASH WITH PEACHES

RED CABBAGE WITH APPLES

Corn & Pepper Orzo F S M

PREP/TOTAL TIME: 30 min. **YIELD:** 6 servings

ANGELA HANKS • ST. ALBANS, WEST VIRGINIA

This fragrant side packs in flavor but keeps out extra fat, calories and sodium. Red pepper lends sweetness and color to the eye-catching dish.

3/4	cup uncooked orzo pasta
1	large sweet red pepper, chopped
1	medium onion, chopped
1	Tbsp. olive oil
2	cups frozen corn, thawed
2	tsp. Italian seasoning
1/8	tsp. salt
1/8	tsp. pepper

1. Cook pasta according to package directions.

2. Meanwhile, in a large nonstick skillet coated with cooking spray, saute red pepper and onion in oil for 2 minutes. Add the corn, Italian seasoning, salt and pepper; cook and stir until vegetables are tender. Drain pasta; stir into the pan.

Nutrition Facts: 3/4 cup equals 178 calories, 3 g fat (trace saturated fat), 0 cholesterol, 55 mg sodium, 34 g carbohydrate, 3 g fiber, 6 g protein. **Diabetic Exchanges:** 2 starch, 1/2 fat.

Broccoli Souffle C M

PREP: 25 min. **BAKE:** 35 min. **YIELD:** 4 servings

JANE SHAPTON • TUSTIN, CALIFORNIA

Many people are intimidated by souffles. But the change-of-pace recipes are simpler than you'd think. This curry-flavored side dish is light, airy and beginner-easy.

4	egg whites
2	tsp. plus 3 Tbsp. all-purpose flour, *divided*
1	cup chopped fresh broccoli
1/4	cup water
1	Tbsp. lemon juice
2	Tbsp. butter
1/4	tsp. salt
1	cup soy milk
1/2	cup minced fresh cilantro
1	tsp. curry powder

1. Place egg whites in a small mixing bowl; let stand at room temperature for 30 minutes. Coat a 1-qt. baking dish with cooking spray and sprinkle with 2 teaspoons flour; set aside.

2. Place broccoli and water in a microwave-safe bowl; cover and microwave on high for 2-3 minutes or until tender. Let stand for 5 minutes; drain. Place broccoli and lemon juice in a small food processor; cover and process until blended.

3. In a small saucepan over medium heat, melt butter. Stir in salt and remaining flour until blended. Gradually whisk in soy milk. Bring to a boil; cook and stir for 1-2 minutes or until thickened. Transfer to a small bowl; stir in the broccoli mixture, cilantro and curry.

4. Beat egg whites until stiff peaks form. With a spatula, fold a fourth of egg whites into broccoli mixture until no white streaks remain. Fold in remain-ing egg whites until combined.

5. Transfer to prepared dish. Bake at 350° for 35-40 minutes or until top is puffed and center appears set. Serve immediately.

Editor's Note: This recipe was tested in a 1,100-watt microwave.

Nutrition Facts: 1 serving equals 121 calories, 7 g fat (4 g saturated fat), 15 mg cholesterol, 285 mg sodium, 8 g carbohydrate, 1 g fiber, 7 g protein. **Diabetic Exchanges:** 1 very lean meat, 1 fat, 1/2 starch.

CORN & PEPPER ORZO

MULTIGRAIN & VEGGIE SIDE DISH

Multigrain & Veggie Side Dish M

PREP/TOTAL TIME: 30 min. **YIELD:** 8 servings

MARIAN PLATT • SEQUIM, WASHINGTON

Packed with all the good things we're supposed to eat, this dish is delicious and so nice in appearance. It's fun to make, too.

2-2/3 cups water
2/3 cup uncooked long grain rice
2/3 cup quick-cooking barley
1/2 tsp. salt
1 large onion, chopped
2 medium carrots, chopped
1 medium sweet red pepper, chopped
1 small turnip, chopped
1/2 cup chopped celery or celery root
1 Tbsp. minced fresh gingerroot
2 Tbsp. olive oil
1 pkg. (10 oz.) fresh spinach, torn
1 cup canned pinto beans, rinsed and drained
2 Tbsp. reduced-sodium soy sauce

1. In a small saucepan, bring water to a boil. Stir in the rice, barley and salt. Reduce heat; cover and simmer for 12-18 minutes or until grains are tender. Remove from the heat; let stand for 5 minutes.

2. In a Dutch oven, saute the onion, carrots, red pepper, turnip, celery and ginger in oil until crisp-tender. Stir in the spinach, beans, soy sauce and rice mixture; cook and stir until heated through and spinach is wilted.

Nutrition Facts: 1-1/4 cups equals 199 calories, 4 g fat (1 g saturated fat), 0 cholesterol, 387 mg sodium, 35 g carbohydrate, 6 g fiber, 6 g protein. **Diabetic Exchanges:** 2 starch, 1 vegetable, 1/2 fat.

Southwestern Baked Beans F M

PREP: 20 min. **BAKE:** 1 hour **YIELD:** 12 servings

LESLIE ADAMS • SPRINGFIELD, MISSOURI

Three kinds of beans and a host of seasonings make this version of baked beans a real winner.

2 cans (16 oz. *each*) kidney beans, rinsed and drained
1 can (15-1/2 oz.) great northern beans, rinsed and drained
1 can (15 oz.) black beans, rinsed and drained
2 cans (14-1/2 oz. *each*) Italian stewed tomatoes, drained and chopped
1 large onion, chopped
1/4 cup packed brown sugar
1/4 cup cider vinegar
2 Tbsp. honey
2 tsp. dried oregano
2 tsp. ground cumin
2 tsp. ground mustard
1-1/2 tsp. ground ginger
1 tsp. garlic powder
1 tsp. chili powder
1/2 tsp. salt

1. In a large bowl, combine the beans, tomatoes and onion. Combine the remaining ingredients; stir into bean mixture.

2. Transfer to a 3-qt. baking dish coated with cooking spray. Cover and bake at 350° for 45 minutes; stir. Bake, uncovered, 15-30 minutes longer or until heated through.

Nutrition Facts: 3/4 cup equals 178 calories, trace fat (trace saturated fat), 0 cholesterol, 502 mg sodium, 35 g carbohydrate, 8 g fiber, 9 g protein. **Diabetic Exchanges:** 2 starch, 1 vegetable.

MAKEOVER CHICKEN ROMAINE SALAD

Makeover Chicken Romaine Salad

PREP/TOTAL TIME: 25 min. **YIELD:** 12 servings

AMY BRANTLEY • RALEIGH, NORTH CAROLINA

I loved a chicken salad, but I wanted to cut its fat and calories. By coating the chicken in panko crumbs instead of frying it, this recipe is now so much healthier.

> 1 egg white
> 2 Tbsp. water
> 1/4 cup all-purpose flour
> 1/4 cup panko (Japanese) bread crumbs
> 1/2 pound boneless skinless chicken breasts, cut into 1-in. pieces

Butter-flavored cooking spray

> 1/4 cup chopped pecans
> 1/4 tsp. salt
> 7 cups torn romaine
> 1 cup seedless red grapes
> 1/2 cup dried cranberries
> 1/2 cup salted soy nuts
> 1/2 cup shredded sharp cheddar cheese
> 1 bottle (8 oz.) Vidalia onion *or* honey mustard salad dressing

1. In a shallow bowl, whisk egg white and water. Place flour and bread crumbs in separate shallow bowls. Coat chicken with flour, then dip in egg white mixture and coat with crumbs. Place on a baking sheet coated with butter-flavored cooking spray. Bake at 425° for 8-12 minutes or until no longer pink, turning once.

2. In a small nonstick skillet coated with butter-flavored cooking spray, cook and stir pecans and salt until toasted. Remove from the heat; set aside.

3. In a salad bowl, combine the romaine, grapes, cranberries, soy nuts and cheese. Add chicken and reserved pecans; toss to combine. Serve with dressing.

Nutrition Facts: 3/4 cup salad with 4 teaspoons dressing equals 226 calories, 12 g fat (3 g saturated fat), 19 mg cholesterol, 212 mg sodium, 21 g carbohydrate, 3 g fiber, 9 g protein.

Tabbouleh Salad with Shrimp

PREP: 20 min. + standing **YIELD:** 5 servings

SANDRA BIENZ • CALGARY, ALBERTA

My co-workers love when I bring this dish to get-togethers. It's terrific as a side dish, but good enough to stand alone.

> 1 cup bulgur
> 2 cups boiling water
> 1 medium cucumber, peeled, seeded and chopped
> 8 green onions, chopped
> 1 cup minced fresh parsley
> 1/4 cup minced fresh mint
> 1/4 cup lemon juice
> 3 Tbsp. olive oil
> 1 to 2 tsp. minced fresh gingerroot
> 1 to 2 tsp. ground coriander
> 1/2 tsp. salt
> 1/4 tsp. pepper
> 1-1/4 lbs. cooked medium shrimp, peeled and deveined

1. Place the bulgur in a small bowl; stir in boiling water. Cover and let stand for 30 minutes or until most of the liquid is absorbed; drain.

2. In a large bowl, combine the bulgur, cucumber, onions, parsley and mint. In a small bowl, whisk the lemon juice, oil, ginger, coriander, salt and pepper. Pour over bulgur mixture and toss to coat. Transfer to a serving bowl; top with shrimp.

Editor's Note: Look for bulgur, quinoa and other whole grains in the cereal, rice or organic food aisle of your grocery store.

Nutrition Facts: 1 cup with about 8 shrimp equals 314 calories, 11 g fat (2 g saturated fat), 172 mg cholesterol, 419 mg sodium, 28 g carbohydrate, 7 g fiber, 28 g protein. **Diabetic Exchanges:** 3 very lean meat, 2 starch, 1-1/2 fat.

Flavorful Mashed Potatoes F M

PREP: 20 min. **COOK:** 25 min. **YIELD:** 12 servings

MARY RELYEA • CANASTOTA, NEW YORK

Classic herbs bring extra flavor to creamy red potatoes, making this side dish anything but ordinary.

- 4 lbs. red potatoes (about 12 medium)
- 6 garlic cloves, peeled and thinly sliced
- 1/2 cup fat-free milk
- 1/2 cup reduced-fat sour cream
- 2 Tbsp. butter, melted
- 2 Tbsp. minced fresh parsley *or* 2 tsp. dried parsley flakes
- 2 Tbsp. minced fresh thyme *or* 2 tsp. dried thyme
- 1 Tbsp. minced fresh rosemary *or* 1 tsp. dried rosemary, crushed
- 1-1/4 tsp. salt

1. Scrub and quarter potatoes; place in a large saucepan and cover with water. Add garlic. Bring to a boil. Reduce heat; cover and cook for 15-20 minutes or until potatoes are tender; drain.

2. In a large bowl, mash potato mixture. Stir in the remaining ingredients.

Nutrition Facts: 3/4 cup equals 146 calories, 3 g fat (2 g saturated fat), 9 mg cholesterol, 280 mg sodium, 26 g carbohydrate, 3 g fiber, 4 g protein. **Diabetic Exchanges:** 2 starch, 1/2 fat.

Creamy Spinach Casserole

PREP: 10 min. **BAKE:** 35 min. **YIELD:** 10 servings

ANNETTE MARIE YOUNG • WEST LAFAYETTE, INDIANA

Rich and comforting, this savory spinach casserole will be a welcome addition to the any table. Busy hostesses will love the short prep time and decadent taste.

- 2 cans (10-3/4 oz. *each*) reduced-fat reduced-sodium condensed cream of chicken soup, undiluted
- 1 pkg. (8 oz.) reduced-fat cream cheese, cubed
- 1/2 cup fat-free milk
- 1/2 cup grated Parmesan cheese
- 4 cups herb seasoned stuffing cubes
- 2 pkg. (10 oz. *each*) frozen chopped spinach, thawed and squeezed dry

1. In a large mixing bowl, beat the soup, cream cheese, milk and Parmesan cheese until blended. Stir in stuffing cubes and spinach.

2. Spoon into a 2-qt. baking dish coated with cooking spray. Bake, uncovered, at 350° for 35-40 minutes or until heated through.

Nutrition Facts: 2/3 cup equals 205 calories, 8 g fat (4 g saturated fat), 25 mg cholesterol, 723 mg sodium, 25 g carbohydrate, 3 g fiber, 9 g protein.

Good news! Not only does the **Creamy Spinach Casserole** offer lots of great flavor, but it includes a healthy dose of vitamin A as well.

FLAVORFUL MASHED POTATOES

CREAMY SPINACH CASSEROLE

Seasoned Baked Potatoes M

PREP: 5 min. **BAKE:** 35 min. **YIELD:** 4 servings

RUTH ANDREWSON • PECK, IDAHO

Everyone is sure to enjoy these crisp, delicious potatoes brushed with basil, garlic and onion salt. Try them alongside poultry or most any main course.

> 4 medium baking potatoes
> 1 Tbsp. olive oil
> 1-1/2 tsp. dried basil
> 1/2 tsp. onion salt
> 1/2 tsp. garlic powder

1. Scrub potatoes and cut in half lengthwise; place cut side up on an ungreased baking sheet. Brush with oil. Sprinkle with basil, onion salt and garlic powder. Bake at 400° for 35-40 minutes or until tender.

Nutrition Facts: 2 potato halves equals 167 calories, 4 g fat (1 g saturated fat), 0 cholesterol, 237 mg sodium, 31 g carbohydrate, 3 g fiber, 4 g protein. **Diabetic Exchanges:** 2 starch, 1/2 fat.

Zucchini Fritters F C M

PREP: 20 min. **BAKE:** 20 min.
YIELD: 10 servings (3/4 cup sauce)

TRISHA KRUSE • EAGLE, IDAHO

To create an authentic "fried" texture, I turn to a technique combined with readily available panko. Baking these fritters at a fairly high heat turns the bread crumbs a nice golden brown.

> 1/4 cup buttermilk
> 1/4 cup egg substitute
> 1/2 cup panko (Japanese) bread crumbs
> 1/2 cup seasoned bread crumbs
> 1/4 cup grated Parmesan cheese
> 1-1/2 tsp. taco seasoning
> 1/4 tsp. garlic salt

> 3 medium zucchini, cut into 1/4-in. slices
> 1/4 cup fat-free sour cream
> 1/4 cup prepared fat-free ranch salad dressing
> 1/4 cup salsa

1. In a shallow bowl, combine buttermilk and egg substitute. In another shallow bowl, combine the bread crumbs, cheese, taco seasoning and garlic salt. Dip zucchini in buttermilk mixture, then bread crumb mixture.

2. Place on baking sheets coated with cooking spray. Bake at 400° for 20-25 minutes or until golden brown, turning once.

3. In a small bowl, combine the sour cream, ranch dressing and salsa. Serve with zucchini.

Nutrition Facts: 1/3 cup zucchini with about 1 tablespoon sauce equals 67 calories, 1 g fat (trace saturated fat), 3 mg cholesterol, 296 mg sodium, 11 g carbohydrate, 1 g fiber, 3 g protein. **Diabetic Exchange:** 1 starch.

Country French Beans F S

PREP: 1-1/4 hours + soaking
BAKE: 1 hour **YIELD:** 12 servings

HEALTHY COOKING TEST KITCHEN

The tender beans in this side dish contribute almost 6 grams of fiber to each serving. Brown sugar, herbs and bacon create a delightful blend of flavors.

> 1 lb. dried navy beans
> 2 qts. water
> 4 turkey bacon strips, diced
> 1 medium onion, chopped
> 1 celery rib, chopped
> 1/4 cup packed brown sugar
> 2 tsp. ground mustard
> 1 tsp. dried thyme
> 1/2 tsp. garlic powder
> 1/4 tsp. salt

1. Sort beans and rinse with cold water. Place in an ovenproof Dutch oven; add water to cover by 2 in. Bring to a boil; boil for 2 minutes. Remove from the heat; cover and let stand for 1-4 hours or until the beans are softened.

2. Drain and rinse beans, discarding liquid. Return beans to the pan; add 2 qts. water. Bring to a boil.

SEASONED BAKED POTATOES

ZUCCHINI FRITTERS

TANGY BARBECUE SAUCE ROASTED TOMATO 'N' GARLIC MAYONNAISE

Reduce heat; cover and simmer for 45-60 minutes or until beans are almost tender.

3. Drain and reserve liquid; set beans aside. Coat the same Dutch oven with cooking spray. Add the bacon, onion and celery; cook and stir until the vegetables are tender. Stir in the beans, brown sugar, mustard, thyme, garlic powder and 2 cups reserved liquid.

4. Cover and bake at 325° for 1 to 1-1/2 hours or until beans are tender and reach desired consistency, stirring every 30 minutes. Add more reserved liquid as needed. Stir in salt before serving.

Nutrition Facts: 1/2 cup equals 164 calories, 2 g fat (trace saturated fat), 4 mg cholesterol, 116 mg sodium, 29 g carbohydrate, 10 g fiber, 10 g protein. **Diabetic Exchange:** 1-1/2 starch.

Tangy Barbecue Sauce F C

PREP: 10 min. **COOK:** 55 min. **YIELD:** 2-1/2 cups

LYNN SAWYER • TWO RIVERS, WISCONSIN

Trying to limit sugar? If you can find sugar-free ketchup, use it in this recipe. It makes a great-tasting barbecue sauce that fits with sugar-sensitive diets.

1	large onion, finely chopped
1	Tbsp. canola oil
1-1/2	cups ketchup
1	cup cider vinegar
3/4	cup water
3/4	cup sugar-free maple-flavored syrup
4-1/2	tsp. Worcestershire sauce

Sugar substitute equivalent to 1 Tbsp. sugar

2	tsp. reduced-sodium beef bouillon granules
1	tsp. salt
1/4	tsp. pepper
1/4	tsp. hot pepper sauce

1. In a large nonstick saucepan, saute onion in oil until tender. Stir in the remaining ingredients. Bring to a boil. Reduce heat; simmer, uncovered, for 45 minutes or until sauce is thickened and reduced to 2-1/2 cups.

Nutrition Facts: 2 tablespoons equals 36 calories, 1 g fat (trace saturated fat), trace cholesterol, 390 mg sodium, 8 g carbohydrate, trace fiber, trace protein.

Roasted Tomato 'n' Garlic Mayonnaise C

PREP: 15 min. **BAKE:** 35 min. + cooling
YIELD: 1-2/3 cups

CINDIE HARAS • BOCA RATON, FLORIDA

We love to use this versatile mayo on any sandwich, but it's especially good on a BLT. I usually make a big batch on the weekends. Leftovers dress up any evening meal.

4	plum tomatoes
3	tsp. olive oil, *divided*
1	tsp. *each* dried basil, oregano and rosemary, crushed
1/4	tsp. coarsely ground pepper
1/2	tsp. salt, *divided*
1	whole garlic bulb
3/4	cup reduced-fat mayonnaise

1. Cut tomatoes in half lengthwise; drizzle cut sides with 1-1/2 teaspoons oil. Combine the herbs, pepper and 1/4 teaspoon salt; sprinkle over tomatoes. Place cut side down on a baking sheet coated with cooking spray.

2. Remove papery outer skin from garlic (do not peel or separate cloves). Cut top off garlic bulb. Brush with 1/2 teaspoon oil. Wrap in heavy-duty foil; place on baking sheet with tomatoes. Bake at 425° for 15 minutes.

3. Turn tomatoes; drizzle with remaining oil. Bake 20-25 minutes longer or until garlic is tender and tomatoes are softened. Cool for 10 minutes.

4. Squeeze softened garlic into a small bowl; chop tomatoes and add to garlic. Stir in mayonnaise and remaining salt until blended.

Nutrition Facts: 2 tablespoons equals 61 calories, 6 g fat (1 g saturated fat), 5 mg cholesterol, 203 mg sodium, 2 g carbohydrate, trace fiber, trace protein. **Diabetic Exchange:** 1 fat.

Makeover Favorite Corn Bake Ⓜ

PREP: 20 min. **BAKE:** 30 min. + standing
YIELD: 12 servings

RUTHANN CLORE• WEST PEORIA, ILLINOIS

To cut sodium even further from this casserole, replace the canned corn with 1-1/3 cups fresh corn.

1	cup all-purpose flour
1	cup cornmeal
3	Tbsp. sugar
1/2	tsp. salt
1/2	tsp. baking soda
1	egg
1	cup (8 oz.) reduced-fat sour cream
1/4	cup unsweetened applesauce
1/4	cup butter, melted
1	can (15-1/4 oz.) whole kernel corn, undrained
1	can (14-3/4 oz.) cream-style corn

1. In a large bowl, combine the first five ingredients. In a small bowl, whisk the egg, sour cream, applesauce and butter. Stir in corn. Stir into dry ingredients just until moistened. Transfer to a 13-in. x 9-in. baking dish coated with cooking spray.

2. Bake at 350° for 30-35 minutes or until a toothpick inserted near the center comes out clean. Serve warm. Refrigerate leftovers.

Nutrition Facts: 1 serving equals 211 calories, 7 g fat (4 g saturated fat), 34 mg cholesterol, 395 mg sodium, 32 g carbohydrate, 2 g fiber, 5 g protein. **Diabetic Exchanges:** 2 starch, 1 fat.

Baked Barley and Wild Rice Ⓕ

PREP: 70 min. **BAKE:** 65 min. **YIELD:** 12 servings

EDNA WOODARD • FREDERICKSBURG, TEXAS

We eat many whole grain dishes, but this is our favorite. It also delivers 4 grams of heart-healthy fiber per serving.

1/3	cup uncooked wild rice
4	cups water, *divided*
1	cup medium pearl barley
1	Tbsp. butter
1	cup sliced fresh mushrooms
2	cups reduced-sodium chicken broth
1	can (8 oz.) sliced water chestnuts, drained
1/4	cup slivered almonds
1	envelope onion soup mix
1/2	tsp. garlic salt
1/2	tsp. onion powder

1. In a small saucepan, combine wild rice and 1 cup water. Bring to a boil. Reduce heat; cover and simmer for 50-60 minutes or until rice is tender.

2. In a large skillet over medium heat, cook and stir barley in butter for 2 minutes. Add mushrooms; cook 2 minutes longer or until mushrooms are tender. Transfer to a 2-1/2-qt. baking dish coated with cooking spray. Stir in the broth, water chestnuts, almonds, soup mix, garlic salt, onion powder, cooked rice and remaining water.

3. Cover and bake at 350° for 1 hour, stirring twice. Uncover; bake 5-10 minutes longer or until barley is tender. Let stand for 5 minutes before serving.

Nutrition Facts: 2/3 cup equals 119 calories, 2 g fat (1 g saturated fat), 3 mg cholesterol, 386 mg sodium, 22 g carbohydrate, 4 g fiber, 4 g protein. **Diabetic Exchanges:** 1-1/2 starch, 1/2 fat.

Makeover Southern Favorite Sweet Potatoes S M

PREP: 15 min. **BAKE:** 40 min. **YIELD:** 12 servings

SONIA CHIMENTI • CONCORD, CALIFORNIA

Thanksgiving just wouldn't be the same without our family's pecan-topped sweet potato bake. This version offers 43 percent less fat and 32 percent fewer calories than the original, but it has all of the buttery flavor we love most!

- 2 eggs, beaten
- 1/2 cup fat-free milk
- 1/3 cup sugar
- 1/3 cup unsweetened pineapple juice
- 1/4 cup reduced-fat butter, melted
- 1 tsp. vanilla extract
- 2 cans (40 oz. *each*) sweet potatoes, drained and coarsely chopped

TOPPING:
- 1 cup chopped pecans
- 2/3 cup packed brown sugar
- 1/4 cup reduced-fat butter, melted

1. In a large bowl, combine the eggs, milk, sugar, pineapple juice, butter and vanilla. Gently stir in sweet potatoes. Transfer to a 3-qt. baking dish coated with cooking spray.

2. Combine the topping ingredients; spoon over sweet potato mixture. Bake, uncovered, at 350° for 40-50 minutes or until bubbly and golden brown.

Editor's Note: This recipe was tested with Land O'Lakes light stick butter.

Nutrition Facts: 1/2 cup equals 302 calories, 12 g fat (3 g saturated fat), 45 mg cholesterol, 140 mg sodium, 47 g carbohydrate, 4 g fiber, 4 g protein.

Whipped Autumn Vegetables F M

PREP/TOTAL TIME: 30 min. **YIELD:** 9 servings

KATHY RAIRIGH • MILFORD, INDIANA

This puts my sweet potato crop to delicious use. I've used butternut squash instead of sweet potatoes with equally yummy results.

- 2 lbs. sweet potatoes, peeled and cubed (about 3 large)
- 3 medium parsnips, peeled and sliced
- 1/2 cup chopped dried apricots
- 1 cup apple cider *or* unsweetened apple juice
- 2 Tbsp. butter, melted
- 1/2 tsp. salt
- 1/8 tsp. pepper

1. Place the sweet potatoes, parsnips and apricots in a large saucepan; cover with water. Bring to a boil. Reduce heat; cover and cook for 10-15 minutes or until vegetables are tender.

2. Meanwhile, in a small saucepan, bring apple cider to a boil; cook until reduced to 1/4 cup.

3. Drain vegetable mixture; cool slightly. Transfer to a food processor. Add the butter, salt, pepper and reduced cider. Cover and process for 1-2 minutes or until blended.

Nutrition Facts: 1/2 cup equals 159 calories, 3 g fat (2 g saturated fat), 7 mg cholesterol, 163 mg sodium, 33 g carbohydrate, 5 g fiber, 2 g protein. **Diabetic Exchange:** 2 starch.

Spanish Lima Beans S M

PREP: 15 min. + soaking
COOK: 1-3/4 hours **YIELD:** 6 servings

PEGGY BURDICK • BURLINGTON, MICHIGAN

This simple recipe makes a tasty side that's low in sodium and fat but high in fiber. Tomatoes and sauteed onions create a pleasing sweet and tangy combination.

- 1 cup dried lima beans
- 1 bay leaf
- 2 medium onions, chopped
- 2 Tbsp. canola oil
- 1 can (14-1/2 oz.) diced tomatoes, undrained
- 1 tsp. sugar

Dash pepper

1. Sort beans and rinse with cold water. Place in a large saucepan; add water to cover by 2 in. Bring to a boil; boil for 2 minutes. Remove from the heat; cover and let stand for 1-4 hours or until beans are softened.

2. Drain and rinse beans, discarding liquid. Return beans to the pan; add bay leaf and water to cover by 2 in. Bring to a boil. Reduce heat; cover and simmer for 1-1/4 to 1-1/2 hours or until beans are tender.

3. Drain, discarding liquid and bay leaf. In a large skillet, saute onions in oil until tender. Stir in the tomatoes, sugar, pepper and beans. Cook for 8-10 minutes or until heated through.

Nutrition Facts: 1/2 cup equals 190 calories, 5 g fat (trace saturated fat), 0 cholesterol, 93 mg sodium, 30 g carbohydrate, 9 g fiber, 8 g protein. **Diabetic Exchanges:** 2 starch, 1 fat.

SPANISH LIMA BEANS

Vegetables in Dill Sauce C M

PREP/TOTAL TIME: 30 min. **YIELD:** 6 servings

EDIE DESPAIN • LOGAN, UTAH

This recipe is ideal for using up vegetables from your garden. It's a great side dish for grilled chicken.

4	cups water
1-1/2	cups pearl onions
1	medium carrot, sliced
1	Tbsp. butter
1/2	pound sliced fresh mushrooms
2	small zucchini, sliced
2	tsp. lemon juice
1	tsp. dried marjoram
1/4	tsp. salt

SAUCE:

2	Tbsp. plus 2 tsp. fat-free sour cream
2	Tbsp. plus 2 tsp. reduced-fat mayonnaise
2	Tbsp. fat-free milk
2-1/4	tsp. finely chopped onion
1/2	tsp. snipped fresh dill

Dash white pepper

1. In a large saucepan, bring water to a boil. Add pearl onions; boil for 3 minutes. Drain and rinse in cold water; peel.

2. In a large nonstick skillet coated with cooking spray, saute onions and carrot in butter for 1 minute. Add mushrooms and zucchini; saute 6-8 minutes longer or until vegetables are tender. Stir in the lemon juice, marjoram and salt.

3. In a small microwave-safe bowl, combine the sauce ingredients. Cover and microwave on high until heated through, stirring once. Serve with vegetables.

Nutrition Facts: 1/2 cup vegetables with 1 tablespoon sauce equals 80 calories, 4 g fat (2 g saturated fat), 9 mg cholesterol, 186 mg sodium, 9 g carbohydrate, 2 g fiber, 3 g protein. **Diabetic Exchanges:** 1 vegetable, 1 fat.

Garden Zucchini Chutney F S

PREP: 20 min. **COOK:** 50 min. **YIELD:** 4 cups

TAREN WEYER • HUDSON, WISCONSIN

At my wit's end with grating my harvest of zucchini, I was determined to make something other than zucchini bread and zucchini cake. I found this recipe and altered it to our taste.

6	cups chopped seeded zucchini (about 7 medium)
2	medium tart apples, peeled and chopped
1-1/2	cups raisins *or* dried currants
1-1/2	cups white vinegar
1	cup honey
1	medium sweet red pepper, chopped
1	small onion, chopped
1/3	cup orange juice concentrate
2	Tbsp. lemon juice

1. In a Dutch oven, bring all ingredients to a boil.

2. Reduce heat; simmer, uncovered, for 45-55 minutes or until thickened. Serve warm or cold. Refrigerate leftovers.

Nutrition Facts: 2 tablespoons equals 67 calories, trace fat (trace saturated fat), 0 cholesterol, 4 mg sodium, 18 g carbohydrate, 1 g fiber, 1 g protein. **Diabetic Exchange:** 1 starch.

Vegetable Barley M

PREP: 10 min. **COOK:** 50 min. **YIELD:** 4 servings

ELLEN GOVERTSEN • WHEATON, ILLINOIS

This hearty side dish has colorful green snow peas, red pepper and just a hint of lemon to give it a fresh springtime taste. It can be served either warm or cool.

2-2/3	cups water
1/2	cup medium pearl barley
1/2	tsp. salt
1	cup fresh snow peas
1	small sweet red pepper, chopped
1	Tbsp. canola oil
4	green onions, thinly sliced
2	Tbsp. lemon juice
1	tsp. grated lemon peel

GARDEN ZUCCHINI CHUTNEY

VEGETABLE BARLEY

1. In a large saucepan, bring water to a boil. Stir in barley and salt. Reduce heat; cover and simmer for 45-50 minutes or until tender.

2. In a small skillet, saute snow peas and red pepper in oil for 2 minutes. Add onions; saute 2 minutes longer or until vegetables are tender.

3. Remove barley from the heat; stir in the lemon juice, lemon peel and vegetable mixture.

Nutrition Facts: 3/4 cup equals 148 calories, 4 g fat (trace saturated fat), 0 cholesterol, 302 mg sodium, 25 g carbohydrate, 6 g fiber, 4 g protein. **Diabetic Exchanges:** 1-1/2 starch, 1 vegetable, 1/2 fat.

Sweet Potato Casserole S M

PREP: 30 min. **BAKE:** 35 min. **YIELD:** 8 servings

KATHY RAIRIGH • MILFORD, INDIANA

I am always looking for ways to use our abundant sweet potatoes. This recipe is my own creation, and I've made it many times. I take it to family potlucks; it never fails to bring compliments!

2-1/4	lbs. sweet potatoes (about 3 large), peeled and cubed
3	egg whites, beaten
3	Tbsp. maple syrup
1	tsp. vanilla extract

TOPPING:

1/4	cup chopped pecans
1	Tbsp. brown sugar
1	Tbsp. butter, melted
1/8	tsp. ground cinnamon
1/3	cup dried apricots, chopped
1/3	cup dried cherries, chopped

1. Place sweet potatoes in a Dutch oven and cover with water. Bring to a boil. Reduce heat; cover and simmer for 15-20 minutes or until tender. Drain and place in a large bowl; mash. Cool slightly. Stir in the egg whites, syrup and vanilla.

2. Transfer to an 8-in. square baking dish coated with cooking spray. Combine the pecans, brown sugar, butter and cinnamon; sprinkle over the top. Bake, uncovered, at 350° for 30 minutes. Sprinkle with apricots and cherries. Bake 5-7 minutes longer or until a thermometer reads 160° and the fruits are heated through.

Nutrition Facts: 1 serving equals 186 calories, 4 g fat (1 g saturated fat), 4 mg cholesterol, 40 mg sodium, 34 g carbohydrate, 3 g fiber, 3 g protein. **Diabetic Exchanges:** 1-1/2 starch, 1 fat, 1/2 fruit.

Two varieties of **sweet potatoes** are readily available. One has a pale skin with a light yellow flesh. The other has dark skin with a dark orange flesh that cooks to a moist texture. This variety is often called a yam.

ASIAN GRILLED GREEN BEANS

Asian Grilled Green Beans
F M S C

PREP: 20 min. **GRILL:** 20 min. **YIELD:** 8 servings

TRISHA KRUSE • EAGLE, IDAHO

You'll love the great flavor and easy preparation of this fresh side dish. It features bright green beans tossed in a sweet sauce with subtle kick.

1	Tbsp. brown sugar
1	Tbsp. sesame oil
1	Tbsp. reduced-sodium soy sauce
2	garlic cloves, minced
1/2	tsp. crushed red pepper flakes
1-1/2	lbs. fresh green beans, trimmed
1	medium red onion, halved and thinly sliced
6	medium fresh mushrooms, quartered

1. In a large bowl, combine the first five ingredients. Add the beans, onion and mushrooms; toss to coat. Place half of the vegetables on a double thickness of heavy-duty foil (about 18 in. square); fold foil around vegetables and seal tightly. Repeat with remaining vegetables.

2. Grill, covered, over medium heat for 18-22 minutes or until beans are tender, turning packets over once. Open foil carefully to allow steam to escape.

Nutrition Facts: 3/4 cup equals 55 calories, 2 g fat (trace saturated fat), 0 cholesterol, 82 mg sodium, 9 g carbohydrate, 3 g fiber, 2 g protein. **Diabetic Exchanges:** 1 vegetable, 1/2 fat.

Barley Pilaf with Bacon F

PREP: 15 min. **BAKE:** 65 min. **YIELD:** 6 servings

LILI HILL • ATHENS, GEORGIA

This is a tried-and-true recipe from my days working in an oat-and-barley flour mill. Chicken broth, onion and bacon lend wonderful flavor to the fiber-rich grain.

2	bacon strips, diced
1	cup uncooked pearl barley
1	small onion, chopped
1/2	cup sliced fresh mushrooms
3	cups reduced-sodium chicken broth
1/4	tsp. pepper

1. In a small nonstick skillet, cook bacon over medium heat until crisp. Using a slotted spoon, remove to paper towels. Cool, then refrigerate.

2. Drain skillet, reserving 2 teaspoons drippings. In the drippings, saute the barley, onion and mushrooms until barley is lightly browned and vegetables are tender.

3. Transfer to a 1-1/2-qt. baking dish coated with cooking spray. Stir in broth and pepper. Cover and bake at 350° for 1 hour.

4. Stir in bacon; bake 5-10 minutes longer or until the barley is tender and the liquid is absorbed.

Nutrition Facts: 2/3 cup equals 157 calories, 3 g fat (1 g saturated fat), 3 mg cholesterol, 356 mg sodium, 28 g carbohydrate, 6 g fiber, 6 g protein. **Diabetic Exchanges:** 2 starch, 1/2 fat.

Spinach Vermicelli

PREP/TOTAL TIME: 30 min. **YIELD:** 6 servings

CHARLEEN BERKERS • PALGRAVE, ONTARIO

Not only is this easy side dish nutritious and meatless, it also offers the goodness of spinach.

- 8 oz. uncooked vermicelli
- 1 large red onion, sliced and separated into rings
- 1 Tbsp. olive oil
- 2 garlic cloves, minced
- 1 pkg. (10 oz.) fresh spinach, torn
- 2 Tbsp. lemon juice
- 1 Tbsp. minced fresh tarragon *or* 1 tsp. dried tarragon
- 1/4 tsp. salt
- 1/8 tsp. pepper
- 1/3 cup crumbled Gorgonzola cheese

1. Cook vermicelli according to package directions. Meanwhile, in a large nonstick skillet, saute onion in oil until crisp-tender. Add garlic; saute 1 minute longer. Add the spinach, lemon juice, tarragon, salt and pepper; saute for 2 minutes or until spinach is wilted.

2. Drain vermicelli; toss with spinach mixture. Sprinkle with cheese.

Nutrition Facts: 1 cup pasta with about 1 tablespoon cheese equals 220 calories, 6 g fat (3 g saturated fat), 8 mg cholesterol, 296 mg sodium, 33 g carbohydrate, 3 g fiber, 9 g protein. **Diabetic Exchanges:** 2 starch, vegetable, 1 fat.

Snappy Herbed Spinach

PREP/TOTAL TIME: 20 min. **YIELD:** 4 servings

EVA BROOKMAN • DAVIS, ILLINOIS

We have a small group that meets once a week for exercise and to share ideas on "light and tasty" foods that are good for us but also quick. This is one of our favorite recipes.

- 1 tsp. butter
- 2 Tbsp. finely chopped onion
- 2 eggs
- 1/3 cup fat-free milk
- 1/2 tsp. Worcestershire sauce
- 1/2 tsp. salt
- 1/4 tsp. dried rosemary, crushed
- 1 pkg. (10 oz.) frozen chopped spinach, thawed and squeezed dry
- 1 cup cooked long grain rice
- 1/2 cup shredded cheddar cheese, *divided*

1. In a small microwave-safe bowl, melt butter. Add onion; cover and microwave at 50% power for 1 minute, stirring after 30 seconds. Set aside.

2. In a large bowl, whisk the eggs, milk, Worcestershire sauce, salt and rosemary. Stir in the spinach, rice, onion mixture and 1/4 cup cheese. Transfer to an 8-in. x 4-in. microwave-safe dish coated with cooking spray.

3. Microwave, uncovered, on high for 6-8 minutes. Sprinkle with remaining cheese; microwave 1-2 minutes longer or until firm and a thermometer reads 160°. Cover and let stand for 5 minutes before cutting.

Editor's Note: This recipe was tested in a 1,100-watt microwave.

Nutrition Facts: 1 piece equals 174 calories, 8 g fat (4 g saturated fat), 124 mg cholesterol, 492 mg sodium, 16 g carbohydrate, 2 g fiber, 10 g protein. **Diabetic Exchanges:** 1 starch, 1 lean meat, 1 vegetable, 1 fat.

When considering **Snappy Herbed Spinach**, keep in mind that you can replace the spinach with chopped broccoli for an equally tasty dish.

SNAPPY HERBED SPINACH

SPINACH VERMICELLI

Vegetable Rice Skillet

PREP: 10 min. **COOK:** 30 min. **YIELD:** 8 servings

ARLENE LEE • HOLLAND, MANITOBA

This is a favorite dish of ours. It's very filling with the rice, and the cheese gives the veggies extra flavor. Great warmed up the next day—if any is left!

1	medium onion, chopped
1	Tbsp. butter
2	medium carrots, sliced
1-1/2	cups cauliflowerets
1-1/2	cups broccoli florets
1	cup uncooked long grain rice
2	garlic cloves, minced
1-1/2	cups reduced-sodium chicken broth
1	cup (4 oz.) shredded reduced-fat cheddar cheese
1	Tbsp. minced fresh parsley
3/4	tsp. salt
1/4	tsp. pepper

1. In a large nonstick skillet over medium heat, cook onion in butter until tender. Add carrots; cook 5 minutes longer. Stir in the cauliflower, broccoli, rice and garlic. Add broth; bring mixture to a boil.

2. Reduce heat; cover and simmer for 20-25 minutes or until rice is tender. Remove from the heat; stir in the cheese, parsley, salt and pepper.

Nutrition Facts: 3/4 cup equals 164 calories, 5 g fat (3 g saturated fat), 14 mg cholesterol, 459 mg sodium, 24 g carbohydrate, 2 g fiber, 7 g protein. **Diabetic Exchanges:** 1 starch, 1 vegetable, 1 fat.

VEGETABLE RICE SKILLET

Acorn Squash Puree

PREP: 1 hour **BAKE:** 20 min. **YIELD:** 8 servings

ANN HENNESSY • BURNSVILLE, MINNESOTA

I created this recipe as a healthy alternative on our Thanksgiving menu. It's become a much-requested favorite.

4	medium acorn squash
8	oz. fat-free cream cheese, cubed
1/2	cup fat-free milk
2	Tbsp. reduced-fat butter, melted
2	Tbsp. dried minced onion
2	Tbsp. minced chives
2	tsp. dried basil
3	Tbsp. chopped pecans

1. Cut squash in half; discard seeds. Place squash cut side down in a 15-in. x 10-in. baking pan; add 1/2 in. of hot water. Bake, uncovered, at 350° for 35 minutes. Drain water from pan; turn squash cut side up. Bake 5-10 minutes longer or until tender. Cool slightly.

2. Carefully scoop out squash; add to food processor. Add the cream cheese, milk, butter, onion, chives and basil; cover and process until blended. Transfer to a 2-qt. baking dish coated with cooking spray; sprinkle with pecans.

3. Cover and bake at 350° for 20-25 minutes or until heated through.

Editor's Note: This recipe was tested with Land O'Lakes light stick butter.

Nutrition Facts: 3/4 cup equals 160 calories, 4 g fat (1 g saturated fat), 8 mg cholesterol, 187 mg sodium, 28 g carbohydrate, 4 g fiber, 7 g protein. **Diabetic Exchanges:** 1-1/2 starch, 1 fat.

Roasted Fennel & Peppers F M

PREP: 10 min. **BAKE:** 20 min. **YIELD:** 6 servings

HEALTHY COOKING TEST KITCHEN

Fennel makes for a tasty change of pace in this versatile side that goes great with grilled meats. Best of all, it's full of flavor and easy to do, and it doesn't seem light at all!

2	fennel bulbs, halved and sliced
2	medium sweet red peppers, cut into 1-in. pieces
1	medium onion, cut into 1-in. pieces
3	garlic cloves, minced
1	Tbsp. olive oil
1/2	tsp. salt
1/2	tsp. pepper
1/2	tsp. rubbed sage

Fresh sage leaves, thinly sliced, optional

1. Place the fennel, peppers, onion and garlic in a 15-in. x 10-in. baking pan coated with cooking spray. Drizzle with oil; sprinkle with salt, pepper and rubbed sage. Toss to coat.

2. Bake, uncovered, at 425° for 20-25 minutes or until tender, stirring twice. Garnish with fresh sage if desired.

Nutrition Facts: 2/3 cup equals 90 calories, 3 g fat (trace saturated fat), 0 cholesterol, 277 mg sodium, 17 g carbohydrate, 6 g fiber, 3 g protein. **Diabetic Exchanges:** 1 starch, 1/2 fat.

ROASTED FENNEL & PEPPERS

So-Good Pilaf M

PREP: 10 min. **COOK:** 50 min. **YIELD:** 6 servings

LINDA NICESWANGER • COLUMBUS, OHIO

Loaded with heart-healthy, fiber-packed grains, this hearty side dish certainly sticks to your ribs.

1	medium onion, chopped
1	medium carrot, chopped
2	garlic cloves, minced
1	Tbsp. butter
1/3	cup uncooked medium pearl barley
1/3	cup uncooked brown rice
1/3	cup uncooked bulgur
2-1/2	cups reduced-sodium chicken broth *or* vegetable broth
1/4	cup white wine *or* additional broth
1	Tbsp. minced fresh sage *or* 1 tsp. rubbed sage
1/4	tsp. white pepper
1/3	cup minced fresh parsley
1/3	cup chopped almonds, toasted
1/4	cup canned chopped green chilies
2	cups fresh baby spinach, optional

1. In a large nonstick skillet, saute the onion, carrot and garlic in butter until tender. Add the barley, rice and bulgur; saute 3 minutes longer.

2. Add the broth, wine, sage and pepper; bring to a boil. Reduce heat; cover and simmer for 40-45 minutes or until the grains are tender. Remove from the heat. Stir in the parsley, almonds and chilies. Serve immediately over spinach if desired.

Nutrition Facts: 2/3 cup equals 195 calories, 6 g fat (2 g saturated fat), 5 mg cholesterol, 287 mg sodium, 29 g carbohydrate, 5 g fiber, 6 g protein. **Diabetic Exchanges:** 2 starch, 1 fat.

Don't forget the pearl barley in **So-Good Pilaf.** It's the most common form of barley because it cooks quickly and is less chewy than other varieties. Where nutrition is concerned, pearl barley is similar to wheat in its calorie, protein and vitamin content.

MAKEOVER FRUITED WILD RICE PILAF

Makeover Fruited Wild Rice Pilaf M

PREP: 15 min. **COOK:** 1 hour **YIELD:** 5 servings

CAROLYN KEITH • EVANSTON, ILLINOIS

The original version of this dish called for a rice mix. I felt funny serving all that sodium and those artificial ingredients. This recipe revamp is a healthy from-scratch delight.

1	small onion, chopped
1	celery rib, chopped
1	small carrot, finely chopped
1	garlic clove, minced
1	Tbsp. butter
3/4	cup uncooked brown rice
1/3	cup uncooked wild rice
1	can (14-1/2 oz.) reduced-sodium beef broth *or* vegetable broth
1-1/4	cups water
3/4	cup *each* golden raisins and cherries
1	Tbsp. minced fresh parsley
1/4	tsp. salt
1/8	tsp. dried thyme
1/8	tsp. rubbed sage
1/8	tsp. pepper
1/4	cup chopped pecans, toasted

1. In a large saucepan, saute the onion, celery, carrot and garlic in butter until tender. Add brown rice and wild rice; stir to coat.

2. Stir in the broth, water, fruit, parsley, salt, thyme, sage and pepper. Bring to a boil. Reduce heat; cover and simmer for 50-60 minutes or until liquid is absorbed and rice is tender.

3. Remove from the heat; stir in pecans. Cover and let stand for 5 minutes. Fluff mixture with a fork before serving.

Nutrition Facts: 3/4 cup equals 286 calories, 8 g fat (2 g saturated fat), 8 mg cholesterol, 305 mg sodium, 49 g carbohydrate, 4 g fiber, 6 g protein.

Spruced-Up Sprouts C

PREP/TOTAL TIME: 30 min. **YIELD:** 6 servings

AGNES WARD • STRATFORD, ONTARIO

Crunchy water chestnuts and earthy thyme stand up beautifully to tasty brussels sprouts in my no-fuss dish. Feel free to add your favorite herb if you'd like. Add some chopped sweet red pepper for a dash of color.

1	pound fresh brussels sprouts, halved
2	cups water
2	tsp. reduced-sodium chicken bouillon granules
1	can (8 oz.) sliced water chestnuts, drained
2	Tbsp. butter
1/2	tsp. dried thyme
1/4	tsp. salt
1/8	tsp. pepper
1/8	tsp. sugar
1	Tbsp. lemon juice

1. Place the brussels sprouts, water and bouillon in a large saucepan. Bring to a boil. Reduce heat; cover and simmer for 8-10 minutes or until tender. Drain.

2. Stir in water chestnuts, butter, seasonings and sugar; cook and stir over medium heat for 2-3 minutes or until butter is melted and water chestnuts are heated through. Stir in lemon juice.

Nutrition Facts: 2/3 cup equals 87 calories, 4 g fat (2 g saturated fat), 10 mg cholesterol, 193 mg sodium, 12 g carbohydrate, 4 g fiber, 3 g protein. **Diabetic Exchanges:** 2 vegetable, 1 fat.

Festive Fruit Gelatin S

PREP: 15 min. + chilling **YIELD:** 12 servings

BARBARA KNAPP • BENNINGTON, VERMONT

I make this during the holidays because of the color combination, but it's good anytime! With cranberry sauce, pineapple and cream cheese, it offers a simply wonderful variety of flavors.

- 1 pkg. (.3 oz.) sugar-free lime gelatin
- 3 cups boiling water, *divided*
- 1 can (8 oz.) unsweetened crushed pineapple, undrained
- 1-1/2 tsp. unflavored gelatin
- 2 Tbsp. cold water
- 1 pkg. (8 oz.) reduced-fat cream cheese
- 1/4 cup fat-free milk
- 2 pkg. (.3 ounce *each*) sugar-free strawberry gelatin
- 1 can (16 oz.) jellied cranberry sauce

1. In a small bowl, dissolve lime gelatin in 1 cup boiling water; stir in pineapple. Pour into a 13-in. x 9-in. dish coated with cooking spray. Refrigerate until set but not firm.

2. Sprinkle gelatin over cold water; let stand for 1 minute. Microwave on high for 15 seconds. Stir and let stand for 1 minute or until gelatin is completely dissolved.

3. In a small mixing bowl, beat cream cheese until fluffy. Gradually add milk and gelatin mixture; beat until smooth. Gently spread over lime layer. Refrigerate until set but not firm.

4. In a large bowl, dissolve strawberry gelatin in remaining boiling water. Whisk in cranberry sauce until smooth. Refrigerate until partially set. Gently spread over cream cheese layer. Refrigerate until firm.

Nutrition Facts: 1 piece equals 122 calories, 4 g fat (3 g saturated fat), 13 mg cholesterol, 139 mg sodium, 18 g carbohydrate, 1 g fiber, 4 g protein. **Diabetic Exchanges:** 1 starch, 1 fat.

Pretty Almond Green Beans S C M

PREP/TOTAL TIME: 25 min. **YIELD:** 6 servings

VIKKI PECK • POLAND, OHIO

The traditional flavors of green beans, mushrooms and onion are in this recipe without the calories of traditional green bean casseroles! The dish is light, festive and easy to put together. It's become a holiday tradition at our house.

- 1 lb. fresh green beans, trimmed
- 1 medium sweet red pepper, julienned
- 1 cup sliced fresh mushrooms
- 1 small onion, chopped
- 1 Tbsp. olive oil
- 1/4 cup sliced almonds, toasted

1. Place beans in a large saucepan and cover with water. Bring to a boil. Cover and cook for 4-7 minutes or until crisp-tender.

2. Meanwhile, in a large nonstick skillet, saute the pepper, mushrooms and onion in oil until tender. Drain beans; stir into vegetable mixture. Sprinkle with almonds.

Nutrition Facts: 3/4 cup equals 78 calories, 4 g fat (1 g saturated fat), 0 cholesterol, 6 mg sodium, 9 g carbohydrate, 4 g fiber, 3 g protein. **Diabetic Exchanges:** 1 vegetable, 1 fat.

PRETTY ALMOND GREEN BEANS

FESTIVE FRUIT GELATIN

SPICED PEAR CRUMBLE

TROPICAL FRUIT SALAD

EGG-FREE SPICED PANCAKES

Good Mornings

You've heard it all before...breakfast is the most important meal of the day. The old saying is particularly true, however, when it comes to losing weight. Jump-start your metabolism with these eye-opening delights. You'll be glad you did.

Spiced Pear Crumble **S**

PREP: 25 min. **BAKE:** 20 min. **YIELD:** 6 servings

BARBRA ANNINO • GALENA, ILLINOIS

Guests at my bed-and-breakfast rave about this. They love to enjoy a sweet treat that doesn't expand their waistlines.

- 4 medium pears, peeled and chopped
- 1/4 cup dried cranberries
- 2 tsp. lemon juice
- 2 Tbsp. reduced-fat butter
- 1/2 cup reduced-sugar orange marmalade
- 1/4 cup sugar-free maple-flavored syrup
- 1/2 tsp. ground cinnamon
- 1/4 tsp. ground ginger
- 1/8 tsp. ground allspice
- 1 tsp. vanilla extract
- 1-1/2 cups crushed reduced-fat vanilla wafers (about 45 wafers)
- 1/4 cup chopped almonds
- 1-1/2 cups reduced-fat vanilla ice cream

1. In a small bowl, combine the pears, cranberries and lemon juice. Transfer to an 8-in. square baking dish coated with cooking spray; set aside.

2. In a small saucepan, melt butter over medium heat. Stir in the marmalade, syrup, cinnamon, ginger and allspice until blended. Bring to a boil. Remove from the heat; stir in vanilla. Drizzle evenly over pear mixture. Sprinkle with vanilla wafers and almonds.

3. Bake, uncovered, at 375° for 20-25 minutes or until pears are tender and topping is golden brown. Serve warm with ice cream.

Editor's Note: This recipe was tested with Land O'Lakes light stick butter.

Nutrition Facts: 1 serving equals 268 calories, 7 g fat (2 g saturated fat), 11 mg cholesterol, 113 mg sodium, 50 g carbohydrate, 4 g fiber, 4 g protein.

Egg-Free Spiced Pancakes **M**

PREP: 10 min. **COOK:** 10 min./batch **YIELD:** 8 pancakes

HEALTHY COOKING TEST KITCHEN

Golden brown and fluffy, these mildly spiced pancakes are ideal with syrup or berries. You'll never guess the eggs are missing!

- 1 cup all-purpose flour
- 2 Tbsp. brown sugar
- 2-1/2 tsp. baking powder
- 1/2 tsp. pumpkin pie spice
- 1/4 tsp. salt
- 1 cup fat-free milk
- 2 Tbsp. canola oil
- Maple syrup, optional

1. In a large bowl, combine flour, brown sugar, baking powder, pie spice and salt. In another bowl, combine milk and oil; stir into dry ingredients just until moistened. Pour batter by 1/4 cupfuls onto a hot griddle coated with cooking spray; turn when bubbles form on top.

2. Cook until the second side is golden brown. Serve with syrup if desired.

Nutrition Facts: 2 pancakes (calculated without syrup) equals 223 calories, 7 g fat (1 g saturated fat), 1 mg cholesterol, 427 mg sodium, 34 g carbohydrate, 1 g fiber, 5 g protein. **Diabetic Exchanges:** 2 starch, 1-1/2 fat.

Tropical Fruit Salad **F** **S** **M**

PREP/TOTAL TIME: 25 min. **YIELD:** 8 servings

KATIE COVINGTON • BLACKSBURG, SOUTH CAROLINA

Bring tropical flavor to your table with toasted coconut, mango, bananas and more. This makes an excellent breakfast or dessert!

- 1 medium mango, peeled and cubed
- 1 medium green apple, cubed
- 1 medium red apple, cubed
- 1 medium pear, cubed
- 1 medium navel orange, peeled and chopped
- 2 medium kiwifruit, peeled and chopped
- 10 seedless red grapes, halved
- 2 Tbsp. orange juice
- 1 firm medium banana, sliced
- 1/4 cup flaked coconut, toasted

1. In a large bowl, combine the first seven ingredients. Drizzle with orange juice; toss gently to coat.

2. Refrigerate until serving. Just before serving, fold in banana and sprinkle with coconut.

Nutrition Facts: 3/4 cup equals 101 calories, 1 g fat (1 g saturated fat), 0 cholesterol, 10 mg sodium, 24 g carbohydrate, 3 g fiber, 1 g protein. **Diabetic Exchange:** 1-1/2 fruit.

Creamy Peaches F C M

PREP/TOTAL TIME: 10 min. **YIELD:** 4 servings

DON PROKIDANSKY • NEW PORT RICHEY, FLORIDA

Smooth and rich, this pretty, refreshing breakfast treat is high in protein and virtually fat-free. Best of all, it goes together in just a few minutes.

  1 can (15 oz.) sliced peaches in extra-light syrup, drained
1-1/2 cups (12 oz.) fat-free cottage cheese
  4 oz. fat-free cream cheese, cubed
Sugar substitute equivalent to 1 tbsp. sugar

1. Thinly slice four peach slices; set aside for garnish. Place remaining peaches in a food processor; add cottage cheese. Cover and process until blended. Add cream cheese and sugar substitute; cover and process until blended.

2. Spoon into four serving dishes. Top with reserved peaches. Refrigerate until serving.

Editor's Note: This recipe was tested with Splenda No Calorie Sweetener.

Nutrition Facts: 1 cup equals 127 calories, trace fat (trace saturated fat), 6 mg cholesterol, 443 mg sodium, 15 g carbohydrate, 1 g fiber, 15 g protein. **Diabetic Exchanges:** 2 very lean meat, 1/2 starch, 1/2 fruit.

CREAMY PEACHES

Makeover Spiced Cocoa-Apple Cake

PREP: 30 min. **BAKE:** 50 min. + cooling
YIELD: 16 servings

WENDY KEYS • RENO, NEVADA

Nearly half the fat was removed from this recipe when I asked "Healthy Cooking" magazine to lighten it for me. Now I don't feel bad about baking it.

  1/3 cup butter, softened
1-2/3 cups sugar
  2 eggs
  2 egg whites
  1/2 cup buttermilk
  1/2 cup unsweetened applesauce
  3 tsp. vanilla extract
2-1/2 cups all-purpose flour
  1/2 cup baking cocoa
  1 tsp. baking powder
  1 tsp. ground cinnamon
  3/4 tsp. baking soda
  1/2 tsp. salt
  1/2 tsp. ground allspice
  2 cups grated peeled tart apples
  1/2 cup chopped walnuts, toasted
  1/2 cup miniature semisweet chocolate chips
  1/2 tsp. confectioners' sugar

1. In a large mixing bowl, beat butter and sugar until crumbly, about 2 minutes. Add eggs, then egg whites, beating well after each addition. Beat in the buttermilk, applesauce and vanilla (mixture will appear curdled).

2. Combine the flour, cocoa, baking powder, cinnamon, baking soda, salt and allspice; stir into butter mixture just until blended. Stir in the apples, walnuts and chips.

3. Transfer to a 10-in. fluted tube pan coated with cooking spray. Bake at 325° for 50-60 minutes or until a toothpick inserted near the center comes out

MAKEOVER SPICED COCOA-APPLE CAKE

clean. Cool for 10 minutes before removing from pan to a wire rack to cool completely. Sprinkle with confectioners' sugar.

Nutrition Facts: 1 slice equals 270 calories, 9 g fat (4 g saturated fat), 37 mg cholesterol, 220 mg sodium, 45 g carbohydrate, 2 g fiber, 5 g protein.

Makeover Multigrain Waffles M

PREP: 15 min. **COOK:** 5 min./batch **YIELD:** 28 waffles

BETTY BLAIR • BARTLETT, TENNESSEE

My waffle recipe is good, but I wanted a healthier version for my husband who is diabetic. These waffles do the trick. In addition, the leftovers freeze great for busy mornings.

1	cup all-purpose flour
1	cup whole wheat flour
1	cup cornmeal
1	Tbsp. sugar
1	Tbsp. baking powder
3/4	tsp. baking soda
1/2	tsp. salt
3	eggs
4	egg whites
3	cups buttermilk
1/2	cup unsweetened applesauce
3	Tbsp. canola oil
2	Tbsp. butter, melted

Butter and maple syrup, optional

1. In a large bowl, combine the first seven ingredients. In another bowl, whisk the eggs, egg whites, buttermilk, applesauce, oil and butter; whisk into dry ingredients just until blended.

2. Bake in a preheated waffle iron according to manufacturer's directions until golden brown. Serve with butter and syrup if desired.

Nutrition Facts: 2 waffles (calculated without butter and syrup) equals 187 calories, 7 g fat (2 g saturated fat), 52 mg cholesterol, 336 mg sodium, 25 g carbohydrate, 2 g fiber, 7 g protein. **Diabetic Exchanges:** 1-1/2 starch, 1 fat.

Heartwarming Chai F S

PREP/TOTAL TIME: 20 min. **YIELD:** 6 servings

HEALTHY COOKING TEST KITCHEN

This guilt-free coffeehouse drink perfectly captures the essence of winter!

3	whole cloves
3	whole allspice
8	individual tea bags
1	tsp. minced fresh gingerroot
1/8	tsp. ground nutmeg
3	cups boiling water
3	cups fat-free milk
1/3	cup honey
1/4	tsp. vanilla extract

Ground cinnamon

1. Place cloves and allspice in a small bowl. With the end of a wooden spoon handle, crush spices until aromas are released. Add the tea bags, ginger, nutmeg and boiling water. Cover and steep for 6 minutes. Meanwhile, in a large saucepan, heat the milk.

2. Strain tea into the pan, discarding tea bags and spices. Stir in honey and vanilla. Ladle into mugs. Sprinkle with cinnamon.

Nutrition Facts: 1 cup equals 100 calories, trace fat (trace saturated fat), 2 mg cholesterol, 52 mg sodium, 22 g carbohydrate, trace fiber, 4 g protein.

Blueberry French Toast F M

PREP: 20 min. **BAKE:** 20 min. **YIELD:** 6 servings

NANCY ARGO • UNIONTOWN, OHIO

The original recipe for this French toast called for heavy cream and whole eggs. But this delicious makeover has a lighter touch with egg substitute and fat-free milk.

1/2	cup sugar
2-1/2	tsp. cornstarch
1	tsp. ground cinnamon
1/4	tsp. ground allspice
3/4	cup water
4	cups fresh or frozen blueberries
1	cup egg substitute
1	cup fat-free milk
1	tsp. vanilla extract
1/2	tsp. salt
12	slices French bread (1 in. thick)

1. In a large bowl, combine the sugar, cornstarch, cinnamon and allspice; stir in water until smooth. Add blueberries; mix well. Transfer to a 13-in. x 9-in. baking dish coated with cooking spray.

2. In a large bowl, beat the egg substitute, milk, vanilla and salt. Dip each slice of bread into egg mixture; arrange slices over the berries. Bake at 400° for 20-25 minutes or until the toast is golden brown and blueberries are bubbly.

Nutrition Facts: 2 slices with about 1/2 cup blueberries equals 285 calories, 2 g fat (trace saturated fat), 1 mg cholesterol, 575 mg sodium, 58 g carbohydrate, 4 g fiber, 10 g protein.

Good-Morning Granola S

PREP: 15 min. **BAKE:** 20 min. + cooling **YIELD:** 7-1/2 cups

MARY BILYEU • ANN ARBOR, MICHIGAN

A great way to start your morning and keep you going, this recipe is ridiculously easy to make! Crunchy, sweet and packed with healthy ingredients, it also makes a nutritious gift.

4	cups old-fashioned oats
1/2	cup toasted wheat germ
1/2	cup sliced almonds
2	tsp. ground cinnamon
1/8	tsp. salt
1/2	cup orange juice
1/2	cup honey
2	tsp. canola oil
1	tsp. vanilla extract
1	cup dried cherries
1	cup dried cranberries

Reduced-fat plain yogurt, optional

1. In a large bowl, combine the first five ingredients; set aside. In a small saucepan, combine the orange juice, honey and oil. Bring to a boil, stirring constantly. Remove from the heat; stir in vanilla. Pour over oat mixture and mix well.

2. Transfer to a 15-in. x 10-in. x 1-in. baking pan coated with cooking spray. Bake at 350° for 20-25 minutes or until golden brown, stirring every 10 minutes. Cool completely on a wire rack. Stir in dried fruits. Store in an airtight container. Serve with yogurt if desired.

Nutrition Facts: 1/2 cup (calculated without yogurt) equals 206 calories, 4 g fat (trace saturated fat), 0 cholesterol, 21 mg sodium, 40 g carbohydrate, 4 g fiber, 5 g protein. **Diabetic Exchanges:** 2 starch, 1/2 fruit, 1/2 fat.

Gluten-Free Pancakes M

PREP: 15 min. **COOK:** 10 min./batch
YIELD: 12 pancakes

KATHY RAIRIGH • MILFORD, INDIANA

I've made this recipe dozens of times since being diagnosed with celiac disease. My kids like them best with chocolate chips (of course!) and maple syrup.

1	cup brown rice flour
1/2	cup potato starch
1/2	cup ground almonds
3	tsp. sugar
3	tsp. baking powder
1/2	tsp. salt
2	eggs
1	cup fat-free milk
2	Tbsp. butter, melted
1	tsp. vanilla extract
1/3	cup miniature semisweet chocolate chips, optional

1. In a large bowl, combine the rice flour, potato starch, almonds, sugar, baking powder and salt. In another bowl, whisk the eggs, milk, butter and vanilla; stir into dry ingredients just until moistened. Stir in chocolate chips if desired.

2. Pour batter by 1/4 cupfuls onto a hot griddle coated with cooking spray; turn when bubbles form on top. Cook until the second side is golden brown.

Nutrition Facts: 2 pancakes (calculated without chocolate chips) equals 242 calories, 10 g fat (3 g saturated fat), 81 mg cholesterol, 464 mg sodium, 33 g carbohydrate, 2 g fiber, 7 g protein. **Diabetic Exchanges:** 2 starch, 2 fat.

Hearty Baked Oatmeal F M

PREP: 15 min. **BAKE:** 50 min. **YIELD:** 6 servings

CYNTHIA RODGERS • BREWTON, ALABAMA

This is a breakfast that will stick with you. Cranberries, apples and cinnamon bring comforting flavor, not fat, to each bite.

2	cups old-fashioned oats
1-3/4	cups boiling water
2	cups fat-free milk
1-1/2	cups chopped peeled tart apples
3/4	cup dried cranberries
1/4	cup maple syrup
1	tsp. ground cinnamon
1/2	tsp. salt

1. Place oats in a large bowl; add boiling water. Let stand for 5 minutes. Stir in the remaining ingredients.

2. Transfer to an 11-in. x 7-in. baking dish coated with cooking spray (dish will be full). Cover and bake at 350° for 40 minutes. Uncover; bake 10-15 minutes longer or until bubbly and set.

Nutrition Facts: 1 cup equals 224 calories, 2 g fat (trace saturated fat), 2 mg cholesterol, 241 mg sodium, 48 g carbohydrate, 4 g fiber, 7 g protein.

GOOD-MORNING GRANOLA

GLUTEN-FREE PANCAKES

Oh-So-Good Oatmeal S M

PREP/TOTAL TIME: 20 min. **YIELD:** 4 servings

DANIELLE PEPA • ELGIN, ILLINOIS

I pack extra nutrition into fiber-rich oatmeal by adding chopped apples with the peel and chopped almonds. My two boys demand seconds! At 1-1/2 cups per serving, it's hearty and filling; and at zero cholesterol, what's not to love?

3	cups water
2	medium tart apples, chopped
1-1/2	cups old-fashioned oats

Dash salt

1/4	cup packed brown sugar
1/2	tsp. ground cinnamon
1/2	tsp. vanilla extract
1/4	cup chopped almonds

Maple syrup *and/or* fat-free milk, optional

1. In a large saucepan over medium heat, bring water to a boil. Add the apples, oats and salt; cook and stir for 5 minutes. Remove from the heat; stir in the brown sugar, cinnamon and vanilla.

2. Cover and let stand for 2 minutes. Sprinkle each serving with almonds. Serve with maple syrup and/or milk if desired.

Nutrition Facts: 1-1/2 cups (calculated without syrup and milk) equals 245 calories, 6 g fat (1 g saturated fat), 0 cholesterol, 44 mg sodium, 44 g carbohydrate, 5 g fiber, 6 g protein. **Diabetic Exchanges:** 2-1/2 starch, 1 fat, 1/2 fruit.

OH-SO-GOOD OATMEAL

Makeover Easy Apple Cake

PREP: 25 min. **BAKE:** 30 min. + cooling
YIELD: 20 servings

SHERRY ASHENFELTER • WATERVILLE, OHIO

This is a long-time favorite, but the original recipe called for a cup of vegetable oil. I'm happy that this version is so much healthier for my family.

3/4	cup sugar
2/3	cup unsweetened applesauce
1/2	cup sugar blend for baking
3	eggs
1/4	cup canola oil
1-1/4	tsp. vanilla extract
2	cups all-purpose flour
1/2	cup ground flaxseed
1-1/4	tsp. baking powder
1-1/4	tsp. ground cinnamon
1	tsp. salt
1/4	tsp. baking soda
2	cups finely chopped peeled tart apples
1/2	cup chopped walnuts, toasted
1-1/4	cups reduced-fat whipped topping

1. In a large mixing bowl, beat the sugar, applesauce, sugar blend, eggs, oil and vanilla until well blended. Combine the flour, flaxseed, baking powder, cinnamon, salt and baking soda; gradually beat into sugar mixture until blended. Fold in the apples and walnuts.

2. Transfer to a 13-in. x 9-in. baking dish coated with cooking spray. Bake at 350° for 28-35 minutes or until a toothpick inserted near the center comes out clean. Cool on a wire rack. Serve with whipped topping.

Editor's Note: This recipe was tested with Splenda Sugar Blend for Baking.

Nutrition Facts: 1 piece with 1 tablespoon topping equals 184 calories, 7 g fat (2 g saturated fat), 32 mg cholesterol, 170 mg sodium, 27 g carbohydrate, 2 g fiber, 4 g protein. **Diabetic Exchanges:** 2 starch, 1 fat.

MAKEOVER EASY APPLE CAKE

BROCCOLI-TURKEY BRUNCH CASSEROLE

Broccoli-Turkey Brunch Casserole

PREP: 20 min. **BAKE:** 45 min. **YIELD:** 6 servings

KELLIE MULLEAVY • LAMBERTVILLE, MICHIGAN

I came up with this terrific casserole as a great way to use up leftover Thanksgiving turkey and decrease my time in the kitchen. No leftover turkey? Use cooked chicken instead. It's even great for dinner with a simple green salad.

1-1/2	cups fat-free milk
1	can (10-3/4 oz.) reduced-fat reduced-sodium condensed cream of chicken soup, undiluted
1	carton (8 oz.) egg substitute
1/4	cup reduced-fat sour cream
1/2	tsp. pepper
1/4	tsp. poultry seasoning
1/8	tsp. salt
2-1/2	cups cubed cooked turkey breast
1	pkg. (16 oz.) frozen chopped broccoli, thawed and drained
2	cups seasoned stuffing cubes
1	cup (4 oz.) shredded reduced-fat cheddar cheese, *divided*

1. In a large bowl, combine the milk, soup, egg substitute, sour cream, pepper, poultry seasoning and salt. Stir in the turkey, broccoli, stuffing cubes and 3/4 cup cheese. Transfer to a 13-in. x 9-in. baking dish coated with cooking spray.

2. Bake, uncovered, at 350° for 40 minutes. Sprinkle with remaining cheese. Bake 5-10 minutes longer or until a knife inserted near the center comes out clean. Let stand for 5 minutes before serving.

Nutrition Facts: 1 serving equals 303 calories, 7 g fat (4 g saturated fat), 72 mg cholesterol, 762 mg sodium, 26 g carbohydrate, 3 g fiber, 33 g protein. **Diabetic Exchanges:** 3 very lean meat, 1-1/2 starch, 1 vegetable, 1 fat.

For added convenience, **Broccoli-Turkey Brunch Casserole** can be made the night before and simply refrigerated. Let it stand at room temperature for 30 minutes before baking.

Banana Blueberry Pancakes F M

PREP: 15 min. **COOK:** 5 min./batch **YIELD:** 14 pancakes

KELLY REINICKE • WISCONSIN RAPIDS, WISCONSIN

This recipe is a favorite in our home; my kids don't even realize how healthy it is!

1	cup whole wheat flour
1/2	cup all-purpose flour
2	Tbsp. sugar
2	tsp. baking powder
1/2	tsp. salt
1	egg, lightly beaten
1-1/4	cups fat-free milk
3	medium ripe bananas, mashed
1	tsp. vanilla extract
1-1/2	cups fresh or frozen blueberries

Maple syrup, optional

1. In a large bowl, combine the flours, sugar, baking powder and salt. Combine the egg, milk, bananas and vanilla; stir into dry ingredients just until moistened.

2. Pour batter by 1/4 cupfuls onto a hot griddle coated with cooking spray; sprinkle with blueberries. Turn when bubbles form on top; cook until second side is golden brown. Serve with syrup if desired.

Editor's Note: If using frozen blueberries, do not thaw.

Nutrition Facts: 2 pancakes (calculated without syrup) equals 195 calories, 2 g fat (trace saturated fat), 31 mg cholesterol, 317 mg sodium, 41 g carbohydrate, 4 g fiber, 6 g protein. **Diabetic Exchanges**: 1-1/2 starch, 1 fruit.

Cran-Orange Waffles M

PREP: 25 min. **COOK:** 5 min./batch
YIELD: 6 waffles (3/4 cup syrup)

NANCY ZIMMERMAN • CAPE MAY COURT HOUSE, NEW JERSEY

These fluffy waffles are a real breakfast treat. You can also serve them for dessert with a scoop of frozen yogurt and the syrup drizzled over the top.

1-1/4	cups all-purpose flour
1/4	cup whole wheat flour
4-1/2	tsp. sugar
4	tsp. baking powder
1/2	tsp. salt
1/4	tsp. baking soda
1	egg
1	egg white
1	cup fat-free evaporated milk
1/2	cup orange juice
2	Tbsp. canola oil
1	tsp. grated orange peel
1/3	cup dried cranberries
3	Tbsp. chopped pecans

CRAN-ORANGE SYRUP:

1	cup fresh or frozen cranberries
1/4	cup sugar
1/2	cup orange juice
2	Tbsp. water
2	Tbsp. maple syrup

1. In a large bowl, combine the flours, sugar, baking powder, salt and baking soda. In another bowl, whisk the egg, egg white, milk, orange juice, oil and orange peel; stir into dry ingredients just until blended. Fold in cranberries and pecans.

2. Bake in a preheated waffle iron according to manufacturer's directions until golden brown.

3. For syrup, in a small saucepan, combine the cranberries, sugar and orange juice. Bring to a boil. Reduce heat; simmer, uncovered, for 5 minutes. Remove from the heat; cool slightly.

4. Remove 1/2 cup cranberries with a slotted spoon; set aside. In a blender, combine the water, syrup and remaining cranberry mixture; cover and process until smooth. Pour into a serving dish; stir in reserved cranberries. Serve with waffles.

Nutrition Facts: 1 waffle with 2 tablespoons syrup equals 336 calories, 9 g fat (1 g saturated fat), 37 mg cholesterol, 586 mg sodium, 57 g carbohydrate, 3 g fiber, 9 g protein.

Egg-Free Apple Cake

PREP: 20 min. + cooling **BAKE:** 40 min. + cooling
YIELD: 16 servings

CHRISTINE HOLMES • MINERAL, VIRGINIA

This apple cake originated during the Depression, when staples were scarce, but I made a few changes to make it healthier and add some extra zip. Everyone who eats it requests the recipe. It's great for cold weather and travels well.

4	cups diced peeled apples
2	cups golden raisins
2	cups unsweetened apple juice
1-1/2	cups packed brown sugar
6	Tbsp. butter, cubed
2	tsp. salt
1-1/2	tsp. ground cinnamon
1/2	tsp. ground cloves
3	cups all-purpose flour
2	tsp. baking soda

1. In a large saucepan, bring the first eight ingredients to a boil. Reduce heat; simmer, uncovered, for 5 minutes. Remove from the heat; cool to room temperature.

2. In a large bowl, combine flour and baking soda; fold in the apple mixture. Transfer to a 10-in. fluted tube pan coated with cooking spray. Bake at 350° for 40-45 minutes or until a toothpick inserted near the center comes out clean. Cool for 10 minutes before removing from the pan to a wire rack to cool completely.

Nutrition Facts: 1 slice equals 286 calories, 5 g fat (3 g saturated fat), 11 mg cholesterol, 508 mg sodium, 60 g carbohydrate, 2 g fiber, 3 g protein.

Recipes such as **Egg-Free Apple Cake** help people with egg allergies enjoy delicious foods. After all, allergy to eggs is one of the most common allergies in young children. Fortunately, most kids outgrow it by the age of 5. The allergic reaction is typically triggered by protein in egg whites but sometime the yolk is the culprit.

EGG-FREE APPLE CAKE

CRAN-ORANGE WAFFLES

Bird's Nest Breakfast Cups C

PREP/TOTAL TIME: 30 min. **YIELD:** 6 servings

ARIS GONZALEZ • DELTONA, FLORIDA

This lightened-up recipe originally called for regular bacon and eggs. Everyone loves it and thinks I fussed, but it's so easy!

- 12 turkey bacon strips
- 1-1/2 cups egg substitute
- 6 Tbsp. shredded reduced-fat Mexican cheese blend
- 1 Tbsp. minced fresh parsley

1. In a large skillet, cook bacon over medium heat for 2 minutes on each side or until partially set but not crisp. Coat six muffin cups with cooking spray; wrap two bacon strips around the inside of each cup. Fill each with 1/4 cup egg substitute; top with the cheese.

2. Bake at 350° for 18-20 minutes or until set. Cool for 5 minutes before removing from pan. Sprinkle with parsley.

Nutrition Facts: 1 breakfast cup equals 120 calories, 7 g fat (2 g saturated fat), 30 mg cholesterol, 515 mg sodium, 2 g carbohydrate, trace fiber, 12 g protein. **Diabetic Exchange:** 2 lean meat.

Ultimate Breakfast Burritos M

PREP/TOTAL TIME: 20 min. **YIELD:** 2 servings

PAMELA SHANK • PARKERSBURG, WEST VIRGINIA

We are just starting a healthier-eating practice, and this is one of our favorite breakfast meals. It's simple to make and really satisfying, too.

- 1/2 cup chopped fresh mushrooms
- 1/4 cup chopped green pepper
- 1/4 cup chopped sweet red pepper
- 1 tsp. olive oil
- 1 cup egg substitute
- 1/4 tsp. pepper
- 2 whole wheat tortillas (8 in.), warmed
- 1/4 cup shredded reduced-fat cheddar cheese
- 2 Tbsp. salsa
- 2 Tbsp. fat-free sour cream

1. In a small nonstick skillet coated with cooking spray, saute mushrooms and peppers in oil until tender. Transfer to a small bowl; keep warm.

2. Add egg substitute and pepper to the pan; cook and stir over medium heat until the eggs are set.

3. Spoon vegetable mixture and eggs off-center on each tortilla; top with cheese, salsa and sour cream. Fold sides and ends over filling and roll up.

Nutrition Facts: 1 burrito equals 231 calories, 6 g fat (2 g saturated fat), 13 mg cholesterol, 595 mg sodium, 29 g carbohydrate, 3 g fiber, 20 g protein. **Diabetic Exchanges:** 2 very lean meat, 1-1/2 starch, 1 vegetable, 1 fat.

Orange Strawberry Sippers F S

PREP/TOTAL TIME: 10 min. **YIELD:** 4 servings

LINDA EVANCOE-COBLE • LEOLA, PENNSYLVANIA

What could be better on a warm day than a frosty smoothie? This recipe eliminates a trip to the mall to get one, plus it's chock-full of fruit, vitamins and nutrition.

- 1 cup water
- 1 cup fat-free milk
- 1 can (6 oz.) frozen orange juice concentrate, thawed
- 2 cups fresh strawberries, hulled
- 10 to 12 ice cubes

Sugar substitute equivalent to 1/4 cup sugar

- 1 tsp. vanilla extract

1. In a blender, combine all ingredients; cover and process until smooth.

BIRD'S NEST BREAKFAST CUPS

ORANGE STRAWBERRY SIPPERS

2. Pour into chilled glasses; serve immediately.

Editor's Note: This recipe was tested with Splenda No Calorie Sweetener.

Nutrition Facts: 1-1/4 cups equals 119 calories, trace fat (trace saturated fat), 1 mg cholesterol, 34 mg sodium, 26 g carbohydrate, 2 g fiber, 4 g protein. **Diabetic Exchange:** 1-1/2 fruit.

Sunrise Frittata C

PREP: 20 min. **COOK:** 15 min. **YIELD:** 6 servings

JOSEPHINE PIRO • EASTON, PENNSYLVANIA

My family and friends find this impressive dish hard to resist...but it's actually simple to prepare. Colorful and hearty, it's meant for a brunch crowd!

2	tsp. canola oil
1-1/2	cups frozen O'Brien potatoes
1-1/2	cups cubed fully cooked lean ham
8	egg whites
4	eggs
1/2	cup shredded fontina cheese, *divided*
1/3	cup fat-free milk
1	tsp. minced fresh oregano *or* 1/4 tsp. dried oregano
3/4	cup julienned roasted sweet red pepper
3/4	cup salsa
1/4	cup minced fresh cilantro

1. In a large ovenproof skillet coated with cooking spray, cook and stir the potatoes in oil over medium heat until tender. Stir in ham; heat through.

2. In a small bowl, whisk the egg whites, eggs, 1/4 cup cheese, milk and oregano; add to the pan. Arrange red pepper strips over egg mixture to resemble the spokes of a wheel. Cover and cook over low heat for 8-12 minutes or until almost set.

3. Uncover; broil 6 in. from the heat for 3-5 minutes or until eggs are set and frittata is golden brown. Sprinkle with remaining cheese; let stand until melted. Cut into wedges.

4. Meanwhile, in a small saucepan, combine salsa and cilantro; heat through. Serve with frittata.

Nutrition Facts: 1 wedge with 2 tablespoons salsa equals 213 calories, 9 g fat (4 g saturated fat), 166 mg cholesterol, 817 mg sodium, 11 g carbohydrate, 1 g fiber, 19 g protein. **Diabetic Exchanges:** 2 lean meat, 1 starch, 1/2 fat.

Feel free to get creative with **Sunrise Frittata. If you** have any leftover cooked chicken, use it in place of the ham. Fresh mushrooms make a fantastic (and healthy) addition as do green onions.

Honey Wheat Pancakes Ⓜ

PREP: 10 min. **COOK:** 5 min./batch **YIELD:** 12 pancakes

MARTINA BIAS • BELLEVILLE, ILLINOIS

Even my kids love these wholesome pancakes! These thick and tender breakfast treats have a delightful hint of honey and cinnamon you'll love.

1-1/2	cups reduced-fat biscuit/baking mix
1/2	cup whole wheat flour
1/4	cup wheat germ
1	tsp. baking powder
1	tsp. ground cinnamon
2	eggs, lightly beaten
1-1/2	cups buttermilk
1	medium ripe banana, mashed
2	Tbsp. honey

Assorted fresh fruit *and/or* maple syrup, optional

1. In a small bowl, combine the first five ingredients. Combine the eggs, buttermilk, banana and honey; add to dry ingredients just until moistened.

2. Pour batter by 1/4 cupfuls onto a hot griddle coated with cooking spray; turn when bubbles form on top. Cook until the second side is golden brown. Serve with fruit and/or syrup if desired.

Nutrition Facts: 2 pancakes (calculated without optional toppings) equals 253 calories, 5 g fat (1 g saturated fat), 73 mg cholesterol, 502 mg sodium, 44 g carbohydrate, 3 g fiber, 9 g protein.

French Toast With Blueberries Ⓜ

PREP/TOTAL TIME: 15 min. **YIELD:** 4 servings

KATHLEEN LINDENBERG • SHARON, MASSACHUSETTS

We love this no-guilt dish made with whole grain bread and egg substitute. The best part is that it's so delicious; you don't even miss the syrup!

1	cup egg substitute
1/4	cup fat-free milk

Sugar substitute equivalent to 2 Tbsp. sugar

2	tsp. ground cinnamon
1-1/2	tsp. vanilla extract
1/8	tsp. salt
1/8	tsp. ground nutmeg

Dash pepper

8	slices whole wheat bread
1	Tbsp. confectioners' sugar
1	cup frozen blueberries

1. In a shallow bowl, combine the first eight ingredients. Dip both sides of each slice of bread in egg mixture. In a large nonstick skillet coated with cooking spray, cook bread over medium-high heat for 2 minutes on each side or until golden brown. Sprinkle with confectioners' sugar.

2. In a small microwave-safe bowl, heat the blueberries until warmed. Serve over French toast.

Nutrition Facts: 2 slices French toast with 1/4 cup blueberries equals 210 calories, 3 g fat (1 g saturated fat), trace cholesterol, 503 mg sodium, 36 g carbohydrate, 6 g fiber, 12 g protein. **Diabetic Exchanges:** 2 starch, 1 very lean meat, 1/2 fruit.

Sausage and Egg Pizza

PREP/TOTAL TIME: 30 min. **YIELD:** 6 slices

VICKI MEYERS • CASTALIA, OHIO

Using turkey sausage, fat-free cheddar cheese, egg substitute and reduced-fat crescent rolls really helps cut calories and fat in this delicious recipe.

1	tube (8 oz.) refrigerated reduced-fat crescent rolls
1/2	pound Italian turkey sausage links, casings removed
1-3/4	cups sliced fresh mushrooms
1-1/4	cups frozen shredded hash brown potatoes
1/4	tsp. garlic salt
1/4	tsp. pepper
2	green onions, chopped
2	Tbsp. finely chopped sweet red pepper
1/2	cup shredded fat-free cheddar cheese
3/4	cup egg substitute

1. Separate dough into eight triangles; place on an ungreased 12-in. pizza pan with points toward center. Press onto the bottom and up sides of pan to form a crust; seal perforations. Bake at 375° for 8 minutes.

2. Meanwhile, crumble sausage into a large nonstick skillet coated with cooking spray. Add mushrooms; cook and stir over medium heat until meat is no longer pink. Drain and set aside. In the same skillet, cook the potatoes, garlic salt and pepper over medium heat until browned.

3. Sprinkle sausage mixture over crust. Layer with potatoes, onions, red pepper and cheese; pour egg substitute over the top. Bake for 10-12 minutes or until egg is set and cheese is melted.

Nutrition Facts: 1 slice equals 241 calories, 10 g fat (2 g saturated fat), 24 mg cholesterol, 744 mg sodium, 22 g carbohydrate, 1 g fiber, 16 g protein. **Diabetic Exchanges:** 2 lean meat, 1-1/2 starch, 1/2 fat.

Fruit Smoothies F S

PREP/TOTAL TIME: 10 min. **YIELD:** 4 servings

SUSAN MCCARTNEY • ONALASKA, WISCONSIN

My children like smoothies, so I make them quite often—I almost know this recipe by heart! It's great as a snack, breakfast or dessert.

1	cup fat-free milk
1/2	cup plain yogurt
1/4	tsp. vanilla extract
1-1/2	cups fresh or frozen strawberries, thawed
1/2	cup canned unsweetened pineapple chunks
1/4	cup nonfat dry milk powder
4	ice cubes
2	Tbsp. sugar

1. In a blender, combine all ingredients; cover and process for 30-45 seconds or until smooth. Stir if necessary.

2. Pour into chilled glasses; serve immediately.

Nutrition Facts: 1 cup equals 122 calories, 1 g fat (1 g saturated fat), 7 mg cholesterol, 81 mg sodium, 22 g carbohydrate, 1 g fiber, 6 g protein. **Diabetic Exchanges:** 1 starch, 1/2 fruit.

FRUIT SMOOTHIES

SAUSAGE AND EGG PIZZA

KID-PLEASING TACO PIZZA

CHICKEN WITH RED PEPPER SAUCE

GREEN TEA TERIYAKI CHICKEN

Cooking healthy doesn't mean spending hours in the kitchen. Take a look at the effortless entrees found here. From pork chops to pizzas and from spaghetti to salads, a nutritious meal is always within reach...even on your busiest day!

Chicken with Red Pepper Sauce C

PREP/TOTAL TIME: 30 min. **YIELD:** 4 servings

MARTHA POLLOCK • OREGONIA, OHIO

This dish is weeknight-quick, simple and very pretty. It's also filled with veggies and wonderful flavor...and elegant enough to serve company.

1	egg white
1/2	cup seasoned bread crumbs
1/4	tsp. salt
4	boneless skinless chicken breast halves (4 oz. *each*)
1	Tbsp. olive oil
1	pkg. (6 oz.) fresh baby spinach
1	jar (7 oz.) roasted sweet red peppers, drained
1	garlic clove, peeled
1/2	tsp. Italian seasoning
1/2	cup crumbled feta cheese

Fresh basil leaves, thinly sliced, optional

1. Whisk egg white in a shallow bowl. Combine bread crumbs and salt in another shallow bowl. Dip chicken in egg white, then roll in crumb mixture.

2. In a large skillet over medium heat, cook the chicken in olive oil for 4-5 minutes on each side or until juices run clear.

3. Meanwhile, place spinach in a steamer basket; place in a large saucepan over 1 in. of water. Bring to a boil; cover and steam for 3-4 minutes or until tender.

4. Place the peppers, garlic and Italian seasoning in a food processor; cover and process until smooth. Transfer to a small microwave-safe bowl; cover and microwave until heated through.

5. Divide the spinach among four plates; top each with a chicken breast half, about 2 tablespoons red pepper sauce and 2 tablespoons feta cheese. Garnish with basil if desired.

Nutrition Facts: 1 serving equals 245 calories, 9 g fat (3 g saturated fat), 70 mg cholesterol, 600 mg sodium, 9 g carbohydrate, 2 g fiber, 29 g protein. **Diabetic Exchanges:** 4 very lean meat, 1 vegetable, 1 fat, 1/2 starch.

Green Tea Teriyaki Chicken F

PREP/TOTAL TIME: 25 min. **YIELD:** 4 servings

HEALTHY COOKING TEST KITCHEN

Tender chicken is treated to an Asian-inspired sauce with green tea for this low-fat entree that really stands out. Serve it with fragrant rice, like jasmine or basmati, for a restaurant-quality meal.

3-1/2	tsp. green tea leaves, *divided*
1	cup boiling water
4	green onions, chopped, *divided*
3	Tbsp. honey
2	Tbsp. cider vinegar
2	Tbsp. reduced-sodium soy sauce
4	garlic cloves, minced
1/2	tsp. minced fresh gingerroot
1/8	tsp. sesame oil
4	boneless skinless chicken breast halves (4 oz. *each*)

1. Place 2-1/2 teaspoons tea leaves in a small bowl; add boiling water. Cover and steep for 5-6 minutes.

2. Strain and discard leaves; pour tea into a large skillet. Add half of the onions. Stir in the honey, vinegar, soy sauce, garlic, ginger and sesame oil. Bring to a boil. Reduce heat; simmer, uncovered, until sauce is reduced to about 3/4 cup.

3. Add chicken and remaining tea leaves; cover and cook over medium heat for 4-5 minutes on each side or until a meat thermometer reads 170°. Cut chicken into thin slices; serve with sauce. Garnish with remaining onions.

Nutrition Facts: 1 chicken breast half with 3 Tbsp. sauce equals 184 calories, 3 g fat (1 g saturated fat), 63 mg cholesterol, 359 mg sodium, 16 g carbohydrate, trace fiber, 24 g protein. **Diabetic Exchanges:** 3 very lean meat, 1 starch.

When you prepare the **Green Tea Teriyaki Chicken** recipe, keep in mind that one tea bag contains 1-1/4 teaspoons of loose tea leaves.

CHICKEN BROCCOLI FETTUCCINE

Chicken Broccoli Fettuccine

PREP/TOTAL TIME: 25 min. **YIELD:** 4 servings

DEBBIE MAIER • LYNDEN, WASHINGTON

My family loves pasta, but often the sauces are loaded with calories, so I came up with this. The soup, milk and cheese are much lighter and taste just as rich.

6	oz. uncooked fettuccine
3	cups fresh broccoli florets
1	lb. boneless skinless chicken breasts, cut into strips
1/4	tsp. salt
1/4	tsp. pepper
1	medium onion, chopped
1	cup sliced fresh mushrooms
2	tsp. olive oil
1	can (10-3/4 oz.) reduced-fat reduced-sodium condensed cream of mushroom soup, undiluted
2/3	cup fat-free milk
1/4	cup shredded Parmesan cheese

1. In a Dutch oven, cook fettuccine according to package directions, adding the broccoli during the last 5 minutes of cooking.

2. Meanwhile, sprinkle chicken with salt and pepper. In a large nonstick skillet, saute chicken, onion and mushrooms in oil until chicken is no longer pink. Remove from the heat; set aside.

3. Drain fettuccine; stir in the soup, milk and reserved chicken mixture. Cook and stir over low heat until heated through. Sprinkle with cheese.

Nutrition Facts: 1-1/4 cups equals 398 calories, 9 g fat (3 g saturated fat), 74 mg cholesterol, 637 mg sodium, 44 g carbohydrate, 4 g fiber, 35 g protein. **Diabetic Exchanges:** 3 very lean meat, 2-1/2 starch, 1 vegetable, 1 fat.

Dijon Chicken with Grapes

PREP/TOTAL TIME: 20 min. **YIELD:** 4 servings

MARGARET WILSON • HEMET, CALIFORNIA

Red and green grapes add color to this quick, dressed-up chicken in a creamy Dijon sauce.

4	boneless skinless chicken breast halves (4 oz. *each*)
1	tsp. olive oil
1/2	cup refrigerated nondairy creamer
2	Tbsp. Dijon mustard
3/4	cup seedless red grapes, halved
3/4	cup seedless green grapes, halved

1. In a large nonstick skillet coated with cooking spray, cook chicken in oil over medium heat for 4-5 minutes on each side or until juices run clear. Remove and keep warm.

2. Add creamer to skillet; cook over medium-low heat, stirring to loosen browned bits from pan. Whisk in mustard until blended. Add grapes; cook and stir until heated through. Serve over chicken.

Nutrition Facts: 1 serving equals 224 calories, 7 g fat (1 g saturated fat), 63 mg cholesterol, 245 mg sodium, 16 g carbohydrate, 1 g fiber, 24 g protein. **Diabetic Exchanges:** 3 lean meat, 1 fruit, 1 fat.

Makeover Garlic Chicken Spaghetti

PREP/TOTAL TIME: 30 min. **YIELD:** 8 servings

JUDY CRAWFORD • DEMING, NEW MEXICO

I tasted a great entree at a restaurant. I got the recipe but cringed at the cup of olive oil it called for. This makeover cut the oil down greatly, decreasing the fat by two-thirds.

1	pkg. (1 lb.) spaghetti
1/2	cup sun-dried tomatoes (not packed in oil)
1	cup boiling water
1/4	cup all-purpose flour
1/2	tsp. garlic salt
1	lb. boneless skinless chicken breasts, cut into 1-in. cubes
1/4	cup olive oil, *divided*
2-3/4	cups sliced fresh mushrooms
5	garlic cloves, minced
1/4	cup reduced-sodium chicken broth
1/2	cup white wine *or* additional reduced-sodium chicken broth
1/4	cup minced fresh parsley
1/2	tsp. dried basil
1/4	tsp. salt
1/4	tsp. pepper
1/8	tsp. crushed red pepper flakes
1/2	cup grated Parmesan cheese

1. Cook spaghetti according to package directions. Meanwhile, place tomatoes in a small bowl; add boiling water. Cover and let stand for 5 minutes. Drain and chop tomatoes; set aside. In a large resealable plastic bag, combine flour and garlic salt. Add chicken, a few pieces at a time, and shake to coat.

2. In a large skillet, saute chicken in 2 tablespoons oil until no longer pink. Remove and keep warm. In the same skillet, saute mushrooms and garlic in remaining oil until tender. Add the broth, wine or additional broth, parsley, basil, salt, pepper and pepper flakes. Stir in the reserved tomatoes and chicken; heat through.

3. Drain spaghetti. Add chicken mixture and cheese; toss to coat.

Nutrition Facts: 1-1/2 cups equals 398 calories, 11 g fat (2 g saturated fat), 36 mg cholesterol, 386 mg sodium, 50 g carbohydrate, 3 g fiber, 23 g protein.

Tortellini Chicken Salad

PREP/TOTAL TIME: 25 min. **YIELD:** 9 servings

LINDA LUNDMARK • MARTINTON, ILLINOIS

My very-simple-to-make salad has just six ingredients, but a great blend of textures and a nice crunch. It also travels well for potlucks or family gatherings.

1	pkg. (19 oz.) frozen cheese tortellini
1	can (16 oz.) kidney beans, rinsed and drained
2	celery ribs, thinly sliced
1	cup cubed cooked chicken breast
4	bacon strips, cooked and crumbled
1	cup fat-free ranch salad dressing

1. Cook tortellini according to package directions; drain and rinse in cold water. Transfer to a large bowl. Add the beans, celery, chicken and bacon. Pour dressing over mixture and toss to coat. Refrigerate until serving.

Nutrition Facts: 3/4 cup equals 247 calories, 6 g fat (2 g saturated fat), 24 mg cholesterol, 611 mg sodium, 34 g carbohydrate, 3 g fiber, 14 g protein. **Diabetic Exchanges:** 2 starch, 2 lean meat.

TORTELLINI CHICKEN SALAD

MAKEOVER GARLIC CHICKEN SPAGHETTI

Thai Restaurant Chicken

PREP/TOTAL TIME: 30 min. **YIELD:** 4 servings

TRISHA KRUSE • EAGLE, IDAHO

This delicious recipe reminds me of the chicken satay I've had at restaurants. It features stir-fried chicken with a savory sauce and healthy veggies.

2	Tbsp. cornstarch
1	Tbsp. brown sugar
1/4	tsp. pepper
1	can (14-1/2 oz.) reduced-sodium chicken broth
2	Tbsp. rice vinegar
2	Tbsp. reduced-sodium soy sauce
2	Tbsp. reduced-fat peanut butter
1	lb. boneless skinless chicken breasts, cut into 1-in. cubes
2	tsp. sesame oil, *divided*
1	large onion, halved and sliced
1	medium sweet red pepper, julienned
1	cup sliced fresh mushrooms
2	garlic cloves, minced
2	cups hot cooked rice

1. In a large bowl, combine the cornstarch, brown sugar and pepper. Add broth; stir until smooth. Stir in the vinegar, soy sauce and peanut butter; set aside.

2. In a large nonstick skillet or wok, stir-fry chicken in 1 teaspoon oil until no longer pink. Remove and keep warm.

3. Stir-fry the onion and red pepper in remaining oil for 2 minutes. Add mushrooms and garlic; stir-fry 2-3 minutes longer or until crisp-tender.

4. Stir cornstarch mixture and add to the pan. Bring to a boil; cook and stir for 1-2 minutes or until thickened. Add chicken; heat through. Serve with rice.

Nutrition Facts: 1 cup stir-fry with 1/2 cup rice equals 359 calories, 8 g fat (2 g saturated fat), 63 mg cholesterol, 704 mg sodium, 40 g carbohydrate, 2 g fiber, 31 g protein. **Diabetic Exchanges:** 3 very lean meat, 2 starch, 1 vegetable, 1 fat.

Prosciutto-Pepper Pork Chops C

PREP/TOTAL TIME: 20 min. **YIELD:** 4 servings

DONNA PRISCO • RANDOLPH, NEW JERSEY

This dish is simple, fast and most importantly, delicious. It's especially easy to make for two, six, eight or more.

4	boneless pork loin chops (4 oz. *each*)
1/8	tsp. garlic powder
1/8	tsp. pepper
2	tsp. canola oil
4	thin slices prosciutto *or* deli ham
1/2	cup julienned roasted sweet red peppers
2	slices reduced-fat provolone cheese, cut in half

1. Sprinkle pork chops with garlic powder and pepper. In a large nonstick skillet, cook chops in oil over medium heat for 4-5 minutes on each side or until a meat thermometer reads 160°.

2. Top each pork chop with prosciutto, red peppers and cheese. Cover and cook for 1-2 minutes or until cheese is melted.

Nutrition Facts: 1 pork chop equals 237 calories, 12 g fat (4 g saturated fat), 72 mg cholesterol, 483 mg sodium, 1 g carbohydrate, trace fiber, 28 g protein. **Diabetic Exchanges:** 4 lean meat, 1/2 fat.

Turkey with Cran-Orange Sauce

PREP/TOTAL TIME: 30 min. **YIELD:** 4 servings

MARY RELYEA • CANASTOTA, NEW YORK

Packed with protein, this turkey dish is a weekday throwback to Thanksgiving. With its fruity glaze, it's an ideal fast entree.

1	pkg. (17.6 oz.) turkey breast tenderloins, cut into 1/4-in. slices
1	Tbsp. canola oil
1/2	cup reduced-sodium chicken broth
1/2	cup orange juice
1	Tbsp. Dijon mustard
1	Tbsp. honey
1/2	tsp. dried tarragon
1	Tbsp. cornstarch
1	Tbsp. cold water
1/3	cup dried cranberries

THAI RESTAURANT CHICKEN

PROSCIUTTO-PEPPER PORK CHOPS

1. In a large skillet, brown turkey in oil. In a small bowl, combine the broth, orange juice, mustard, honey and tarragon; pour over turkey. Bring to a boil. Reduce heat; cover and simmer for 7 minutes or until turkey is no longer pink.

2. Combine cornstarch and water until smooth; stir into turkey mixture. Stir in cranberries. Bring to a boil; cook and stir for 2 minutes or until thickened.

Nutrition Facts: 1 serving equals 237 calories, 6 g fat (1 g saturated fat), 61 mg cholesterol, 239 mg sodium, 18 g carbohydrate, 1 g fiber, 30 g protein. **Diabetic Exchanges:** 4 very lean meat, 1 starch, 1/2 fat.

Chicken Artichoke Pasta

PREP/TOTAL TIME: 30 min. **YIELD:** 4 servings

CATHY DICK • ROANOKE, VIRGINIA

Here's a colorful chicken entree that's easy enough for weeknights but special enough for guests. Oregano, garlic and a light wine sauce add lovely flavor.

2-1/4	cups uncooked ziti *or* small tube pasta
1	lb. boneless skinless chicken breasts, cut into thin strips
3	tsp. olive oil, *divided*
1/2	cup fresh broccoli florets
1/2	cup sliced fresh mushrooms
1/2	cup cherry tomatoes, halved
2	garlic cloves, minced
1	can (14 oz.) water-packed artichoke hearts, rinsed, drained and halved
1/2	tsp. salt
1/2	tsp. dried oregano
2	tsp. all-purpose flour
1/4	cup reduced-sodium chicken broth
1/3	cup white wine *or* additional reduced-sodium chicken broth
1	Tbsp. minced fresh parsley
1	Tbsp. shredded Parmesan cheese

1. Cook ziti according to package directions. Meanwhile, in a large nonstick skillet coated with cooking spray, cook chicken in 2 teaspoons oil over medium heat until no longer pink. Remove and keep warm.

2. In the same skillet, cook and stir broccoli in remaining oil for 2 minutes. Stir in the mushrooms, tomatoes and garlic; cook 2 minutes longer. Add the artichokes, salt and oregano; heat through.

3. Combine the flour with broth and wine or additional broth until smooth; stir into the pan. Bring to a boil; cook and stir for 1-2 minutes or until thickened. Add parsley and reserved chicken.

4. Drain ziti; add to chicken mixture and toss to coat. Sprinkle with cheese.

Nutrition Facts: 2 cups equals 378 calories, 8 g fat (2 g saturated fat), 64 mg cholesterol, 668 mg sodium, 41 g carbohydrate, 2 g fiber, 33 g protein. **Diabetic Exchanges:** 3 very lean meat, 2 starch, 2 vegetable, 1 fat.

ASIAN TURKEY LETTUCE WRAPS

Asian Turkey Lettuce Wraps

PREP/TOTAL TIME: 20 min. **YIELD:** 5 servings

SUSAN RILEY • ALLEN, TEXAS

This is one of my favorite recipes! Frozen chopped vegetables make the wraps a snap. Add some Asian chili sauce if you want to spice it up a bit.

1-1/4	lbs. extra-lean ground turkey
1	pkg. (16 oz.) frozen Oriental mixed vegetables, thawed
1/3	cup reduced-sodium teriyaki sauce
1/4	cup hoisin sauce
3	Tbsp. reduced-fat creamy peanut butter
2	Tbsp. minced fresh gingerroot
3	garlic cloves, minced
1	Tbsp. rice wine vinegar
1	Tbsp. sesame oil
4	green onions, chopped
10	Boston lettuce leaves

Additional hoisin sauce, optional

1. In a large nonstick skillet coated with cooking spray, cook and stir the turkey over medium-high heat until no longer pink.

2. Coarsely chop mixed vegetables; add to the pan. Stir in teriyaki sauce, hoisin sauce, peanut butter, ginger, garlic, vinegar and oil. Cook and stir over medium-high heat for 5 minutes or until heated through.

3. Remove from heat; stir in onions. Place a scant 1/2 cup turkey mixture on each lettuce leaf; fold lettuce over filling. Serve with additional hoisin sauce if desired.

Nutrition Facts: 2 wraps (calculated without additional hoisin sauce) equals 275 calories, 8 g fat (1 g saturated fat), 45 mg cholesterol, 686 mg sodium, 19 g carbohydrate, 4 g fiber, 34 g protein. **Diabetic Exchanges:** 3 very lean meat, 1-1/2 fat, 1 starch, 1 vegetable.

Lemon Mushroom Chicken [c]

PREP/TOTAL TIME: 30 min. **YIELD:** 4 servings

CARRIE PALMQUIST • CANOVA, SOUTH DAKOTA

Yum! Our taste panel loved this version of lemon chicken. Its refreshing taste makes for a terrific weeknight meal.

4	boneless skinless chicken breast halves (4 oz. *each*)
1/4	cup plus 2 tsp. all-purpose flour, *divided*
1/2	tsp. salt
1/4	tsp. pepper
2	Tbsp. butter
1/3	cup plus 3 Tbsp. reduced-sodium chicken broth, *divided*
1/2	lb. sliced fresh mushrooms
1	Tbsp. lemon juice

1. Flatten chicken to 1/2-in. thickness. In a large resealable plastic bag, combine 1/4 cup flour, salt and pepper. Add chicken, one piece at a time, shake to coat.

2. In a large nonstick skillet over medium heat, cook chicken in butter for 5-6 minutes on each side or until no longer pink. Remove and keep warm.

3. Add 1/3 cup broth to the pan, stirring to loosen browned bits. Bring to a boil. Add mushrooms; cook and stir for 3-5 minutes or until tender.

4. Combine the remaining flour and broth until smooth; stir into the mushroom mixture. Bring to a boil; cook and stir for 2 minutes or until thickened. Stir in lemon juice. Serve with chicken.

Nutrition Facts: 1 chicken breast half with 1/4 cup sauce equals 213 calories, 9 g fat (4 g saturated fat), 78 mg cholesterol, 368 mg sodium, 8 g carbohydrate, 1 g fiber, 26 g protein. **Diabetic Exchanges:** 3 very lean meat, 1-1/2 fat, 1/2 starch.

Citrus Chicken with Peppers

PREP/TOTAL TIME: 30 min. **YIELD:** 4 servings

MARY WILHELM • SPARTA, WISCONSIN

This dish is so attractive and healthy. I tried a similar recipe, but adding citrus and honey makes this so much better.

- 1 cup uncooked instant brown rice
- 4 boneless skinless chicken breast halves (4 oz. *each*)
- 1 Tbsp. canola oil
- 1 medium sweet orange pepper, sliced
- 1 medium sweet red pepper, sliced
- 1 Tbsp. cornstarch
- 1/3 cup orange juice
- 2 Tbsp. water
- 2 Tbsp. lime juice
- 2 Tbsp. honey
- 1/4 tsp. salt
- 1/4 tsp. paprika
- Dash pepper
- Minced fresh basil, optional

1. Prepare rice according to package directions. Meanwhile, in a large skillet over medium heat, cook chicken in oil for 4-5 minutes on each side or until juices run clear. Remove and keep warm.

2. In the same skillet, saute peppers until tender. In a small bowl, combine the cornstarch, orange juice, water and lime juice until smooth; stir in the honey, salt, paprika and pepper. Stir into the pan. Bring to a boil; cook and stir for 2 minutes or until thickened.

3. Return chicken to the pan; heat through. Serve with rice. Sprinkle with basil if desired.

Nutrition Facts: 1 chicken breast half with peppers and 1/2 cup rice equals 330 calories, 7 g fat (1 g saturated fat), 63 mg cholesterol, 206 mg sodium, 41 g carbohydrate, 2 g fiber, 26 g protein. **Diabetic Exchanges:** 3 starch, 3 very lean meat, 1/2 fat.

Pronto Penne Pasta

PREP/TOTAL TIME: 30 min. **YIELD:** 6 servings

TOMISSA HUART • UNION, ILLINOIS

I have four boys and have to trick them into eating healthy! Not an easy task, but this is a favorite.

- 2-1/4 cups uncooked whole wheat penne pasta
- 1 lb. Italian turkey sausage links, casings removed
- 1 medium red onion, chopped
- 1 medium green pepper, chopped
- 1 can (14-1/2 oz.) no-salt-added diced tomatoes, undrained
- 1 can (14-1/2 oz.) reduced-sodium chicken broth
- 2 garlic cloves, minced
- 2 tsp. dried tarragon
- 2 tsp. dried basil
- 1/4 tsp. cayenne pepper
- 1/4 cup all-purpose flour
- 1/2 cup fat-free milk
- 1/2 cup shredded reduced-fat cheddar cheese
- 1/4 cup grated Parmesan cheese

1. Cook pasta according to package directions. Meanwhile, crumble sausage into a large nonstick skillet coated with cooking spray. Add onion and green pepper; cook and stir over medium heat until meat is no longer pink. Drain. Stir in the tomatoes, broth, garlic, tarragon, basil and cayenne.

2. In a small bowl, combine flour and milk until smooth; stir into sausage mixture. Bring to a boil; cook and stir for 2 minutes or until thickened.

3. Remove from the heat. Stir in cheddar cheese until melted. Drain pasta; toss with sausage mixture. Sprinkle each serving with 2 teaspoons Parmesan cheese.

Nutrition Facts: about 1 cup equals 373 calories, 11 g fat (3 g saturated fat), 55 mg cholesterol, 800 mg sodium, 45 g carbohydrate, 4 g fiber, 24 g protein. **Diabetic Exchanges:** 2-1/2 starch, 2 lean meat, 1 vegetable, 1 fat.

PRONTO PENNE PASTA

LEMON MUSHROOM CHICKEN

Jalapeno Chicken Pizza

PREP/TOTAL TIME: 25 min. **YIELD:** 12 servings

LINDA EWANKOWICH • RALEIGH, NORTH CAROLINA

This is one of our favorite pizza recipes. It comes together quickly since it uses a premade crust, so it's really handy on busy nights.

- 2 plum tomatoes, quartered
- 1/2 cup fresh cilantro leaves
- 1 Tbsp. tomato paste
- 1 tsp. chopped chipotle peppers in adobo sauce
- 1 garlic clove, peeled and quartered
- 1/2 tsp. salt
- 1 prebaked thin Italian bread shell crust (10 oz.)
- 2 cups shredded cooked chicken breast
- 3/4 cup shredded reduced-fat Monterey Jack cheese *or* Mexican cheese blend
- 2 jalapeno peppers, seeded and sliced into rings

1. Place the first six ingredients in a food processor; cover and process until blended. Place the crust on an ungreased 12-in. pizza pan; spread with tomato mixture. Top with chicken, cheese and jalapenos.

2. Bake at 450° for 10-12 minutes or until heated through and the cheese is melted.

Editor's Note: When cutting hot peppers, disposable gloves are recommended. Avoid touching your face.

Nutrition Facts: 2 pieces equals 262 calories, 8 g fat (2 g saturated fat), 46 mg cholesterol, 613 mg sodium, 26 g carbohydrate, 1 g fiber, 23 g protein. **Diabetic Exchanges:** 3 lean meat, 1-1/2 starch.

Beefstro Bruschetta Burgers

PREP/TOTAL TIME: 30 min. **YIELD:** 4 servings

DEVON DELANEY • PRINCETON, NEW JERSEY

My mom always ate her hamburger on top of a salad. As a child, I thought it was unusual, but I adjusted the concept to make it a light and tasty meal for the whole family!

- 3 Tbsp. Dijon mustard
- 3 Tbsp. reduced-sugar apricot preserves
- 1 Tbsp. prepared horseradish
- 2 thin slices prosciutto *or* deli ham, chopped
- 1 lb. lean ground beef
- 3/4 tsp. salt-free lemon-pepper seasoning
- 8 slices French bread (1/2 in. thick)
- 1 cup fresh arugula *or* baby spinach
- 2 oz. Brie *or* Camembert cheese, cut into eight thin slices
- 1/4 cup julienned roasted sweet red peppers

1. In a small bowl, combine the mustard, preserves and horseradish. In a small skillet coated with cooking spray, cook and stir prosciutto over medium heat until lightly browned. Set aside.

2. In a large bowl, combine ground beef and lemon-pepper. Shape into eight patties. If grilling the burgers, coat grill rack with cooking spray before starting the grill. Grill burgers, covered, over medium heat or broil 4 in. from heat for 3-4 minutes on each side or until no longer pink. Remove and keep warm.

3. Grill or broil bread for 1-2 minutes on each side or until toasted. Spread each slice of toast with 1-1/4 teaspoons reserved mustard sauce. Layer each with arugula, a burger, a cheese slice and 1-1/4 teaspoons additional sauce. Garnish with peppers and prosciutto. Serve immediately.

Nutrition Facts: 2 bruschetta burgers equals 329 calories, 14 g fat (6 g saturated fat), 76 mg cholesterol, 767 mg sodium, 20 g carbohydrate, 1 g fiber, 29 g protein.

JALAPENO CHICKEN PIZZA

BEEFSTRO BRUSCHETTA BURGERS

Scrumptious Scramble C M

PREP/TOTAL TIME: 15 min. **YIELD:** 3 servings

LYNN WINKLER • CHATSWORTH, GEORGIA

By substituting four egg whites for two whole eggs here, you save 25 calories, 3 g fat and a whopping 141 mg cholesterol per serving! The eggs are seasoned with veggies and dill, so you won't miss any flavor at all.

1/2	cup finely chopped red onion
1	tsp. olive oil
1	medium tomato, seeded and finely chopped
4	eggs
4	egg whites
2	Tbsp. water
1-1/2	tsp. snipped fresh dill *or* 1/2 tsp. dill weed
1/4	tsp. salt
1/8	tsp. pepper

1. In a large nonstick skillet coated with cooking spray, saute the onion in the olive oil for 2 minutes. Add the tomato; saute 1-2 minutes longer or until the vegetables are tender. Transfer mixture to a small bowl; set aside.

2. In a large bowl, whisk the remaining ingredients. Coat the same skillet with additional cooking spray; add egg mixture. Cook and stir over medium heat until eggs are nearly set.

3. Add reserved onion mixture; cook and stir until heated through and eggs are completely set.

Nutrition Facts: 3/4 cup equals 156 calories, 8 g fat (2 g saturated fat), 283 mg cholesterol, 359 mg sodium, 6 g carbohydrate, 1 g fiber, 14 g protein.

Tomato-Walnut Pesto On Linguine

PREP/TOTAL TIME: 30 min. **YIELD:** 8 servings

HEALTHY COOKING TEST KITCHEN

Our Test Kitchen uses sun-dried tomatoes to make this tangy alternative to traditional pesto.

1/2	cup sun-dried tomatoes (not packed in oil)
1/2	cup boiling water
12	oz. uncooked linguine
2	cups loosely packed basil leaves
1/4	cup grated Parmesan cheese
1	garlic clove, peeled
1/3	cup reduced-sodium chicken broth
1/4	cup chopped walnuts, toasted
1/4	tsp. salt
1/8	tsp. pepper
3	Tbsp. olive oil

1. Place the tomatoes in a small bowl; add boiling water. Cover and let stand for 5 minutes. Meanwhile, cook linguine according to package directions.

2. Place the basil, Parmesan cheese and garlic in a food processor; cover and pulse until chopped. Add the tomatoes with liquid, broth, walnuts, salt and pepper; cover and process until blended. While processing, gradually add oil in a steady stream.

3. Drain linguine; toss with pesto. Serve immediately.

Nutrition Facts: 3/4 cup equals 244 calories, 9 g fat (2 g saturated fat), 2 mg cholesterol, 212 mg sodium, 33 g carbohydrate, 3 g fiber, 7 g protein.

Italian Spinach & Chicken Skillet

PREP/TOTAL TIME: 30 min. **YIELD:** 4 servings

SARAH NEWMAN • BROOKLYN CENTER, MINNESOTA

This is a flavorful entree that's hearty enough to be a one-dish meal. My husband and 2-year-old both love it, even with the spinach mixed in!

- 2 cups uncooked yolk-free whole wheat noodles
- 2 cups sliced fresh mushrooms
- 2 tsp. olive oil
- 1 garlic clove, minced
- 1 can (14-1/2 oz.) no-salt-added diced tomatoes, undrained
- 1 can (10-3/4 oz.) reduced-fat reduced-sodium condensed cream of chicken soup, undiluted
- 3/4 cup spaghetti sauce
- 2 cups cubed cooked chicken breast
- 1 pkg. (10 oz.) frozen chopped spinach, thawed and squeezed dry
- 1/4 cup shredded Parmesan cheese
- 1-1/2 tsp. Italian seasoning
- 1/2 cup shredded part-skim mozzarella cheese

1. Cook noodles according to package directions. Meanwhile, in a large skillet, saute mushrooms in oil until tender. Add garlic; saute 30 seconds longer. Stir in the tomatoes, soup, spaghetti sauce, chicken, spinach, Parmesan cheese and Italian seasoning. Cook for 5-8 minutes or until heated through, stirring occasionally.

2. Drain noodles; toss with chicken mixture. Sprinkle with mozzarella cheese.

Nutrition Facts: 1-1/2 cups equals 389 calories, 12 g fat (4 g saturated fat), 73 mg cholesterol, 821 mg sodium, 38 g carbohydrate, 8 g fiber, 35 g protein.

Presto Stew & Garlic Mashed Potatoes

PREP/TOTAL TIME: 30 min. **YIELD:** 4 servings

MARY TALLMAN • ARBOR VITAE, WISCONSIN

To lighten this recipe, I use fat-free gravy and less butter in the potatoes. The robust stew is also good served over pasta, biscuits or leftover mashed potatoes.

- 1 lb. lean ground beef
- 1/4 cup chopped onion
- 1 can (14-1/2 oz.) diced tomatoes, drained
- 1 jar (12 oz.) fat-free beef gravy
- 1 cup frozen mixed vegetables
- 1/2 tsp. dried marjoram
- 1/2 tsp. pepper

POTATOES:
- 1 cup water
- 1/2 cup fat-free milk
- 1 Tbsp. butter
- 1/2 tsp. garlic powder
- 1/4 tsp. pepper
- 1-1/3 cups mashed potato flakes
- 1 Tbsp. minced fresh parsley

1. In a large nonstick skillet, cook beef and onion over medium heat until meat is no longer pink; drain. Stir in the tomatoes, gravy, vegetables, marjoram and pepper. Bring to a boil. Reduce heat; cover and simmer for 5-8 minutes or until the vegetables are tender.

2. Meanwhile, in a small saucepan, bring the water, milk, butter, garlic powder and pepper just to a boil. Remove from the heat; stir in potato flakes and parsley. Cover and let stand for 5 minutes. Fluff with a fork. Serve with stew.

Nutrition Facts: 1 cup stew with 1/2 cup potatoes equals 368 calories, 11 g fat (5 g saturated fat), 71 mg cholesterol, 751 mg sodium, 39 g carbohydrate, 5 g fiber, 27 g protein. **Diabetic Exchanges:** 3 lean meat, 2 starch, 1 vegetable, 1/2 fat.

Fiesta Ranch Burgers

PREP/TOTAL TIME: 30 min. **YIELD:** 5 servings

CAROL BREWER • FAIRBORN, OHIO

These always satisfy my burger cravings. I typically freeze extra cooked patties so that these are always on hand and ready to eat at a moment's notice.

2	egg whites, lightly beaten
1/2	cup canned diced tomatoes, drained
1/2	cup canned black beans, rinsed and drained
1	small onion, chopped
1	Tbsp. lime juice
1 to 2	Tbsp. chopped chipotle peppers in adobo sauce
1	garlic clove, minced
1/4	tsp. salt
1-1/4	lbs. lean ground turkey
1/3	cup prepared fat-free ranch salad dressing
1	Tbsp. minced fresh cilantro
5	lettuce leaves
5	hamburger buns, split

1. In a large bowl, combine the first eight ingredients. Crumble turkey over mixture and mix well. Shape into five burgers.

2. Broil 4 in. from the heat for 7-9 minutes on each side or until a meat thermometer reads 165° and juices run clear. In a small bowl, combine the salad dressing and cilantro. Serve burgers with dressing on lettuce-lined buns.

Nutrition Facts: 1 burger equals 357 calories, 12 g fat (3 g saturated fat), 90 mg cholesterol, 745 mg sodium, 34 g carbohydrate, 3 g fiber, 27 g protein. **Diabetic Exchanges:** 3 lean meat, 2 starch.

Thai Chicken Pizzas

PREP/TOTAL TIME: 20 min. **YIELD:** 4 servings

LYNETTE RANDLEMAN • BUFFALO, WYOMING

I found a recipe like this in a cookbook and modified it by cutting down on the peanut butter and adding cilantro for more flavor.

4	whole wheat tortillas (8 in.)
1/4	cup reduced-fat creamy peanut butter
2	Tbsp. reduced-sodium soy sauce
4-1/2	tsp. honey
2-1/4	tsp. rice wine vinegar
2	cups shredded cooked chicken breast
2	small carrots, shredded
1/2	cup minced fresh cilantro
1	cup (4 oz.) shredded part-skim mozzarella cheese

1. Coat both sides of tortillas with cooking spray; place on ungreased baking sheets. In a small bowl, combine the peanut butter, soy sauce, honey and vinegar. Stir in chicken until blended. Spread over tortillas. Top with carrots, cilantro and cheese.

2. Bake at 400° for 10-12 minutes or until cheese is melted.

Nutrition Facts: 1 pizza equals 374 calories, 12 g fat (4 g saturated fat), 70 mg cholesterol, 748 mg sodium, 36 g carbohydrate, 4 g fiber, 35 g protein. **Diabetic Exchanges:** 4 lean meat, 2 starch.

Count on **Thai Chicken Pizzas** to use up last night's leftover chicken. Save time by buying shredded carrots from the supermarket's produce department.

FIESTA RANCH BURGERS

THAI CHICKEN PIZZAS

Kid-Pleasing Taco Pizza

PREP/TOTAL TIME: 30 min. **YIELD:** 10 servings

KIMBERLY THEOBALD • GALESBURG, ILLINOIS

Kids will love this quick-and-easy take on both tacos and pizza. And you'll love that it's healthful, full of flavor and lower in fat and calories!

1	tube (13.8 oz.) refrigerated pizza crust
1	lb. lean ground turkey
3/4	cup water
1	envelope reduced-sodium taco seasoning
1	can (16 oz.) fat-free refried beans
1-1/2	cups (6 oz.) shredded pizza cheese blend
3	medium tomatoes, chopped
7	cups shredded lettuce
2	cups crushed baked tortilla chip scoops

1. Unroll crust into a 15-in. x 10-in. x 1-in. baking pan coated with cooking spray; flatten dough and build up edges slightly. Bake at 425° for 8-10 minutes or until the edges are lightly browned.

2. Meanwhile, in a large nonstick skillet, cook turkey over medium heat until no longer pink; drain. Stir in water and taco seasoning. Bring to a boil. Reduce heat; simmer, uncovered, for 5 minutes. Stir in refried beans until blended.

3. Spread the turkey mixture over crust; sprinkle with cheese. Bake at 425° for 5-7 minutes or until the cheese is melted. Top with tomatoes, lettuce and chips. Serve immediately.

Nutrition Facts: 1 piece equals 345 calories, 11 g fat (4 g saturated fat), 48 mg cholesterol, 873 mg sodium, 42 g carbohydrate, 5 g fiber, 20 g protein.

KID-PLEASING TACO PIZZA

Scrambled Egg Wraps Ⓜ

PREP/TOTAL TIME: 20 min. **YIELD:** 6 servings

JANE SHAPTON • TUSTIN, CALIFORNIA

This tasty morning meal will satisfy your family with protein and veggies. Try using flavored wraps to jazz things up.

1	medium sweet red pepper, chopped
1	medium green pepper, chopped
2	tsp. canola oil
5	plum tomatoes, seeded and chopped
6	eggs
1/2	cup soy milk
1/4	tsp. salt
6	flour tortillas (8 in.), warmed

1. In a large nonstick skillet, saute peppers in oil until tender. Add tomatoes; saute 1-2 minutes longer.

2. Meanwhile, in a large bowl, whisk the eggs, soy milk and salt. Reduce heat to medium; add egg mixture to skillet. Cook and stir until eggs are completely set. Spoon 2/3 cup mixture down the center of each tortilla; roll up.

Nutrition Facts: 1 wrap equals 258 calories, 10 g fat (2 g saturated fat), 212 mg cholesterol, 427 mg sodium, 30 g carbohydrate, 1 g fiber, 12 g protein. **Diabetic Exchanges:** 1-1/2 starch, 1 lean meat, 1 vegetable, 1 fat.

Busy-Day Pork Chops Ⓒ

PREP/TOTAL TIME: 25 min. **YIELD:** 4 servings

DEE MALTBY • WAYNE, OHIO

I developed this recipe one day when I had thawed pork chops and needed to find a quick fix for them. It's extremely simple, and the response was a rave review!

1/4	cup fat-free milk
1/4	cup grated Parmesan cheese
1/4	cup seasoned bread crumbs
1/4	tsp. salt
1/4	tsp. garlic powder
1/8	tsp. pepper
4	boneless pork loin chops (4 oz. *each*)

Cooking spray

SCRAMBLED EGG WRAPS

1. Place milk in a shallow bowl. In another shallow bowl, combine the cheese, bread crumbs, salt, garlic powder and pepper. Dip pork chops in milk, then coat with crumb mixture.

2. Place on a baking sheet coated with cooking spray; spritz the pork chops with cooking spray. Bake at 375° for 9-11 minutes on each side or until a meat thermometer reads 160°.

Nutrition Facts: 1 pork chop equals 178 calories, 7 g fat (3 g saturated fat), 57 mg cholesterol, 207 mg sodium, 3 g carbohydrate, trace fiber, 23 g protein. **Diabetic Exchange:** 3 lean meat.

Turkey a la King

PREP/TOTAL TIME: 30 min. **YIELD:** 4 servings

PAT LEMKE • BRANDON, WISCONSIN

I like to make this dish with our leftover turkey. It's a nice change from casseroles and so simple. Serve over rice, noodles, biscuits or toast.

1-3/4	cups sliced fresh mushrooms
1	celery rib, chopped
1/4	cup chopped onion
1/4	cup chopped green pepper
2	Tbsp. butter
1/4	cup all-purpose flour
1	cup reduced-sodium chicken broth
1	cup fat-free milk
2	cups cubed cooked turkey breast
1	cup frozen peas
1/2	tsp. salt
2	cups hot cooked rice

1. In a large nonstick skillet, saute the mushrooms, celery, onion and pepper in butter until tender.

2. Combine flour and broth until smooth; stir into vegetable mixture. Stir in milk. Bring to a boil. Cook and stir for 2 minutes or until thickened. Add the turkey, peas and salt; heat through. Serve with rice.

Nutrition Facts: 1-1/4 cups turkey mixture with 1/2 cup rice equals 350 calories, 7 g fat (4 g saturated fat), 76 mg cholesterol, 594 mg sodium, 40 g carbohydrate, 3 g fiber, 30 g protein. **Diabetic Exchanges:** 3 very lean meat, 2 starch, 2 vegetable.

For a great meal-in-one give Turkey a la King a try. Round out the menu with a spinach salad topped with sesame or Asian dressing. For dessert, stop by the ethnic aisle of your grocery store for some fortune cookies. The sweet, little treats are surprising low in fat.

Chicken Veggie Wraps

PREP/TOTAL TIME: 30 min. **YIELD:** 6 servings

KENDRA KATT • ALBUQUERQUE, NEW MEXICO

I gathered bits and pieces of things I like about Southwestern cooking to come up with this economical recipe. Serve with a green salad and vinaigrette dressing for a refreshing meal.

1-1/2	cups uncooked instant rice
1	medium tomato, chopped
2	cans (4 oz. *each*) chopped green chilies
7	Tbsp. lime juice, *divided*
1-1/2	tsp. chili powder
1-1/2	tsp. ground cumin
1/2	tsp. salt
1	lb. boneless skinless chicken breasts, cubed
3	tsp. canola oil, *divided*
1	large onion, halved and sliced
1	large green pepper, julienned
1	large sweet red pepper, julienned
3	garlic cloves, minced
1	Tbsp. brown sugar
6	flour tortillas (8 in.), warmed

1. Cook rice according to package directions. Stir in the tomato, chilies and 3 tablespoons lime juice.

2. Meanwhile, combine the chili powder, cumin and salt; sprinkle over chicken. In a large nonstick skillet coated with cooking spray, saute chicken in 2 teaspoons oil until no longer pink. Remove and keep warm.

3. In the same skillet, cook the onion, peppers and garlic in remaining oil until crisp-tender. Stir in the brown sugar, cooked chicken and remaining lime juice; heat through.

4. Spoon 2/3 cup each of rice mixture and chicken mixture down the center of each tortilla; roll up.

Nutrition Facts: 1 wrap equals 395 calories, 8 g fat (1 g saturated fat), 42 mg cholesterol, 646 mg sodium, 59 g carbohydrate, 3 g fiber, 23 g protein.

Cumin Chicken C

PREP/TOTAL TIME: 30 min. **YIELD:** 4 servings

MARGARET ALLEN • ABINGDON, VIRGINIA

This zesty chicken dish comes together in a flash. Saucy and delicious, it's great for company or a special family dinner.

2	tsp. ground cumin, *divided*
1/2	tsp. dried oregano
1/4	tsp. garlic salt
4	boneless skinless chicken breast halves (4 oz. *each*)
1	Tbsp. canola oil
1/2	cup picante sauce
1/4	cup water
1	tsp. reduced-sodium chicken bouillon granules

1. Combine 1 teaspoon cumin, oregano and garlic salt; sprinkle over both sides of chicken. In a large nonstick skillet, brown chicken in oil on both sides.

2. Combine the picante sauce, water, bouillon and remaining cumin; pour over chicken. Bring to a boil. Reduce heat; cover and simmer for 8-12 minutes or until chicken is no longer pink.

3. Remove chicken and keep warm. Cook and stir the sauce over medium-high heat for 3-5 minutes or until thickened. Serve with chicken.

Nutrition Facts: 1 chicken breast half with 3 tablespoons sauce equals 170 calories, 6 g fat (1 g saturated fat), 63 mg cholesterol, 377 mg sodium, 3 g carbohydrate, trace fiber, 23 g protein. **Diabetic Exchanges:** 3 very lean meat, 1 fat.

Couscous Chicken Salad

PREP/TOTAL TIME: 25 min. **YIELD:** 6 servings

LINDA BAGGETT • ARCATA, CALIFORNIA

This is perfect for a speedy lunch. It's easy to make, and you can keep most of the ingredients on hand for a nutritious meal.

1	can (14-1/2 oz.) reduced-sodium chicken broth
1/3	cup water
1-3/4	cups uncooked couscous
3	cups cubed cooked chicken breast
1	can (14 oz.) water-packed artichoke hearts, rinsed, drained and chopped
2	medium tomatoes, chopped
1	medium sweet red pepper, chopped
1	small cucumber, sliced
1/2	cup minced fresh parsley
1/2	cup crumbled feta cheese
3	green onions, sliced
1/4	tsp. salt
1/4	tsp. pepper
3/4	cup fat-free Italian salad dressing

1. In a large saucepan, bring broth and water to a boil. Stir in couscous. Cover and remove from the heat; let stand for 5 minutes. Fluff with a fork.

2. Stir in the chicken, artichokes, tomatoes, red pepper, cucumber, parsley, cheese, onions, salt and pepper. Drizzle with dressing and toss to coat. Refrigerate until serving.

Nutrition Facts: 1-1/2 cups equals 388 calories, 5 g fat (2 g saturated fat), 60 mg cholesterol, 923 mg sodium, 53 g carbohydrate, 4 g fiber, 33 g protein.

Turkey Luncheon Salad F

PREP/TOTAL TIME: 25 min. **YIELD:** 7 servings

JOAN CANNON • NOBLESVILLE, INDIANA

I received this recipe as a newlywed and made it healthier by using brown rice, fat-free mayo and sour cream. Think ladies' luncheon...with a light, refreshing Asian twist!

2	cups cubed cooked turkey breast
2	cups cooked brown rice
1	can (14 oz.) bean sprouts, drained
1	can (8 oz.) sliced water chestnuts, drained
1	celery rib, chopped
1	small carrot, shredded
1/4	cup finely chopped onion
1/2	cup fat-free mayonnaise
1/2	cup fat-free sour cream
1	Tbsp. reduced-sodium soy sauce
3/4	tsp. salt
7	lettuce leaves
1/4	cup dried cranberries

1. In a large bowl, combine the first seven ingredients. In a small bowl, combine the mayonnaise, sour cream, soy sauce and salt; pour over salad and gently stir to coat. Serve over lettuce leaves. Sprinkle with cranberries.

Nutrition Facts: 1 cup equals 195 calories, 2 g fat (trace saturated fat), 39 mg cholesterol, 545 mg sodium, 29 g carbohydrate, 4 g fiber, 16 g protein. **Diabetic Exchanges:** 1 starch, 1 very lean meat, 1 vegetable.

TURKEY LUNCHEON SALAD

COUSCOUS CHICKEN SALAD

BEEF ROAST DINNER

BEEFY RED PEPPER PASTA

SESAME BEEF 'N' VEGGIE KABOBS

Beef Entrees

Watching your weight doesn't mean foregoing meaty main courses. Just dig into the hearty dinners featured here. Loaded with flavor and comforting appeal, these heart-smart beef recipes give new meaning to good eating.

Sesame Beef 'n' Veggie Kabobs C

PREP: 25 min. + marinating
GRILL: 10 min. **YIELD:** 16 kabobs

FRANCES KLINGEMANN • OMAHA, NEBRASKA

This is a favorite with my entire family. It offers wonderful flavor and a beautiful presentation, too!

1/2	cup reduced-sodium soy sauce
1/4	cup white wine or unsweetened apple juice
3	medium green peppers, cut into 1-in. pieces, *divided*
1	medium onion, cut into wedges
1	garlic clove, peeled
1/2	tsp. ground ginger
1	Tbsp. sesame seeds
2	lbs. boneless beef sirloin steak, cut into 1-in. pieces
32	medium fresh mushrooms
32	cherry tomatoes
1	Tbsp. canola oil

1. In a blender, combine the soy sauce, wine or juice, 1/2 cup green pepper, onion, garlic and ginger; cover and process until smooth. Stir in sesame seeds.

2. Cover and refrigerate 1/3 cup of mixture for basting. Pour remaining mixture into a large resealable plastic bag; add the beef. Seal bag and turn to coat; refrigerate overnight. Refrigerate remaining peppers.

3. If grilling the kabobs, coat grill rack with cooking spray before starting the grill. Drain and discard marinade. On 16 metal or soaked wooden skewers, alternately thread the beef, mushrooms, tomatoes and remaining peppers. Brush lightly with oil.

4. Grill, covered, over medium heat or broil 4 in. from the heat for 10-15 minutes or until beef reaches desired doneness, turning occasionally and basting with reserved marinade.

Nutrition Facts: 2 kabobs equals 211 calories, 8 g fat (2 g saturated fat), 64 mg cholesterol, 361 mg sodium, 10 g carbohydrate, 3 g fiber, 26 g protein. **Diabetic Exchanges:** 3 lean meat, 2 vegetable, 1/2 fat.

Beef Roast Dinner

PREP: 20 min. **COOK:** 8 hours **YIELD:** 10 servings

SANDRA DUDLEY • BEMIDJI, MINNESOTA

Here's a healthy dish that's so easy to prepare. Because it's slow cooked, you can use less-expensive roasts with mouthwatering results that equal costly cuts.

1	lb. red potatoes (about 4 medium), cubed
1/4	lb. small fresh mushrooms
1-1/2	cups fresh baby carrots
1	medium green pepper, chopped
1	medium parsnip, chopped
1	small red onion, chopped
1	boneless beef rump roast (3 lbs.)
1	can (14-1/2 oz.) beef broth
3/4	tsp. salt
3/4	tsp. dried oregano
1/4	tsp. pepper
3	Tbsp. cornstarch
1/4	cup cold water

1. Place vegetables in a 5-qt. slow cooker. Cut roast in half; place in slow cooker. Combine the broth, salt, oregano and pepper; pour over meat. Cover and cook on low for 8 hours or until meat is tender.

2. Remove meat and vegetables to a serving platter; keep warm. Skim fat from cooking juices; transfer to a small saucepan. Bring liquid to a boil. Combine cornstarch and water until smooth. Gradually stir into the pan. Bring to a boil; cook and stir for 2 minutes or until thickened. Serve with meat and vegetables.

Nutrition Facts: 4 ounces cooked beef with 2/3 cup vegetables and 1/4 cup gravy equals 245 calories, 7 g fat (2 g saturated fat), 82 mg cholesterol, 427 mg sodium, 16 g carbohydrate, 2 g fiber, 29 g protein. **Diabetic Exchanges:** 4 lean meat, 1 starch.

> **Save money when shopping for Beef Roast Dinner.**
> **Look for cuts of beef such as rump roast, round roast, chuck shoulder roast or lean beef stew meat.**

Jamaican-Style Beef Stew

PREP: 25 min. **COOK:** 1-1/2 hours **YIELD:** 5 servings

JAMES HAYES • RIDGECREST, CALIFORNIA

I rely on lean meats, a variety of herbs and seasonings, fresh vegetables, and rice or potatoes for this satisfying stew.

1	Tbsp. canola oil
1	Tbsp. sugar
1-1/2	lbs. boneless beef sirloin steak, cut into 3/4-in. cubes
5	plum tomatoes, finely chopped
3	large carrots, cut into 1/2-in. slices
3	celery ribs, cut into 1/2-in. slices
4	green onions, chopped
3/4	cup reduced-sodium beef broth
1/4	cup barbecue sauce
1/4	cup reduced-sodium soy sauce
2	Tbsp. steak sauce
1	Tbsp. garlic powder
1	tsp. dried thyme
1/4	tsp. ground allspice
1/4	tsp. pepper
1/8	tsp. hot pepper sauce
1	Tbsp. cornstarch
2	Tbsp. cold water

Hot cooked rice *or* mashed potatoes, optional

1. In a Dutch oven, heat oil over medium-high heat. Add sugar; cook and stir for 1 minute or until lightly browned. Add beef and brown on all sides.

2. Stir in the vegetables, broth, barbecue sauce, soy sauce, steak sauce and seasonings. Bring to a boil. Reduce heat; cover and simmer for 1 to 1-1/4 hours or until meat and vegetables are tender.

3. Combine cornstarch and water until smooth; stir into stew. Bring to a boil; cook and stir for 2 minutes or until thickened. Serve with rice or potatoes if desired.

Nutrition Facts: 1 cup (calculated without rice or potatoes) equals 282 calories, 10 g fat (3 g saturated fat), 77 mg cholesterol, 866 mg sodium, 19 g carbohydrate, 3 g fiber, 29 g protein.

Inside-Out Cabbage Rolls

PREP: 15 min. **COOK:** 30 min. **YIELD:** 6 servings

LISA WILLIAMS • COMSTOCK PARK, MICHIGAN

Here's a hearty, one-dish meal that's lower in fat but very filling. The cabbage, ground beef and brown rice give it a comforting, down-home feel.

1	lb. lean ground beef
1	large onion, chopped
1	large green pepper, chopped
1	small head cabbage, chopped
1	can (10 oz.) diced tomatoes and green chilies
1	cup reduced-sodium beef broth
1	can (8 oz.) pizza sauce
1	cup cooked brown rice
1/2	cup shredded reduced-fat cheddar cheese

1. In a Dutch oven, cook the beef, onion and green pepper over medium heat until meat is no longer pink; drain.

2. Stir in the cabbage, tomatoes, broth and pizza sauce. Bring mixture to a boil. Reduce heat; cover and simmer for 20-25 minutes or until cabbage is tender, stirring occasionally.

3. Stir in rice; heat through. Remove from the heat. Sprinkle with cheese; cover and let stand until cheese is melted.

Nutrition Facts: 1-1/3 cups equals 244 calories, 8 g fat (4 g saturated fat), 45 mg cholesterol, 502 mg sodium, 23 g carbohydrate, 5 g fiber, 21 g protein. **Diabetic Exchanges:** 2 lean meat, 1-1/2 starch, 1/2 fat.

Barbecues for the Bunch

PREP: 25 min. **COOK:** 6 hours **YIELD:** 16 servings

LOUISE WATKINS • SPARTA, WISCONSIN

When I worked full-time, this slow-cooker staple was an easy way to have dinner ready when I got home. It's fall-apart tender and makes enough to freeze for another night!

- 2 lbs. boneless beef sirloin steak, cubed
- 1-1/2 lbs. boneless pork loin roast, cubed
- 2 large onions, chopped
- 3/4 cup chopped celery
- 1 can (6 oz.) tomato paste
- 1/2 cup packed brown sugar
- 1/4 cup cider vinegar
- 1/4 cup chili sauce
- 2 Tbsp. Worcestershire sauce
- 1 Tbsp. ground mustard
- 16 hamburger buns, split

1. In a 5-qt. slow cooker, combine the beef, pork, onions and celery. In a small bowl, combine the tomato paste, brown sugar, vinegar, chili sauce, Worcestershire sauce and mustard. Pour over meat mixture.

2. Cover and cook on high for 6-8 hours or until meat is very tender. Shred meat in the slow cooker with two forks. With a slotted spoon, serve 1/2 cup meat mixture on each bun.

Nutrition Facts: 1 sandwich equals 297 calories, 7 g fat (2 g saturated fat), 53 mg cholesterol, 336 mg sodium, 34 g carbohydrate, 2 g fiber, 24 g protein. **Diabetic Exchanges:** 3 lean meat, 2 starch.

Skillet Beef Tamales

PREP/TOTAL TIME: 30 min. **YIELD:** 5 servings

DEBORAH WILLIAMS • WILDWOOD, MISSOURI

This skillet dinner is cheesy and delicious, and it doesn't taste light at all! It's sure to be a family favorite!

- 1 lb. lean ground beef
- 1/3 cup chopped green pepper
- 1/3 cup chopped sweet red pepper
- 2 cups salsa
- 3/4 cup frozen corn
- 2 Tbsp. water
- 6 corn tortillas (6 in.), halved and cut into 1/2-in. strips
- 3/4 cup shredded reduced-fat cheddar cheese
- 5 Tbsp. fat-free sour cream

1. In a large nonstick skillet coated with cooking spray, cook beef and peppers over medium heat until meat is no longer pink; drain. Stir in the salsa, corn and water; bring to a boil.

2. Stir in tortilla strips. Reduce heat; cover and simmer for 10-15 minutes or until tortillas are softened. Sprinkle with cheese; cover and cook 2-3 minutes longer or until cheese is melted. Serve with sour cream.

Nutrition Facts: 1 cup beef mixture with 1 tablespoon sour cream equals 329 calories, 11 g fat (5 g saturated fat), 59 mg cholesterol, 679 mg sodium, 28 g carbohydrate, 6 g fiber, 25 g protein. **Diabetic Exchanges:** 3 lean meat, 1-1/2 starch, 1 vegetable, 1/2 fat.

Hamburger Stir-Fry

PREP/TOTAL TIME: 25 min. **YIELD:** 4 servings

JOHN HORST • WESTFIELD, NEW YORK

Here's a quick, easy teriyaki stir-fry that uses hamburger instead of the traditional beef strips. It has a nice sauce and is different enough to be a treat for the taste buds!

- 1 Tbsp. sugar
- 1 Tbsp. cornstarch
- 1 Tbsp. ground mustard
- 1/3 cup water
- 1/3 cup reduced-sodium teriyaki sauce
- 1 lb. lean ground beef
- 1 pkg. (16 oz.) frozen asparagus stir-fry vegetable blend
- 1 medium onion, halved and thinly sliced
- 2 tsp. canola oil
- 2 cups hot cooked rice
- 2 tsp. sesame seeds

1. In a small bowl, combine the sugar, cornstarch and mustard. Stir in water and teriyaki sauce until smooth; set aside.

2. In a large skillet or wok, stir-fry beef until no longer pink; drain and set aside. In the same pan, stir-fry the vegetable blend and onion in oil until crisp-tender.

3. Stir cornstarch mixture and add to the pan. Bring to a boil; cook and stir for 1-2 minutes or until thickened. Add beef; heat through. Serve with rice. Sprinkle with sesame seeds.

Nutrition Facts: 1 cup stir-fry with 1/2 cup rice equals 399 calories, 12 g fat (4 g saturated fat), 56 mg cholesterol, 516 mg sodium, 42 g carbohydrate, 3 g fiber, 28 g protein. **Diabetic Exchanges:** 3 lean meat, 2 starch, 2 vegetable, 1/2 fat.

SKILLET BEEF TAMALES

Chili Beef Quesadillas

PREP: 30 min. **BAKE:** 10 min. **YIELD:** 4 servings

ROBYN LARABEE • LUCKNOW, ONTARIO

Served in whole wheat tortillas, these scrumptious beef-and-veggie quesadillas pack a healthy dose of fiber. They're spicy enough to suit my husband, but mild enough to please our 2-year-old son.

3/4	pound lean ground beef
1	medium onion, chopped
3/4	cup finely chopped fresh mushrooms
1	medium zucchini, shredded
1	medium carrot, shredded
2	garlic cloves, minced
2	tsp. chili powder
1/4	tsp. salt
1/4	tsp. hot pepper sauce
2	medium tomatoes, seeded and chopped
1/4	cup minced fresh cilantro
4	whole wheat tortillas (8 in.), warmed

Cooking spray

1/2	cup shredded part-skim mozzarella cheese

1. In a large nonstick skillet over medium heat, cook beef and onion until meat is no longer pink; drain. Remove and keep warm. In the same skillet, cook and stir the mushrooms, zucchini, carrot, garlic, chili powder, salt and pepper sauce until vegetables are tender. Stir in tomatoes, cilantro and beef mixture.

2. Spritz one side of each tortilla with cooking spray; place plain side up in a 15-in. x 10-in. x 1-in. baking pan coated with cooking spray. Spoon beef mixture over half of each tortilla; sprinkle with cheese. Fold tortillas over filling.

3. Bake at 400° for 5 minutes. Carefully turn over; bake 5-6 minutes longer or until cheese is melted. Cut into wedges.

Nutrition Facts: 1 quesadilla equals 353 calories, 12 g fat (4 g saturated fat), 50 mg cholesterol, 475 mg sodium, 33 g carbohydrate, 5 g fiber, 26 g protein. **Diabetic Exchanges:** 3 lean meat, 2 vegetable, 1-1/2 starch.

Southwestern Goulash

PREP/TOTAL TIME: 30 min. **YIELD:** 6 servings

VIKKI REBHOLZ • WEST CHESTER, OHIO

I had some extra cilantro in the fridge and didn't want to throw it away. Instead, I came up with this delightful and filling recipe. Everyone just loved it!

1	cup uncooked elbow macaroni
1	lb. lean ground beef
1	medium onion, chopped
1	can (28 oz.) diced tomatoes, undrained
2/3	cup frozen corn
1	can (8 oz.) tomato sauce
1	can (4 oz.) chopped green chilies
1/2	tsp. ground cumin
1/2	tsp. pepper
1/4	tsp. salt
1/4	cup minced fresh cilantro

1. Cook macaroni according to package directions. Meanwhile, in a Dutch oven over medium heat, cook beef and onion until meat is no longer pink; drain. Stir in the tomatoes, corn, tomato sauce, chilies, cumin, pepper and salt. Bring to a boil. Reduce heat; simmer, uncovered, for 3-4 minutes or until mixture is heated through.

2. Drain macaroni; add to meat mixture. Stir in cilantro and heat through.

Nutrition Facts: 1-1/3 cups equals 224 calories, 6 g fat (2 g saturated fat), 37 mg cholesterol, 567 mg sodium, 24 g carbohydrate, 4 g fiber, 19 g protein. **Diabetic Exchanges:** 2 lean meat, 2 vegetable, 1 starch.

Spoon Bread Tamale Bake

PREP: 25 min. **BAKE:** 30 min. **YIELD:** 8 servings

MARJORIE MERSEREAU • CORVALLIS, OREGON

This is a favorite comfort food for my family on winter nights—and all year-round! Make it ahead for convenience, then reheat it in the oven to bake about an hour before dinner.

1-1/2	lbs. lean ground beef
1	large onion, chopped
1	small green pepper, chopped
1	garlic clove, minced
1	can (28 oz.) diced tomatoes, undrained
1-1/2	cups frozen corn
1	can (2-1/4 oz.) sliced ripe olives, drained
4-1/2	tsp. chili powder
1/2	tsp. salt
1/4	tsp. pepper
1/2	cup cornmeal
1	cup water

TOPPING:

1-1/2	cups fat-free milk, *divided*
1/2	cup cornmeal
1/2	tsp. salt
1/2	cup shredded reduced-fat cheddar cheese
2	Tbsp. butter
1/2	cup egg substitute

SOUTHWESTERN GOULASH

ITALIAN PASTA CASSEROLE

1. In a Dutch oven coated with cooking spray, cook beef, onion, green pepper and garlic over medium heat until meat is no longer pink; drain. Stir in tomatoes, corn, olives, chili powder, salt and pepper. Bring to a boil. Reduce heat; simmer, uncovered, for 5 minutes.

2. Combine cornmeal and water until smooth; gradually stir into the pan. Bring to a boil. Reduce heat; simmer, uncovered, for 10 minutes, stirring occasionally. Transfer to a 2-1/2-qt. baking dish coated with cooking spray.

3. In a small saucepan, bring 1 cup milk to a boil. Combine the cornmeal, salt and remaining milk; slowly whisk into the boiling milk. Cook and stir until mixture returns to a boil. Reduce heat; cook and stir for 3-4 minutes or until slightly thickened.

4. Remove from heat; stir in cheese and butter until melted. Stir in egg substitute. Pour over meat mixture. Bake, uncovered, at 375° for 30-40 minutes or until topping is lightly browned.

Nutrition Facts: 1 serving equals 331 calories, 12 g fat (6 g saturated fat), 55 mg cholesterol, 754 mg sodium, 30 g carbohydrate, 4 g fiber, 25 g protein. **Diabetic Exchanges:** 3 lean meat, 1-1/2 starch, 1 vegetable, 1/2 fat.

Italian Pasta Casserole

PREP: 30 min. **BAKE:** 20 min. **YIELD:** 6 servings

DENISE RASMUSSEN • SALINA, KANSAS

Some simple meat substitutions and a host of seasonings make this traditional, lasagna-style dish a healthy meal.

- 2 cups uncooked spiral pasta
- 1/2 lb. lean ground beef
- 1/2 lb. Italian turkey sausage links, casings removed
- 1 small onion, finely chopped
- 1 garlic clove, minced
- 2 cans (14-1/2 oz. *each*) diced tomatoes, undrained
- 1/3 cup tomato paste
- 3/4 tsp. Italian seasoning
- 1/2 tsp. chili powder
- 1/4 tsp. dried oregano
- 1/8 tsp. salt
- 1/8 tsp. garlic powder
- 1/8 tsp. dried thyme
- 1/8 tsp. pepper
- 2 oz. sliced turkey pepperoni
- 1 cup (4 ounces) shredded part-skim mozzarella cheese

1. Cook pasta according to package directions. Meanwhile, crumble beef and sausage into a large skillet; add onion and garlic. Cook and stir over medium heat until meat is no longer pink; drain. Stir in the tomatoes, tomato paste and seasonings. Bring to a boil. Reduce heat; simmer, uncovered, for 5 minutes.

2. Drain pasta; stir in meat mixture and pepperoni. Transfer half of pasta mixture to a 2-qt. baking dish coated with cooking spray. Sprinkle with half of cheese; repeat layers. Cover and bake at 350° for 20-25 minutes or until bubbly.

Nutrition Facts: 1 cup equals 335 calories, 11 g fat (4 g saturated fat), 64 mg cholesterol, 752 mg sodium, 33 g carbohydrate, 4 g fiber, 26 g protein. **Diabetic Exchanges:** 2 starch, 2 lean meat, 1-1/2 fat.

Italian Cabbage Casserole

PREP: 35 min. **BAKE:** 15 min. **YIELD:** 6 servings

DEBRA SANDERS • BREVARD, NORTH CAROLINA

If your gang likes stuffed cabbage, they'll love this hearty, beefy recipe. And you'll love that it has all the taste—with a lot less work than stuffed cabbage!

1	medium head cabbage, coarsely shredded
1	lb. lean ground beef
1	large green pepper, chopped
1	medium onion, chopped
1	can (14-1/2 oz.) diced tomatoes, undrained
1	can (8 oz.) tomato sauce
3	Tbsp. tomato paste
1-1/2	tsp. dried oregano
1/2	tsp. garlic powder
1/2	tsp. pepper
1/8	tsp. salt
1/2	cup shredded part-skim mozzarella cheese

1. Place cabbage in a steamer basket; place in a large saucepan over 1 in. of water. Bring to a boil; cover and steam for 6-8 minutes or until tender. Drain and set aside.

2. In a large nonstick skillet over medium heat, cook and stir the beef, green pepper and onion until meat is no longer pink; drain. Stir in the tomatoes, tomato sauce, tomato paste and seasonings. Bring to a boil. Reduce heat; simmer, uncovered, for 10 minutes.

3. Place half of the cabbage in an 11-in. x 7-in. baking dish coated with cooking spray; top with half of beef mixture. Repeat layers (dish will be full). Sprinkle with cheese. Bake, uncovered, at 350° for 15-20 minutes or until heated through.

Nutrition Facts: 1-1/3 cups equals 223 calories, 7 g fat (3 g saturated fat), 42 mg cholesterol, 438 mg sodium, 20 g carbohydrate, 7 g fiber, 21 g protein. **Diabetic Exchanges:** 2 lean meat, 1 starch.

Asian Orange Beef

PREP: 20 min. **COOK:** 20 min. **YIELD:** 6 servings

NANCY BELLOMO • ST. CHARLES, MISSOURI

Here is the fastest stir-fry ever! Fresh ginger is a must for this recipe and really sparks it up. Our test panel agreed and just raved about the splash of orange flavor. Try it the next time you need a change-of-pace beef dish.

3	large navel oranges
1	bunch green onions
3	Tbsp. sugar
2	Tbsp. cornstarch
3	Tbsp. reduced-sodium soy sauce
3	garlic cloves, minced
1	Tbsp. minced fresh gingerroot
1-1/2	lbs. boneless beef sirloin steak, cut into 1/2-in. cubes
1	Tbsp. canola oil
3	cups hot cooked rice

1. Finely grate the peel from two oranges; set aside. Cut thin strips of orange peel from the remaining orange for garnish; set aside. Squeeze juice from all oranges. Cut onions to separate the white and green parts. Thinly slice white parts; cut green parts into 1-in. lengths for garnish.

2. For sauce, in a small bowl, combine sugar and cornstarch; stir in orange juice until smooth. Stir in the soy sauce, garlic, ginger, grated orange peel and white parts of onions; set aside.

3. In a large nonstick skillet or wok coated with cooking spray, stir-fry beef in oil until no longer pink. Stir the sauce and add to the pan. Bring to a boil; cook and stir for 2 minutes or until thickened. Serve with rice. Garnish with orange peel strips and remaining onions.

Nutrition Facts: 1 slice equals 104 calories, 1 g fat (1 g saturated fat), 3 mg cholesterol, 219 mg sodium, 19 g carbohydrate, 1 g fiber, 4 g protein. **Diabetic Exchange:** 1 starch.

Wintertime Braised Beef Stew

PREP: 40 min. **BAKE:** 2 hours
YIELD: 8 servings (2 quarts)

MICHAELA ROSENTHAL • INDIO, CALIFORNIA

This easy beef stew has a deep, rich taste. Since it's even better a day or two later, you may want to make a double batch.

- 2 Tbsp. all-purpose flour
- 2 tsp. steak seasoning
- 2 lbs. boneless beef sirloin steak, cut into 1-in. cubes
- 2 Tbsp. olive oil, *divided*
- 1 large onion, chopped
- 2 celery ribs, chopped
- 2 medium parsnips, peeled and cut into 1-1/2-in. pieces
- 2 medium carrots, peeled and cut into 1-1/2-in. pieces
- 2 garlic cloves, minced
- 1 can (14-1/2 oz.) diced tomatoes, undrained
- 1 cup dry red wine *or* reduced-sodium beef broth
- 2 Tbsp. red currant jelly
- 2 bay leaves
- 2 fresh oregano sprigs
- 1 can (15 oz.) white kidney *or* cannellini beans, rinsed and drained

1. In a large resealable plastic bag, combine flour and steak seasoning. Add beef, a few pieces at a time, and shake to coat. Heat 1 tablespoon oil in an ovenproof Dutch oven; brown beef in batches on all sides. Remove and keep warm.

2. In the same pan, saute the onion, celery, parsnips and carrots in remaining oil until crisp-tender. Add garlic; cook 1 minute longer. Add the tomatoes, wine, jelly, bay leaves, oregano and beef; bring to a boil.

3. Cover and bake at 350° for 1-1/2 hours. Stir in beans; cover and bake 30-40 minutes longer or until the beef and vegetables are tender. Discard bay leaves and oregano.

Editor's Note: This recipe was tested with McCormick's Montreal Steak Seasoning. Look for it in the spice aisle.

Nutrition Facts: 1 cup equals 310 calories, 9 g fat (3 g saturated fat), 64 mg cholesterol, 373 mg sodium, 26 g carbohydrate, 5 g fiber, 25 g protein. **Diabetic Exchanges:** 3 lean meat, 1 starch, 1 vegetable, 1 fat.

Beef 'n' Bean Chili

PREP: 20 min. **COOK:** 1-1/4 hours
YIELD: 10 servings (2-3/4 quarts)

LINDA CHARLIER • EAST CLEVELAND, OHIO

My tangy chili is chock-full of beef, beans and rich tomato flavor. Leftovers freeze well and make a yummy filling for homemade burritos later.

- 1 lb. lean ground beef
- 1 medium onion, chopped
- 1/2 lb. boneless beef sirloin steak, cut into 1/2-in. cubes
- 1 Tbsp. olive oil
- 1/2 lb. fresh mushrooms, quartered
- 1 medium zucchini, shredded
- 6 garlic cloves, minced
- 2 cans (15 oz. *each*) tomato sauce
- 1 can (28 oz.) crushed tomatoes
- 1 can (16 oz.) light red kidney beans, rinsed and drained
- 1 can (15 oz.) black beans, rinsed and drained
- 2/3 cup water
- 2 Tbsp. chili powder
- 4-1/2 tsp. dried parsley flakes
- 1 Tbsp. Italian seasoning
- 1 tsp. ground cumin
- 1/2 tsp. crushed red pepper flakes
- 1/2 tsp. pepper
- 1 can (16 ounces) dark red kidney beans, rinsed and drained, *divided*

1. In a Dutch oven, cook ground beef and onion over medium heat until meat is no longer pink; drain and set aside.

2. In the same pan, brown steak in oil on all sides. Add the mushrooms, zucchini and garlic; saute until mushrooms are tender. Drain. Stir in the tomato sauce, crushed tomatoes, light red kidney beans, black beans, water, seasonings and ground beef mixture.

3. In a small bowl, mash 1/2 cup dark red kidney beans with a fork. Stir into chili. Add remaining kidney beans. Bring to a boil. Reduce heat; cover and simmer for 40 minutes. Uncover; simmer 20 minutes longer or until slightly thickened and meat is tender.

Nutrition Facts: 1-1/2 cups equals 290 calories, 6 g fat (2 g saturated fat), 35 mg cholesterol, 766 mg sodium, 35 g carbohydrate, 10 g fiber, 25 g protein. **Diabetic Exchanges:** 2 starch, 2 lean meat, 1 vegetable.

WINTERTIME BRAISED BEEF STEW

Easy Beef Stroganoff

PREP/TOTAL TIME: 30 min. **YIELD:** 6 servings

JENNIFER RIORDAN • ST. LOUIS, MISSOURI

I lightened my mother-in-law's wonderful Stroganoff and came up with this one. My family loves it—it's called "special noodles" in my house.

4-1/2	cups uncooked yolk-free noodles
1	lb. lean ground beef
1/2	lb. sliced fresh mushrooms
1	large onion, halved and sliced
3	garlic cloves, minced
1	Tbsp. reduced-fat butter
2	Tbsp. all-purpose flour
1	can (14-1/2 oz.) reduced-sodium beef broth
2	Tbsp. tomato paste
1	cup (8 oz.) fat-free sour cream
1/4	tsp. salt
1/4	tsp. pepper

1. Cook noodles according to package directions. Meanwhile, in a Dutch oven, cook the beef, mushrooms, onion and garlic over medium heat until meat is no longer pink; drain. Remove and keep warm.

2. In the same pan, melt butter. Stir in flour until smooth; gradually add broth and tomato paste. Bring to a boil; cook and stir for 2 minutes or until thickened.

3. Carefully return beef mixture to the pan. Add sour cream, salt and pepper; cook and stir until heated through (do not boil). Drain noodles; serve with beef mixture.

Editor's Note: This recipe was tested with Land O'Lakes light stick butter.

Nutrition Facts: 2/3 cup beef mixture with 3/4 cup noodles equals 326 calories, 7 g fat (3 g saturated fat), 48 mg cholesterol, 342 mg sodium, 39 g carbohydrate, 3 g fiber, 24 g protein. **Diabetic Exchanges:** 2 starch, 2 lean meat, 1 vegetable.

All-American Beef Stew

PREP: 40 min. **COOK:** 1-3/4 hours
YIELD: 8 servings (2-1/2 quarts)

FRANCES ALDAL • ANTELOPE, CALIFORNIA

Born and raised in Japan, my mother wasn't familiar with many American dishes when she married my father and moved to the States. Her mother-in-law gave her this recipe. It was always one of my favorites.

3/4	cup all-purpose flour, *divided*
1/2	tsp. seasoned salt
1/2	tsp. pepper, *divided*
2	lbs. lean beef stew meat, cut into 1-in. cubes
1	Tbsp. olive oil
4-1/2	cups water, *divided*
1	large onion, halved and sliced
2	Tbsp. Worcestershire sauce
1	Tbsp. lemon juice
2	garlic cloves, minced
1	tsp. sugar
1/2	tsp. salt
1/2	tsp. paprika
1/8	tsp. ground allspice
1	bay leaf
4	medium potatoes, cubed
6	medium carrots, sliced

1. Place 1/2 cup flour, seasoned salt and 1/4 teaspoon pepper in a large resealable plastic bag. Add beef, a few pieces at a time, and shake to coat.

2. In a Dutch oven, brown meat in oil in batches. Remove and set aside. Add 4 cups water to the pan, stirring to loosen browned bits. Add the onion, Worcestershire sauce, lemon juice, garlic, sugar, salt, paprika, allspice, bay leaf and remaining pepper. Return beef to the pan. Bring to a boil. Reduce heat; cover and simmer for 1 hour.

3. Stir in potatoes and carrots. Bring to a boil. Reduce heat; cover and simmer for 30-35 minutes or until meat and vegetables are tender. Combine remaining flour and water until smooth; stir into the pan. Bring to a boil; cook and stir for 2 minutes or until thickened. Discard bay leaf.

Nutrition Facts: 1-1/4 cups equals 324 calories, 10 g fat (3 g saturated fat), 70 mg cholesterol, 322 mg sodium, 33 g carbohydrate, 4 g fiber, 25 g protein. **Diabetic Exchanges:** 3 lean meat, 2 starch, 1 vegetable.

ALL-AMERICAN BEEF STEW

EASY BEEF STROGANOFF

Beefy Red Pepper Pasta

PREP: 20 min. **COOK:** 25 min. **YIELD:** 6 servings

MARGE WERNER • BROKEN ARROW, OKLAHOMA

Chock-full of veggies and gooey with cheese, this hearty one-dish meal will warm your loved ones to their toes! Pureed roasted red peppers add zing and color to the sauce.

1	jar (12 oz.) roasted sweet red peppers, drained
1	lb. lean ground beef
1	small onion, chopped
1	can (14-1/2 oz.) diced tomatoes, undrained
2	garlic cloves, minced
1	tsp. dried oregano
1	tsp. dried basil
3/4	tsp. salt
8	oz. uncooked ziti or small tube pasta
1-1/2	cups cut fresh green beans
1-1/2	cups (6 ounces) shredded part-skim mozzarella cheese

1. Place peppers in a food processor; cover and process until smooth. In a large skillet, cook beef and onion until meat is no longer pink; drain. Stir in the pepper puree, tomatoes, garlic, oregano, basil and salt. Bring to a boil. Reduce heat; simmer, uncovered, for 15 minutes.

2. Meanwhile, in a Dutch oven, cook pasta according to package directions, adding green beans during the last 5 minutes of cooking. Cook until pasta and green beans are tender; drain. Return to the pan; stir in meat sauce. Sprinkle with cheese; stir until melted.

Nutrition Facts: 1-2/3 cups equals 362 calories, 11 g fat (5 g saturated fat), 53 mg cholesterol, 739 mg sodium, 38 g carbohydrate, 4 g fiber, 28 g protein. **Diabetic Exchanges:** 3 lean meat, 2 starch, 1 vegetable.

Makeover Li'l Cheddar Meat Loaves

PREP: 15 min. **BAKE:** 25 min. **YIELD:** 8 servings

JODIE MITCHELL • DENVER, PENNSYLVANIA

My husband goes wild for my meat loaf, but I didn't think it was very healthy. I asked the team at "Healthy Cooking" magazine to lighten it up, and this was the result. They cut about half the fat from my original recipe as well as 46 milligrams of cholesterol.

2	egg whites, beaten
3/4	cup fat-free milk
1	cup (4 oz.) shredded reduced-fat cheddar cheese
3/4	cup quick-cooking oats
1	medium onion, chopped
1	medium carrot, shredded
1/2	tsp. salt
3/4	lb. lean ground beef
2/3	cup ketchup
2	Tbsp. brown sugar
1-1/2	tsp. prepared mustard

1. In a large bowl, whisk egg whites and milk. Stir in the cheese, oats, onion, carrot and salt. Crumble beef over mixture and mix well. Shape into eight loaves; place in a 13-in. x 9-in. baking dish coated with cooking spray. In a small bowl, combine the ketchup, brown sugar and mustard; spoon over loaves.

2. Bake, uncovered, at 350° for 25-30 minutes or until no pink remains and a meat thermometer reads 160°.

Nutrition Facts: 1 meat loaf equals 187 calories, 7 g fat (3 g saturated fat), 36 mg cholesterol, 550 mg sodium, 18 g carbohydrate, 1 g fiber, 15 g protein. **Diabetic Exchanges:** 2 lean meat, 1 starch.

BURGUNDY BEEF STEW

Barbecued Beef Roast c

PREP: 15 min. **BAKE:** 2-1/2 hours
YIELD: 10 servings

LUANA KEMPF • ASHLEY, NORTH DAKOTA

My daughter makes this dish in the slow cooker, and it turns out just as great that way. Try the leftovers on sandwich buns.

1/2	cup ketchup
3	Tbsp. brown sugar
1	Tbsp. ground mustard
1	Tbsp. lemon juice
2	tsp. Worcestershire sauce
2	tsp. celery salt
2	tsp. pepper
1/2	tsp. garlic powder
1/2	tsp. onion powder

Dash ground nutmeg

3	drops hot pepper sauce
1	Tbsp. Liquid Smoke, optional
1	boneless beef top sirloin roast (3-1/2 lbs.)

1. In a bowl, combine the first 11 ingredients. Stir in Liquid Smoke if desired. Place roast on a rack in a shallow roasting pan; pour ketchup mixture over the top.

2. Cover and bake at 325° for 2-1/2 to 3 hours or until meat is tender. Remove meat to a serving platter and keep warm. Skim fat from pan juices and thicken juices if desired. Serve with beef.

Nutrition Facts: 4 ounces cooked beef with 2 tablespoons pan juices equals 228 calories, 8 g fat (3 g saturated fat), 84 mg cholesterol, 520 mg sodium, 8 g carbohydrate, trace fiber, 30 g protein. **Diabetic Exchanges:** 4 lean meat, 1/2 starch.

Burgundy Beef Stew

PREP: 25 min. **COOK:** 8 hours **YIELD:** 6 servings

MINDY ILAR • ST. ALBANS, WEST VIRGINIA

My stew brims with home-cooked comfort. I dress it up with sirloin, turkey bacon and a variety of herbs for a company-special dish.

1/2	cup all-purpose flour
1	lb. boneless beef sirloin steak, cut into 1/2-in. pieces
3	turkey bacon strips, diced
8	small red potatoes, halved
2	medium carrots, cut into 1-in. pieces
1	cup sliced fresh mushrooms
3/4	cup frozen pearl onions, thawed
3	garlic cloves, minced
1	bay leaf
1	tsp. dried marjoram
1/2	tsp. salt
1/2	tsp. dried thyme
1/4	tsp. pepper
1/2	cup reduced-sodium beef broth
1	cup Burgundy wine *or* additional reduced-sodium beef broth
6	cups hot cooked egg noodles

1. Place flour in a large resealable plastic bag. Add beef, a few pieces at a time, and shake to coat. In a large skillet coated with cooking spray, brown beef and bacon in batches on all sides.

2. Place beef and bacon in a 5-qt. slow cooker. Stir in the vegetables, garlic, seasonings, broth and wine or additional broth. Cover and cook on low for 8-9 hours or until the meat is tender.

3. Discard bay leaf. Thicken cooking juices if desired. Serve with noodles.

Nutrition Facts: 1 cup stew with 1 cup noodles equals 386 calories, 7 g fat (2 g saturated fat), 85 mg cholesterol, 415 mg sodium, 49 g carbohydrate, 4 g fiber, 24 g protein.

Makeover Cheese-Stuffed Shells

PREP: 35 min. **BAKE:** 50 min. **YIELD:** 12 servings

BETH FLEMING • DOWNERS GROVE, ILLINOIS

The original recipe behind this dish was one I found in a magazine. I asked for a lighter version and was happy to find this dish as the result. Most surprisingly, the revamped recipe doesn't call for any reduced-fat products.

- 3/4 lb. lean ground beef
- 1 Italian turkey sausage link (4 oz.), casing removed
- 1 large onion, chopped
- 1 pkg. (10 oz.) frozen chopped spinach, thawed and squeezed dry
- 1 cup ricotta cheese
- 1 egg, beaten
- 1-1/2 cups (6 oz.) shredded part-skim mozzarella cheese, *divided*
- 1-1/2 cups 4% cottage cheese
- 1 cup grated Parmesan cheese
- 1 cup (4 oz.) shredded sharp cheddar cheese
- 1 tsp. Italian seasoning
- 1/4 tsp. pepper
- 1/8 tsp. ground cinnamon, optional
- 24 jumbo pasta shells, cooked and drained

SAUCE:
- 3 cans (8 oz. *each*) no-salt-added tomato sauce
- 1 Tbsp. dried minced onion
- 1-1/2 tsp. dried basil
- 1-1/2 tsp. dried parsley flakes
- 2 garlic cloves, minced
- 1 tsp. sugar
- 1 tsp. dried oregano
- 1/4 tsp. pepper

1. Crumble beef and sausage into a large nonstick skillet; add onion. Cook and stir over medium heat until meat is no longer pink; drain.

2. Transfer to a large bowl. Stir in spinach, ricotta and egg. Add 1 cup mozzarella, cottage cheese, Parmesan, cheddar, Italian seasoning, pepper and cinnamon if desired; mix well.

3. Stuff pasta shells with meat mixture. Arrange in two 11-in. x 7-in. baking dishes coated with cooking spray. Combine sauce ingredients; spoon over shells. Cover and bake at 350° for 45 minutes. Uncover; sprinkle with remaining mozzarella. Bake 5-10 minutes longer or until bubbly and cheese is melted. Let stand for 5 minutes before serving.

Nutrition Facts: 2 stuffed shells equals 318 calories, 14 g fat (8 g saturated fat), 79 mg cholesterol, 714 mg sodium, 23 g carbohydrate, 2 g fiber, 25 g protein.

Freezer Burritos

PREP: 35 min. **COOK:** 15 min. **YIELD:** 12 servings

LAURA WINEMILLER • DELTA, PENNSYLVANIA

I love burritos, but the frozen ones are high in salt and chemicals, so I created these. They're great for fast dinners.

- 1-1/4 lbs. lean ground beef
- 1/4 cup finely chopped onion
- 1-1/4 cups salsa
- 2 Tbsp. reduced-sodium taco seasoning
- 2 cans (15 oz. *each*) pinto beans, rinsed and drained
- 1/2 cup water
- 2 cups (8 oz.) shredded reduced-fat cheddar cheese
- 12 flour tortillas (8 in.), warmed

1. In a large skillet, cook beef and onion over medium heat until the meat is no longer pink; drain. Stir in salsa and taco seasoning. Bring to a boil. Reduce heat; simmer, uncovered, for 2-3 minutes. Transfer to a large bowl; set aside.

2. In a food processor, combine pinto beans and water. Cover and process until almost smooth. Add to beef mixture. Stir in cheese.

3. Spoon 1/2 cup beef mixture down the center of each tortilla. Fold ends and sides over filling; roll up. Wrap each burrito in waxed paper and foil. Freeze for up to 1 month.

4. To use frozen burritos: Remove foil and waxed paper. Place one burrito on a microwave-safe plate. Microwave on high for 2-1/2 to 2-3/4 minutes or until a meat thermometer reads 165°, turning burrito over once. Let stand for 20 seconds.

Editor's Note: This recipe was tested in a 1,100-watt microwave.

Nutrition Facts: 1 burrito equals 345 calories, 11 g fat (4 g saturated fat), 36 mg cholesterol, 677 mg sodium, 40 g carbohydrate, 3 g fiber, 22 g protein. **Diabetic Exchanges:** 2-1/2 starch, 2 lean meat, 1/2 fat.

MAKEOVER CHEESE-STUFFED SHELLS

Asian Steak Wraps

PREP: 20 min. + marinating
COOK: 10 min. **YIELD:** 4 servings

TRISHA KRUSE • EAGLE, IDAHO

A zesty marinade with a splash of fresh lime juice makes these sesame-flavored wraps a treat. To speed prep time, use a 1-pound package of frozen onion-and-pepper mix.

1/4	cup lime juice
3	Tbsp. honey
1	Tbsp. reduced-sodium soy sauce
2	tsp. sesame oil
2	tsp. minced fresh gingerroot
1-1/2	tsp. minced fresh cilantro
1	lb. boneless beef sirloin steak, cut into thin strips
1/4	tsp. salt
1/4	tsp. pepper
1	medium onion, halved and thinly sliced
1	large green pepper, julienned
1	large sweet red pepper, julienned
4	flour tortillas (8 in.), warmed
2	oz. reduced-fat cream cheese
2	tsp. sesame seeds, toasted

1. In a small bowl, combine the first six ingredients. Pour 1/3 cup marinade into a large resealable plastic bag; add the beef. Seal bag and turn to coat; refrigerate for 1 hour. Add salt and pepper to remaining marinade; cover and refrigerate.

2. Drain beef and discard marinade. In a large nonstick skillet or wok coated with cooking spray, stir-fry beef until no longer pink; remove and keep warm. In the same pan, stir-fry onion and peppers until crisp-tender. Stir in reserved marinade. Return beef to the pan; heat through.

3. Spread tortillas with cream cheese; top with beef mixture and sprinkle with sesame seeds. Roll up.

Nutrition Facts: 1 wrap equals 402 calories, 14 g fat (5 g saturated fat), 74 mg cholesterol, 575 mg sodium, 41 g carbohydrate, 3 g fiber, 29 g protein. **Diabetic Exchanges:** 3 lean meat, 2 starch, 1 vegetable, 1 fat.

ASIAN STEAK WRAPS

Warm Beef & Spinach Salad C

PREP/TOTAL TIME: 20 min. **YIELD:** 4 servings

LINDA EGGERS • ALBANY, CALIFORNIA

Sliced beef and onion top this simple spinach salad. The dressing is thick, hearty and tangy—just the thing to bring it all together.

1/2	cup reduced-fat sour cream
2	Tbsp. fat-free milk
1	Tbsp. horseradish
1	Tbsp. prepared mustard

SALAD:

1	small red onion, sliced and separated into rings
1	lb. deli roast beef, cut into thin strips
1	pkg. (6 oz.) fresh baby spinach
2	plum tomatoes, cut into 1/4-in. slices

1. In a small bowl, combine the sour cream, milk, horseradish and mustard; set aside.

2. In a large nonstick skillet coated with cooking spray, cook and stir onion over medium-high heat until tender. Add beef; cook and stir until heated through.

3. In a salad bowl, combine spinach and tomatoes. Add beef mixture and dressing; toss to coat. Serve immediately.

Nutrition Facts: 1-3/4 cups equals 192 calories, 7 g fat (3 g saturated fat), 73 mg cholesterol, 733 mg sodium, 7 g carbohydrate, 2 g fiber, 27 g protein. **Diabetic Exchanges:** 3 lean meat, 1 vegetable, 1/2 fat.

Grilled Italian Meatball Burgers

PREP: 25 min. **GRILL:** 15 min. **YIELD:** 8 servings

PRISCILLA GILBERT • INDIAN HARBOUR BEACH, FLORIDA

These burgers are a big hit with kids and adults. I serve them with sliced green peppers, tomato, onions and a jar of crushed red peppers on the side for adults. Kids enjoy them best as is.

1	egg, lightly beaten
1/3	cup seasoned bread crumbs
3	garlic cloves, minced
1	tsp. dried oregano
1	tsp. dried basil
1/4	tsp. salt
1/4	tsp. dried thyme
1-1/2	lbs. lean ground beef
1/2	lb. Italian turkey sausage links, casings removed
3/4	cup shredded part-skim mozzarella cheese
8	kaiser rolls, split
1	cup roasted garlic Parmesan spaghetti sauce, warmed

1. In a large bowl, combine the first seven ingredients. Crumble beef and sausage over mixture and mix well. Shape into eight burgers.

2. Coat grill rack with cooking spray before starting the grill. Grill burgers, covered, over medium heat for 5-7 minutes on each side or until a meat thermometer reads 165° and juices run clear. Sprinkle burgers with cheese; cover and grill 2-3 minutes longer or until cheese is melted. Remove and keep warm.

3. Grill rolls, uncovered, for 1-2 minutes or until toasted. Serve burgers on rolls with spaghetti sauce.

EASY GRILLED FLANK STEAK

Nutrition Facts: 1 burger equals 399 calories, 14 g fat (5 g saturated fat), 102 mg cholesterol, 743 mg sodium, 35 g carbohydrate, 2 g fiber, 30 g protein.

Easy Grilled Flank Steak C

PREP: 20 min. + marinating
GRILL: 15 min. **YIELD:** 4 servings

VALERIE CHIPMAN • LISBON, MAINE

We've made this over an open fire pit, which is really yummy, and also on a gas grill. Try serving it with onions, peppers and potatoes grilled in a foil pack.

- 1 small onion, chopped
- 1/2 cup dry red wine or reduced-sodium beef broth
- 2 Tbsp. olive oil
- 2 garlic cloves, minced
- 1 tsp. brown sugar
- 1/4 tsp. pepper
- 2 fresh sage leaves, thinly sliced or 3/4 tsp. dried sage leaves
- 1/2 tsp. salt
- 1/2 tsp. minced fresh gingerroot
- 1 beef flank steak (1 lb.)

1. In a large resealable plastic bag, combine the first nine ingredients. Score the surface of the beef, making diamond shapes 1/4 in. deep; place in bag. Seal bag and turn to coat; refrigerate for 8 hours or overnight.

2. Coat grill rack with cooking spray before starting the grill. Drain and discard marinade. Grill beef, covered, over medium heat for 6-8 minutes on each side or until meat reaches desired doneness (for medium-rare, a meat thermometer should read 145°; medium, 160°; well-done, 170°).

3. Let stand for 5 minutes; thinly slice across the grain.

Nutrition Facts: 3 ounces cooked beef equals 205 calories, 11 g fat (4 g saturated fat), 54 mg cholesterol, 179 mg sodium, 2 g carbohydrate, trace fiber, 22 g protein. **Diabetic Exchanges:** 3 lean meat, 1/2 fat.

Sweet & Sour Meatballs

PREP: 20 min. **COOK:** 20 min. **YIELD:** 4 servings

MERYL BISZICK • ORLANDO, FLORIDA

This is one of the first things my mother taught me to make, and it's still one of my family's favorites.

- 1 can (15 ounces) tomato sauce
- 1 cup water, *divided*
- 1/2 cup raisins
- 3 Tbsp. brown sugar
- 1 Tbsp. lemon juice
- 1/4 cup seasoned bread crumbs
- 1/2 tsp. garlic powder
- 1/2 tsp. onion powder
- 1/2 tsp. pepper
- 1/8 tsp. seasoned salt
- 1/4 cup egg substitute
- 2 Tbsp. fat-free milk
- 1 lb. lean ground beef
- 1 Tbsp. all-purpose flour
- 2 cups hot cooked rice

1. In a Dutch oven, combine the tomato sauce, 3/4 cup water, raisins, brown sugar and lemon juice. Bring to a boil. Reduce heat; simmer, uncovered, for 10-15 minutes.

2. Meanwhile, in a large bowl, combine the bread crumbs, seasonings, egg substitute and milk. Crumble beef over mixture and mix well. Shape into 1-1/2-in. balls. Carefully add to tomato mixture. Cover and simmer for 20-25 minutes or until meatballs are no longer pink.

3. In a small bowl, combine flour and remaining water; stir into meatball mixture. Bring to a boil; cook and stir for 2 minutes or until slightly thickened. Serve with rice.

Nutrition Facts: about 5 meatballs with 1/2 cup sauce and 1/2 cup rice equals 442 calories, 10 g fat (4 g saturated fat), 69 mg cholesterol, 734 mg sodium, 60 g carbohydrate, 2 g fiber, 29 g protein.

ZESTY CHICKEN WITH ARTICHOKES

CHICKEN BROCCOLI STIR-FRY

SKINNY CACCIATORE

Chicken & Turkey

Whether whipping up a fast supper or preparing dinner for weekend guests, chicken and turkey make healthy choices that everyone enjoys. And with all of the poultry products available today, cooking right has never been so satisfying.

Skinny Cacciatore

PREP: 20 min. **COOK:** 25 min. **YIELD:** 6 servings

ANITA WEBB • HARTSVILLE, TENNESSEE

I needed a menu light on calories but heavy on flavor for my husband's associates. They weren't watching calories, but I was and wanted to eat, too. This recipe was a big success, and no one guessed I "skinnied" it down!

- 1-1/2 lbs. boneless skinless chicken breasts, cut into 1-in. pieces
- 3 tsp. canola oil, *divided*
- 1 large green pepper, chopped
- 2 celery ribs, thinly sliced
- 1 medium onion, chopped
- 1-3/4 cups sliced fresh mushrooms
- 1 medium carrot, shredded
- 3 garlic cloves, minced
- 1 can (29 oz.) tomato sauce
- 1 can (14-1/2 oz.) Italian diced tomatoes, undrained
- 1 bay leaf
- 3 tsp. dried oregano
- 2 tsp. dried basil
- 1/4 tsp. pepper
- 9 oz. uncooked spaghetti

Additional shredded carrot, optional

1. In a large nonstick skillet coated with cooking spray, brown chicken in 2 teaspoons oil; drain. Remove and keep warm. In the same skillet, saute the green pepper, celery and onion in remaining oil for 3 minutes. Add the mushrooms, carrot and garlic; saute 2-4 minutes longer or until vegetables are tender.

2. Stir in the tomato sauce, tomatoes and seasonings. Bring to a boil. Reduce heat; simmer, uncovered, for 10-12 minutes or until thickened. Meanwhile, cook spaghetti according to package directions.

3. Stir chicken into tomato mixture; cook for 8-12 minutes or until chicken is no longer pink. Discard bay leaf. Drain spaghetti; serve with chicken mixture. Garnish with additional carrot if desired.

Nutrition Facts: 1-1/3 cups chicken mixture with 2/3 cup spaghetti equals 393 calories, 6 g fat (1 g saturated fat), 63 mg cholesterol, 968 mg sodium, 52 g carbohydrate, 5 g fiber, 33 g protein.

Chicken Broccoli Stir-Fry

PREP: 20 min. + marinating
COOK: 15 min. **YIELD:** 4 servings

CLARA COULSTON • WASHINGTON COURT HOUSE, OHIO

This easily prepared recipe offers scrumptious but mild Asian flavor. It makes a nicely balanced meal the whole family will love.

- 1/2 cup reduced-sodium chicken broth
- 6 Tbsp. reduced-sodium soy sauce
- 1/4 cup water
- 1/4 cup rice vinegar
- 2 garlic cloves, minced

Dash cayenne pepper

- 1 lb. boneless skinless chicken breasts, cut into 3/4-in. cubes
- 2 tsp. cornstarch
- 4 tsp. canola oil, *divided*
- 2 cups fresh broccoli florets
- 1 cup sliced fresh mushrooms
- 1/2 cup canned sliced water chestnuts
- 1/2 cup canned bamboo shoots
- 2 green onions, thinly sliced
- 2 cups hot cooked rice

1. In a small bowl, combine the first six ingredients. Cover and refrigerate 3/4 cup. Pour remaining marinade into a large resealable plastic bag; add the chicken. Seal bag and turn to coat; refrigerate for 1-2 hours. Drain chicken and discard marinade.

2. In a small bowl, combine cornstarch and reserved marinade until smooth; set aside.

3. In a large skillet or wok, stir-fry chicken in 2 teaspoons oil until no longer pink. Remove and keep warm. Stir-fry broccoli in remaining oil for 2 minutes. Add mushrooms; stir-fry 2 minutes longer. Add the water chestnuts, bamboo shoots and onions; cook 1-2 minutes longer or until vegetables are crisp-tender.

4. Stir cornstarch mixture and add to the pan. Bring to a boil; cook and stir for 2 minutes or until thickened. Add chicken; heat through. Serve with rice.

Nutrition Facts: 1 cup stir-fry with 1/2 cup rice equals 316 calories, 8 g fat (1 g saturated fat), 63 mg cholesterol, 719 mg sodium, 32 g carbohydrate, 2 g fiber, 28 g protein. **Diabetic Exchanges:** 3 very lean meat, 1-1/2 starch, 1 vegetable, 1 fat.

Grilled Apple Chicken C

PREP: 10 min. + marinating
GRILL: 10 min. **YIELD:** 6 servings

EILEEN RANDE • FARMINGTON HILLS, MICHIGAN

I like to slice this chicken into strips, and serve them on a bed of salad greens on hot summer days. Light on fat and sodium and a good source of lean protein, this dish is a great fit for a heart-healthy diet.

3/4	cup unsweetened apple juice *or* apple cider
1/3	cup lemon juice
3	Tbsp. reduced-sodium soy sauce
3	Tbsp. honey
1/4	tsp. garlic powder
1/4	tsp. ground ginger
4-1/2	tsp. canola oil
6	boneless skinless chicken breast halves (4 oz. *each*)

1. In a small bowl, combine the first six ingredients. Set aside 1/3 cup juice mixture. Add oil to the remaining juice mixture; pour into a large resealable bag. Add the chicken. Seal bag and turn to coat; refrigerate for at least 4 hours. Cover and refrigerate reserved juice mixture.

2. Coat grill rack with cooking spray before starting the grill. Drain chicken and discard marinade. Grill, covered, over medium heat for 5-7 minutes on each side or until juices run clear, basting occasionally with reserved juice mixture.

Nutrition Facts: 1 chicken breast half equals 160 calories, 4 g fat (1 g saturated fat), 63 mg cholesterol, 207 mg sodium, 7 g carbohydrate, trace fiber, 23 g protein. **Diabetic Exchanges:** 3 very lean meat, 1/2 starch.

Chicken Pesto Pizza

PREP: 35 min. + rising
BAKE: 20 min. **YIELD:** 8 slices

HEATHER THOMPSON • WOODLAND HILLS, CALIFORNIA

This is the only pizza I make anymore. We love it! Keeping the spices simple helps the flavor of the chicken and vegetables to come through.

2	tsp. active dry yeast
1	cup warm water (110° to 115°)
2-3/4	cups bread flour
1	Tbsp. plus 2 tsp. olive oil, *divided*
1	Tbsp. sugar
1-1/2	tsp. salt, *divided*
1/2	lb. boneless skinless chicken breasts, cut into 1/2-in. pieces
1	small onion, halved and thinly sliced
1/2	*each* small green, sweet red and yellow peppers, julienned
1/2	cup sliced fresh mushrooms
3	Tbsp. prepared pesto
1-1/2	cups (6 oz.) shredded part-skim mozzarella cheese
1/4	tsp. pepper

1. In a large mixing bowl, dissolve yeast in warm water. Beat in the flour, 1 tablespoon oil, sugar and 1 teaspoon salt.

2. Turn onto a lightly floured surface; knead until smooth and elastic, about 6-8 minutes. Place in a bowl coated with cooking spray, turning once to coat top. Cover and let rise in a warm place until doubled, about 1 hour.

3. In a large nonstick skillet over medium heat, cook the chicken, onion, peppers and mushrooms in remaining oil until chicken is no longer pink and vegetables are tender. Remove chicken mixture from the heat; set aside.

4. Punch dough down; roll into a 15-in. circle. Transfer to a 14-in. pizza pan. Build up edges slightly. Spread with pesto. Top with chicken mixture and cheese. Sprinkle with pepper and remaining salt.

5. Bake at 400° for 18-20 minutes or until crust and cheese are lightly browned.

Nutrition Facts: 1 slice equals 293 calories, 10 g fat (3 g saturated fat), 30 mg cholesterol, 601 mg sodium, 35 g carbohydrate, 2 g fiber, 18 g protein. **Diabetic Exchanges:** 2 starch, 1 lean meat, 1 fat.

Slow-Cooked Curry Chicken

PREP: 25 min. **COOK:** 4 hours **YIELD:** 6 servings

HELEN TOULANTIS • WANTAGH, NEW YORK

We adopted three children from Thailand, and we all love the spicy flavors in this entree.

6	boneless skinless chicken breast halves (6 oz. *each*)
1-1/4	tsp. salt
1	can (14 oz.) light coconut milk
1	tsp. curry powder
1/2	tsp. ground turmeric
1/2	tsp. cayenne pepper
3	green onions, sliced, *divided*
2	Tbsp. cornstarch
2	Tbsp. cold water
1 to 2	Tbsp. lime juice
3	cups hot cooked rice

1. Sprinkle chicken with salt. In a large nonstick skillet coated with cooking spray, brown chicken on both sides. Place in a 5-qt. slow cooker.

2. Combine the coconut milk, curry, turmeric and cayenne; pour over chicken. Sprinkle with half of the onions. Cover and cook on low for 3-1/2 to 4-1/2 hours or until chicken is tender.

3. Combine cornstarch and water until smooth; stir into slow cooker. Cover and cook on high for 30 minutes or until sauce is thickened. Stir in lime juice.

Serve chicken and sauce over rice; sprinkle with remaining onions.

Nutrition Facts: 1 chicken breast half with 1/4 cup sauce and 1/2 cup rice equals 351 calories, 9 g fat (5 g saturated fat), 94 mg cholesterol, 589 mg sodium, 27 g carbohydrate, 1 g fiber, 37 g protein. **Diabetic Exchanges:** 5 very lean meat, 1-1/2 starch, 1 fat.

Baked Chicken Chimichangas

PREP: 20 min. **BAKE:** 20 min. **YIELD:** 6 servings

RICKEY MADDEN • CLINTON, SOUTH CAROLINA

I developed this quick and easy recipe through trial and error. I used to garnish with sour cream, but eliminated it to lighten the dish. My friends all love this; it's much healthier than the fried version of chimichangas.

1-1/2	cups cubed cooked chicken breast
1-1/2	cups picante sauce, *divided*
1/2	cup shredded reduced-fat cheddar cheese
2/3	cup chopped green onions, *divided*
1	tsp. ground cumin
1	tsp. dried oregano
6	flour tortillas (8 in.)
1	Tbsp. butter, melted

1. In a small bowl, combine the chicken, 3/4 cup picante sauce, cheese, 1/4 cup onions, cumin and oregano. Spoon 1/2 cup mixture down the center of each tortilla. Fold sides and ends over filling and roll up. Place seam side down in a 15-in. x 10-in. baking pan coated with cooking spray. Brush with butter.

2. Bake, uncovered, at 375° for 20-25 minutes or until heated through. Top with remaining picante sauce and onions.

Nutrition Facts: 1 chimichanga equals 269 calories, 8 g fat (3 g saturated fat), 39 mg cholesterol, 613 mg sodium, 31 g carbohydrate, 1 g fiber, 17 g protein. **Diabetic Exchanges:** 2 very lean meat, 1-1/2 starch, 1 vegetable, 1 fat.

BAKED CHICKEN CHIMICHANGAS

CHICKEN PESTO PIZZA

Oregano Olive Chicken C

PREP: 15 min. **COOK:** 30 min. **YIELD:** 8 servings

CONSUELO LEWTER • MURFREESBORO, TENNESSEE

Capers, olives, oregano and mint combine to give this dish a wonderful taste and aroma as it simmers on the stovetop. Hard to believe this is light.

- 1   broiler/fryer chicken (4 lbs.), cut up and skin removed
- 1/4   tsp. pepper
- 2   Tbsp. olive oil
- 1/2   cup white wine *or* reduced-sodium chicken broth
- 1/2   cup chopped pimiento-stuffed olives
- 1/4   cup capers, drained
- 2   Tbsp. minced fresh oregano
- 1   Tbsp. minced fresh mint
- 1   Tbsp. cider vinegar
- 2   garlic cloves, minced
- 1   tsp. minced fresh thyme

1. Sprinkle chicken with pepper. In a large nonstick skillet coated with cooking spray, brown chicken on all sides in oil. Remove and keep warm. Drain drippings from skillet.

Removing the skin from chicken wings can be tricky. When buying chicken for **Oregano Olive Chicken** you may want to ask the butcher to do it for you.

OREGANO OLIVE CHICKEN

2. Combine the remaining ingredients; pour into skillet, stirring to loosen browned bits. Bring to a boil. Carefully return chicken to the pan. Reduce heat; cover and simmer for 20-25 minutes or until chicken juices run clear.

Nutrition Facts: 3 ounces cooked chicken with 2 tablespoons olive mixture equals 217 calories, 11 g fat (2 g saturated fat), 73 mg cholesterol, 370 mg sodium, 2 g carbohydrate, trace fiber, 24 g protein. **Diabetic Exchanges:** 3 lean meat, 1 fat.

Marinara Turkey Meatballs

PREP: 20 min. **COOK:** 25 min. **YIELD:** 6 servings

HEALTHY COOKING TEST KITCHEN

Frozen spinach and a jar of spaghetti sauce speed up the prep time for these meatballs. You can even freeze the leftovers.

- 1   pkg. (10 oz.) frozen chopped spinach, thawed and squeezed dry
- 1/2   cup seasoned bread crumbs
- 1   small onion, finely chopped
- 3   Tbsp. minced fresh parsley
- 2   garlic cloves, minced
- 1/4   tsp. ground nutmeg
- 1/4   tsp. ground allspice
- 1/4   tsp. pepper
- 1-1/4   lbs. lean ground turkey
- 1   jar (26 oz.) meatless spaghetti sauce
- 9   oz. uncooked spaghetti

1. In a large bowl, combine the spinach, bread crumbs, onion, parsley, garlic, nutmeg, allspice and pepper. Crumble turkey over mixture and mix well.

2. Shape into 24 meatballs. Place on a broiler pan coated with cooking spray. Broil 4-6 in. from the heat for 8 minutes. Turn; broil 3-5 minutes longer or until meat is no longer pink.

3. Transfer meatballs to a Dutch oven; add spaghetti sauce. Bring to a boil. Reduce heat; cover and simmer for 10 minutes. Meanwhile, cook spaghetti according to package directions; drain. Serve spaghetti with meatballs and sauce.

Nutrition Facts: 4 meatballs with 1/3 cup sauce and 2/3 cup spaghetti equals 405 calories, 9 g fat (2 g saturated fat), 75 mg cholesterol, 812 mg sodium, 53 g carbohydrate, 5 g fiber, 27 g protein.

MARINARA TURKEY MEATBALLS

Grilled Jerk Turkey C

PREP: 15 min. + marinating
GRILL: 15 min. **YIELD:** 4 servings

DIANE HALFERTY • CORPUS CHRISTI, TEXAS

Seasoned with ginger, Caribbean jerk spices and jalapeno pepper, this simple grilled main dish is more tangy than hot and spicy. It's wonderful for backyard barbecues!

1/4	cup rice vinegar
1/4	cup orange juice
2	Tbsp. canola oil
2	Tbsp. reduced-sodium soy sauce
2	green onions, chopped
2	garlic cloves, minced
4	tsp. chopped jalapeno pepper
1	Tbsp. Caribbean jerk seasoning
1-1/2	tsp. packed brown sugar
1-1/2	tsp. minced fresh gingerroot
1/2	tsp. salt
1	pkg. (20 oz.) turkey breast tenderloins

1. In a small bowl, combine the first 11 ingredients. Pour 1/2 cup marinade into a large resealable plastic bag; add the turkey. Seal bag and turn to coat; refrigerate for 2 hours. Cover and refrigerate remaining marinade.

2. Coat grill rack with cooking spray before starting the grill. Drain turkey and discard marinade. Grill, covered, over medium heat for 7-10 minutes on each side or until a meat thermometer reads 170°, basting occasionally with reserved marinade. Cut into slices.

Editor's Note: When cutting hot peppers, disposable gloves are recommended. Avoid touching your face.

Nutrition Facts: 4 ounces cooked turkey equals 195 calories, 5 g fat (1 g saturated fat), 69 mg cholesterol, 481 mg sodium, 3 g carbohydrate, trace fiber, 33 g protein. **Diabetic Exchanges:** 5 very lean meat, 1/2 fat.

Turkey Fruit Kabobs

PREP: 15 min. + marinating
GRILL: 10 min. **YIELD:** 4 servings

EDIE DESPAIN • LOGAN, UTAH

This is a citrusy favorite for the grill; it's very simple to prepare and absolutely delicious. It makes a healthy dish for summer picnics and family get-togethers.

3/4	cup lemonade concentrate
3	Tbsp. canola oil
3	Tbsp. reduced-sodium soy sauce
1	lb. turkey breast tenderloins, cut into 1-in. cubes
1	honeydew half, seeded, peeled and cut into 1-1/2-in. cubes
1	medium mango, peeled and cut into 1-1/2-in. cubes

1. In a small bowl, combine the lemonade concentrate, oil and soy sauce. Pour 1/2 cup marinade into a large resealable plastic bag; add the turkey. Seal bag and turn to coat; refrigerate for 2 hours. Cover and refrigerate remaining marinade.

2. Coat grill rack with cooking spray before starting the grill. Drain and discard marinade. On four metal or soaked wooden skewers, alternately thread turkey and fruits. Grill, covered, over medium-hot heat for 3-4 minutes on each side or until juices run clear, basting frequently with reserved marinade.

Nutrition Facts: 1 kabob equals 330 calories, 9 g fat (1 g saturated fat), 56 mg cholesterol, 380 mg sodium, 38 g carbohydrate, 2 g fiber, 28 g protein. **Diabetic Exchanges:** 3 very lean meat, 1-1/2 fat, 1 starch, 1 fruit.

DIJON-CRUSTED CHICKEN BREASTS

Dijon-Crusted Chicken Breasts C

PREP/TOTAL TIME: 25 min. **YIELD:** 4 servings

JACQUI CORREA • LANDING, NEW JERSEY

If you're craving fried chicken, this will hit the spot! A crisp, flavorful coating makes this easy weeknight entree feel special and indulgent.

1/3	cup dry bread crumbs
1	Tbsp. grated Parmesan cheese
1	tsp. Italian seasoning
1/2	tsp. dried thyme
1/4	tsp. salt
1/4	tsp. pepper
4	boneless skinless chicken breast halves (4 oz. *each*)
2	Tbsp. Dijon mustard
1	tsp. olive oil
1	tsp. reduced-fat margarine

1. Place the first six ingredients in a shallow bowl. Brush chicken with mustard; roll in crumb mixture.

2. In a large skillet, cook chicken in oil and margarine over medium heat for 5-6 minutes on each side or until juices run clear.

Editor's Note: This recipe was tested with Parkay Light stick margarine.

Nutrition Facts: 1 chicken breast half equals 169 calories, 5 g fat (1 g saturated fat), 63 mg cholesterol, 380 mg sodium, 6 g carbohydrate, trace fiber, 24 g protein. **Diabetic Exchanges:** 3 very lean meat, 1/2 starch, 1/2 fat.

Red Beans and Rice

PREP: 20 min. + soaking
COOK: 2-1/2 hours **YIELD:** 4 servings

HEALTHY COOKING TEST KITCHEN

Turkey kielbasa is right at home with red beans and rice in this lighter main dish. The hearty meal will satisfy on cool nights.

1	cup dried red beans
6	oz. smoked turkey kielbasa, halved and cut into 1/4-in. slices
1	celery rib, chopped
1	small onion, chopped
1	small green pepper, chopped
2	tsp. canola oil
2	garlic cloves, minced
3	cups water
2	bay leaves
1/2	tsp. dried thyme
1/2	tsp. hot pepper sauce
2	cups hot cooked rice

1. Sort beans and rinse with cold water. Place in a Dutch oven; add water to cover by 2 in. Bring to a boil; boil for 2 minutes. Remove from the heat; cover and let stand for 1-4 hours or until beans are softened.

2. Drain and rinse beans, discarding liquid; set beans aside. In the same pan, saute the kielbasa, celery, onion and green pepper in oil until vegetables are crisp-tender. Add garlic; saute 2 minutes longer.

3. Stir in the beans, water, bay leaves, thyme and hot pepper sauce. Bring to a boil. Reduce heat; cover and simmer for 2 hours or until the beans are tender, stirring occasionally.

4. Uncover and simmer 10-15 minutes longer or until the beans reach desired consistency. Discard the bay leaves. Serve with rice.

Nutrition Facts: 3/4 cup beans with 1/2 cup rice equals 347 calories, 4 g fat (1 g saturated fat), 15 mg cholesterol, 380 mg sodium, 59 g carbohydrate, 8 g fiber, 18 g protein.

Hearty Chicken Casserole

PREP: 15 min. **BAKE:** 25 min. **YIELD:** 6 servings

JENNY EBERT • EAU CLAIRE, WISCONSIN

This delectable high-fiber dish with Southwest flavors is sure to win over your family.

2	celery ribs, chopped
1	small onion, chopped
1-1/2	tsp. olive oil
3	cups cubed cooked chicken breast
1	can (16 oz.) kidney beans, rinsed and drained
1	can (15 oz.) black beans, rinsed and drained
1	Tbsp. chili powder
2	tsp. ground cumin
1	can (14-1/2 oz.) no-salt-added diced tomatoes, undrained
1	can (10-3/4 oz.) reduced-fat reduced-sodium condensed cream of mushroom soup, undiluted
1	cup (4 oz.) shredded reduced-fat cheddar cheese

1. In a large nonstick skillet coated with cooking spray, saute celery and onion in oil until tender. Stir in chicken, beans, chili powder and cumin; heat through.

2. Transfer to a shallow 2-1/2-qt. baking dish coated with cooking spray. Combine the tomatoes and soup; pour over the chicken mixture.

3. Bake, uncovered, at 350° for 20 minutes. Sprinkle with cheese. Bake 5-10 minutes longer or until heated through and the cheese is melted.

Nutrition Facts: 1-1/2 cups equals 346 calories, 9 g fat (4 g saturated fat), 71 mg cholesterol, 670 mg sodium, 32 g carbohydrate, 9 g fiber, 35 g protein. **Diabetic Exchanges:** 4 very lean meat, 2 starch, 1 vegetable, 1 fat.

Chicken Athena **C**

PREP: 15 min. **COOK:** 4 hours **YIELD:** 6 servings

RADELLE KNAPPENBERGER • OVIEDO, FLORIDA

Greek flavors abound in this tasty, tender slow cooker chicken. It makes a great weeknight meal over rice or noodles.

6	boneless skinless chicken breast halves (6 oz. *each*)
2	medium onions, chopped
1/3	cup sun-dried tomatoes (not packed in oil), chopped
1/3	cup pitted Greek olives, chopped
2	Tbsp. lemon juice
1	Tbsp. balsamic vinegar
3	garlic cloves, minced
1/2	teaspoon salt

1. Place chicken in a 3-qt. slow cooker. Add the remaining ingredients.

2. Cover and cook on low for 4 hours or until a meat thermometer reads 170°.

Nutrition Facts: 1 chicken breast half equals 237 calories, 6 g fat (1 g saturated fat), 94 mg cholesterol, 467 mg sodium, 8 g carbohydrate, 1 g fiber, 36 g protein. **Diabetic Exchanges:** 5 very lean meat, 1 vegetable, 1 fat.

Overcooking chicken breasts in a slow cooker can lead to rubbery meat. When simmering **Chicken Athena**, use a thermometer to ensure the dish is just right.

CHICKEN ATHENA

HEARTY CHICKEN CASSEROLE

Sausage 'n' Chicken Skillet

PREP: 15 min. **COOK:** 40 min. **YIELD:** 4 servings

JOANNA IOVINO • COMMACK, NEW YORK

Chicken and rice was a staple at my parents' house, but the chicken never turned out quite right. I enjoy this recipe much more now that I use skinless chicken and kielbasa.

1/2	lb. boneless skinless chicken breasts, cubed
1/2	tsp. dried thyme, *divided*
1/4	tsp. pepper, *divided*
1-1/2	tsp. canola oil
1/4	lb. smoked turkey kielbasa, cut into 1/4-in. slices
1	small onion, finely chopped
1	small green pepper, finely chopped
2	garlic cloves, minced
2	cups water
1	cup uncooked long grain rice
1/2	tsp. reduced-sodium chicken bouillon granules
1/2	tsp. hot pepper sauce

1. Sprinkle chicken with 1/4 teaspoon thyme and 1/8 teaspoon pepper. In a large nonstick skillet, saute chicken in oil until no longer pink. Remove chicken and keep warm.

2. In the same skillet, saute the kielbasa, onion, green pepper and garlic until vegetables are tender. Stir in the water, rice, bouillon, hot pepper sauce, and remaining thyme and pepper. Bring to a boil. Reduce heat; cover and simmer for 18-20 minutes or until liquid is absorbed and rice is tender.

3. Return chicken to the pan; heat through.

Nutrition Facts: 1-1/4 cups equals 296 calories, 5 g fat (1 g saturated fat), 49 mg cholesterol, 352 mg sodium, 41 g carbohydrate, 1 g fiber, 20 g protein. **Diabetic Exchanges:** 2-1/2 starch, 2 very lean meat, 1/2 fat.

Turkey-Stuffed Bell Peppers

PREP: 30 min. **BAKE:** 20 min. **YIELD:** 5 servings

JUDY HAND-TRUITT • BIRMINGHAM, ALABAMA

This dish is so tasty, no one even realizes I don't use real cheddar cheese. Round out the entree with a side of rice or a healthy salad of spinach greens.

5	medium green peppers
1	large onion, chopped
2	tsp. olive oil
1-1/4	lbs. extra-lean ground turkey
2	tsp. ground cumin
1	tsp. Italian seasoning
1	garlic clove, minced
1/2	tsp. salt
1/2	tsp. pepper
1	pkg. (7 oz.) shredded cheddar-flavored soy cheese
2	medium tomatoes, finely chopped
1-1/2	cups soft bread crumbs
1/4	tsp. paprika

1. Cut peppers in half lengthwise and discard seeds. In a large kettle, cook peppers in boiling water for 3-5 minutes. Drain and rinse in cold water; set aside.

2. In a large skillet, saute onion in oil until tender. Add turkey, cumin, Italian seasoning, garlic, salt and pepper; cook and stir over medium heat until meat is no longer pink.

3. Transfer to a large bowl; stir in the soy cheese, tomatoes and bread crumbs. Spoon into pepper halves. Place in a 15-in. x 10-in. baking pan coated with cooking spray. Sprinkle with paprika.

4. Bake, uncovered, at 325° for 20-25 minutes or until heated through and peppers are tender.

Editor's Note: Some breads/bread crumbs are made with milk. To ensure this recipe is lactose-free, read the label or ask your baker.

Nutrition Facts: 2 filled pepper halves equals 323 calories, 10 g fat (trace saturated fat), 45 mg cholesterol, 771 mg sodium, 20 g carbohydrate, 4 g fiber, 40 g protein. **Diabetic Exchanges:** 5 very lean meat, 2 vegetable, 1 starch, 1/2 fat.

TURKEY-STUFFED BELL PEPPERS

SAUSAGE 'N' CHICKEN SKILLET

Zesty Chicken With Artichokes

PREP: 15 min. **COOK:** 25 min. **YIELD:** 4 servings

CHRISTINE ECKER • LINWOOD, NEW JERSEY

Our children love chicken. Both can be finicky eaters and they're not crazy about sauces, but they adore this no-fuss dish!

2	tsp. dried thyme
2	tsp. grated lemon peel
1/4	tsp. salt
1/4	tsp. pepper
4	boneless skinless chicken breast halves (4 oz. *each*)
4	tsp. olive oil, *divided*
1	large onion, chopped
2	garlic cloves, minced
1	can (14 oz.) water-packed artichoke hearts, rinsed, drained and halved
3/4	cup white wine *or* reduced-sodium chicken broth
1/4	cup sliced pimiento-stuffed olives, drained
1/4	cup sliced ripe olives, drained

1. Combine the thyme, lemon peel, salt and pepper; rub over chicken. In a large nonstick skillet, brown chicken in 2 teaspoons oil; remove and set aside.

2. In the same skillet, saute onion and garlic in remaining oil until tender. Stir in the artichokes, wine and olives. Return chicken to the pan. Bring to a boil. Reduce heat; cover and simmer for 6-8 minutes or until the chicken juices run clear.

3. Remove chicken and keep warm. Simmer artichoke mixture, uncovered, for 2-3 minutes or until liquid has evaporated; serve with chicken.

Nutrition Facts: 1 chicken breast half with 1/2 cup artichoke mixture equals 256 calories, 10 g fat (1 g saturated fat), 63 mg cholesterol, 706 mg sodium, 12 g carbohydrate, 2 g fiber, 26 g protein. **Diabetic Exchanges:** 3 very lean meat, 2 vegetable, 1-1/2 fat.

Chicken Broccoli Bake

PREP: 25 min. **BAKE:** 35 min. **YIELD:** 6 servings

PHYLLIS SCHMALZ • KANSAS CITY, KANSAS

Get the benefits of broccoli while enjoying this guilt-free casserole. It's perfect when cool weather sets in.

4	cups uncooked egg noodles
1	medium onion, chopped
4	tsp. butter
5	Tbsp. all-purpose flour
1/2	tsp. salt
1/2	tsp. pepper
1	can (14-1/2 oz.) reduced-sodium chicken broth
1	cup fat-free milk
3	cups cubed cooked chicken breast
3	cups frozen chopped broccoli, thawed and drained
1	cup (4 oz.) shredded reduced-fat cheddar cheese

1. Cook the noodles according to package directions. Meanwhile, in a large nonstick saucepan over medium heat, cook the chopped onion in butter until tender.

2. Stir in the flour, salt and pepper until blended. Gradually stir in broth and milk. Bring to a boil; cook and stir for 1-2 minutes or until thickened.

3. Remove from the heat. Drain noodles; place in a 2-qt. baking dish coated with cooking spray. Stir in 1 cup sauce. Layer with chicken, broccoli and remaining sauce.

4. Cover and bake at 350° for 30 minutes. Uncover; sprinkle the casserole with cheese. Bake 5-10 minutes longer or until the casserole is heated through and the cheese is melted.

Nutrition Facts: 1 cup equals 354 calories, 10 g fat (5 g saturated fat), 102 mg cholesterol, 601 mg sodium, 33 g carbohydrate, 3 g fiber, 34 g protein. **Diabetic Exchanges:** 4 very lean meat, 2 starch, 1 vegetable, 1 fat.

Garlic Cranberry Chicken C

PREP: 30 min. **BAKE:** 70 min. **YIELD:** 6 servings

LESLEY PEW • LYNN, MASSACHUSETTS

I enjoy serving this tender main dish with a savory garlic sauce to family and friends. It's perfect alongside a simple salad of mixed greens.

8	green onions, chopped
2	celery ribs, chopped
2	medium carrots, chopped
1/2	cup dried cranberries
1	whole garlic bulb, cloves separated and peeled
1	bay leaf
1-1/2	cups white wine *or* reduced-sodium chicken broth
1/2	tsp. salt
1/2	tsp. white pepper
1/2	tsp. dried basil
6	bone-in chicken breast halves (7 oz. *each*)

SAUCE:

1/4	cup dried cranberries
1/4	cup boiling water
4-1/2	tsp. butter
3	Tbsp. all-purpose flour
1/4	tsp. salt
1/8	tsp. white pepper
1/4	cup fat-free half-and-half

1. Place onions, celery, carrots, cranberries, garlic and bay leaf in a 13-in. x 9-in. baking dish coated with cooking spray. Add wine or broth. Combine salt, pepper and basil; sprinkle over chicken. Place over vegetable mixture.

2. Bake, uncovered, at 350° for 70-80 minutes or until juices run clear. Remove chicken; keep warm. Strain cooking liquid; discard vegetable mixture. Skim fat and set aside 1-1/3 cups.

3. For sauce, place cranberries in a small bowl; add boiling water. Let stand for 3 minutes; drain and discard liquid. Set berries aside.

4. In a nonstick saucepan coated with cooking spray, melt butter. Stir in flour, salt and pepper until smooth. Gradually whisk in reserved cooking liquid. Bring to a boil; cook 1-2 minutes longer or until thickened. Stir in half-and-half and reserved cranberries; heat through. Serve with chicken.

Nutrition Facts: 1 chicken breast half (skin removed) with 1/4 cup sauce equals 224 calories, 6 g fat (3 g saturated fat), 86 mg cholesterol, 393 mg sodium, 9 g carbohydrate, trace fiber, 30 g protein. **Diabetic Exchanges:** 4 very lean meat, 1/2 starch, 1/2 fat.

Turkey Meat Loaf

PREP: 20 min. **BAKE:** 50 min. **YIELD:** 6 servings

JOHN COTTI-DIAZ • DEL RIO, TEXAS

I added sweet red pepper, garlic and a sweet-and-sour sauce to my mom's basic recipe for this tasty entree.

1	egg, lightly beaten
1	can (8 oz.) tomato sauce, *divided*
1	cup soft bread crumbs
1/4	cup finely chopped onion
1/4	cup finely chopped green pepper
1/4	cup finely chopped sweet red pepper
1-1/2	tsp. garlic powder
1/4	tsp. salt
1/8	tsp. pepper
1-1/2	lbs. lean ground turkey
1	can (10-3/4 oz.) reduced-sodium condensed tomato soup, undiluted
2	Tbsp. brown sugar
2	Tbsp. cider vinegar
2	Tbsp. ketchup
2	Tbsp. prepared mustard

1. In a large bowl, combine the egg, 1/2 cup tomato sauce, bread crumbs, onion, peppers, garlic powder, salt and pepper. Crumble turkey over mixture and mix well.

2. In an 11-in. x 7-in. baking dish coated with cooking spray, pat turkey mixture into a 9-in. x 4-in. loaf. Bake, uncovered, at 350° for 30 minutes; drain if necessary.

3. Meanwhile, combine the soup, brown sugar, vinegar, ketchup, mustard and remaining tomato sauce. Pour 1/2 cup over meat loaf. Bake 20-30 minutes longer or until a meat thermometer reads 165°. Warm remaining sauce; serve with meat loaf.

Nutrition Facts: 1 slice with 2 tablespoons sauce equals 282 calories, 11 g fat (3 g saturated fat), 125 mg cholesterol, 736 mg sodium, 21 g carbohydrate, 2 g fiber, 23 g protein. **Diabetic Exchanges:** 3 lean meat, 1-1/2 starch.

Turkey & Bulgur Salad

PREP: 25 min. + standing **YIELD:** 6 servings

CAROLE RESNICK • CLEVELAND, OHIO

Cranberry juice concentrate gives this wonderful luncheon salad a burst of flavor. Line a serving platter with lettuce leaves and mound the salad in the center for a pretty presentation.

1-1/2	cups reduced-sodium chicken broth
1/2	cup water
1	cup bulgur
2	cups cubed cooked turkey breast
1	small cucumber, finely chopped
1	cup garbanzo beans *or* chickpeas, rinsed and drained
3	green onions, thinly sliced
1/4	cup sliced ripe olives
3	Tbsp. dried cranberries
1/4	cup olive oil
3	Tbsp. lime juice
2	Tbsp. cranberry juice concentrate
1	cup cherry tomatoes, halved
3	Tbsp. minced fresh parsley

1. In a small saucepan, bring broth and water to a boil. Place bulgur in a large bowl. Stir in broth mixture. Cover and let stand for 30 minutes or until most of the liquid is absorbed. Drain. Stir in the turkey, cucumber, beans, onions, olives and cranberries.

2. In a small bowl, whisk the oil, lime juice and cranberry juice concentrate. Stir into bulgur mixture.

Add tomatoes and parsley; gently toss to coat. Serve at room temperature or chilled.

Nutrition Facts: 1-1/2 cups equals 302 calories, 11 g fat (2 g saturated fat), 40 mg cholesterol, 283 mg sodium, 32 g carbohydrate, 7 g fiber, 20 g protein. **Diabetic Exchanges:** 2 starch, 2 very lean meat, 2 fat.

Island Jerk Chicken C

PREP: 15 min. + marinating
GRILL: 10 min. **YIELD:** 4 servings

LYNN DAVIS • ST. LOUIS PARK, MINNESOTA

My husband's crazy about hot sauce and I'm not, but I absolutely love this spicy chicken!

3/4	cup water
4	green onions, chopped
2	Tbsp. canola oil
1	Tbsp. hot pepper sauce
4	tsp. ground allspice
3	garlic cloves, minced
2	tsp. ground cinnamon
1	tsp. salt
1	tsp. ground nutmeg
4	boneless skinless chicken breast halves (4 oz. *each*)

1. In a small saucepan, combine the first nine ingredients; bring to a boil. Reduce heat; simmer, uncovered, for 10 minutes. Cool to room temperature.

2. Pour 1/2 cup marinade into a large resealable plastic bag; add chicken. Seal bag and turn to coat; refrigerate overnight. Transfer remaining marinade to a small bowl; cover and refrigerate for basting.

3. Coat grill rack with cooking spray before starting. Drain and discard marinade. Grill chicken, covered, over medium heat for 4-7 minutes on each side or until juices run clear, basting occasionally with reserved marinade.

Nutrition Facts: 1 chicken breast half equals 168 calories, 7 g fat (1 g saturated fat), 63 mg cholesterol, 437 mg sodium, 2 g carbohydrate, 1 g fiber, 23 g protein. **Diabetic Exchanges:** 3 very lean meat, 1 fat.

ISLAND JERK CHICKEN

TURKEY & BULGUR SALAD

Harvest Chicken With Walnut Gremolata

PREP: 25 min. **COOK:** 5-1/4 hours **YIELD:** 6 servings

PATRICIA HARMON • BADEN, PENNSYLVANIA

I lightened up the recipe by using fat-free chicken broth and removing the skin and excess fat from the chicken legs. It makes such an elegant, complete dinner!

- 1 medium butternut squash (about 3 lbs.), peeled and cubed
- 1 can (14-1/2 oz.) diced tomatoes, drained
- 1 medium onion, chopped
- 1 celery rib, chopped
- 1/2 cup reduced-sodium chicken broth
- 1/4 cup white wine *or* additional reduced-sodium chicken broth
- 1 garlic clove, minced
- 1 tsp. Italian seasoning
- 1/4 tsp. coarsely ground pepper, *divided*
- 1/4 cup all-purpose flour
- 1 tsp. seasoned salt
- 6 chicken drumsticks, skin removed
- 1 cup uncooked orzo pasta

GREMOLATA:
- 2 Tbsp. finely chopped walnuts
- 2 Tbsp. minced fresh parsley
- 1 garlic clove, minced
- 1 tsp. grated lemon peel

1. In a 5-qt. slow cooker, combine the squash, tomatoes, onion, celery, broth, wine, garlic, Italian seasoning and 1/8 teaspoon pepper.

2. In a large resealable plastic bag, combine the flour, seasoned salt and remaining pepper. Add chicken, a few pieces at a time, and shake to coat. Place chicken on top of vegetables. Cover and cook on low for 5 hours or until chicken juices run clear. Remove chicken and keep warm.

3. Stir orzo into vegetable mixture; cover and cook 15-20 minutes longer or until orzo is tender. Meanwhile, combine gremolata ingredients.

4. Transfer vegetable mixture to a serving platter; top with chicken. Sprinkle with gremolata.

HARVEST CHICKEN WITH WALNUT GREMOLATA

Nutrition Facts: 1 chicken drumstick with 1-1/4 cups vegetable mixture equals 343 calories, 5 g fat (1 g saturated fat), 40 mg cholesterol, 252 mg sodium, 55 g carbohydrate, 9 g fiber, 21 g protein.

Turkey Enchiladas

PREP: 30 min. **BAKE:** 25 min. **YIELD:** 8 servings

KIMBERLY BISH • VANDALIA, OHIO

My husband and I hosted a Mexican-themed party, and this was one of the main dishes. It was a huge success! I was thrilled when four of our friends asked for a copy of the recipe!

- 1 large onion, chopped
- 1 large green pepper, chopped
- 2 tsp. canola oil
- 3 Tbsp. all-purpose flour
- 1-1/4 tsp. ground coriander
- 1/4 tsp. pepper
- 1 can (14-1/2 oz.) reduced-sodium chicken broth
- 1 cup (8 oz.) fat-free sour cream
- 1 cup (4 oz.) shredded reduced-fat cheddar cheese, *divided*
- 3 cups cubed cooked turkey breast
- 3/4 cup salsa
- 8 flour tortillas (6 in.), warmed

1. In a large nonstick saucepan coated with cooking spray, cook and stir onion and green pepper in oil until tender. Sprinkle with flour, coriander and pepper; stir until blended. Gradually stir in broth. Bring to a boil; cook and stir for 2 minutes or until thickened. Remove from the heat. Stir in sour cream and 3/4 cup cheese.

2. In a large bowl, combine the turkey, salsa, and 1 cup cheese mixture. Spoon 1/3 cup turkey mixture down the center of each tortilla. Roll up and place seam side down in a 13-in. x 9-in. baking dish coated with cooking spray. Pour remaining cheese mixture over the top.

3. Cover and bake at 350° for 20 minutes. Sprinkle with remaining cheese. Bake, uncovered, 5-10 minutes longer or until heated through and cheese is melted.

Nutrition Facts: 1 enchilada equals 284 calories, 8 g fat (2 g saturated fat), 60 mg cholesterol, 610 mg sodium, 26 g carbohydrate, 1 g fiber, 26 g protein. **Diabetic Exchanges:** 3 very lean meat, 2 starch, 1 fat.

Makeover Chicken Potpies

PREP: 30 min. + chilling
BAKE: 20 min. **YIELD:** 4 servings

JOHN SLIVON • NAVARRE BEACH, FLORIDA

This is a light take on a favorite dish my wife and I enjoy when dining out. The calories are cut by nearly half!

- 1 cup plus 2 Tbsp. all-purpose flour, *divided*
- 1/4 tsp. baking powder
- 1/4 tsp. salt
- 3 Tbsp. cold butter, *divided*
- 2 Tbsp. buttermilk
- 1 Tbsp. canola oil
- 1 to 2 Tbsp. cold water
- 4 medium carrots, sliced

3 celery ribs, sliced
1 large onion, chopped
2-1/2 cups reduced-sodium chicken broth
2/3 cup fat-free milk
2 cups cubed cooked chicken breast
1 cup frozen peas
1/8 tsp. pepper
1 egg white

1. Combine 3/4 cup flour, baking powder and salt. Cut in 2 tablespoons butter until crumbly. Add buttermilk and oil; toss with a fork. Gradually add water, tossing with a fork until dough forms a ball. Cover and refrigerate for 1 hour.

2. For filling, in a large skillet, melt remaining butter. Add the carrots, celery and onion; saute until crisp-tender. In a small bowl, combine remaining flour with the broth and milk until smooth. Gradually stir into vegetable mixture. Bring to a boil; cook and stir for 2 minutes or until thickened. Stir in the chicken, peas and pepper. Transfer to four 16-oz. ramekins; set aside.

3. Divide dough into four portions. On a lightly floured surface, roll out dough to fit ramekins. Place dough over chicken mixture; trim and seal edges. Cut out a decorative center or cut slits in pastry. Brush with egg white.

4. Place ramekins on a baking sheet. Bake at 425° for 20-25 minutes or until crusts are golden brown.

Nutrition Facts: 1 potpie equals 443 calories, 15 g fat (6 g saturated fat), 78 mg cholesterol, 781 mg sodium, 45 g carbohydrate, 5 g fiber, 31 g protein.

Turkey Noodle Casserole

PREP: 25 min. **BAKE:** 45 min. **YIELD:** 4 servings

RAMONA FISH • COLUMBUS, INDIANA

I blend nutritious spinach with turkey breast and lighter cheese for a hearty and comforting meal. Try it with a simple fruit salad for dessert.

2-1/2 cups uncooked yolk-free noodles
2 cups cubed cooked turkey breast
1 can (10-3/4 oz.) reduced-fat reduced-sodium condensed cream of chicken soup, undiluted
1/8 tsp. garlic salt
1/8 tsp. dried rosemary, crushed
Dash pepper
1 pkg. (10 oz.) frozen chopped spinach, thawed and squeezed dry
1 cup (8 oz.) fat-free cottage cheese
3/4 cup shredded part-skim mozzarella cheese, *divided*
1/8 teaspoon paprika

1. Cook noodles according to package directions. Meanwhile, in a large bowl, combine the turkey, soup, garlic salt, rosemary and pepper. In a small bowl, combine the spinach, cottage cheese and 1/2 cup mozzarella cheese.

2. Drain noodles. Place half of the noodles in a 2-qt. baking dish coated with cooking spray; layer with half of the turkey and cottage cheese mixtures. Repeat layers. Cover and bake at 350° for 35 minutes. Uncover; sprinkle with remaining mozzarella. Bake 10-15 minutes longer until edges are lightly browned. Sprinkle with paprika. Let stand for 5 minutes before serving.

Nutrition Facts: 1-1/2 cups equals 357 calories, 6 g fat (3 g saturated fat), 81 mg cholesterol, 746 mg sodium, 32 g carbohydrate, 4 g fiber, 40 g protein. **Diabetic Exchanges:** 5 very lean meat, 2 starch, 1/2 fat.

Using yolk-free noodles in **Turkey Noodle Casserole** trims 23 mg of cholesterol from the dish, and reduced-fat, reduced-sodium condensed cream of chicken soup saves 3 g of fat and 283 mg of sodium per serving.

Makeover Chicken Fettuccine Alfredo

PREP: 20 min. **COOK:** 20 min. **YIELD:** 9 servings

HEATHER PRIVRATSKY • GREENFIELD, WISCONSIN

My husband and I enjoyed this supper at a friend's house. I wanted to lighten it up, and cutting the salt and using low-fat ingredients did the trick!

1	pkg. (16 oz.) fettuccine
1-1/2	lbs. boneless skinless chicken breasts, cut into 1-in. cubes
1	Tbsp. Italian seasoning
6	garlic cloves, minced, *divided*
3	Tbsp. reduced-fat butter, *divided*
1/2	lb. sliced fresh mushrooms
1	medium onion, chopped
1/3	cup all-purpose flour
1-1/2	tsp. salt
1/4	tsp. pepper
3	cups fat-free milk
1	cup half-and-half cream
1-1/2	cups (6 oz.) shredded reduced-fat Colby-Monterey Jack cheese
3	plum tomatoes, chopped
1/2	cup reduced-fat sour cream
1/4	cup plus 3 Tbsp. shredded Parmesan cheese, *divided*

1. Cook fettuccine according to package directions. Meanwhile, in a large skillet over medium heat, cook the chicken, Italian seasoning and 2 garlic cloves in 1 tablespoon butter until chicken is no longer pink; remove and keep warm.

2. In the same skillet, saute mushrooms and onion in remaining butter until tender. Add remaining garlic; saute 1-2 minutes longer. Stir in the flour, salt and pepper until blended; gradually add milk and cream.

3. Bring to a boil; cook and stir for 1-2 minutes or until thickened. Add the Colby-Monterey Jack cheese, tomatoes, sour cream, 1/4 cup Parmesan cheese and reserved chicken; cook and stir until heated through.

4. Drain fettuccine; serve with sauce. Sprinkle each serving with 1 teaspoon of remaining Parmesan cheese.

Editor's Note: This recipe was tested with Land O'Lakes light stick butter.

Nutrition Facts: 1 cup fettuccine with 1 cup sauce equals 462 calories, 13 g fat (8 g saturated fat), 79 mg cholesterol, 766 mg sodium, 50 g carbohydrate, 3 g fiber, 35 g protein.

Turkey Spaghetti Casserole

PREP: 30 min. **BAKE:** 1-1/4 hours **YIELD:** 6 servings

CASANDRA HETRICK • LINDSEY, OHIO

My mom made this creamy and comforting entree when I was growing up. Whenever I have leftover chicken or turkey, I look forward to making this simple yet tasty dish.

1	medium onion, chopped
1	medium carrot, chopped
1	celery rib, chopped
1/3	cup sliced fresh mushrooms
1	Tbsp. butter
2-1/2	cups reduced-sodium chicken broth
1	can (10-3/4 oz.) reduced-fat reduced-sodium condensed cream of mushroom soup, undiluted
1/4	tsp. salt
1/4	tsp. pepper
2-1/2	cups cubed cooked turkey breast
6	oz. uncooked spaghetti, broken into 2-in. pieces
1/2	cup shredded reduced-fat Colby-Monterey Jack cheese
1/2	teaspoon paprika

1. In a small skillet, saute the vegetables in butter until tender. In a large bowl, combine the broth, soup, salt and pepper.

2. In a 2-1/2-qt. baking dish coated with cooking spray, layer the turkey, spaghetti and vegetable mixture. Pour broth mixture over the top.

3. Cover and bake at 350° for 70-80 minutes or until spaghetti is tender, stirring once. Uncover; sprinkle with cheese and paprika. Bake 5-10 minutes longer or until cheese is melted.

Nutrition Facts: 1 cup equals 284 calories, 6 g fat (3 g saturated fat), 62 mg cholesterol, 702 mg sodium, 30 g carbohydrate, 3 g fiber, 26 g protein. **Diabetic Exchanges:** 3 very lean meat, 1-1/2 starch, 1 vegetable, 1/2 fat.

Sweet & Sassy Turkey Burgers

PREP: 25 min. **GRILL:** 15 min. **YIELD:** 6 servings

MARLA CLARK • MORIARTY, NEW MEXICO

These are scrumptious! I served them at our last family reunion, and they were a huge hit. (Uncle Milton had two!) Cranberry sauce with turkey is a match made in Heaven.

6	turkey bacon strips, diced and cooked
1/4	cup dried cranberries
1	Tbsp. maple syrup
1	tsp. rubbed sage
1/8	tsp. pepper
1-1/4	lbs. extra-lean ground turkey
1	Italian turkey sausage link (4 oz.), casing removed
3	slices part-skim mozzarella cheese, cut in half
6	onion rolls, split
6	Tbsp. jellied cranberry sauce
6	Tbsp. fat-free mayonnaise
6	lettuce leaves

1. In a large bowl, combine the first five ingredients. Crumble turkey and sausage over mixture and mix well. Shape into six burgers.

2. If grilling the burgers, coat the grill rack with cooking spray before starting the grill. Grill burgers, covered, over medium heat or broil 4 in. from the heat for 5-7 minutes on each side or until a meat thermometer reads 165° and juices run clear. Top with cheese; cook 1-2 minutes longer or until the cheese is melted.

3. Toast the rolls; spread warm rolls with cranberry sauce and mayonnaise. Serve burgers on rolls with lettuce.

Nutrition Facts: 1 burger equals 418 calories, 12 g fat (4 g saturated fat), 73 mg cholesterol, 809 mg sodium, 41 g carbohydrate, 2 g fiber, 38 g protein.

Chicken Salad Bake [C]

PREP: 20 min. **BAKE:** 30 min. **YIELD:** 6 servings

DARLA GERMAUX • SAXTON, PENNSYLVANIA

This amazing twist on the classic chicken salad is sure to impress guests and family.

4	cups cubed cooked chicken breast
2	celery ribs, thinly sliced
1	small green or sweet red pepper, chopped
1/2	cup sliced water chestnuts, halved
1/2	cup sliced fresh mushrooms
1/4	cup finely chopped onion
1	cup reduced-fat salad dressing
1/2	tsp. garlic powder
1/2	tsp. pepper
1	cup soft bread crumbs
1	Tbsp. butter, melted
1/4	cup shredded cheddar cheese

1. In a large bowl, combine the first six ingredients. Combine the salad dressing, garlic powder and pepper; stir into chicken mixture.

2. Transfer to a 2-qt. baking dish coated with cooking spray. Bake, uncovered, at 350° for 20 minutes. Toss bread crumbs with butter; sprinkle over chicken mixture. Top with cheese. Bake 7-10 minutes longer or until heated through and top is lightly browned.

Nutrition Facts: 1 cup equals 311 calories, 14 g fat (4 g saturated fat), 93 mg cholesterol, 516 mg sodium, 14 g carbohydrate, 1 g fiber, 30 g protein.

SWEET & SASSY TURKEY BURGERS

CHICKEN SALAD BAKE

Sweet & Sour Chicken

PREP: 20 min. + marinating
COOK: 15 min. **YIELD:** 4 servings

LORI BURTENSHAW • TERRETON, IDAHO

I first tasted this yummy dish at our friends' home. I immediately asked for the recipe, and we've enjoyed it ever since. We call it "favorite chicken" at our house!

- 1 Tbsp. plus 2 tsp. reduced-sodium soy sauce, *divided*
- 1 Tbsp. sherry *or* reduced-sodium chicken broth
- 1/2 tsp. salt
- 1/2 tsp. garlic powder
- 1/2 tsp. ground ginger
- 1 lb. boneless skinless chicken breasts, cut into 1-in. cubes
- 1 can (20 oz.) unsweetened pineapple chunks
- 2 Tbsp. plus 1/3 cup cornstarch, *divided*
- 2 Tbsp. sugar
- 1/4 cup cider vinegar
- 1/4 cup ketchup
- 1 Tbsp. canola oil
- 2 cups hot cooked rice

1. In a large resealable plastic bag, combine 1 tablespoon soy sauce, sherry or broth, salt, garlic powder and ginger; add the chicken. Seal bag and turn to coat; refrigerate for 30 minutes.

2. Drain pineapple, reserving juice; set pineapple aside. Add enough water to juice to measure 1 cup. In a small bowl, combine 2 tablespoons cornstarch, sugar and pineapple juice mixture until smooth; stir in the vinegar, ketchup and remaining soy sauce. Set aside.

3. Drain chicken and discard marinade. Place remaining cornstarch in a large resealable plastic bag. Add chicken, a few pieces at a time, and shake to coat. In a large nonstick skillet or wok coated with cooking spray, stir-fry chicken in oil until no longer pink. Remove and keep warm.

4. Stir pineapple juice mixture and add to the pan. Bring to a boil; cook and stir for 2 minutes or until thickened. Add chicken and reserved pineapple; heat through. Serve with rice.

Nutrition Facts: 1 cup chicken mixture with 1/2 cup rice equals 428 calories, 6 g fat (1 g saturated fat), 63 mg cholesterol, 571 mg sodium, 65 g carbohydrate, 2 g fiber, 26 g protein.

Crab-Stuffed Chicken Breasts Ⓒ

PREP: 45 min. **BAKE:** 30 min. **YIELD:** 6 servings

MARY PLUMMER • DE SOTO, KANSAS

Here's an idea for an elegant rolled-chicken entree. It's stuffed with crabmeat and crunchy water chestnuts and is definitely something special.

- 6 boneless skinless chicken breast halves (5 oz. *each*)
- 1/2 tsp. salt
- 1/4 tsp. pepper
- 1/2 cup canned crabmeat, drained, flaked and cartilage removed
- 1/4 cup sliced water chestnuts, drained and chopped
- 2 Tbsp. dry bread crumbs
- 2 Tbsp. reduced-fat mayonnaise
- 1 Tbsp. minced fresh parsley
- 1 tsp. Dijon mustard
- 6 tsp. Worcestershire sauce for chicken, *divided*
- 2 green onions, thinly sliced, *divided*
- 3 slices reduced-fat Swiss cheese, *divided*

1. Flatten chicken to 1/4-in. thickness; sprinkle with salt and pepper. In a small bowl, combine crab, water chestnuts, bread crumbs, mayonnaise, parsley, mustard, 2 teaspoons Worcestershire sauce and half of the onions.

SWEET & SOUR CHICKEN

CRAB-STUFFED CHICKEN BREASTS

TURKEY BURGERS WITH AVOCADO SAUCE

2. Chop one cheese slice; stir into crab mixture. Spread over chicken; roll up and secure with toothpicks.

3. In a large nonstick skillet coated with cooking spray, brown chicken on all sides. Place seam side down in a shallow 3-qt. baking dish coated with cooking spray. Brush with remaining Worcestershire sauce. Bake, uncovered, at 350° for 25 minutes.

4. Cut each remaining cheese slice into six strips; place two cheese strips over each chicken breast. Bake 5-10 minutes longer or until a meat thermometer reads 170°. Discard toothpicks. Sprinkle remaining onions over chicken.

Nutrition Facts: 1 stuffed chicken breast half equals 225 calories, 7 g fat (2 g saturated fat), 95 mg cholesterol, 469 mg sodium, 5 g carbohydrate, trace fiber, 35 g protein. **Diabetic Exchanges:** 5 very lean meat, 1 fat.

Turkey Burgers With Avocado Sauce

PREP: 30 min. + chilling
GRILL: 10 min. **YIELD:** 4 servings

JAN WARREN-RUCKER • CLEMMONS, NORTH CAROLINA

I love burgers and I love Southwestern food, so why not combine the two in a light and juicy burger? I like to whip these up on a Friday, pop them in the fridge and cook them later for weekend entertaining or an exciting family surprise!

> 1   cup fresh or frozen corn, thawed
> 1/2 cup chopped red onion
> 1   small sweet red pepper, chopped
> 2   jalapeno peppers, seeded and minced
> 2   tsp. olive oil
> 2   Tbsp. lime juice
> 2   garlic cloves, minced
> 1/2 tsp. salt
> 1/2 tsp. ground cumin

> 1/4 tsp. chili powder
> 1/8 tsp. dried oregano
> 1   lb. extra-lean ground turkey

SAUCE:
> 1   medium ripe avocado, peeled
> 1/2 cup fat-free sour cream
> 2   Tbsp. minced fresh cilantro
> 2   tsp. lime juice
> 1   garlic clove, minced
> 1/8 tsp. salt

SERVING:
> 4   whole wheat hamburger buns, split

Shredded lettuce and reduced-fat Mexican cheese blend, optional

Sliced tomato and red onion, optional

1. In a large skillet, saute the corn, onion and peppers in oil until crisp-tender. Stir in the lime juice, garlic, salt, cumin, chili powder and oregano; cook 1 minute longer. Transfer to a large bowl and cool slightly. Crumble turkey over mixture and mix well. Shape into four burgers. Refrigerate for at least 30 minutes.

2. For sauce, in a small bowl, mash avocado with sour cream, cilantro, lime juice, garlic and salt. Refrigerate until serving.

3. If grilling the burgers, coat grill rack with cooking spray before starting the grill. Grill burgers, covered, over medium heat or broil 4 in. from the heat for 5-7 minutes on each side or until a meat thermometer reads 165° and juices run clear.

4. Place on buns; top each with about 1/4 cup sauce. Serve with lettuce, cheese, tomato and onion if desired.

Editor's Note: When cutting hot peppers, disposable gloves are recommended. Avoid touching your face.

Nutrition Facts: 1 burger (calculated without optional toppings) equals 413 calories, 13 g fat (2 g saturated fat), 50 mg cholesterol, 678 mg sodium, 43 g carbohydrate, 8 g fiber, 37 g protein.

Terrific Teriyaki Burgers

PREP: 20 min. **GRILL:** 15 min. **YIELD:** 6 servings

MARGARET WILSON • HEMET, CALIFORNIA

Golden flecks of pineapple give these burgers a touch of sweetness, while the gingerroot adds some spice. Ground chicken works well in this recipe, too.

1/4	cup ketchup
2	Tbsp. reduced-sodium soy sauce
1	Tbsp. brown sugar
1	Tbsp. unsweetened crushed pineapple
1-1/2	tsp. minced fresh gingerroot
1	garlic clove, minced
1/2	tsp. sesame oil

BURGERS:

1	egg white, lightly beaten
1/3	cup dry bread crumbs
3	green onions, chopped
2	Tbsp. unsweetened crushed pineapple
3/4	lb. lean ground beef
3/4	lb. lean ground turkey
6	slices unsweetened pineapple
6	hamburger buns, split and toasted
6	lettuce leaves
6	slices tomato

1. In a small bowl, combine the ketchup, soy sauce, brown sugar, pineapple, ginger, garlic and sesame oil; set aside.

2. In a large bowl, combine the egg white, bread crumbs, onions, crushed pineapple and 3 tablespoons reserved ketchup mixture. Crumble beef and turkey over mixture and mix well. Shape into six burgers.

3. Coat grill rack with cooking spray before starting the grill. Grill burgers, covered, over medium heat for 5-7 minutes on each side or until a meat thermometer reads 165° and juices run clear, brushing occasionally with remaining ketchup mixture.

4. Grill pineapple slices for 2-3 minutes on each side or until heated through. Serve burgers and pineapple on buns with lettuce and tomato.

Nutrition Facts: 1 burger equals 386 calories, 12 g fat (4 g saturated fat), 79 mg cholesterol, 677 mg sodium, 41 g carbohydrate, 2 g fiber, 27 g protein. **Diabetic Exchanges:** 3 lean meat, 2 starch, 1/2 fruit.

Makeover Chicken Noodle Delight

PREP: 25 min. **BAKE:** 40 min. **YIELD:** 6 servings

GAIL SCHUMACHER • BERTHOUD, COLORADO

I loved this original casserole, but I knew it needed to be lightened-up for me to enjoy regularly. The "Healthy Cooking" team took advantage of low-fat and reduced-sodium items to eliminate 27 grams of fat and 1,000 milligrams of sodium. Now I can serve this hot bake without the guilt.

4	cups uncooked yolk-free noodles
1	can (10-3/4 oz.) reduced-fat reduced-sodium condensed cream of chicken soup, undiluted
4	oz. reduced-fat cream cheese, cubed
1	cup (8 oz.) reduced-fat sour cream
1	cup (8 oz.) plain yogurt
1/4	cup fat-free milk
3	Tbsp. minced fresh parsley or 1 Tbsp. dried parsley flakes
1	tsp. onion powder

1/4 tsp. salt
2 cups cubed cooked chicken breast
1 cup crushed reduced-fat butter-flavored crackers (about 25 crackers)
3 Tbsp. reduced-fat butter, melted

1. Cook noodles according to package directions. Meanwhile, in a large bowl, combine the soup, cream cheese, sour cream, yogurt, milk, parsley, onion powder and salt. Stir in the chicken.

2. Drain noodles; toss with chicken mixture. Transfer to a 2-qt. baking dish coated with cooking spray.

3. Combine cracker crumbs and butter; sprinkle over casserole. Bake, uncovered, at 350° for 40-45 minutes or until heated through.

Editor's Note: This recipe was tested with Land O'Lakes light stick butter.

Nutrition Facts: 1 cup equals 432 calories, 17 g fat (9 g saturated fat), 86 mg cholesterol, 637 mg sodium, 41 g carbohydrate, 2 g fiber, 27 g protein.

Malibu Chicken Bundles

PREP: 25 min. **BAKE:** 45 min. **YIELD:** 4 servings

BEVERLY NORRIS • EVANSTON, WYOMING

The first time I made this, it was an instant hit and we agreed I wouldn't change a thing. Mustard may seem like a unique ingredient, but it adds a really nice touch.

4 boneless skinless chicken breast halves (4 oz. *each*)
1/2 cup honey Dijon mustard, *divided*
4 thin slices deli ham
4 slices reduced-fat Swiss cheese
1 can (8 oz.) unsweetened crushed pineapple, well drained
1-1/2 cups panko (Japanese) bread crumbs
1/4 tsp. salt
1/4 tsp. pepper
SAUCE:
1 can (10-3/4 oz.) reduced-fat reduced-sodium condensed cream of chicken soup, undiluted
1/4 cup reduced-fat sour cream
1/8 tsp. dried tarragon

1. Flatten chicken breasts to 1/4-in. thickness. Spread 1 tablespoon mustard over each; layer with ham, cheese and pineapple. Fold chicken over pineapple; secure with toothpicks. Brush bundles with remaining mustard.

2. In a shallow bowl, combine the bread crumbs, salt and pepper. Roll bundles in bread crumb mixture; place in an 11-in. x 7-in. baking dish coated with cooking spray. Bake, uncovered, at 350° for 45-50 minutes or until a meat thermometer reads 170°. Discard toothpicks.

3. Meanwhile, in a small saucepan, combine the sauce ingredients. Cook, stirring occasionally, until heated through. Serve with chicken.

Nutrition Facts: 1 chicken bundle with 1/3 cup sauce equals 400 calories, 12 g fat (4 g saturated fat), 86 mg cholesterol, 784 mg sodium, 41 g carbohydrate, 2 g fiber, 36 g protein. **Diabetic Exchanges:** 3 very lean meat, 2 starch, 1-1/2 fat, 1/2 fruit.

Chicken Pasta Dinner

PREP: 15 min. **COOK:** 20 min. **YIELD:** 5 servings

HEALTHY COOKING TEST KITCHEN
Green beans add crunch and a bit of color to this tasty pasta-and-chicken dish that appeals to all ages.

4 cups uncooked spiral pasta
1/2 lb. fresh green beans, trimmed and cut into 1/4-in. pieces
3/4 lb. boneless skinless chicken breasts, cut into 1/2-in. pieces
3 tsp. olive oil, *divided*
1 jar (7 oz.) roasted sweet red peppers, drained
1 garlic clove, minced
3/4 cup reduced-sodium chicken broth
3/4 cup fat-free evaporated milk, *divided*
1/4 cup minced fresh basil *or* 4 tsp. dried basil
1/2 tsp. salt
1/4 tsp. pepper
2 tsp. cornstarch
5 Tbsp. shredded Parmesan cheese

1. Cook pasta according to package directions, adding green beans during the last 2 minutes.

2. Meanwhile, in a large nonstick skillet, saute chicken in 2 teaspoons oil until no longer pink. Remove and keep warm. In the same pan, saute red peppers and garlic in remaining oil for 1 minute.

3. Stir in the broth, 1/2 cup milk, basil, salt and pepper. Bring to a boil. Reduce heat; simmer, uncovered, for 3 minutes or until slightly thickened. Remove from the heat; cool slightly. Transfer to a blender; cover and process until smooth. Return to the pan.

4. Add chicken to the pepper mixture. Combine cornstarch and remaining milk until smooth; gradually stir into the chicken mixture. Bring to a boil; cook and stir for 2 minutes or until thickened.

5. Drain pasta mixture; toss with sauce. Sprinkle each serving with 1 tablespoon Parmesan cheese.

Nutrition Facts: 1-1/4 cups equals 345 calories, 6 g fat (2 g saturated fat), 42 mg cholesterol, 625 mg sodium, 44 g carbohydrate, 3 g fiber, 25 g protein. **Diabetic Exchanges:** 2-1/2 starch, 2 lean meat, 1 vegetable, 1/2 fat.

CHICKEN PASTA DINNER

Citrus Chicken Fajitas

PREP: 20 min. + marinating
COOK: 15 min. **YIELD:** 4 servings

DEBRA KAPITAN • SACRAMENTO, CALIFORNIA

I've tried several variations of this recipe, choosing chicken for lighter fare and just the perfect blend of spices. I've prepared it for many "themed" dinners with friends, and everyone raves about these fajitas.

- 6 Tbsp. lemon juice
- 1/4 cup lime juice
- 2 Tbsp. minced fresh cilantro
- 1 Tbsp. olive oil
- 1 tsp. sugar
- 1/2 tsp. garlic powder
- 1/2 tsp. ground cumin
- 1 lb. boneless skinless chicken breasts, cut into strips
- 1 *each* medium green, sweet red and yellow peppers, julienned
- 1 large red onion, halved and thinly sliced
- 4 flour tortillas (8 in.), warmed
- 1/2 cup shredded lettuce
- 1/4 cup sliced ripe olives
- 1/4 cup shredded reduced-fat cheddar cheese

1. In a small bowl, combine the first seven ingredients. Divide marinade equally between two large resealable plastic bags; add the chicken to one bag. Add peppers and onion to remaining bag. Seal bags and turn to coat; refrigerate for several hours or overnight.

2. Drain chicken and vegetables, discarding the marinade. In a large nonstick skillet coated with cooking spray, cook and stir chicken over medium heat for 3 minutes. Add vegetables; cook 3-5 minutes longer or until chicken is no longer pink and vegetables are crisp-tender. Spoon filling onto tortillas; top with lettuce, olives and cheese. Roll up.

Nutrition Facts: 1 fajita equals 360 calories, 10 g fat (2 g saturated fat), 68 mg cholesterol, 426 mg sodium, 38 g carbohydrate, 3 g fiber, 31 g protein. **Diabetic Exchanges:** 3 very lean meat, 2 vegetable, 1-1/2 starch, 1 fat.

Honey-Grilled Chicken Breasts [C]

PREP: 15 min. + marinating
GRILL: 10 min. **YIELD:** 8 servings

JENNIFER PETERSEN • MURRAY, UTAH

Orange juice and soy sauce make such a tasty combination. The longer this chicken marinates, the fuller the flavor!

- 1/2 cup orange juice
- 1/3 cup honey
- 1/4 cup lemon juice
- 1/4 cup reduced-sodium soy sauce
- 2 Tbsp. minced fresh gingerroot
- 12 garlic cloves, minced
- 1/2 tsp. pepper
- 1/4 tsp. salt
- 8 boneless skinless chicken breast halves (6 oz. *each*)

1. In a small bowl, combine the first eight ingredients. Pour 1/2 cup marinade into a large resealable plastic bag; add the chicken. Seal bag and turn to coat; refrigerate for 8 hours or overnight. Cover and refrigerate remaining marinade.

2. Coat grill rack with cooking spray before starting the grill. Drain chicken and discard marinade. Grill, covered, over medium heat for 5-7 minutes on each side or until juices run clear, basting frequently with reserved marinade.

Nutrition Facts: 1 chicken breast half equals 221 calories, 4 g fat (1 g saturated fat), 94 mg cholesterol, 331 mg sodium, 10 g carbohydrate, trace fiber, 35 g protein. **Diabetic Exchanges:** 5 very lean meat, 1/2 starch.

Gouda-Stuffed Chicken

PREP: 15 min. **COOK:** 40 min. **YIELD:** 4 servings

MARY ANN DELL • PHOENIXVILLE, PENNSYLVANIA

My brother gave me the recipe for this hearty dish we often serve at family gatherings. Men, especially, seem to enjoy it, and it's become one of our special favorites.

- 4 boneless skinless chicken breast halves (6 oz. *each*)
- 2 oz. smoked Gouda cheese, cut into thin pieces

CITRUS CHICKEN FAJITAS

HONEY-GRILLED CHICKEN BREASTS

GOUDA-STUFFED CHICKEN

2 Tbsp. all-purpose flour

1/4 tsp. salt

1/8 tsp. pepper

2 tsp. canola oil, *divided*

1 garlic clove, minced

1 cup reduced-sodium chicken broth

1 cup apple cider *or* unsweetened apple juice

2 large tart apples, thinly sliced

1 Tbsp. honey

1. Cut a slit lengthwise through the thickest part of each chicken breast; fill with cheese. In a shallow bowl, combine the flour, salt and pepper. Dip the chicken in the flour mixture on both sides; shake off excess.

2. In a large nonstick skillet coated with cooking spray, cook chicken in 1-1/2 teaspoons oil over medium heat for 8-10 minutes on each side or until juices run clear. Remove and keep warm.

3. In the same skillet, saute garlic in remaining oil for 30 seconds. Add broth and cider, stirring to loosen browned bits. Bring to a boil. Reduce heat; simmer, uncovered, for 12-14 minutes or until mixture is reduced to about 1 cup.

4. Stir in apples and honey; return to a boil. Reduce heat; simmer, uncovered, for 5-7 minutes or until apples are crisp-tender. Serve with chicken.

Nutrition Facts: 1 chicken breast half with 1/3 cup apple mixture equals 350 calories, 10 g fat (4 g saturated fat), 110 mg cholesterol, 507 mg sodium, 24 g carbohydrate, 1 g fiber, 39 g protein. **Diabetic Exchanges:** 5 very lean meat, 1 fruit, 1 fat, 1/2 starch.

Green Chili Luncheon Bake

PREP: 30 min. **BAKE:** 55 min. **YIELD:** 6 servings

KATHLEEN SMITH • PITTSBURGH, PENNSYLVANIA

This is a warm, comforting, low-fat entree that we always enjoy. Try it with a green salad.

1/2 lb. lean ground turkey

1 large onion, chopped

1 can (16 oz.) fat-free refried beans

1-3/4 tsp. ground cumin

1-1/2 tsp. dried oregano

1/2 tsp. garlic powder

1/2 tsp. salt, *divided*

1/4 tsp. pepper

2 cans (4 oz. *each*) chopped green chilies

1 cup (4 oz.) shredded reduced-fat Mexican cheese blend

1 cup frozen corn, thawed

1/3 cup all-purpose flour

2 eggs

2 egg whites

1-1/3 cups fat-free milk

1/8 tsp. hot pepper sauce

1/4 cup thinly sliced red onion

3 Tbsp. fresh cilantro leaves

1. In a large nonstick skillet coated with cooking spray, cook turkey and onion over medium heat until meat is no longer pink; drain. Stir in the beans, cumin, oregano, garlic powder, 1/4 teaspoon salt and pepper.

2. Sprinkle half of the chilies and cheese into a 2-qt. baking dish coated with cooking spray. Layer with bean mixture, corn and remaining chilies and cheese.

3. In a small bowl, combine flour and remaining salt. In another small bowl, whisk the eggs, egg whites, milk and pepper sauce; gradually whisk into flour mixture until smooth. Pour over the top. Bake, uncovered, at 350° for 55-65 minutes or until set. Sprinkle with red onion and cilantro.

Nutrition Facts: 1 piece equals 312 calories, 9 g fat (3 g saturated fat), 115 mg cholesterol, 884 mg sodium, 34 g carbohydrate, 7 g fiber, 25 g protein. **Diabetic Exchanges:** 3 lean meat, 2 reduced-fat milk.

BAKED MOSTACCIOLI

Baked Mostaccioli

PREP: 35 min. **BAKE:** 30 min. **YIELD:** 6 servings

DONNA EBERT • RICHFIELD, WISCONSIN

I often serve this for dinner parties and always get rave reviews. Two tomato products give this casserole extra healthy appeal and loads of flavor.

8	oz. uncooked mostaccioli
1/2	lb. lean ground turkey
1	small onion, chopped
1	can (14-1/2 oz.) diced tomatoes, undrained
1	can (6 oz.) tomato paste
1/3	cup water
1	tsp. dried oregano
1/2	tsp. salt
1/8	tsp. pepper
2	cups (16 oz.) fat-free cottage cheese
1	tsp. dried marjoram
1-1/2	cups (6 oz.) shredded part-skim mozzarella cheese
1/4	cup grated Parmesan cheese

1. Cook mostaccioli according to package directions. Meanwhile, in a large saucepan, cook the turkey and onion over medium heat until the meat is no longer pink; drain if necessary.

2. Stir in the tomatoes, tomato paste, water, oregano, salt and pepper. Bring to a boil. Reduce heat; cover and simmer for 15 minutes.

3. In a small bowl, combine cottage cheese and marjoram; set aside. Drain mostaccioli.

4. Spread 1/2 cup meat sauce into an 11-in. x 7-in. baking dish coated with cooking spray. Layer with half of the mostaccioli, meat sauce and mozzarella cheese. Top with cottage cheese mixture. Layer with remaining mostaccioli, meat sauce and mozzarella cheese. Sprinkle with the Parmesan cheese (dish will be full).

5. Bake, uncovered, at 350° for 30-40 minutes or until bubbly and heated through.

Nutrition Facts: 1 serving equals 278 calories, 7 g fat (3 g saturated fat), 39 mg cholesterol, 607 mg sodium, 32 g carbohydrate, 3 g fiber, 23 g protein. **Diabetic Exchanges:** 2 lean meat, 2 vegetable, 1-1/2 starch.

Penne Chicken

PREP: 10 min. **COOK:** 25 min. **YIELD:** 6 servings

HEALTHY COOKING TEST KITCHEN

A rich sun-dried tomato sauce brings a little excitement to pasta, chicken, portobello mushrooms and peas in this satisfying and healthful meal-in-one.

1	cup water
1/4	cup white wine *or* reduced-sodium chicken broth
1	tsp. reduced-sodium chicken bouillon granules
2	boneless skinless chicken breast halves (6 oz. *each*)
2	cups uncooked penne pasta
1	cup sliced baby portobello mushrooms
1	cup sun-dried tomatoes (not packed in oil), cut in half
3	Tbsp. chopped shallots
1	Tbsp. cornstarch
1/2	cup fat-free milk
1/4	cup tomato paste
1/2	tsp. salt
1	cup (4 oz.) shredded Parmesan cheese
1	cup frozen peas, thawed
2	Tbsp. minced fresh basil *or* 2 tsp. dried basil

1. In a large nonstick skillet, bring the water, wine and bouillon to a boil. Reduce heat; carefully add chicken. Cover and cook for 15 minutes or until a meat thermometer reads 170°. Meanwhile, in a large saucepan, cook pasta according to package directions.

2. Remove chicken from the pan, reserving the cooking liquid; set chicken aside to cool slightly. Add the mushrooms, tomatoes and shallots to the cooking liquid. Bring to a boil. Reduce heat; simmer, uncovered, for 5 minutes or until tender.

3. Combine the cornstarch, milk, tomato paste and salt

until smooth; stir into the pan until blended. Bring to a boil. Cook and stir for 2 minutes or until thickened.

4. Shred chicken with two forks; add to the sauce. Drain pasta; add to sauce. Add the cheese, peas and basil; cook and stir until heated through.

Nutrition Facts: 1-1/3 cups equals 281 calories, 6 g fat (3 g saturated fat), 41 mg cholesterol, 739 mg sodium, 32 g carbohydrate, 4 g fiber, 24 g protein. **Diabetic Exchanges:** 3 very lean meat, 2 vegetable, 1-1/2 starch, 1/2 fat.

Mexican Corn Bread Pizza

PREP: 25 min. **BAKE:** 20 min. **YIELD:** 6 servings

CHRISTY WEST • GREENFIELD, INDIANA

The combination of sweet corn bread and spicy taco flavors livens up this meal. Using extra-lean ground turkey instead of beef cuts the fat for a delicious dinner that's guilt-free.

1	pkg. (8-1/2 oz.) corn bread/muffin mix
1/3	cup fat-free milk
1	egg, beaten
1	cup frozen corn, thawed
3/4	lb. extra-lean ground turkey
1	small onion, chopped
1	small sweet red pepper, chopped
2	jalapeno peppers, seeded and chopped
3	Tbsp. reduced-sodium taco seasoning
1/2	cup water
3/4	cup shredded reduced-fat Mexican cheese blend
1	small tomato, chopped
1/4	cup sliced ripe olives
2	green onions, chopped
6	Tbsp. reduced-fat sour cream

1. In a small bowl, combine the corn bread mix, milk and egg. Stir in corn just until blended. Spread evenly into a 10-in. ovenproof skillet coated with cooking spray. Bake at 400° for 14-18 minutes or until a toothpick inserted near the center comes out clean.

2. Meanwhile, in a large nonstick skillet, cook the turkey, onion, red pepper and jalapenos over medium heat until meat is no longer pink; drain. Stir in taco seasoning and water; bring to a boil. Reduce heat; simmer, uncovered, for 5 minutes.

3. Spoon turkey mixture over corn bread; sprinkle with cheese. Bake for 5-10 minutes or until cheese is melted. Sprinkle with tomato, olives and green onions. Cut into six wedges; top each with sour cream.

Editor's Note: When cutting or seeding hot peppers, use rubber or plastic gloves to protect your hands. Avoid touching your face.

Nutrition Facts: 1 wedge equals 354 calories, 11 g fat (4 g saturated fat),82 mg cholesterol, 793 mg sodium, 43 g carbohydrate, 2 g fiber, 25 g protein. **Diabetic Exchanges:** 3 starch, 2 lean meat.

Buffalo Chicken Burgers With Tangy Slaw

PREP: 25 min. **BROIL:** 10 min. **YIELD:** 4 servings

JEANNE HOLT • MENDOTA HEIGHTS, MINNESOTA

These burgers are my way of enjoying the flavors of Buffalo chicken wings while avoiding some of the fat and calories.

SLAW:

1/4	cup thinly sliced celery
1/4	cup shredded apple
2	Tbsp. prepared fat-free blue cheese salad dressing
1	tsp. finely chopped walnuts

SAUCE:

3	Tbsp. Louisiana-style hot sauce
2	tsp. ketchup
2	tsp. reduced-fat butter, melted

BURGERS:

2	Tbsp. chopped sweet red pepper
2	Tbsp. plus 4 tsp. thinly sliced green onions, *divided*
1	Tbsp. unsweetened applesauce
1/4	tsp. salt
1/4	tsp. garlic salt
1/4	tsp. pepper
1	lb. ground chicken
4	lettuce leaves
4	hamburger buns, split

1. In a small bowl, combine celery, apple, salad dressing and walnuts. In another small bowl, combine the hot sauce, ketchup and butter; set aside.

2. In a large bowl, combine the red pepper, 2 tablespoons green onions, applesauce, salt, garlic salt and pepper. Crumble chicken over mixture and mix well. Shape into four burgers.

3. Broil 6 in. from the heat for 5-7 minutes on each side or until a meat thermometer reads 165° and juices run clear, basting occasionally with reserved sauce. Serve on lettuce-lined buns; top each with 2 tablespoons slaw and sprinkle with remaining green onions.

Editor's Note: This recipe was tested with Land O'Lakes light stick butter.

Nutrition Facts: 1 burger equals 312 calories, 12 g fat (4 g saturated fat), 78 mg cholesterol, 682 mg sodium, 29 g carbohydrate, 2 g fiber, 23 g protein. **Diabetic Exchanges:** 3 lean meat, 2 starch.

BUFFALO CHICKEN BURGERS WITH TANGY SLAW

Cashew Chicken

PREP: 20 min. + marinating
BAKE: 15 min. **YIELD:** 4 servings

LINDA AVILA • TOONE, TENNESSEE

Whenever my friends and I get together for a potluck, they ask me to bring this dish. The recipe came from my brother; it has a distinct Asian flavor from the seasonings.

3	Tbsp. reduced-sodium soy sauce, *divided*
1	Tbsp. sherry *or* reduced-sodium chicken broth
3/4	tsp. sesame oil, *divided*
1	lb. boneless skinless chicken breasts, cut into 1-in. pieces
1	Tbsp. cornstarch
1/3	cup reduced-sodium chicken broth
1	Tbsp. sugar
1	Tbsp. rice wine vinegar
1	Tbsp. hoisin sauce
1/2	tsp. minced fresh gingerroot
1/4	tsp. salt
2	tsp. canola oil, *divided*
1-1/2	cups fresh snow peas
2	medium carrots, julienned
1	can (8 oz.) sliced water chestnuts, drained
1/4	cup unsalted cashews, toasted

Hot cooked rice, optional

1. In a large resealable plastic bag, combine 2 tablespoons soy sauce, sherry or broth, and 1/2 teaspoon sesame oil; add the chicken. Seal bag and turn to coat. Refrigerate for 30 minutes.

2. In a small bowl, combine cornstarch and broth until smooth. Stir in the sugar, vinegar, hoisin sauce, ginger, salt, and remaining soy sauce and sesame oil; set aside.

3. Drain chicken and discard marinade. In a large nonstick wok or skillet, stir-fry chicken in 1 teaspoon oil until no longer pink. Remove and keep warm. In the same pan, stir-fry peas and carrots in remaining oil until crisp-tender. Add water chestnuts.

4. Return chicken to the pan. Stir sauce mixture and stir into chicken mixture. Bring to a boil; cook and stir for 1 minute or until thickened. Sprinkle with cashews. Serve with rice if desired.

Nutrition Facts: 1 cup (calculated without rice) equals 301 calories, 10 g fat (2 g saturated fat), 63 mg cholesterol, 590 mg sodium, 25 g carbohydrate, 4 g fiber, 28 g protein. **Diabetic Exchanges:** 3 very lean meat, 3 vegetable, 1-1/2 fat, 1/2 starch.

Greek-Style Chicken Burgers

PREP: 25 min. + chilling
GRILL: 10 min. **YIELD:** 4 servings

JUDY PUSKAS • WALLACEBURG, ONTARIO

The original recipe called for lamb or beef, but I decided to try ground chicken to decrease the fat. The sauce easily doubles as a great dip for veggies and toasted pita bread.

1/2	cup fat-free plain yogurt
1/4	cup chopped peeled cucumber
1/4	cup crumbled reduced-fat feta cheese
1-1/2	tsp. snipped fresh dill
1-1/2	tsp. lemon juice
1	small garlic clove, minced

BURGERS:

1	medium onion, finely chopped
1/4	cup dry bread crumbs
1	Tbsp. dried oregano
1	Tbsp. lemon juice
2	garlic cloves, minced
1/2	tsp. salt
1/4	tsp. pepper
1	lb. ground chicken
4	hamburger buns, split
4	lettuce leaves
4	tomato slices

1. Line a strainer with four layers of cheesecloth or one coffee filter and place over a bowl. Place yogurt in prepared strainer; cover yogurt with edges of cheesecloth. Refrigerate for 8 hours or overnight.

CASHEW CHICKEN

GREEK-STYLE CHICKEN BURGERS

MEXICAN MEAT LOAF

2. Remove yogurt from cheesecloth and discard liquid from bowl. Stir in the cucumber, feta cheese, dill, lemon juice and garlic; set aside.

3. In a bowl, combine onion, bread crumbs, oregano, lemon juice, garlic, salt and pepper. Crumble chicken over mixture and mix well. Shape into four burgers.

4. Coat grill rack with cooking spray before starting the grill. Grill burgers, covered, over medium heat for 5-7 minutes on each side or until a meat thermometer reads 165° and juices run clear. Serve each on a bun with lettuce, tomato and 2 tablespoons yogurt sauce.

Nutrition Facts: 1 burger equals 350 calories, 12 g fat (4 g saturated fat), 78 mg cholesterol, 732 mg sodium, 35 g carbohydrate, 3 g fiber, 27 g protein. **Diabetic Exchanges:** 3 lean meat, 2 starch, 1 vegetable.

Mexican Meat Loaf

PREP: 20 min. **BAKE:** 45 min. **YIELD:** 6 servings

CONNIE STAAL • GREENBRIER, ARKANSAS

This great-tasting meat loaf is moist, tender and chock-full of green pepper, onion and zesty tomato flavor! Why not make two? Tuck one in the oven for supper, the other in the freezer for another night.

- 1 large onion, chopped
- 1 medium green pepper, chopped
- 2 garlic cloves, minced
- 2 tsp. olive oil
- 3/4 cup dry bread crumbs
- 3/4 cup shredded reduced-fat cheddar cheese
- 1/2 cup tomato sauce
- 1/4 cup fat-free plain yogurt
- 2 Tbsp. minced fresh parsley

- 2 tsp. Worcestershire sauce
- 1 tsp. chili powder
- 3/4 lb. lean ground turkey
- 1/4 lb. lean ground beef

TOPPING:
- 1/4 cup tomato sauce
- 1 tsp. Worcestershire sauce
- 1/2 tsp. chili powder
- 1/4 cup shredded reduced-fat cheddar cheese

1. In a large nonstick skillet, saute the onion, green pepper and garlic in oil until tender. Transfer to a large bowl. Stir in the bread crumbs, cheese, tomato sauce, yogurt, parsley, Worcestershire sauce and chili powder. Crumble turkey and beef over mixture and mix well.

2. Shape into a loaf. Place in an 11-in. x 7-in. baking dish coated with cooking spray. Bake, uncovered, at 350° for 25 minutes; drain.

3. Combine the tomato sauce, Worcestershire sauce and chili powder; spread over meat loaf. Bake for 15 minutes or until a meat thermometer reads 165°. Sprinkle with cheese; bake 2-3 minutes longer or until cheese is melted.

Nutrition Facts: 1 slice equals 266 calories, 13 g fat (5 g saturated fat), 70 mg cholesterol, 480 mg sodium, 17 g carbohydrate, 2 g fiber, 21 g protein.

If you freeze **Mexican Meat Loaf** for a future use, simply thaw it in the refrigerator overnight and then bake it as directed.

PORK CUTLETS WITH CAPERS

HERBED GRILLED PORK TENDERLOIN

MONTEGO BAY PORK CHOPS

Pork, Ham & More

Sink your teeth into thick, juicy pork chops. Enjoy a hearty sausage stir-fry. Dig into a creamy pasta dish that's loaded with chunks of ham. You can savor these dishes and more with the specialties found in this heartwarming chapter.

Montego Bay Pork Chops C

PREP: 20 min. + marinating **GRILL:** 10 min.
YIELD: 8 servings (1-3/4 cups salsa)

HEATHER KENNEY • ARLINGTON, VIRGINIA

When the weather gets warmer, I inevitably want to move the party outside and away from the hot stove. This is a fun, light dish that's full of flavor.

  1 can (11.3 oz.) mango nectar
1/4 cup white wine vinegar
  3 garlic cloves, minced
1/2 habanero pepper, seeded and chopped
  2 tsp. ground allspice
  1 tsp. ground cinnamon
1/2 tsp. salt
1/2 tsp. ground cloves
1/2 tsp. cayenne pepper
1/4 tsp. ground nutmeg
1/4 tsp. pepper
  8 boneless pork loin chops (4 oz. *each*)

SALSA:
  1 medium mango, finely chopped
  1 small onion, finely chopped
  1 small sweet red pepper, finely chopped
  2 Tbsp. lime juice
1/2 habanero pepper, seeded and finely chopped
1/4 tsp. salt

1. In a large resealable plastic bag, combine the first 11 ingredients. Add pork chops; seal bag and turn to coat. Refrigerate for at least 4 hours. Meanwhile, combine salsa ingredients in a small bowl. Refrigerate until serving.

2. Drain and discard marinade. Coat grill rack with cooking spray before starting the grill. Grill pork chops, covered, over medium heat or broil 4 in. from the heat for 4-5 minutes on each side or until a meat thermometer reads 160°. Serve with salsa.

Editor's Note: When cutting hot peppers, disposable gloves are recommended. Avoid touching your face.

Nutrition Facts: 1 pork chop with about 3 tablespoons salsa equals 184 calories, 7 g fat (2 g saturated fat), 55 mg cholesterol, 142 mg sodium, 8 g carbohydrate, 1 g fiber, 22 g protein. **Diabetic Exchanges:** 3 lean meat, 1/2 starch.

Herb Grilled Pork Tenderloin C

PREP: 10 min. + marinating
GRILL: 25 min. **YIELD:** 6 servings

JUDY NEIL • ROYAL OAK, MICHIGAN

A flavorful herb marinade gives a lovely glaze and lots of savory grilled taste to this moist, melt-in-your-mouth tenderloin. The marinade's also great on chicken.

1/2 cup sherry *or* reduced-sodium chicken broth
  3 Tbsp. lemon juice
  3 Tbsp. reduced-sodium soy sauce
  3 Tbsp. honey
  1 Tbsp. canola oil
  3 garlic cloves, minced
4-1/2 tsp. minced fresh sage *or* 1-1/2 tsp. rubbed sage
  1 Tbsp. minced fresh thyme *or* 1 tsp. dried thyme
  1 bay leaf
  2 pork tenderloins (1 lb. *each*)

1. In a small bowl, combine the first nine ingredients. Pour 3/4 cup marinade into a large resealable plastic bag; add the pork. Seal the bag and turn to coat; refrigerate pork for at least 4 hours. Cover and refrigerate the remaining marinade.

2. Coat grill rack with cooking spray before starting the grill. Prepare grill for indirect heat. Drain the pork and discard marinade. Grill, covered, over indirect medium-hot heat for 25-40 minutes or until a meat thermometer reads 160°, basting occasionally with reserved marinade. Let meat stand for 5 minutes before slicing.

Nutrition Facts: 4 ounces cooked pork equals 226 calories, 7 g fat (2 g saturated fat), 84 mg cholesterol, 261 mg sodium, 7 g carbohydrate, trace fiber, 30 g protein. **Diabetic Exchanges:** 4 lean meat, 1/2 starch.

Is your gang getting tired of chicken? Trying to cut back on red meat a bit? Consider a pork entree. Recipes such as **Montego Bay Pork Chops** are low in fat and are good sources of essential B vitamins.

Ham & Corn Souffle

PREP: 25 min. **BAKE:** 50 min. **YIELD:** 4 servings

MARGARET HAUGH HEILMAN • HOUSTON, TEXAS

Start that special day with this puffy, ham-egg-and-cheese souffle I whip up for family and friends. It's almost too pretty to eat!

4	egg whites
2	tsp. dry bread crumbs
1-1/2	cups frozen corn, thawed
2	green onions, thinly sliced
2/3	cup diced fully cooked lean ham
1/4	cup all-purpose flour
1/4	tsp. salt
1/8	tsp. cayenne pepper
1	cup fat-free milk
1/2	cup shredded reduced-fat sharp cheddar cheese
2	egg yolks
1/2	tsp. cream of tartar

1. Place egg whites in a large mixing bowl; let stand at room temperature for 30 minutes. Coat a 1-1/2-qt. baking dish with cooking spray and lightly sprinkle with bread crumbs; set aside.

2. In a large nonstick skillet coated with cooking spray, cook corn and onions until tender. Remove from the heat; stir in ham and set aside.

3. In a small saucepan, combine the flour, salt and cayenne; gradually whisk in milk until smooth. Bring to a boil; cook and stir for 2 minutes or until thickened. Remove from the heat; stir in cheese until melted. Transfer to a large bowl; stir in corn mixture. Stir a small amount of hot mixture into egg yolks; return all to the bowl, stirring constantly. Cool slightly.

4. Add cream of tartar to egg whites; beat until stiff peaks form. With a spatula, fold a fourth of the egg whites into the milk mixture until no white streaks remain. Fold in remaining egg whites until combined.

5. Transfer to prepared dish. Bake at 325° for 50-55 minutes or until top is puffed and center appears set. Serve immediately.

Nutrition Facts: 1 serving equals 248 calories, 7 g fat (3 g saturated fat), 123 mg cholesterol, 577 mg sodium, 28 g carbohydrate, 2 g fiber, 20 g protein. **Diabetic Exchanges:** 2 starch, 2 lean meat.

Gingered Pork Tenderloin ⒸC

PREP: 10 min. + marinating **GRILL:** 25 min.
YIELD: 6 servings

MICHELLE SANDERS • FRASER LAKE, BRITISH COLUMBIA

This pork tenderloin is absolutely delicious and great for entertaining. Why? The quick prep is done ahead of time, and the grilling is so simple. This one's foolproof!

2	Tbsp. reduced-sodium soy sauce
1/4	cup sherry or reduced-sodium chicken broth
2	Tbsp. canola oil
2	Tbsp. minced fresh gingerroot
2	tsp. sugar
2	garlic cloves, minced
2	pork tenderloins (1 lb. *each*)

1. In a large resealable plastic bag, combine the first six ingredients; add the pork. Seal bag and turn to coat; refrigerate for 8 hours or overnight.

2. Coat grill rack with cooking spray before starting the grill. Prepare grill for indirect heat. Drain pork and discard marinade. Grill, covered, over indirect medium-hot heat for 25-40 minutes or until a meat thermometer reads 160°. Let stand for 5 minutes before slicing.

Nutrition Facts: 4 ounces cooked pork equals 214 calories, 8 g fat (2 g saturated fat), 84 mg cholesterol, 194 mg sodium, 2 g carbohydrate, trace fiber, 30 g protein. **Diabetic Exchanges:** 4 lean meat, 1/2 fat.

HAM & CORN SOUFFLE

GINGERED PORK TENDERLOIN

Marinated Lamb Chops ⓈⒸ

PREP: 10 min. + marinating **GRILL:** 10 min.
YIELD: 4 servings

JILL HEATWOLE • PITTSVILLE, MARYLAND

These lean little lamb chops are packed with the flavors of rosemary, ginger and mustard. Marinating makes them so tender. They're something special for spring.

- 1 small onion, sliced
- 2 Tbsp. red wine vinegar
- 1 Tbsp. lemon juice
- 1 Tbsp. olive oil
- 2 tsp. minced fresh rosemary or 3/4 tsp. dried rosemary, crushed
- 2 tsp. Dijon mustard
- 1 garlic clove, minced
- 1/2 tsp. pepper
- 1/4 tsp. salt
- 1/4 tsp. ground ginger
- 8 lamb loin chops (3 oz. *each*)

1. In a large resealable plastic bag, combine the first 10 ingredients; add the lamb chops. Seal bag and turn to coat; refrigerate for several hours or overnight.

2. Coat grill rack with cooking spray before starting the grill. Remove chops from marinade, discarding marinade and onion.

3. Grill chops, covered, over medium heat for 5-7 minutes on each side or until meat reaches desired doneness (for medium-rare, a meat thermometer should read 145°; medium, 160°; well-done, 170°).

Nutrition Facts: 2 lamb chops equals 164 calories, 8 g fat (3 g saturated fat), 68 mg cholesterol, 112 mg sodium, trace carbohydrate, trace fiber, 21 g protein. **Diabetic Exchange:** 3 lean meat.

Serve **Marinated Lamb Chops** with freshly steamed asparagus that is lightly seasoned with thyme.

Pork Cutlets with Capers [C]

PREP/TOTAL TIME: 30 min. **YIELD:** 4 servings

LISA SNEAD • FRANKLIN, OHIO

Capers add a touch of elegance to this tender pork lightly laced with white wine. Enjoy!

1	pork tenderloin (1 lb.)
1/4	cup all-purpose flour
1/2	tsp. salt
1/2	tsp. pepper
1	Tbsp. olive oil, *divided*
1/2	cup reduced-sodium chicken broth
1/2	cup white wine *or* reduced-sodium chicken broth
2	Tbsp. capers, drained
1	Tbsp. minced fresh parsley

1. Cut pork into eight slices; flatten to 1/4-in. thickness. In a large resealable plastic bag, combine the flour, salt and pepper. Add pork, one piece at a time, and shake to coat. In a large nonstick skillet over medium heat, cook pork in oil in batches for 2-3 minutes on each side or until juices run clear. Remove and keep warm.

2. Add broth and wine to the pan, stirring to loosen browned bits. Stir in capers. Bring to a boil. Reduce heat; simmer, uncovered, for 4-6 minutes or until juices are slightly thickened. Stir in parsley. Drizzle over pork.

Nutrition Facts: 2 pork cutlets with 4 teaspoons pan juices equals 204 calories, 7 g fat (2 g saturated fat), 63 mg cholesterol, 541 mg sodium, 4 g carbohydrate, trace fiber, 23 g protein. **Diabetic Exchanges:** 3 lean meat, 1/2 fat.

Pork Chops with Blue Cheese Sauce [C]

PREP/TOTAL TIME: 30 min. **YIELD:** 4 servings

KATHY SPECHT • CAMBRIA, CALIFORNIA

These wonderful chops have a unique kick. Not a blue-cheese fan? You'll still love the mild sauce. They're perfect for weekdays but nice enough for company.

4	bone-in pork loin chops (7 oz. *each*)
1	tsp. coarsely ground pepper

SAUCE:

1	green onion, finely chopped
1	garlic clove, minced
1	tsp. butter
1	Tbsp. all-purpose flour
2/3	cup fat-free milk
3	Tbsp. crumbled blue cheese
1	Tbsp. white wine *or* reduced-sodium chicken broth

1. Sprinkle pork chops on both sides with pepper. Broil 3-4 in. from the heat for 4-6 minutes on each side or until a meat thermometer reads 160°.

2. Meanwhile, in a small saucepan, saute onion and garlic in butter until tender. Sprinkle with flour; stir until blended. Gradually add milk. Bring to a boil; cook and stir for 2 minutes or until thickened. Add cheese and wine; heat through. Serve sauce with chops.

Nutrition Facts: 1 pork chop with 3 tablespoons sauce equals 263 calories, 11 g fat (5 g saturated fat), 94 mg cholesterol, 176 mg sodium, 5 g carbohydrate, trace fiber, 33 g protein. **Diabetic Exchanges:** 4 lean meat, 2 fat.

Spinach Pork Tenderloin

PREP: 25 min. **BAKE:** 25 min. + standing
YIELD: 4 servings

LINDA RAE LEE • SAN FRANCISCO, CALIFORNIA

Stuffed with fresh spinach and artichoke hearts, these pork slices look fancy enough for guests. A sweet-sour sauce enhances the entree.

    2 cups torn fresh baby spinach
  1/4 cup water
  1/2 cup frozen artichoke hearts, thawed and chopped
  1/3 cup shredded Parmesan cheese
  1/4 tsp. dried rosemary, crushed
    1 pork tenderloin (1 lb.)
  1/2 tsp. salt, *divided*
  1/8 tsp. pepper

SAUCE:
  1/2 cup apple-cranberry juice concentrate
  1/4 cup balsamic vinegar
    1 Tbsp. sugar

1. In a large nonstick skillet, cook the spinach in water over medium heat for 3-4 minutes or until wilted; drain well. In a large bowl, combine the spinach, artichokes, Parmesan cheese and rosemary; set aside.

2. Cut a lengthwise slit down center of tenderloin to within 1/2 in. of bottom. Open meat so it lies flat; cover with plastic wrap. Flatten to 1/4-in. thickness; remove plastic. Sprinkle meat with 1/2 teaspoon salt; top with spinach mixture.

3. Close meat; tie with kitchen string and secure ends with toothpicks. Sprinkle with pepper and remaining salt. Place in a shallow baking pan. Bake at 425° for 15 minutes.

4. Meanwhile, in a small saucepan, combine the sauce ingredients. Bring to a boil over medium heat. Reduce heat; simmer, uncovered, for 15 minutes. Pour over the meat. Bake 10 minutes longer or until a meat thermometer reads 160°. Let stand for 10 minutes before slicing. Discard toothpicks.

Nutritional Facts: One serving (3 ounces cooked meat with about 2 tablespoons sauce) equals 262 calories, 6 g fat (3 g saturated fat), 72 mg cholesterol, 517 mg sodium, 22 g carbohydrate, 1 g fiber, 29 g protein. **Diabetic Exchanges:** 4 very lean meat, 1 vegetable, 1 fruit, 1/2 fat.

Glazed Pork Roast C

PREP: 30 min. **COOK:** 4 hours **YIELD:** 16 servings

RADELLE KNAPPENBERGER • OVIEDO, FLORIDA

This light recipe is always popular with adults and children alike. It's an excellent take-along meal for potlucks. Serve it alongside a simple rice pilaf for guests.

    1 boneless whole pork loin roast (4 lbs.), trimmed
    1 Tbsp. olive oil
    1 Tbsp. butter, melted
  2/3 cup orange juice concentrate
  1/3 cup water
    3 garlic cloves, minced
1-1/2 tsp. salt

  1/2 tsp. pepper
GLAZE:
  1/4 cup packed brown sugar
    2 Tbsp. balsamic vinegar
    1 Tbsp. orange juice concentrate
    1 garlic clove, minced
    1 can (11 oz.) mandarin oranges, drained, optional

1. Cut roast in half. In a large skillet, brown roast in oil and butter on all sides. Transfer to a 5-qt. slow cooker. Add the orange juice concentrate, water, garlic, salt and pepper. Cover and cook on low for 4-6 hours or until a meat thermometer reads 160° and the meat is tender.

2. For glaze, in a small saucepan, combine the brown sugar, vinegar, orange juice concentrate and garlic. Bring to a boil. Reduce heat; simmer, uncovered, for 3-5 minutes or until reduced to about 1/4 cup. Brush over roast. Garnish with oranges if desired.

Nutrition Facts: 3 ounces cooked pork (calculated without oranges) equals 190 calories, 7 g fat (2 g saturated fat), 58 mg cholesterol, 263 mg sodium, 9 g carbohydrate, trace fiber, 22 g protein. **Diabetic Exchanges:** 3 lean meat, 1/2 starch.

If you plan to double the recipe for **Spinach Pork Tenderloin,** or any pork tenderloin dish, you can cook the 1-pound tenderloins side by side, leaving space between them. Follow the cooking time noted in the recipe.

PORK CHOPS WITH BLUE CHEESE SAUCE

Cinnamon-Apple Pork Chops

PREP/TOTAL TIME: 25 min. **YIELD:** 4 servings

CHRISTINA PRICE • PITTSBURGH, PENNSYLVANIA

I skip the pecans in this dish to keep my portion even lighter calorie-wise, but my boyfriend loves to add them.

4	boneless pork loin chops (4 oz. *each*)
2	Tbsp. reduced-fat butter, *divided*
3	Tbsp. brown sugar
1	tsp. ground cinnamon
1/2	tsp. ground nutmeg
1/4	tsp. salt
4	medium tart apples, thinly sliced
2	Tbsp. chopped pecans

1. In a large skillet over medium heat, cook pork chops in 1 tablespoon butter for 4-5 minutes on each side or until juices run clear. Meanwhile, in a small bowl, combine the brown sugar, cinnamon, nutmeg and salt.

2. Remove chops and keep warm. Add the apples, pecans, brown sugar mixture and remaining butter to the pan; cook and stir until apples are tender. Serve with chops.

Editor's Note: This recipe was tested with Land O'Lakes light stick butter.

Nutrition Facts: 1 pork chop with 2/3 cup apples equals 316 calories, 12 g fat (4 g saturated fat), 62 mg cholesterol, 232 mg sodium, 31 g carbohydrate, 4 g fiber, 22 g protein. **Diabetic Exchanges:** 3 lean meat, 1 starch, 1 fruit, 1 fat.

Pork Medallions with Asian Flair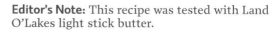

PREP/TOTAL TIME: 25 min. **YIELD:** 4 servings

DIANNE JAMES • EDMOND, OKLAHOMA

When I got serious about losing weight and getting healthy, my kids missed the Chinese delivery I often ordered. I combined a few recipes to come up with this tasty winner.

1	pork tenderloin (1 lb.), halved and thinly sliced
1	Tbsp. sesame oil
1/4	cup sherry or reduced-sodium chicken broth
3	Tbsp. reduced-sodium soy sauce
1	Tbsp. brown sugar
1	Tbsp. hoisin sauce
1	garlic clove, minced
1/8	tsp. cayenne pepper

Hot cooked brown rice, optional

1. In a large nonstick skillet, saute pork in oil in batches until no longer pink. Remove and keep warm.

2. Add the remaining ingredients to the pan; cook and stir over medium heat for 3-4 minutes or until thickened. Return pork to the pan; heat through. Serve with rice if desired.

Nutrition Facts: 3 ounces cooked pork (calculated without rice) equals 202 calories, 7 g fat (2 g saturated fat), 63 mg cholesterol, 566 mg sodium, 6 g carbohydrate, trace fiber, 23 g protein. **Diabetic Exchanges:** 3 lean meat, 1/2 starch, 1/2 fat.

PORK MEDALLIONS WITH ASIAN FLAIR

CINNAMON-APPLE PORK CHOPS

Sausage Zucchini Skillet

PREP/TOTAL TIME: 25 min. **YIELD:** 4 servings

DEBBY ABEL • FLAT ROCK, NORTH CAROLINA

I began serving a version of this as a side with grilled salmon. One day, a lightbulb went off, and I added sausage for a one-dish supper with rice or noodles.

1	lb. Italian turkey sausage links, casings removed
2	large zucchini, chopped
1	large sweet onion, chopped
2	garlic cloves, minced
1	can (14-1/2 oz.) no-salt-added diced tomatoes, undrained
1/4	tsp. pepper
2	cups hot cooked rice

1. Crumble sausage into a large nonstick skillet coated with cooking spray. Add the zucchini and onion; cook and stir over medium heat for 4 minutes.

Add the garlic; cook and stir until meat is no longer pink. Drain.

2. Stir in tomatoes and pepper; bring to a boil. Reduce heat; simmer, uncovered, for 4-5 minutes or until liquid is evaporated. Serve with rice.

Nutrition Facts: 1-1/4 cups sausage mixture with 1/2 cup rice equals 329 calories, 11 g fat (2 g saturated fat), 68 mg cholesterol, 724 mg sodium, 36 g carbohydrate, 5 g fiber, 23 g protein.
Diabetic Exchanges: 3 lean meat, 2 vegetable, 1-1/2 starch.

When it's time to mix up your supper standbys, consider the zesty flavor of **Sausage Zucchini Skillet**. If you don't have the Italian turkey sausage links on hand, try using cubed chicken instead. Feel free to toss in some frozen corn kernels or peas for extra nutrition as well.

Pork Chops with Ginger Maple Sauce

PREP: 20 min. **COOK:** 20 min. **YIELD:** 4 servings

RUTH GOODING • LOS ANGELES, CALIFORNIA

An unusual combination of cinnamon, chili powder, ginger and maple syrup gives these tender pork chops a fantastic taste! No one will believe the recipe is light.

1	medium onion, chopped
4	tsp. canola oil, *divided*
1	Tbsp. minced fresh gingerroot
1	tsp. chili powder
1/2	tsp. salt
1/2	tsp. pepper
1/2	tsp. ground cinnamon
4	bone-in pork loin chops (6 oz. *each*)
1/2	cup reduced-sodium chicken broth
1/4	cup maple syrup
2	cups hot cooked rice

1. In a small skillet over medium-low heat, cook onion in 2 teaspoons oil until golden brown and very tender, about 10 minutes. Add ginger; cook and stir 2 minutes longer.

2. Meanwhile, combine the chili powder, salt, pepper and cinnamon; rub over both sides of pork chops. In a large skillet over medium heat, brown chops in remaining oil for 2-3 minutes on each side.

3. Add the broth, syrup and onion mixture. Bring to a boil. Reduce heat; cover and simmer for 8-10 minutes or until meat is tender. Remove chops and keep warm. Bring broth mixture to a boil; cook, uncovered, until liquid is thickened and reduced to 1/2 cup. Serve chops with rice and sauce.

Nutrition Facts: 1 pork chop with 1/2 cup rice and 2 tablespoons sauce equals 393 calories, 12 g fat (3 g saturated fat), 74 mg cholesterol, 431 mg sodium, 40 g carbohydrate, 2 g fiber, 29 g protein. **Diabetic Exchanges:** 3 lean meat, 2-1/2 starch, 1 fat.

Zesty Pork Chops C

PREP: 25 min. **BAKE:** 35 min. **YIELD:** 4 servings

CHERYL BOAK • ROTHESAY, NEW BRUNSWICK

My own creation, this recipe is light, flavorful and simple to make. I sometimes top these chops with bread crumbs and shredded mozzarella for the last 10 minutes of baking. They're a favorite with family and friends.

4	boneless pork loin chops (4 oz. *each*)
1/4	tsp. pepper
1/8	tsp. salt
1/4	cup all-purpose flour
1	can (14-1/2 oz.) diced tomatoes, undrained
1-3/4	cups sliced fresh mushrooms
4	green onions, chopped
1/2	cup pimiento-stuffed olives

1 garlic clove, minced
1 tsp. minced fresh basil *or* 1/4 tsp. dried basil
1 tsp. minced fresh oregano *or* 1/4 tsp. dried oregano

1. Sprinkle pork chops with pepper and salt. Place flour in a large resealable plastic bag; add the pork chops, one at a time, and shake to coat.

2. In a large nonstick skillet coated with cooking spray, brown chops on both sides. Transfer to an ungreased 11-in. x 7-in. baking dish. Top with tomatoes, mushrooms, onions and olives. Sprinkle with garlic, basil and oregano.

3. Cover and bake at 350° for 35-40 minutes or until a meat thermometer reads 160°.

Nutrition Facts: 1 pork chop equals 251 calories, 10 g fat (3 g saturated fat), 57 mg cholesterol, 670 mg sodium, 15 g carbohydrate, 2 g fiber, 25 g protein. **Diabetic Exchanges:** 3 lean meat, 2 vegetable, 1/2 fat.

German Deli Pizza

PREP: 40 min. + rising **BAKE:** 15 min. **YIELD:** 6 slices

CINDY REAMS • PHILIPSBURG, PENNSYLVANIA

Take the chill off and serve up great German deli flavor with this savory, cheesy pizza. It has a tender crust and mild, mustardy bite that all ages can appreciate.

DOUGH:
2/3 cup water (70° to 80°)
1 Tbsp. olive oil
1 tsp. caraway seeds
1/4 tsp. salt
1-1/2 cups bread flour
1/2 cup rye flour
1 tsp. active dry yeast

SAUCE:
1/3 cup chopped red onion
1 Tbsp. butter
1 Tbsp. all-purpose flour
1 cup fat-free evaporated milk
1 Tbsp. spicy brown mustard
1/4 cup shredded Swiss cheese

TOPPINGS:
1/3 cup thinly sliced red onion
1 cup cubed fully cooked lean ham
1 cup (4 oz.) shredded Swiss cheese

1. In bread machine pan, place dough ingredients in order suggested by manufacturer. Select dough setting (check dough after 5 minutes of mixing; add 1 to 2 tablespoons of water or flour if needed).

2. When cycle is completed, turn dough onto a lightly floured surface. Punch dough down; roll into a 13-in. circle. Transfer to a 12-in. pizza pan coated with cooking spray; build up edges slightly. Cover and let rest for 10 minutes.

3. Prick dough thoroughly with a fork. Bake at 400° for 6-8 minutes or until edges are lightly browned.

4. Meanwhile, for sauce, in a small saucepan, saute chopped onion in butter until tender. Stir in flour until blended; gradually add evaporated milk and mustard. Bring to a boil; cook and stir for 2 minutes or until thickened. Remove from the heat; stir in cheese. Spread over crust. Top with sliced onion, ham and cheese. Bake for 12-15 minutes or until crust and cheese are lightly browned.

Nutrition Facts: 1 slice equals 330 calories, 12 g fat (6 g saturated fat), 36 mg cholesterol, 546 mg sodium, 37 g carbohydrate, 3 g fiber, 19 g protein. **Diabetic Exchanges:** 2-1/2 starch, 2 lean meat, 1 fat.

It's the unique rye crust that makes the recipe for **German Deli Pizza** a hit. Keep the crust recipe in mind the next time you'd like to experiment in the kitchen.

GERMAN DELI PIZZA

ZESTY PORK CHOPS

Greek Pork Chops ⓒ

PREP: 15 min. + marinating
GRILL: 10 min. **YIELD:** 4 servings

GERI LIPCZYNSKI • OAK LAWN, ILLINOIS

My in-laws taught me a lot about cooking, so any time I come across a great new recipe, I enjoy making it for them. These tasty grilled chops always get rave reviews.

2	Tbsp. olive oil
4	tsp. lemon juice
1	Tbsp. Worcestershire sauce
2	tsp. dried oregano
1	tsp. salt
1	tsp. onion powder
1	tsp. garlic powder
1	tsp. pepper
1/2	tsp. ground mustard
4	boneless pork loin chops (3/4 in. thick and 4 oz. *each*)

1. In a large resealable plastic bag, combine the first nine ingredients; add the pork. Seal bag and turn to coat; refrigerate for 8 hours or overnight.

2. Coat grill rack with cooking spray before starting the grill. Drain pork and discard marinade. Grill pork, covered, over medium heat for 4-5 minutes on each side or until a meat thermometer reads 160°.

Nutrition Facts: 1 pork chop equals 193 calories, 10 g fat (3 g saturated fat), 55 mg cholesterol, 348 mg sodium , 2 g carbohydrate, 1 g fiber, 22 g protein. **Diabetic Exchanges:** 3 lean meat, 1/2 fat.

Mandarin Pork Chops

PREP/TOTAL TIME: 30 min. **YIELD:** 6 servings

MARY ANN MARINO • BARDSTOWN, KENTUCKY

This sweet and tangy sauce is perfect with pork. Oranges, cloves and cinnamon give each bite wonderful flavor.

1	can (11 oz.) mandarin oranges
1	Tbsp. cornstarch
5	green onions, sliced
1/4	cup packed brown sugar
1/4	cup ketchup
1	Tbsp. cider vinegar
1	tsp. prepared mustard
1/2	tsp. salt
1/2	tsp. ground cinnamon
3	whole cloves
6	boneless pork loin chops (4 oz. *each*)
1	Tbsp. butter

1. Drain oranges, reserving juice; set oranges aside. In a small bowl, combine cornstarch and 3 tablespoons reserved juice until smooth; set aside. In another small bowl, combine the onions, brown sugar, ketchup, vinegar, mustard, salt, cinnamon, cloves and remaining juice; set aside.

2. In a large nonstick skillet, brown pork chops in butter on both sides. Add onion mixture; bring to a boil. Reduce heat; simmer, uncovered, for 8-10 minutes or until a meat thermometer reads 160°, turning chops once.

3. Remove pork and keep warm. Discard cloves. Stir cornstarch mixture into pan juices. Bring to a boil; cook and stir for 1-2 minutes or until thickened. Stir in oranges. Serve with pork chops.

Nutrition Facts: 1 pork chop with 3 tablespoons sauce equals 255 calories, 8 g fat (4 g saturated fat), 60 mg cholesterol, 384 mg sodium, 23 g carbohydrate, 1 g fiber, 22 g protein. **Diabetic Exchanges:** 3 lean meat, 1-1/2 starch.

GREEK PORK CHOPS

MANDARIN PORK CHOPS

Makeover Pork Chops With Gravy

PREP: 30 min. **BAKE:** 10 min. **YIELD:** 4 servings

BETTY SLIVON • SUN CITY, ARIZONA

I wanted to impress guests with an elegant dish that was simple and light. When the staff at "Healthy Cooking" revised my recipe, I knew I had a hit on my hands!

1	egg
1-1/4	cups 2% milk, *divided*
1-1/2	cups soft bread crumbs
3	tsp. minced fresh parsley, *divided*
1	tsp. minced fresh thyme
4	bone-in pork loin chops (7 oz. *each*)
3/4	tsp. salt, *divided*
1/2	tsp. pepper, *divided*
3	Tbsp. reduced-fat butter, *divided*
3	Tbsp. plus 1 tsp. all-purpose flour
1/3	cup half-and-half cream
1/3	cup reduced-sodium beef broth

1. In a shallow bowl, whisk egg and 1/2 cup milk. Combine the bread crumbs, 1 teaspoon parsley and thyme in another shallow bowl. Sprinkle pork chops with 1/2 teaspoon salt and 1/4 teaspoon pepper. Dip chops in egg mixture, then crumb mixture.

2. In a large skillet over medium-high heat, cook pork chops in 2 tablespoons butter for 4 minutes on each side. Transfer to an ungreased 13-in. x 9-in. baking pan. Bake, uncovered, at 425° for 10-15 minutes or until a meat thermometer reads 160°.

3. Meanwhile, in the same skillet, melt remaining butter. Stir in flour and remaining salt and pepper until smooth; gradually stir in the cream, broth and remaining milk. Bring to a boil; cook and stir for 2 minutes or until thickened. Serve gravy with chops; sprinkle with remaining parsley.

Editor's Note: This recipe was tested with Land O'Lakes light stick butter.

Nutrition Facts: 1 pork chop with 1/3 cup gravy equals 392 calories, 19 g fat (9 g saturated fat), 126 mg cholesterol, 799 mg sodium, 18 g carbohydrate, 1 g fiber, 35 g protein.

The home economist at "Healthy Cooking" created **Makeover Pork Chops with Gravy** by cooking the chops in reduced-fat butter instead of the oil the recipe originally called for. In addition, they relied on half-and-half to eliminate nearly two-thirds of the fat.

Makeover Tempting Tortellini & Ham

PREP: 20 min. **COOK:** 15 min. **YIELD:** 6 servings

LISA BURKE • HOPKINSVILLE, KENTUCKY

When I decided to eat healther, this was one recipe I knew needed a makeover. By creating a low-fat roux using light butter and fat-free milk, this dish still offers all of its creamy goodness with far less fat than my original.

1	pkg. (9 oz.) refrigerated cheese tortellini
1	cup chopped fresh broccoli
1/4	cup reduced-fat butter, cubed
1/4	cup all-purpose flour
3/4	cup fat-free milk
1/4	cup half-and-half cream
1-1/2	cups cubed fully cooked lean ham
4	oz. reduced-fat cream cheese, cubed
1/2	cup grated Parmigiano-Reggiano cheese
1	tsp. dried basil
1/2	tsp. garlic powder
1/4	tsp. pepper
1	medium tomato, seeded and chopped

1. In a large saucepan, cook tortellini according to package directions, adding the broccoli during the last 5 minutes of cooking.

2. In a large nonstick skillet over medium heat, melt butter. Stir in flour until smooth; gradually add milk and cream. Bring to a boil; cook and stir for 1 minute or until thickened.

3. Add the ham, cheeses, basil, garlic powder and pepper; cook and stir until cream cheese is melted.

Stir in tomato. Drain tortellini mixture; add to the pan and heat through.

Editor's Note: This recipe was tested with Land O'Lakes light stick butter.

Nutrition Facts: 3/4 cup equals 334 calories, 16 g fat (9 g saturated fat), 66 mg cholesterol, 865 mg sodium, 29 g carbohydrate, 2 g fiber, 19 g protein.

Slow-Cooked Pork Roast Dinner

PREP: 25 min. **COOK:** 6 hours **YIELD:** 8 servings

JANE MONTGOMERY • PIQUA, OHIO

This easy, delicious recipe will give you the moistest pork you have ever tasted! You can cut it with a fork, and leftovers are just as tender the next day.

1	large onion, halved and sliced
1	boneless pork loin roast (2-1/2 lbs.)
4	medium potatoes, peeled and cubed
1	pkg. (16 oz.) frozen sliced carrots
1	cup hot water
1/4	cup sugar
3	Tbsp. cider vinegar
2	Tbsp. reduced-sodium soy sauce
1	Tbsp. ketchup
1/2	tsp. salt
1/2	tsp. pepper
1/4	tsp. garlic powder
1/4	tsp. chili powder
2	Tbsp. cornstarch
2	Tbsp. cold water

1. Place onion in the bottom of a 5-qt. slow cooker. Add the pork, potatoes and carrots. Whisk the hot water, sugar, vinegar, soy sauce, ketchup, salt, pepper, garlic powder and chili powder; pour over pork and vegetables.

2. Cover and cook on low for 6-8 hours or until a meat thermometer reads 160° and the pork and potatoes are tender.

3. Remove pork and vegetables and keep warm. Pour cooking juices into a small saucepan and skim fat. Combine cornstarch and cold water until smooth; stir into cooking juices. Bring to a boil; cook and stir for 1-2 minutes or until thickened. Serve with pork and vegetables.

Nutrition Facts: 4 ounces cooked pork with 2/3 cup vegetables and 1/3 cup gravy equals 304 calories, 7 g fat (2 g saturated fat), 70 mg cholesterol, 401 mg sodium, 30 g carbohydrate, 3 g fiber, 29 g protein. **Diabetic Exchanges:** 4 lean meat, 1-1/2 starch, 1 vegetable.

Pork Medallions In Orange Sauce c

PREP: 15 min. **COOK:** 25 min. **YIELD:** 4 servings

DIANE ZALEWSKI • FREEHOLD, NEW JERSEY

This pork recipe is my family's favorite dinner. My children absolutely love it, and there are never any extras. I garnish with orange slices and parsley.

1/2	cup orange juice
1/4	cup sherry or reduced-sodium chicken broth
2	Tbsp. ketchup
1	Tbsp. light corn syrup
1	tsp. grated orange peel
1	pork tenderloin (1 lb.), cut into 1/2-in. slices
1/4 to 1/2	tsp. dried rosemary, crushed
1/4	tsp. salt
1/8	tsp. pepper
1-1/2	tsp. canola oil

1. In a small bowl, combine the orange juice, sherry or broth, ketchup, corn syrup and orange peel; set aside.

2. Flatten pork to 1/4-in. thickness; sprinkle with rosemary, salt and pepper. In a large nonstick skillet, brown pork in oil. Remove and keep warm.

3. Pour juice mixture into the skillet, stirring to loosen browned bits. Bring to a boil. Reduce heat; simmer, uncovered, for 10-15 minutes or until liquid is reduced to 1 cup. Return pork to the pan; cover and simmer for 4-5 minutes or until meat is no longer pink.

Nutrition Facts: 3 ounces cooked pork with 2 tablespoons sauce equals 194 calories, 6 g fat (1 g saturated fat), 63 mg cholesterol, 289 mg sodium, 10 g carbohydrate, trace fiber, 23 g protein. **Diabetic Exchanges:** 3 lean meat, 1/2 starch.

Pork Chops & Acorn Squash

PREP: 15 min. **COOK:** 4 hours **YIELD:** 6 servings

MARY JOHNSON • COLOMA, WISCONSIN

My husband and I can never get enough fresh buttery squash from our garden. These chops cook up so sweet and tender in the slow cooker. Best of all, the classic, "comfort food" doesn't take me a whole day to prepare!

6	boneless pork loin chops (4 oz. *each*)
2	medium acorn squash, peeled and cubed
1/2	cup packed brown sugar
2	Tbsp. butter, melted
1	Tbsp. orange juice
3/4	tsp. salt
1/2	tsp. grated orange peel
3/4	tsp. browning sauce, optional

1. Place pork chops in a 5-qt. slow cooker; add the squash. Combine the brown sugar, butter, orange juice, salt, orange peel and browning sauce if desired; pour over squash.

2. Cover and cook on low for 4 hours or until meat and squash are tender.

Nutrition Facts: 1 pork chop with 2/3 cup squash (calculated without browning sauce) equals 317 calories, 10 g fat (5 g saturated fat), 65 mg cholesterol, 365 mg sodium, 34 g carbohydrate, 2 g fiber, 23 g protein. **Diabetic Exchanges:** 3 lean meat, 2 starch, 1 fat.

SLOW-COOKED PORK ROAST DINNER

PORK MEDALLIONS IN ORANGE SAUCE

FLORIBBEAN FISH BURGERS WITH TROPICAL SAUCE

CREOLE SHRIMP & RICE

TORTELLINI WITH SALMON-RICOTTA SAUCE

Fish & Seafood

When it comes to eating light, fish is a natural choice. With the many options available today, family cooks no longer feel the need to reserve this refreshing option for guests, so surprise your gang tonight with one of these sensations.

Creole Shrimp & Rice

PREP: 25 min. **COOK:** 20 min. **YIELD:** 4 servings

ELSIE EPP • NEWTON, KANSAS

Running late for dinner? Here's a light weekday supper recipe with lots of Creole flavor that my family always loves. It couldn't be much quicker or easier to prepare.

- 1 celery rib, chopped
- 1 small onion, chopped
- 1 small green pepper, chopped
- 1 Tbsp. canola oil
- 1 can (14-1/2 oz.) diced tomatoes, undrained
- 2 Tbsp. savory herb with garlic soup mix
- 1 garlic clove, minced
- 1 tsp. Worcestershire sauce
- 1 bay leaf
- 1/8 tsp. cayenne pepper
- 1 lb. cooked medium shrimp, peeled and deveined
- 2 cups hot cooked rice

1. In a large skillet, saute the celery, onion and green pepper in oil until tender. Add the tomatoes, soup mix, garlic, Worcestershire sauce, bay leaf and cayenne. Bring to a boil. Reduce heat; cover and simmer for 15 minutes.

2. Add shrimp; heat through. Discard bay leaf. Serve with rice.

Nutrition Facts: 3/4 cup shrimp mixture with 1/2 cup rice equals 304 calories, 6 g fat (1 g saturated fat), 172 mg cholesterol, 622 mg sodium, 34 g carbohydrate, 3 g fiber, 27 g protein. **Diabetic Exchanges:** 3 very lean meat, 2 starch, 1 vegetable.

Floribbean Fish Burgers With Tropical Sauce

PREP: 35 min. **COOK:** 10 min. **YIELD:** 6 servings

VIRGINIA ANTHONY • JACKSONVILLE, FLORIDA

I like to make fish burgers because they're lower in saturated fat and cholesterol than other varieties. I can use some avocado because there's not a lot of other fat in these burgers.

- 1/2 cup fat-free mayonnaise
- 1 Tbsp. minced fresh cilantro
- 1 Tbsp. minced chives
- 1 Tbsp. sweet pickle relish
- 1 Tbsp. lime juice
- 1 tsp. grated lime peel
- 1-1/2 tsp. Caribbean jerk seasoning
- 1/8 tsp. hot pepper sauce

BURGERS:
- 1 egg white, lightly beaten
- 4 green onions, chopped
- 1/3 cup soft bread crumbs
- 2 Tbsp. minced fresh cilantro
- 2 tsp. Caribbean jerk seasoning
- 1 garlic clove, minced
- 1/8 tsp. salt
- 1-1/2 lbs. grouper or red snapper fillets
- 6 kaiser rolls, split
- 6 lettuce leaves
- 1 medium ripe avocado, peeled and cut into 12 slices

1. In a small bowl, combine the first eight ingredients; cover and refrigerate until serving.

2. In a large bowl, combine the egg white, onions, bread crumbs, cilantro, jerk seasoning, garlic and salt. Place fish in a food processor; cover and process until finely chopped. Add to egg white mixture and mix well. Shape into six burgers.

3. Coat grill rack with cooking spray before starting the grill. Spray both sides of burgers with cooking spray. Grill burgers, covered, over medium heat for 4-5 minutes on each side or until a meat thermometer reads 160°. Serve each on a roll with lettuce, avocado and 5 teaspoons tropical sauce.

Nutrition Facts: 1 burger equals 353 calories, 9 g fat (1 g saturated fat), 44 mg cholesterol, 797 mg sodium, 39 g carbohydrate, 4 g fiber, 29 g protein. **Diabetic Exchanges:** 3 very lean meat, 2-1/2 starch, 1 fat.

Seasoned with hot pepper sauce, herbs and more, the Tropical Sauce from Floribbean Fish Burgers makes a fine addition to chicken and pork entrees, too.

TILAPIA WITH JASMINE RICE

Tilapia with Jasmine Rice

PREP/TOTAL TIME: 30 min.　**YIELD:** 2 servings

SHIRL PARSONS • CAPE CARTERET, NORTH CAROLINA

Here's a tasty meal-in-one that's sized right for two. Bottled salad dressing adds flavor without much effort on my part. Best of all, the recipe is easy to double for guests.

3/4	cup water
1/2	cup uncooked jasmine rice
1-1/2	tsp. butter
1/4	tsp. ground cumin
1/4	tsp. seafood seasoning
1/4	tsp. pepper
1/8	tsp. salt
2	tilapia fillets (6 oz. *each*)
1/4	cup prepared fat-free Italian salad dressing

1. In a large saucepan, bring the water, rice and butter to a boil. Reduce heat; cover and simmer for 15-20 minutes or until liquid is absorbed and rice is tender.

2. Combine the seasonings; sprinkle over fillets. Place salad dressing in a large skillet; cook over medium heat until heated through. Add fish; cook for 3-4 minutes on each side or until fish flakes easily with a fork. Serve with rice.

Nutrition Facts: 1 fillet with 3/4 cup rice equals 356 calories, 5 g fat (3 g saturated fat), 91 mg cholesterol, 743 mg sodium, 41 g carbohydrate, 1 g fiber, 35 g protein. **Diabetic Exchanges:** 4 very lean meat, 3 starch, 1/2 fat.

Mexican Shrimp Salad C

PREP: 20 min. + marinating
GRILL: 10 min.　**YIELD:** 4 servings

MARIE BASON • BEND, OREGON

These terrific shrimp can be served on top of a salad, with tortillas or over rice. And you can use the marinade with chicken or beef, too. How versatile!

1	small onion, halved and thinly sliced
1/4	cup minced fresh cilantro
1	jalapeno pepper, seeded and chopped
2	Tbsp. canola oil
2	tsp. chili powder
1/2	tsp. ground cumin
1/2	tsp. ground coriander
1/2	tsp. pepper
1/4	tsp. salt
1	lb. uncooked medium shrimp, peeled and deveined
6	cups torn leaf lettuce
1/2	cup fat-free ranch salad dressing

1. In a large bowl, combine the first nine ingredients. Add shrimp; toss to coat. Cover and refrigerate for 30 minutes.

2. If grilling shrimp, coat grill rack with cooking spray before starting the grill. Thread shrimp onto four metal or soaked wooden skewers; discard onion mixture. Grill, covered, over medium heat or broil 4 in. from the heat for 3-4 minutes on each side or until shrimp turn pink.

3. Divide lettuce among four plates; top with shrimp. Serve immediately with dressing.

Editor's Note: When cutting hot peppers, disposable gloves are recommended. Avoid touching your face.

Nutrition Facts: 1 serving equals 218 calories, 9 g fat (1 g saturated fat), 168 mg cholesterol, 716 mg sodium, 15 g carbohydrate, 3 g fiber, 20 g protein. **Diabetic Exchanges:** 3 very lean meat, 1-1/2 fat, 1 vegetable, 1/2 starch.

Tasty Tuna Casserole

PREP: 20 min. **BAKE:** 25 min. **YIELD:** 4 servings

ELSIE EPP • NEWTON, KANSAS

Classic tuna casserole gets a tomato-twist in this no-fuss recipe. Rich and creamy, it makes a family-pleasing meal.

2	cups uncooked elbow macaroni
1	can (12 oz.) solid white tuna, drained
1	can (8 oz.) tomato sauce
4	oz. reduced-fat cream cheese, cubed
1	small onion, finely chopped
1/4	tsp. salt
1/2	tsp. dried oregano

1. Cook macaroni according to package directions. Meanwhile, in a large bowl, combine the remaining ingredients. Drain macaroni; stir into tuna mixture. Transfer to a 2-qt. baking dish coated with cooking spray. Cover and bake at 350° for 20-25 minutes or until heated through.

Nutrition Facts: 1-1/2 cups equals 334 calories, 9 g fat (5 g saturated fat), 56 mg cholesterol, 851 mg sodium, 33 g carbohydrate, 2 g fiber, 29 g protein. **Diabetic Exchanges:** 3 very lean meat, 2 starch, 1 fat.

Five-Spice Tuna C

PREP/TOTAL TIME: 30 min. **YIELD:** 4 servings

LINDA MURRAY • ALLENSTOWN, NEW HAMPSHIRE

A bit of five-spice adds Asian flair to tuna steaks with delightful results! For a bolder taste, marinate for 30 minutes.

1	Tbsp. sugar
1	Tbsp. reduced-sodium soy sauce
1	Tbsp. sesame oil
1/2	tsp. Chinese five-spice powder
1/2	tsp. salt
1/4	tsp. pepper
4	tuna steaks (1 in. thick and 6 oz. *each*)

1. In a large resealable plastic bag, combine the first six ingredients. Add the tuna; seal the bag and turn to coat. Refrigerate for 15 minutes.

2. Drain and discard marinade. Place tuna on a broiler pan coated with cooking spray. Broil 3-4 in. from the heat for 3-5 minutes on each side or until the fish flakes easily with a fork.

Nutrition Facts: 1 tuna steak equals 230 calories, 5 g fat (1 g saturated fat), 77 mg cholesterol, 509 mg sodium, 4 g carbohydrate, trace fiber, 40 g protein. **Diabetic Exchanges:** 5 very lean meat, 1/2 fat.

Mediterranean Shrimp & Linguine

PREP/TOTAL TIME: 30 min. **YIELD:** 6 servings

NANCY DEANS • ROCHESTER, NEW YORK

This dish is lower in fat but so rich in vegetables, it looks like it came from an Italian restaurant. It's nice for a healthy diet. You can also make it ahead and reheat later.

9	oz. uncooked linguine
1	lb. uncooked medium shrimp, peeled and deveined
1	cup sliced fresh mushrooms
2	Tbsp. olive oil
3	medium tomatoes, chopped
1	can (14 oz.) water-packed artichoke hearts, rinsed, drained and halved
1	can (6 oz.) pitted ripe olives, drained and halved
2	garlic cloves, minced
1	tsp. dried oregano
1/2	tsp. dried basil
1/2	tsp. salt
1/8	tsp. pepper

1. Cook linguine according to package directions. Meanwhile, in a large nonstick skillet, saute shrimp and mushrooms in oil for 2 minutes. Add the remaining ingredients; cook and stir for 5 minutes or until shrimp turn pink and sauce is heated through.

2. Drain linguine; serve with shrimp mixture.

Nutrition Facts: 1 cup shrimp mixture with 3/4 cup linguine equals 328 calories, 9 g fat (1 g saturated fat), 112 mg cholesterol, 748 mg sodium, 41 g carbohydrate, 3 g fiber, 21 g protein. **Diabetic Exchanges:** 2 starch, 2 very lean meat, 1-1/2 fat, 1 vegetable.

MEDITERRANEAN SHRIMP & LINGUINE

Open-Faced Salmon Sandwiches

PREP/TOTAL TIME: 25 min. **YIELD:** 4 servings

MRS. RALPH CABECEIRAS • SOUTH PRAIRIE, WASHINGTON

I keep several cans of salmon in my pantry at all times so I never have to worry about drop-in guests. This recipe is so tasty and quick...and it doubles easily for company.

- 1 egg, lightly beaten
- 1 small onion, finely chopped
- 1 small green pepper, finely chopped
- 1/3 cup soft bread crumbs
- 1 Tbsp. lemon juice
- 1 tsp. reduced-sodium teriyaki sauce
- 1/4 tsp. dried parsley flakes
- 1/4 tsp. dried basil
- 1/4 tsp. pepper
- 1 can (14-3/4 oz.) salmon, drained, bones and skin removed
- 2 English muffins, split and toasted

Lettuce leaves and tomato slices, optional

1. In a small bowl, combine the first nine ingredients. Add salmon; mix well. Shape into four patties.

2. In a large nonstick skillet coated with cooking spray, cook patties over medium heat for 4-5 minutes on each side or until lightly browned. Serve on English muffin halves with lettuce and tomato if desired.

Nutrition Facts: 1 sandwich equals 270 calories, 10 g fat (2 g saturated fat), 99 mg cholesterol, 757 mg sodium, 19 g carbohydrate, 2 g fiber, 26 g protein. **Diabetic Exchanges:** 3 lean meat, 1 starch.

OPEN-FACED SALMON SANDWICHES

Weeknight Jambalaya

PREP: 20 min. **COOK:** 25 min. **YIELD:** 6 servings

DEBRA MARSHALL • PARK FALLS, WISCONSIN

This is a great way to use up leftovers. You can mix and match any or all of the meats. Feel free to leave out what you don't like and adjust the chilies and cayenne to taste.

- 1/4 lb. boneless skinless chicken breast, cubed
- 3 tsp. canola oil, *divided*
- 1/4 lb. smoked turkey sausage, halved lengthwise and sliced
- 1/4 lb. cubed fully cooked lean ham
- 1 large onion, chopped
- 1 medium green pepper, chopped
- 1 celery rib, chopped
- 2 Tbsp. chopped green chilies
- 2 garlic cloves, minced
- 2 cans (8 oz. *each*) no-salt-added tomato sauce
- 1 can (14-1/2 oz.) no-salt-added diced tomatoes, undrained
- 1/3 cup water
- 3 Tbsp. tomato paste
- 2 tsp. Cajun seasoning
- 1/4 tsp. cayenne pepper
- 1/2 lb. deveined peeled cooked medium shrimp
- 3 cups hot cooked rice

1. In a large saucepan coated with cooking spray, brown chicken in 1-1/2 teaspoons oil. Add sausage and ham; cook and stir for 2 minutes or until browned and chicken is no longer pink. Remove and keep warm.

2. In the same pan, saute the onion, green pepper and celery in remaining oil until tender. Add chilies and garlic; cook 1 minute longer. Stir in the tomato sauce, tomatoes, water, tomato paste, Cajun seasoning and cayenne. Bring to a boil. Reduce heat; cover and simmer for 5 minutes.

3. Stir in shrimp and reserved chicken mixture; heat through. Serve with rice.

Nutrition Facts: 1 cup jambalaya with 1/2 cup rice equals 286 calories, 5 g fat (1 g saturated fat), 103 mg cholesterol, 815 mg sodium, 35 g carbohydrate, 3 g fiber, 22 g protein.

WEEKNIGHT JAMBALAYA

Soy-Ginger Grilled Swordfish C

PREP: 10 min. + marinating
GRILL: 10 min. **YIELD:** 4 servings

MARCY HALL • VISALIA, CALIFORNIA

This is one of my family's favorite recipes that's also delicious with tuna or halibut steaks. I like to use frozen orange juice concentrate for a richer flavor. Best of all, it only marinates for 30 minutes.

2	Tbsp. orange juice
2	Tbsp. reduced-sodium soy sauce
1	Tbsp. minced fresh parsley
1	Tbsp. lemon juice
1	Tbsp. ketchup
1	tsp. minced fresh gingerroot
1/4	tsp. dried oregano
1/4	tsp. pepper
1	tsp. olive oil
2	garlic cloves, minced
1-1/4	lbs. swordfish steak

1. In a small bowl, combine orange juice, soy sauce, parsley, lemon juice, ketchup, ginger, oregano and pepper. Set aside 2 tablespoons mixture for basting.

2. Stir oil and garlic into remaining mixture. Place in a large resealable plastic bag; add the fish. Seal bag and turn to coat; refrigerate for 30 minutes.

3. Drain and discard marinade. Coat grill rack with cooking spray before starting the grill. Grill, covered, over high heat for 3-5 minutes on each side or until fish flakes easily with a fork, basting occasionally with reserved orange juice mixture.

Nutrition Facts: 4 ounces cooked fish equals 178 calories, 6 g fat (2 g saturated fat), 52 mg cholesterol, 328 mg sodium, 2 g carbohydrate, trace fiber, 27 g protein. **Diabetic Exchange:** 4 lean meat.

Chipotle-Sparked Mustard Salmon C

PREP/TOTAL TIME: 25 min. **YIELD:** 6 servings

HELEN CONWELL • FAIRHOPE, ALABAMA

This delicious salmon packs huge flavors—horseradish, stone-ground mustard and chipotle come together in a fantastic blend that's anything but boring.

6	salmon fillets (4 oz. *each*)
1/4	cup reduced-fat mayonnaise
1/4	cup prepared horseradish
1/4	cup stone-ground mustard
1/4	tsp. lemon-pepper seasoning
1	tsp. minced chipotle pepper in adobo sauce
1	tsp. snipped fresh dill

1. Place salmon in a foil-lined 15-in. x 10-in. baking pan. Combine the mayonnaise, horseradish, mustard, lemon-pepper and chipotle pepper; spread over fillets.

2. Bake at 350° for 15-20 minutes or until fish flakes easily with a fork. Sprinkle with dill.

Nutrition Facts: 1 fillet equals 260 calories, 16 g fat (3 g saturated fat), 70 mg cholesterol, 407 mg sodium, 4 g carbohydrate, 1 g fiber, 23 g protein.

Tortellini with Salmon-Ricotta Sauce

PREP/TOTAL TIME: 30 min. **YIELD:** 4 servings

BETH DAUENHAUER • PUEBLO, COLORADO

I like to serve this with a colorful vegetable side, such as a tomato salad or peas and carrots. I often top it with Romano cheese and use fresh basil instead of dill. It's always tasty!

1	pkg. (9 oz.) refrigerated cheese tortellini
2	green onions, sliced
2	garlic cloves, minced
1	tsp. butter
1	tsp. cornstarch
1	cup fat-free milk
1/2	cup shredded part-skim mozzarella cheese
1	cup fat-free ricotta cheese
1	pouch (7.1 oz.) boneless skinless pink salmon
2	Tbsp. snipped fresh dill *or* 2 tsp. dill weed
1-1/2	tsp. grated lemon peel
1-1/2	tsp. lemon juice
1/4	tsp. salt

1. Cook tortellini according to package directions. Meanwhile, in a large saucepan, saute onions and garlic in butter until tender. Combine cornstarch and milk until smooth; gradually stir into the pan. Bring to a boil; cook and stir for 2 minutes or until slightly thickened.

2. Stir in mozzarella cheese until melted. Stir in the ricotta cheese, salmon, dill, lemon peel, lemon juice and salt.

3. Drain tortellini; add to ricotta sauce. Cook and stir until heated through.

Nutrition Facts: 1 cup equals 373 calories, 11 g fat (6 g saturated fat), 67 mg cholesterol, 797 mg sodium, 40 g carbohydrate, 2 g fiber, 28 g protein. **Diabetic Exchanges:** 3 lean meat, 2-1/2 starch, 1/2 fat.

Poached Salmon Steaks C

PREP/TOTAL TIME: 20 min. **YIELD:** 4 servings

CHARLOTTE ELLIOTT • NEENAH, WISCONSIN

If you're looking for a new way to fix salmon, these lemon-pepper steaks are sure to please family and friends.

2	cups water
2	Tbsp. white vinegar
2	Tbsp. lemon juice
1	small onion, halved and sliced
5	thin slices lemon
1	celery rib, chopped
1	tsp. salt
4	whole cloves
1	bay leaf
4	salmon steaks (6 oz. *each*)
1/2	tsp. salt-free lemon-pepper seasoning

1. In an 11-in. x 7-in. microwave-safe dish coated with cooking spray, combine the first nine ingredients. Microwave, uncovered, on high for 4-5 minutes or until mixture comes to a boil.

2. Carefully place salmon in dish. Cover and microwave on high for 4 to 4-1/2 minutes or until fish almost flakes with a fork. Turn steaks over. Cover and let stand for 2 minutes or until fish flakes easily with a fork. Remove salmon from poaching liquid; sprinkle with lemon-pepper.

Editor's Note: This recipe was tested in a 1,100-watt microwave.

Nutrition Facts: 1 salmon steak equals 313 calories, 18 g fat (4 g saturated fat), 100 mg cholesterol, 297 mg sodium, 1 g carbohydrate, trace fiber, 34 g protein.

Shrimp 'n' Noodle Bowls ☐F

PREP/TOTAL TIME: 25 min. **YIELD:** 6 servings

MARY BERGFELD • EUGENE, OREGON

This is a great quick meal that can be made with pick-up ingredients from the grocery store. I often use Japanese soba noodles. Cooked shrimp and bagged slaw reduce the time and work to get it to the table.

8	oz. uncooked angel hair pasta
1	lb. cooked small shrimp
2	cups broccoli coleslaw mix
6	green onions, thinly sliced
1/2	cup minced fresh cilantro
2/3	cup reduced-fat sesame ginger salad dressing

1. Cook pasta according to package directions; drain and rinse in cold water. Transfer to a large bowl. Add the shrimp, coleslaw mix, onions and cilantro. Add dressing; toss to coat. Cover and refrigerate until serving.

Nutrition Facts: 1-1/3 cups equals 260 calories, 3 g fat (trace saturated fat), 147 mg cholesterol, 523 mg sodium, 36 g carbohydrate, 2 g fiber, 22 g protein. **Diabetic Exchanges:** 2 starch, 2 very lean meat, 1/2 fat.

Red Pepper & Parmesan Tilapia ☐C

PREP/TOTAL TIME: 20 min. **YIELD:** 4 servings

MICHELLE MARTIN • DURHAM, NORTH CAROLINA

My husband and I are always looking for light and healthy fish recipes. This one's a hit with him, and we've tried it at dinner parties, too. It's a staple!

1/4	cup egg substitute
1/2	cup grated Parmesan cheese
1	tsp. Italian seasoning
1/2 to 1	tsp. crushed red pepper flakes
1/2	tsp. pepper
4	tilapia fillets (6 oz. *each*)

1. Place egg substitute in a shallow bowl. In another shallow bowl, combine the cheese, Italian seasoning, pepper flakes and pepper. Dip fillets in egg substitute, then cheese mixture.

2. Place in a 15-in. x 10-in. baking pan coated with cooking spray. Bake at 425° for 10-15 minutes or until fish flakes easily with a fork.

Nutrition Facts: 1 fillet equals 179 calories, 4 g fat (2 g saturated fat), 89 mg cholesterol, 191 mg sodium, 1 g carbohydrate, trace fiber, 35 g protein. **Diabetic Exchanges:** 5 very lean meat, 1/2 fat.

For a quick splash of seasoning anytime you need it, always keep **bottled salad dressing** on hand. Just be sure to check the label for fat content before buying.

SHRIMP 'N' NOODLE BOWLS

RED PEPPER & PARMESAN TILAPIA

Pan-Seared Chili Salmon

PREP/TOTAL TIME: 30 min. **YIELD:** 4 servings

CHERYL HERRICK • BURLINGTON, VERMONT

I adapted this recipe from a restaurant dish we had years ago, and it remains a regular in our meal rotation. With shortcuts like peeled baby carrots and instant brown rice, it's ready in 30 minutes from start to finish!

3	cups fresh baby carrots
1	cup instant brown rice
1	cup reduced-sodium chicken broth
1/4	tsp. pepper, *divided*
3	tsp. chili powder
1/2	tsp. salt
4	salmon fillets (4 oz. *each*)
2	tsp. olive oil
1	Tbsp. minced fresh parsley
1	tsp. butter

1. Place carrots in a steamer basket; place in a small saucepan over 1 in. of water. Bring to a boil; cover and steam for 12 minutes or until crisp-tender.

2. Meanwhile, in a small saucepan, bring the rice, broth and 1/8 teaspoon pepper to a boil. Reduce heat; cover and simmer for 5 minutes.

3. Combine chili powder and salt; rub over salmon. In a large nonstick skillet coated with cooking spray, cook salmon in oil over medium-high heat for 4-6 minutes on each side or until fish flakes easily with a fork.

4. Remove rice from the heat; let stand for 5 minutes. Fluff with a fork. In a small bowl, combine the carrots, parsley, butter and remaining pepper. Serve with salmon and rice.

Nutrition Facts: 1 salmon fillet with 2/3 cup carrots and 1/2 cup rice equals 369 calories, 17 g fat (3 g saturated fat), 69 mg cholesterol, 620 mg sodium, 27 g carbohydrate, 4 g fiber, 26 g protein.

Fish Tacos ▣

PREP: 30 min. **COOK:** 20 min. **YIELD:** 8 servings

LENA LIM • SEATTLE, WASHINGTON

A cool sauce with just a bit of zing tops these crispy, spicy fish tacos. I love this recipe. It's good, guilt-free and doesn't break the bank.

3/4	cup fat-free sour cream
1	can (4 oz.) chopped green chilies
1	Tbsp. fresh cilantro leaves
1	Tbsp. lime juice
4	tilapia fillets (4 oz. *each*)
1/2	cup all-purpose flour
1	egg white, beaten
1/2	cup panko (Japanese) bread crumbs
1	Tbsp. canola oil
1/2	tsp. salt
1/2	tsp. *each* white pepper, cayenne pepper and paprika
8	corn tortillas (6 in.), warmed
1	large tomato, finely chopped

1. Place the sour cream, chilies, cilantro and lime juice in a food processor; cover and process until blended. Set aside.

2. Cut each tilapia fillet lengthwise into two portions. Place the flour, egg white and bread crumbs in separate shallow bowls. Dip tilapia in flour, then egg white, then crumbs.

3. In a large skillet over medium heat, cook tilapia in oil in batches for 4-5 minutes on each side or until fish flakes easily with a fork. Combine the seasonings; sprinkle over fish.

4. Place a portion of fish on each tortilla; top with about 2 tablespoons of sour cream mixture. Sprinkle with tomato.

Nutrition Facts: 1 taco equals 196 calories, 3 g fat (trace saturated fat), 31 mg cholesterol, 303 mg sodium, 26 g carbohydrate, 2 g fiber, 16 g protein. **Diabetic Exchanges:** 2 very lean meat, 1-1/2 starch, 1/2 fat.

PAN-SEARED CHILI SALMON

FISH TACOS

Crab Cakes with Fresh Lemon

PREP: 25 min. **COOK:** 10 min./batch
YIELD: 4 servings

EDIE DESPAIN • LOGAN, UTAH

Fresh lemon and lemon juice bring out all the great flavors in these crispy crab cakes. But be careful not to overcook, or they'll be dry—instead of moist and delicate.

2/3	cup yellow cornmeal
1/3	cup fat-free milk
1	small sweet red pepper, finely chopped
4	green onions, chopped
1	tsp. canola oil
3	egg whites, lightly beaten
1/3	cup reduced-fat mayonnaise
1/4	cup all-purpose flour
1/4	cup minced fresh parsley
2	Tbsp. lemon juice
1/4	tsp. seafood seasoning
1/8	tsp. cayenne pepper
4	pouches (3.53 oz. *each*) premium crabmeat, drained
1	cup frozen corn, thawed
8	lemon wedges

1. In a large bowl, combine cornmeal and milk; set aside. In a large nonstick skillet, saute red pepper and onions in oil until tender. Remove from heat.

2. Add the egg whites, mayonnaise, flour, parsley, lemon juice, seafood seasoning and cayenne to the reserved cornmeal mixture; mix well. Fold in the crab, corn and red pepper mixture.

3. Coat the same skillet with cooking spray; drop crab mixture by scant 1/2 cupfuls into the pan. Press into 3/4-in.-thick patties. Cook in batches over medium heat for 4-6 minutes on each side or until golden brown. Serve with lemon wedges.

Nutrition Facts: 2 crab cakes equals 311 calories, 9 g fat (1 g saturated fat), 67 mg cholesterol, 764 mg sodium, 43 g carbohydrate, 5 g fiber, 17 g protein. **Diabetic Exchanges:** 3 starch, 2 very lean meat, 1-1/2 fat.

Teriyaki Salmon With Sesame Ginger Rice

PREP/TOTAL TIME: 20 min. **YIELD:** 6 servings

KATRINA LOPES • LYMAN, SOUTH CAROLINA

This delicious recipe is lighter, super-fast and elegant enough for company. It's packed full of vitamins and antioxidants and is good not only for your waistline, but for your heart, too!

2	cups uncooked instant rice
6	salmon fillets (4 oz. *each*)
1/3	cup reduced-calorie pancake syrup
1/3	cup reduced-sodium teriyaki sauce
4	green onions, thinly sliced
1	Tbsp. butter
1	pkg. (10 oz.) frozen chopped spinach, thawed and squeezed dry
1/2	cup reduced-fat sesame ginger salad dressing

1. Cook rice according to package directions. Meanwhile, place salmon fillets in a 15-in. x 10-in. baking pan coated with cooking spray. Combine syrup and teriyaki sauce; spoon 1/3 cup mixture over fillets.

2. Bake at 400° for 10-15 minutes or until fish flakes easily with a fork, basting frequently with remaining syrup mixture.

3. In a large skillet, saute onions in butter until tender. Add spinach and cooked rice; saute 2 minutes longer. Stir in dressing; heat through. Serve with salmon.

Nutrition Facts: 1 fillet with 3/4 cup rice equals 412 calories, 16 g fat (4 g saturated fat), 72 mg cholesterol, 675 mg sodium, 40 g carbohydrate, 2 g fiber, 27 g protein.

ZUCCHINI TOMATO BAKE

SPRING VEGETABLE QUICHE

SATISFYING CREMINI BARLEY

Meatless Mains

Thinking about cutting back on the amount of red meat you serve your family? You'll be amazed at the variety of sensational items found here. Each dish is so full of hearty flavor, no one will even realize they're eating a meatless main dish.

Spring Vegetable Quiche M

PREP: 15 min. **BAKE:** 40 min. + standing
YIELD: 6 servings

SANDI TUTTLE • HAYWARD, WISCONSIN

Brown rice makes up the crust for this different but very healthy, nutritious and totally delicious main dish. It tastes just as great reheated the next day.

- 7 egg whites, *divided*
- 2 cups cooked brown rice
- 1 Tbsp. all-purpose flour
- 1 cup evaporated fat-free milk
- 1 egg
- 1 cup (4 oz.) shredded part-skim mozzarella cheese
- 1 cup chopped fresh asparagus
- 1/2 cup fresh or frozen corn, thawed
- 1 jar (4-1/2 oz.) sliced mushrooms, drained
- 1/3 cup finely chopped carrot
- 1/4 cup finely chopped red onion
- 2 Tbsp. minced fresh parsley
- 3/4 tsp. dried basil
- 1/2 tsp. salt
- 1/4 tsp. dried oregano
- 2 Tbsp. grated Parmesan cheese

1. In a bowl, whisk 1 egg white. Add rice; stir until blended. Press onto the bottom and up the sides of a 9-in. deep-dish pie plate coated with cooking spray.

2. In a large bowl, whisk flour and milk until smooth. Whisk in egg and remaining egg whites. Stir in the mozzarella cheese, asparagus, corn, mushrooms, carrot, onion, parsley, basil, salt and oregano. Pour into crust; sprinkle with Parmesan cheese.

3. Bake at 375° for 45-50 minutes or until a knife inserted near the center comes out clean. Let stand for 10 minutes before cutting.

Nutrition Facts: 1 piece equals 225 calories, 5 g fat (3 g saturated fat), 49 mg cholesterol, 538 mg sodium, 28 g carbohydrate, 3 g fiber, 17 g protein. **Diabetic Exchanges:** 1-1/2 starch, 1 lean meat, 1 vegetable.

Satisfying Cremini Barley F M

PREP: 20 min. **COOK:** 15 min. **YIELD:** 5 servings

LILLIAN JULOW • GAINESVILLE, FLORIDA

Almost 2 decades ago, I became a pretty strict vegetarian. I've eased up a bit and occasionally eat chicken or fish, but I still enjoy meatless entrees the most. This is one of my very favorites! It also makes a great side dish.

- 2 cups vegetable broth
- 1 cup quick-cooking barley
- 1 medium red onion, finely chopped
- 1 celery rib, finely chopped
- 1 medium carrot, finely chopped
- 2 tsp. olive oil
- 1/2 lb. sliced baby portobello (cremini) mushrooms
- 2 garlic cloves, minced
- 1 pkg. (6 oz.) fresh baby spinach
- 1 can (15 oz.) white kidney or cannellini beans, rinsed and drained
- 1/4 tsp. pepper
- 3 Tbsp. minced fresh parsley

1. In a large saucepan, bring broth to a boil. Stir in barley. Reduce heat; cover and simmer for 10-12 minutes or until barley is tender. Remove from the heat; let stand for 5 minutes.

2. Meanwhile, in a large skillet, saute the onion, celery and carrot in oil for 3 minutes. Add mushrooms and garlic; saute 3-4 minutes longer or until vegetables are tender. Stir in the spinach, beans, pepper and barley; cook and stir until spinach is wilted. Stir in parsley.

Nutrition Facts: 1 cup equals 255 calories, 3 g fat (trace saturated fat), 0 cholesterol, 532 mg sodium, 47 g carbohydrate, 12 g fiber, 11 g protein.

Whether looking for a brunch item or a change-of-pace dinner, try **Spring Vegetable Quiche.** It's wonderful any time of day, particularly with a fresh fruit salad.

White Bean, Sweet Potato & Pepper Ragout Ⓜ

PREP: 20 min. **COOK:** 25 min. **YIELD:** 4 servings

HEATHER SAVAGE • CORYDON, INDIANA

I try to serve a meatless meal two or three nights a week. It's a great way to keep up our intake of veggies—along with all the fiber and nutrients they provide. It even helps save money! This hearty comfort food is a family favorite.

- 1 large sweet red pepper, cut into 1-in. pieces
- 1 large green pepper, cut into 1-in. pieces
- 1 Tbsp. olive oil
- 1 large sweet potato, peeled, quartered and sliced
- 3 garlic cloves, minced
- 1/2 tsp. minced fresh rosemary *or* 1/4 tsp. dried rosemary, crushed
- 1/2 cup water
- 1/4 tsp. pepper
- 2 cans (15 oz. *each*) white kidney *or* cannellini beans, rinsed and drained
- 1 can (14-1/2 oz.) diced tomatoes, undrained
- 1/4 tsp. salt

1. In a Dutch oven over medium heat, cook and stir peppers in oil until tender. Add the sweet potato, garlic and rosemary; cook 4-5 minutes longer.

2. Stir in water and pepper. Bring to a boil. Reduce heat; cover and simmer for 5-7 minutes or until sweet potato is tender. Stir in the beans, tomatoes and salt; heat through.

Nutrition Facts: 1-3/4 cups equals 286 calories, 5 g fat (trace saturated fat), 0 cholesterol, 551 mg sodium, 51 g carbohydrate, 13 g fiber, 11 g protein.

WHITE BEAN, SWEET POTATO & PEPPER RAGOUT

Grilled Black Bean & Pineapple Burgers Ⓜ

PREP: 30 min. + chilling **GRILL:** 10 min. **YIELD:** 6 servings

CAROLE RESNICK • CLEVELAND, OHIO

This filling sandwich contains a whopping 11 g of fiber but only 5 g of fat per serving. Pineapple slices are a perfect topper for this tasty bean burger.

- 2 cans (15 oz. *each*) black beans, rinsed and drained
- 1 medium red onion, finely chopped
- 2 eggs, beaten
- 1/2 cup panko (Japanese) bread crumbs
- 1/2 cup crushed baked tortilla chip scoops
- 1/3 cup chopped green pepper
- 1 Tbsp. minced fresh cilantro
- 1 tsp. ground cumin
- 1 tsp. chili powder
- 1/2 tsp. hot pepper sauce
- 1/2 cup fat-free mayonnaise
- 4 tsp. chopped green onion
- 4 tsp. Dijon mustard
- 2 tsp. honey
- 1-1/2 tsp. orange juice
- 1/2 tsp. reduced-sodium soy sauce
- 6 slices unsweetened pineapple
- 6 whole wheat hamburger buns, split

1. In a large bowl, mash beans. Add the red onion, eggs, bread crumbs, chips, green pepper, cilantro, cumin, chili powder and pepper sauce. Shape into six patties. Refrigerate for 1 hour.

2. In a small bowl, combine the mayonnaise, green onion, mustard, honey, orange juice and soy sauce; refrigerate until serving.

3. Coat grill rack with cooking spray before starting the grill. Grill burgers, covered, over medium heat for 3-5 minutes on each side or until a thermometer reads 160°. Grill pineapple slices for 2-3 minutes on each side or until heated through. Place burgers and pineapple on buns; top each with 1 rounded tablespoon of sauce.

Nutrition Facts: 1 burger equals 357 calories, 5 g fat (1 g saturated fat), 73 mg cholesterol, 807 mg sodium, 65 g carbohydrate, 11 g fiber, 14 g protein.

GRILLED BLACK BEAN & PINEAPPLE BURGERS

Stuffed Portobellos C M

PREP: 15 min. **BAKE:** 20 min. **YIELD:** 4 servings

MALCOLM LEWIS • FREEVILLE, NEW YORK

*I like to turn hearty portobellos into a flavorful meal. The
addition of walnuts adds crunch to the savory topping. If you'd
like, add raisins for a bit of sweetness.*

4	large portobello mushrooms (about 5 in.)
3/4	cup shredded part-skim mozzarella cheese, *divided*
1/3	cup dry bread crumbs
1/3	cup chopped walnuts
1/3	cup finely chopped onion
1/3	cup golden raisins, optional
3	Tbsp. grated Parmesan cheese
1/4	tsp. salt
1/4	tsp. pepper
1	egg, lightly beaten
2	Tbsp. vegetable broth

1. Remove stems from mushrooms (discard or save
for another use); set caps aside. In a small bowl,
combine 1/4 cup mozzarella cheese, bread crumbs,
walnuts, onion, raisins if desired, Parmesan cheese,
salt and pepper. Stir in egg and broth until blended.

2. Spoon into the mushroom caps; sprinkle with
remaining mozzarella cheese. Place in a 15-in. x 10-in.
baking pan coated with cooking spray. Bake,
uncovered, at 350° for 20-25 minutes or until the
mushrooms are tender.

Nutrition Facts: 1 stuffed portobello (calculated without
raisins) equals 221 calories, 12 g fat (4 g saturated fat), 68 mg
cholesterol, 435 mg sodium, 14 g carbohydrate, 2 g fiber, 14 g
protein. **Diabetic Exchanges:** 2 fat, 1 lean meat, 1 vegetable,
1/2 starch.

Black Bean 'n' Corn Quesadillas M

PREP/TOTAL TIME: 25 min. **YIELD:** 6 servings

SUSAN FRANKLIN • LITTLETON, COLORADO

*Black beans partner up with another power food, spinach, in
my easy quesadillas.*

1	can (15 oz.) black beans, rinsed and drained, *divided*
1	small onion, finely chopped
2	tsp. olive oil
1	can (11 oz.) Mexicorn, drained
1	tsp. chili powder
1	tsp. ground cumin
1	pkg. (6 oz.) fresh baby spinach
8	flour tortillas (8 in.)
3/4	cup shredded reduced-fat Monterey Jack cheese *or* Mexican cheese blend

1. In a small bowl, mash 1 cup beans with a fork. In a
large skillet, saute onion in oil until tender. Add the
corn, chili powder, cumin, mashed beans and
remaining beans; cook and stir until heated through.
Stir in spinach just until wilted.

2. Place two tortillas on an ungreased baking sheet;
spread each with a rounded 1/2 cup of bean mixture.
Sprinkle each with 3 tablespoons of cheese; top with
another tortilla. Repeat.

3. Bake at 400° for 8-10 minutes or until the cheese
is melted. Cut each of the quesadillas into six wedges.
Serve warm.

Nutrition Facts: 4 wedges equals 358 calories, 9 g fat (3 g
saturated fat), 10 mg cholesterol, 900 mg sodium, 56 g
carbohydrate, 5 g fiber, 15 g protein.

Black Bean Lasagna M

PREP: 25 min. **BAKE:** 40 min. + standing
YIELD: 12 servings

DUSTY DAVIS • SLIDELL, LOUISIANA

I came up with this lasagna to help my husband lower his cholesterol. It's one of our favorite meals.

9	lasagna noodles
1	large onion, chopped
3	garlic cloves, minced
1	tsp. canola oil
2	cans (16 oz. *each*) black beans, rinsed and drained
1	can (14-1/2 oz.) diced tomatoes, undrained
2	cans (6 oz. *each*) tomato paste
1	cup water
2	Tbsp. minced fresh cilantro
1/4	to 1/2 tsp. crushed red pepper flakes
4	egg whites, beaten
1	carton (15 oz.) reduced-fat ricotta cheese
1/2	cup grated Parmesan cheese
1/4	cup minced fresh parsley
2	cups (8 oz. *each*) shredded reduced-fat Mexican cheese blend

1. Cook noodles according to package directions. Meanwhile, in a large skillet over medium heat, cook onion and garlic in oil until tender. Add the beans, tomatoes, tomato paste, water, cilantro and pepper flakes. Bring to a boil. Reduce heat; simmer, uncovered, for 15 minutes or until slightly thickened.

2. In a small bowl, combine the egg whites, ricotta cheese, Parmesan cheese and parsley.

3. Drain noodles. Spread 1/2 cup bean mixture into a 13-in. x 9-in. baking dish coated with cooking spray. Layer with three noodles, a third of the ricotta mixture, a third of the remaining bean mixture and 2/3 cup cheese blend. Repeat layers twice.

4. Cover and bake at 350° for 30-35 minutes. Uncover; bake 10-15 minutes longer or until bubbly. Let stand for 10 minutes before cutting.

Nutrition Facts: 1 piece equals 279 calories, 7 g fat (4 g saturated fat), 25 mg cholesterol, 455 mg sodium, 36 g carbohydrate, 6 g fiber, 18 g protein. **Diabetic Exchanges:** 2 starch, 1-1/2 lean meat, 1 vegetable.

Zucchini Frittata C M

PREP: 25 min. **BAKE:** 25 min. **YIELD:** 4 servings

AMY CRANE • SWARTZ CREEK, MICHIGAN

Ideal for breakfast or dinner, this delicate frittata hits the spot without being too heavy. I like to prepare it with sharp cheddar cheese for extra flavor.

3	medium zucchini, thinly sliced
3	Tbsp. whole wheat flour
2	tsp. olive oil
6	egg whites
3	eggs
1/2	cup reduced-fat ricotta cheese
1/2	cup shredded cheddar cheese, *divided*

1/3 cup plain yogurt
1 Tbsp. dried parsley flakes
2 garlic cloves, minced
1/2 tsp. salt
1/4 tsp. white pepper
1/2 tsp. poppy seeds

1. Toss zucchini with flour. In a large nonstick skillet coated with cooking spray, saute zucchini in oil until crisp-tender and lightly browned. Remove from heat.

2. In a large bowl, whisk the egg whites, eggs, ricotta cheese, 1/4 cup cheddar cheese, yogurt, parsley, garlic, salt and pepper. Stir in zucchini. Transfer to a 9-in. pie plate coated with cooking spray. Sprinkle with poppy seeds and remaining cheddar cheese.

3. Bake at 350° for 25-30 minutes or until a knife inserted near the center comes out clean. Let stand for 5 minutes before cutting.

Nutrition Facts: 1 piece equals 238 calories, 12 g fat (6 g saturated fat), 185 mg cholesterol, 552 mg sodium, 13 g carbohydrate, 3 g fiber, 19 g protein. **Diabetic Exchanges:** 2 lean meat, 1 vegetable, 1 fat, 1/2 starch.

Mediterranean Pizza M

PREP/TOTAL TIME: 20 min. **YIELD:** 12 pieces

DEBORAH PREVOST • BARNET, VERMONT

Every year, my sisters and I have a "Sisters Day," which includes a special lunch. This fast and easy pizza is one of our favorites. Served with a garden salad, it makes a light and nutritious meal.

1 prebaked thin Italian whole wheat bread shell crust (10 oz.)
3 Tbsp. prepared pesto
2 medium tomatoes, thinly sliced
3/4 cup water-packed artichoke hearts, rinsed, drained and chopped
1/2 cup crumbled reduced-fat feta cheese
1/4 cup sliced ripe olives

1. Place the crust on an ungreased 12-in. pizza pan; spread with pesto. Top with tomatoes, artichokes, feta cheese and olives.

2. Bake at 450° for 10-12 minutes or until heated through.

Nutrition Facts: 2 pieces equals 206 calories, 8 g fat (3 g saturated fat), 6 mg cholesterol, 547 mg sodium, 27 g carbohydrate, 4 g fiber, 10 g protein. **Diabetic Exchanges:** 1-1/2 starch, 1-1/2 fat, 1 vegetable.

Zucchini Corn Bake M

PREP: 20 min. **BAKE:** 25 min. **YIELD:** 4 servings

DIANE CONSER • LAKEWOOD, NEW JERSEY

I found the original version of this recipe in a magazine and decided to lighten it. It's delicious!

1 medium zucchini, quartered lengthwise and sliced
1-3/4 cups frozen corn, thawed
1 small onion, chopped
1 Tbsp. plus 1 tsp. butter, *divided*
1 Tbsp. all-purpose flour
1/4 tsp. salt
1/4 tsp. pepper
1 cup fat-free milk
3/4 cup shredded reduced-fat cheddar cheese
1/4 cup dry bread crumbs
2 garlic cloves, minced
1/4 tsp. dried oregano

1. In a large nonstick skillet over medium heat, cook the zucchini, corn and onion in 1 tablespoon butter until crisp-tender. Stir in the flour, salt and pepper until blended.

2. Gradually add milk. Bring to a boil; cook and stir for 2 minutes or until thickened. Reduce heat; stir in cheese. Cook and stir for 1-2 minutes or until the cheese is melted. Transfer to a 1-qt. baking dish coated with cooking spray.

3. In a small skillet, saute the bread crumbs, garlic and oregano in remaining butter for 2-3 minutes or until crumbs are lightly browned. Sprinkle over vegetable mixture.

4. Bake, uncovered, at 350° for 25-30 minutes or until bubbly.

Nutrition Facts: 3/4 cup equals 229 calories, 10 g fat (6 g saturated fat), 27 mg cholesterol, 417 mg sodium, 29 g carbohydrate, 3 g fiber, 12 g protein. **Diabetic Exchanges:** 2 fat, 1-1/2 starch, 1 vegetable.

MEDITERRANEAN PIZZA

ZUCCHINI FRITTATA

Italian Garden Frittata C M

PREP/TOTAL TIME: 30 min. **YIELD:** 4 servings

SALLY MALONEY • DALLAS, GEORGIA

I like to serve this pretty frittata with melon wedges for a delightful breakfast or brunch.

6	egg whites
4	eggs
1/2	cup grated Romano cheese, *divided*
1	Tbsp. minced fresh sage
1/2	tsp. salt
1/4	tsp. pepper
1	small zucchini, sliced
2	green onions, sliced
1	tsp. olive oil
2	plum tomatoes, thinly sliced

1. In a large bowl, whisk the egg whites, eggs, 1/4 cup Romano cheese, sage, salt and pepper; set aside.

2. In a 10-in. ovenproof skillet coated with cooking spray, saute zucchini and onions in oil for 2 minutes. Add egg mixture; cover and cook for 4-6 minutes or until eggs are nearly set.

3. Uncover; top with tomato slices and remaining cheese. Broil 3-4 in. from the heat for 2-3 minutes or until eggs are completely set. Let stand for 5 minutes. Cut into wedges.

Nutrition Facts: 1 wedge equals 183 calories, 11 g fat (5 g saturated fat), 228 mg cholesterol, 655 mg sodium, 4 g carbohydrate, 1 g fiber, 18 g protein.

Black Bean Veggie Enchiladas M

PREP: 30 min. **BAKE:** 25 min. **YIELD:** 6 servings

NICOLE BARNETT • AURORA, COLORADO

I created this recipe one night when we were in the mood for enchiladas, but didn't want all the traditional version's fat and calories. I used ingredients I had on hand, and now this recipe's a family favorite!

1	small onion, chopped
1	small green pepper, chopped
1/2	cup sliced fresh mushrooms
1	garlic clove, minced
2	tsp. olive oil
1	can (15 oz.) black beans, rinsed and drained
3/4	cup frozen corn, thawed
1	can (4 oz.) chopped green chilies
2	Tbsp. reduced-sodium taco seasoning
1	tsp. dried cilantro flakes
6	whole wheat tortillas (8 in.), warmed
1/2	cup enchilada sauce
3/4	cup shredded reduced-fat Mexican cheese blend

1. In a large skillet, saute the onion, pepper, mushrooms and garlic in oil until crisp-tender. Add the beans, corn, chilies, taco seasoning and cilantro; saute 2-3 minutes longer.

2. Spoon 1/2 cup bean mixture down the center of each tortilla. Roll up and place seam side down in a 13-in. x 9-in. baking dish coated with cooking spray. Pour sauce over the top; sprinkle with cheese. Bake, uncovered, at 350° for 25-30 minutes or until heated through.

Nutrition Facts: 1 enchilada equals 292 calories, 8 g fat (2 g saturated fat),10 mg cholesterol, 759 mg sodium, 43 g carbohydrate, 6 g fiber, 13 g protein.

ITALIAN GARDEN FRITTATA

BLACK BEAN VEGGIE ENCHILADAS

LOADED MEXICAN PIZZA

Loaded Mexican Pizza M

PREP/TOTAL TIME: 25 min. **YIELD:** 6 slices

MARY BARKER • KNOXVILLE, TENNESSEE

My husband, Steve, is a picky eater, but this healthy pizza has lots of flavor and he actually looks forward to it. Try it for parties and other casual get-togethers.

    1   can (15 oz.) black beans, rinsed and drained
    1   medium red onion, chopped
    1   small sweet yellow pepper, chopped
    3   tsp. chili powder
  3/4   tsp. ground cumin
    3   medium tomatoes, chopped
    1   jalapeno pepper, seeded and finely chopped
    1   garlic clove, minced
    1   prebaked thin Italian bread shell crust (10 oz.)
    2   cups chopped fresh spinach
    2   Tbsp. minced fresh cilantro
Hot pepper sauce to taste
  1/2   cup shredded reduced-fat cheddar cheese
  1/2   cup pepper Jack cheese

1. In a small bowl, mash black beans; stir in the onion, yellow pepper, chili powder and cumin. In another bowl, combine the tomatoes, jalapeno and garlic.

2. Place the crust on an ungreased 12-in. pizza pan; spread with bean mixture. Top with tomato mixture and spinach. Sprinkle with cilantro, hot pepper sauce and cheeses.

3. Bake at 400° for 12-15 minutes or until the cheese is melted.

Editor's Note: When cutting or seeding hot peppers, use rubber or plastic gloves to protect your hands. Avoid touching your face.

Nutrition Facts: 1 slice equals 297 calories, 9 g fat (4 g saturated fat), 17 mg cholesterol, 566 mg sodium, 41 g carbohydrate, 6 g fiber, 15 g protein. **Diabetic Exchanges:** 2-1/2 starch, 1 lean meat, 1 vegetable.

Roasted Veggie Tacos M

PREP: 20 min. **BAKE:** 15 min. **YIELD:** 6 servings

SHANNON KOENE • BLACKSBURG, VIRGINIA

When I tried making one vegetarian dish a week, my husband often said, "It would've been better with meat in it." But he doesn't even miss the beef in these tacos!

    2   medium green peppers, julienned
    3   plum tomatoes, cut into wedges
    1   medium onion, halved and sliced
    1   Tbsp. reduced-sodium taco seasoning
    1   Tbsp. olive oil
    1   can (16 oz.) fat-free refried beans, warmed
    6   flour tortillas (8 in.), warmed
  3/4   cup shredded reduced-fat cheddar cheese

1. In a large bowl, combine green peppers, tomatoes, onion, taco seasoning and oil. Arrange in a single layer in an ungreased 15-in. x 10-in. baking pan. Bake at 425° for 15-20 minutes or until tender, stirring once.

2. Spread about 1/4 cup refried beans over each tortilla; top with 1/3 cup vegetable mixture and 2 tablespoons cheese.

Nutrition Facts: 1 taco equals 316 calories, 8 g fat (3 g saturated fat), 10 mg cholesterol, 722 mg sodium, 48 g carbohydrate, 6 g fiber, 14 g protein.

Spinach 'n' Broccoli Enchiladas Ⓜ

PREP: 25 min. **BAKE:** 25 min. **YIELD:** 8 servings

LESLEY TRAGESSER • CHARLESTON, MISSOURI

I slimmed down these enchiladas even more, and now they're sure to satisfy any craving. I like to top them with lettuce and serve with extra picante sauce.

- 1 medium onion, chopped
- 2 tsp. olive oil
- 1 pkg. (10 oz.) frozen chopped spinach, thawed and squeezed dry
- 1 cup finely chopped fresh broccoli
- 1 cup picante sauce, *divided*
- 1/2 tsp. garlic powder
- 1/2 tsp. ground cumin
- 1 cup (8 oz.) 1% cottage cheese
- 1 cup (4 oz.) shredded reduced-fat cheddar cheese, *divided*
- 8 flour tortillas (8 in.), warmed

1. In a large nonstick skillet over medium heat, cook and stir onion in oil until tender. Add the spinach, broccoli, 1/3 cup picante sauce, garlic powder and cumin; heat through.

2. Remove from the heat; stir in cottage cheese and 1/2 cup cheddar cheese. Spoon about 1/3 cup spinach mixture down the center of each tortilla. Roll up and place seam side down in a 13-in. x 9-in. baking dish coated with cooking spray. Spoon remaining picante sauce over the top.

3. Cover and bake at 350° for 20-25 minutes or until heated through. Uncover; sprinkle with remaining cheese. Bake 5 minutes longer or until cheese is melted.

Nutrition Facts: 1 enchilada equals 246 calories, 8 g fat (3 g saturated fat), 11 mg cholesterol, 614 mg sodium, 32 g carbohydrate, 2 g fiber, 13 g protein. **Diabetic Exchanges:** 1-1/2 starch, 1 lean meat, 1 vegetable, 1/2 fat.

Cannellini 'n' Onion Linguine Ⓜ

PREP/TOTAL TIME: 30 min. **YIELD:** 6 servings

TRISHA KRUSE • EAGLE, IDAHO

This pasta dish is very simple, but everyone loves it. The tasty main course also adds protein and fiber to your diet, without too much fat.

- 2 medium onions, halved and thinly sliced
- 1 Tbsp. butter
- 1 Tbsp. olive oil

1/4 cup white wine *or* vegetable broth
1 tsp. brown sugar
10 oz. uncooked linguine
1 can (19 oz.) cannellini *or* white kidney beans, rinsed and drained
1 cup vegetable broth
3 garlic cloves, minced
1 tsp. dried basil
1/4 tsp. pepper
6 Tbsp. shredded Parmesan cheese

1. In a large nonstick skillet over medium-low heat, cook onions in butter and oil until tender. Add wine or broth and brown sugar; cook 5 minutes longer. Meanwhile, cook linguine according to package directions.

2. Add the beans, broth, garlic, basil and pepper to the onions; bring to a boil. Reduce heat; simmer, uncovered, for 10-12 minutes or until slightly thickened.

3. Drain linguine; toss with onion mixture. Sprinkle each serving with Parmesan cheese.

Nutrition Facts: 1 cup equals 332 calories, 7 g fat (3 g saturated fat), 9 mg cholesterol, 388 mg sodium, 54 g carbohydrate, 6 g fiber, 13 g protein.

Southwestern Rice Bake M

PREP: 25 min. BAKE: 30 min. YIELD: 8 servings

BETTY CLAYCOMB • ALVERTON, PENNSYLVANIA

We really enjoy this hearty dish. Just add a side salad for a nutritious, complete meal.

1-2/3 cups uncooked long grain rice
3-1/3 cups water
1 large onion, chopped
1 small green pepper, chopped
3 garlic cloves, minced
1 tsp. olive oil
1 can (15 oz.) garbanzo beans *or* chickpeas, rinsed and drained
1 can (2-1/4 oz.) sliced ripe olives, drained
2 cups (8 oz.) shredded reduced-fat cheddar cheese, *divided*
1 cup reduced-fat ricotta cheese
1/4 cup reduced-fat sour cream
1-1/2 tsp. chili powder
1 cup salsa

1. In a large saucepan, bring rice and water to a boil. Reduce heat; cover and simmer for 15-18 minutes or until water is absorbed and rice is tender.

2. In a large nonstick saucepan, saute the onion, green pepper and garlic in oil until tender. Remove from the heat; stir in the beans, olives and rice. In a small bowl, combine 1-1/2 cups cheddar cheese, ricotta cheese, sour cream and chili powder.

3. Spoon half of the rice mixture into a 13-in. x 9-in. baking dish coated with cooking spray; layer with half of the cheese mixture and salsa. Repeat layers.

4. Bake, uncovered, at 350° for 25 minutes. Sprinkle with remaining cheddar cheese. Bake 3-5 minutes longer or until heated through and cheese is melted.

Nutrition Facts: 1 serving equals 348 calories, 11 g fat (6 g saturated fat), 30 mg cholesterol, 506 mg sodium, 46 g carbohydrate, 5 g fiber, 15 g protein.

Anytime Frittata C M

PREP/TOTAL TIME: 30 min. YIELD: 4 servings

LYNNE VAN WAGENEN • SALT LAKE CITY, UTAH

We enjoy frittatas often at our house. They're a great way to use up leftover vegetables and cheese. We like this dish with fruit and whole wheat toast for a light dinner.

1-1/4 cups egg substitute
2 eggs
1/2 tsp. dried oregano
1/8 tsp. pepper
1 small onion, chopped
1 garlic clove, minced
1 tsp. butter
3 plum tomatoes, chopped
1/2 cup crumbled feta cheese
2 Tbsp. capers, drained

1. In a small bowl, whisk the egg substitute, eggs, oregano and pepper; set aside. In a 10-in. ovenproof skillet, saute onion and garlic in butter for 2 minutes. Stir in tomatoes; heat through.

2. Pour reserved egg mixture into skillet. Reduce heat; cover and cook for 4-6 minutes or until nearly set.

3. Sprinkle with cheese and capers. Broil 3-4 in. from the heat for 2-3 minutes or until eggs are completely set. Let stand for 5 minutes. Cut into wedges.

Nutrition Facts: 1 wedge equals 138 calories, 6 g fat (3 g saturated fat), 116 mg cholesterol, 465 mg sodium, 6 g carbohydrate, 2 g fiber, 14 g protein. **Diabetic Exchanges:** 2 lean meat, 1 vegetable.

ANYTIME FRITTATA

Black Bean Cornmeal Pie M

PREP: 30 min. **BAKE:** 20 min. **YIELD:** 6 servings

TARI AMBLER • SHOREWOOD, ILLINOIS

This hearty, meatless south-of-the-border main dish is delicious. If desired, you can vary the beans used. I like to serve it with salsa and reduced-fat sour cream.

- 1 large onion, chopped
- 1 large green pepper, chopped
- 1 tsp. canola oil
- 1-1/2 tsp. chili powder
- 1 garlic clove, minced
- 3/4 tsp. ground cumin
- 1/4 tsp. pepper
- 1 can (14-1/2 oz.) diced tomatoes, undrained
- 2 cans (15 oz. *each*) black beans, rinsed and drained
- 1 cup frozen corn

TOPPING:
- 3/4 cup whole wheat pastry flour
- 3/4 cup yellow cornmeal
- 2 tsp. sugar
- 2 tsp. baking powder
- 2 tsp. chopped seeded jalapeno pepper
- 1/4 tsp. salt
- 1 egg
- 3/4 cup fat-free milk
- 1 Tbsp. canola oil

Salsa and reduced-fat sour cream, optional

1. In a large skillet, saute onion and green pepper in oil until tender. Add the chili powder, garlic, cumin and pepper; saute 1 minute longer. Add tomatoes and bring to a boil. Reduce heat; cover and simmer for 5 minutes.

2. Stir in beans and corn; heat through. Transfer to an 11-in. x 7-in. baking dish coated with cooking spray.

3. For topping, in a small bowl, combine the flour, cornmeal, sugar, baking powder, jalapeno and salt. Whisk the egg, milk and oil; stir into dry ingredients just until moistened. Spoon over filling; gently spread to cover the top.

4. Bake at 375° for 20-25 minutes or until filling is bubbly and a toothpick inserted into the topping comes out clean. Serve with salsa and sour cream if desired.

Editor's Note: When cutting hot peppers, disposable gloves are recommended. Avoid touching your face.

Nutrition Facts: 1 piece (calculated without salsa and sour cream) equals 329 calories, 5 g fat (1 g saturated fat), 36 mg cholesterol, 621 mg sodium, 58 g carbohydrate, 11 g fiber, 14 g protein.

Southwest Casserole F M

PREP: 25 min. + simmering **BAKE:** 45 min.
YIELD: 8 servings

MELODY DAVIS • OVERLAND PARK, KANSAS

A rainbow of colors and flavors is found in this festive entree. You won't believe how satisfying this casserole is, and at only 3 grams of fat per serving, it's a smart choice, too!

- 1 cup uncooked brown rice
- 1/3 cup uncooked wild rice
- 2-3/4 cups vegetable broth
- 4 cans (14-1/2 oz. *each*) diced tomatoes, drained
- 1 can (15 oz.) black beans, rinsed and drained
- 1-1/2 cups frozen corn, thawed
- 1 medium sweet red pepper, finely chopped
- 1 medium onion, finely chopped
- 6 green onions, chopped
- 1 jalapeno pepper, seeded and chopped
- 2 garlic cloves, minced
- 2 tsp. ground cumin
- 1/4 tsp. cayenne pepper
- 1/4 tsp. pepper
- 1/2 cup shredded reduced-fat Mexican cheese blend

1. In a large saucepan, bring brown rice, wild rice and broth to a boil. Reduce heat; cover and simmer for 50-60 minutes or until liquid is absorbed and rice is tender.

2. In a large bowl, combine the tomatoes, beans, corn, red pepper, onion, green onions, jalapeno, garlic, cumin, cayenne and pepper. Stir in rice.

3. Transfer to a 13-in. x 9-in. baking dish coated with cooking spray. Cover and bake at 325° for 40 minutes. Uncover; sprinkle with cheese. Bake 5-10 minutes longer or until heated through and the cheese is melted.

Editor's Note: When cutting hot peppers, disposable gloves are recommended. Avoid touching your face.

Nutrition Facts: 1-1/4 cups equals 268 calories, 3 g fat (1 g saturated fat), 5 mg cholesterol, 741 mg sodium, 53 g carbohydrate, 8 g fiber, 11 g protein.

BLACK BEAN CORNMEAL PIE

ZUCCHINI LASAGNA

Zucchini Lasagna ⓜ

PREP: 45 min. **BAKE:** 30 min. + standing
YIELD: 9 servings

RUTH VAUGHT • TEMPE, ARIZONA

This meatless lasagna is chock-full of healthy zucchini and delicious cheeses. You'll be surprised that such a generous portion weighs in at under 300 calories!

6	lasagna noodles
1	medium onion, chopped
2	garlic cloves, minced
2	tsp. olive oil
2	cups water
2	cans (6 oz. *each*) tomato paste
2-1/2	tsp. *each* dried thyme, basil and oregano
3/4	tsp. salt
3	medium zucchini, thinly sliced
1	egg, beaten
1	carton (15 oz.) part-skim ricotta cheese
2	cups (8 oz.) shredded part-skim mozzarella cheese
1/4	cup grated Parmesan cheese

1. Cook noodles according to package directions. Meanwhile, in a large nonstick skillet, saute onion and garlic in oil until tender. Stir in the water, tomato paste and seasonings. Bring to a boil. Reduce heat; cover and simmer for 10 minutes.

2. Place zucchini in a large saucepan; add 1/2 in. water. Bring to a boil. Reduce heat; cover and cook for 5 minutes. Drain and set aside. In a small bowl, combine egg and ricotta cheese.

3. Drain noodles. Place 1/2 cup tomato sauce in a 13-in. x 9-in. baking dish coated with cooking spray; top with three noodles. Layer with half of the ricotta mixture and zucchini. Top with half of the remaining tomato sauce and 1 cup mozzarella cheese. Repeat layers.

4. Cover and bake at 375° for 25 minutes. Uncover; sprinkle with Parmesan cheese. Bake 5-10 minutes longer or until bubbly. Let stand for 10 minutes before cutting.

Nutrition Facts: 1 piece equals 272 calories, 10 g fat (6 g saturated fat), 55 mg cholesterol, 454 mg sodium, 28 g carbohydrate, 4 g fiber, 18 g protein. **Diabetic Exchanges:** 2 lean meat, 2 vegetable, 1 starch, 1/2 fat.

You'll love the from-scratch tomato sauce featured in the recipe for **Zucchini Lasagna.** It pares down calories and comes together in moments. If you have a red sauce you enjoy, however, feel free to use it instead.

Warm Roasted Beet Salad M

PREP: 30 min. **BAKE:** 40 min. **YIELD:** 6 servings

JILL ANDERSON • SLEEPY EYE, MINNESOTA

This recipe lets beets shine. It's a hearty salad that's beautiful on the plate. I often use hazelnut oil in the dressing, but olive oil or any nut oil works well, too.

8	whole fresh beets
Cooking spray	
1-1/2	cups orange juice
1	shallot, chopped
2	Tbsp. olive oil
2	Tbsp. balsamic vinegar
1	tsp. minced fresh thyme *or* 1/4 tsp. dried thyme
1/2	tsp. grated orange peel
1/8	tsp. salt
1/8	tsp. pepper
6	cups fresh arugula *or* baby spinach
3	Tbsp. crumbled blue cheese
3	Tbsp. chopped hazelnuts, toasted

1. Scrub beets and cut into wedges; place on a baking sheet coated with cooking spray. Lightly coat beets with additional cooking spray. Bake at 350° for 40-50 minutes or until tender, turning occasionally.

2. Meanwhile, for dressing, place orange juice in a small saucepan. Bring to a boil. Reduce heat; simmer, uncovered, until liquid is syrupy and reduced to about 1/3 cup. Remove from the heat. Whisk in the shallot, oil, vinegar, thyme, orange peel, salt and pepper. Set aside to cool.

3. Just before serving, place arugula in a large bowl. Drizzle with 1/4 cup dressing and toss to coat. Divide mixture among six salad plates. Place beets in the same bowl; add remaining dressing and toss to coat. Arrange on plates. Sprinkle salads with blue cheese and hazelnuts.

Nutrition Facts: 1 serving equals 147 calories, 8 g fat (2 g saturated fat), 3 mg cholesterol, 167 mg sodium, 17 g carbohydrate, 2 g fiber, 4 g protein. **Diabetic Exchanges:** 2 vegetable, 1-1/2 fat, 1/2 fruit.

Chickpea 'n' Red Onion Burgers M

PREP/TOTAL TIME: 30 min. **YIELD:** 6 servings

LILLIAN JULOW • GAINESVILLE, FLORIDA

I like to make this burger when it's chilly outdoors, and the grill has been retired to the garage.

1	large red onion, thinly sliced
1/4	cup fat-free red wine vinaigrette
2	cans (15 oz. *each*) chickpeas or garbanzo beans, rinsed and drained
1/3	cup chopped walnuts
1/4	cup toasted wheat germ
1/4	cup packed fresh parsley sprigs
2	eggs
1	tsp. curry powder
1/2	tsp. pepper
1/3	cup fat-free mayonnaise
2	tsp. Dijon mustard

6 sesame seed hamburger buns, split
6 lettuce leaves
3 Tbsp. thinly sliced fresh basil leaves

1. In a small bowl, combine onion and vinaigrette; set aside. In a food processor, combine the chickpeas, walnuts, wheat germ and parsley; cover and pulse until blended. Add the eggs, curry and pepper; cover and process until smooth.

2. Shape into six patties. Place on a baking sheet coated with cooking spray. Bake at 375° for 10-15 minutes or until firm.

3. Combine mayonnaise and mustard; spread over cut sides of buns. Serve patties on buns with lettuce, basil and reserved onion mixture.

Nutrition Facts: 1 burger equals 386 calories, 12 g fat (2 g saturated fat), 72 mg cholesterol, 732 mg sodium, 54 g carbohydrate, 9 g fiber, 16 g protein.

Vegetarian Sloppy Joes M

PREP/TOTAL TIME: 25 min. **YIELD:** 6 servings

LINDA WINTER • OAK HARBOR, WASHINGTON

The meat won't be missed in this vegetarian version of sloppy joes. I like to preserve the flavor of a classic while adding important nutrients.

1 small onion, finely chopped
2 tsp. butter
1 pkg. (12 oz.) frozen vegetarian meat crumbles
1/2 tsp. pepper
2 Tbsp. all-purpose flour
1 can (8 oz.) no-salt-added tomato sauce
2/3 cup ketchup
6 hamburger buns, split and toasted

1. In a large nonstick skillet coated with cooking spray, saute onion in butter until tender. Stir in meat crumbles and pepper; heat through.

2. Sprinkle flour over mixture and stir until blended. Stir in tomato sauce and ketchup. Bring to a boil; cook and stir for 1-2 minutes or until thickened. Spoon 1/2 cup onto each bun.

Nutrition Facts: 1 sandwich equals 273 calories, 6 g fat (2 g saturated fat), 4 mg cholesterol, 815 mg sodium, 39 g carbohydrate, 5 g fiber, 15 g protein. **Diabetic Exchanges:** 2-1/2 starch, 2 lean meat.

Zucchini Tomato Bake C M

PREP: 30 min. **BAKE:** 25 min. **YIELD:** 6 servings

TINA REPAK • JOHNSTOWN, PENNSYLVANIA

Melted Swiss cheese and sour cream lend decadence to this flavorful side with garden-fresh ingredients.

1 medium onion, chopped
1 Tbsp. butter
3 medium zucchini (about 1 lb.), shredded and patted dry
3 medium tomatoes, seeded and chopped
1 cup (4 oz.) shredded reduced-fat Swiss cheese, *divided*
1/3 cup reduced-fat sour cream
1 tsp. paprika
1/2 tsp. salt
1/2 tsp. garlic powder
1/4 tsp. pepper
2 Tbsp. shredded Parmesan cheese

1. In a large nonstick skillet, saute onion in butter until tender. Transfer to a large bowl. Add the zucchini, tomatoes, 1/2 cup Swiss cheese, sour cream and seasonings; mix well.

2. Transfer to an 11-in. x 7-in. baking dish coated with cooking spray. Sprinkle with Parmesan cheese and remaining Swiss cheese. Bake, uncovered, at 350° for 25-30 minutes or until vegetables are tender.

Nutrition Facts: 1 serving equals 113 calories, 5 g fat (3 g saturated fat), 18 mg cholesterol, 321 mg sodium, 9 g carbohydrate, 2 g fiber, 9 g protein. **Diabetic Exchanges:** 2 vegetable, 1 lean meat, 1/2 fat.

ZUCCHINI TOMATO BAKE

VEGETARIAN SLOPPY JOES

APPLESAUCE BREAD

MILK-FREE CORN BREAD

BLUEBERRY OATMEAL MUFFINS

The Bread Basket

Watching what you eat doesn't mean giving up your favorites. Due to their carbs, breads, muffins and scones were once considered a healthy cook's nightmare; but, with this selection of delights, you can sample the bread basket without worry!

Applesauce Bread

PREP: 20 min. **BAKE:** 50 min. + cooling
YIELD: 1 loaf (16 slices)

SHERRY CRAW • MATTOON, ILLINOIS

Applesauce gives this tasty bread natural sweetness and moisture, so less sugar and oil are required. It's a great treat with a glass of milk or a cup of coffee. Best of all, it curbs my cravings for sweets without resorting to junk food.

1	cup all-purpose flour
1	cup whole wheat flour
1/2	cup sugar
1-1/2	tsp. ground cinnamon, *divided*
1	tsp. baking soda
1/2	tsp. salt
1/2	tsp. baking powder
1/4	tsp. ground nutmeg
2	egg whites
1	egg
1-1/4	cups unsweetened applesauce
1/4	cup canola oil
3	Tbsp. fat-free milk
1/4	cup packed brown sugar

1. In a large bowl, combine the flours, sugar, 1 teaspoon cinnamon, baking soda, salt, baking powder and nutmeg. In a small bowl, whisk the egg whites, egg, applesauce, oil and milk. Stir into dry ingredients just until moistened.

2. Transfer to a 9-in. x 5-in. loaf pan coated with cooking spray. Combine brown sugar and remaining cinnamon; sprinkle over the top.

3. Bake at 350° for 50-60 minutes or until a toothpick inserted near the center comes out clean. Cool for 10 minutes before removing from pan to a wire rack.

Nutrition Facts: 1 slice equals 139 calories, 4 g fat (trace saturated fat), 13 mg cholesterol, 180 mg sodium, 24 g carbohydrate, 1 g fiber, 3 g protein. **Diabetic Exchanges:** 1-1/2 starch, 1/2 fat.

Blueberry Oatmeal Muffins

PREP/TOTAL TIME: 30 min. **YIELD:** 1 dozen

DONNA BROCKETT • KINGFISHER, OKLAHOMA

Talk about a grab-and-go great! These yummy muffins come together in just half an hour and make a perfect bite as you're headed out the door.

1-1/4	cups all-purpose flour
1	cup quick-cooking oats
1/2	cup packed brown sugar
2	tsp. baking powder
1/2	tsp. salt
1/2	tsp. ground cinnamon
1/4	tsp. baking soda
1/4	tsp. ground nutmeg
1	egg, lightly beaten
1	cup (8 oz.) plain yogurt
1/4	cup butter, melted
1	cup fresh blueberries

1. In a large bowl, combine the first eight ingredients. Combine the egg, yogurt and butter; stir into dry ingredients just until moistened. Fold in blueberries.

2. Coat muffin cups with cooking spray or use paper liners; fill three-fourths full with batter. Bake at 400° for 18-22 minutes or until a toothpick comes out clean. Cool for 5 minutes before removing from pan to a wire rack.

Nutrition Facts: 1 muffin equals 167 calories, 6 g fat (3 g saturated fat), 31 mg cholesterol, 249 mg sodium, 26 g carbohydrate, 1 g fiber, 4 g protein. **Diabetic Exchanges:** 1-1/2 starch, 1 fat.

It is easy to keep quick breads light with a few simple substitutes. In **Applesauce Bread,** for instance, unsweetened applesauce replaces the butter usually found in such recipes. Similarly, egg whites cut back on the whole eggs one would expect in a quick bread.

Cranberry Gingerbread Muffins

PREP: 20 min. **BAKE:** 20 min. **YIELD:** 1 dozen

LISA VARNER • GREENVILLE, SOUTH CAROLINA

This wonderful treat can be served for breakfast or even dessert. It's perfect during the holiday season.

2-1/4	cups all-purpose flour
1/2	cup packed brown sugar
2	tsp. ground ginger
1	tsp. baking powder
1	tsp. ground cinnamon
3/4	tsp. salt
1/2	tsp. baking soda
1	egg
3/4	cup water
1/2	cup fat-free plain yogurt
1/3	cup molasses
1/4	cup canola oil
1	cup fresh *or* frozen cranberries, thawed and quartered

1. In a large bowl, combine the first seven ingredients. In a small bowl, combine the egg, water, yogurt, molasses and oil. Stir into dry ingredients just until moistened. Fold in cranberries.

2. Coat muffin cups with cooking spray or use paper liners; fill three-fourths full with batter. Bake at 350° for 18-22 minutes or until a toothpick comes out clean. Cool for 5 minutes before removing from pan to a wire rack.

Nutrition Facts: 1 muffin equals 201 calories, 5 g fat (1 g saturated fat), 18 mg cholesterol, 252 mg sodium, 35 g carbohydrate, 1 g fiber, 3 g protein. **Diabetic Exchanges:** 2 starch, 1 fat.

Pear-Nut Biscuits

PREP: 20 min. **BAKE:** 15 min. **YIELD:** 10 biscuits

MARY ANN DELL • PHOENIXVILLE, PENNSYLVANIA

Pears bring a mild sweetness to these tender biscuits, while chopped pecans lend a little crunch. They're great for an on-the-go breakfast.

1-3/4	cups all-purpose flour
1/3	cup packed brown sugar
2	tsp. baking powder
3/4	tsp. salt
3	Tbsp. cold butter
1	egg
1/2	cup half-and-half cream
1	cup chopped peeled ripe pears
1/4	cup chopped pecans

1. In a large bowl, combine the flour, brown sugar, baking powder and salt. Cut in butter until mixture resembles coarse crumbs. Whisk egg and cream; stir into crumb mixture just until moistened. Fold in pears and pecans. Drop by 1/4 cupfuls onto an ungreased baking sheet.

2. Bake at 400° for 15-18 minutes or until golden brown. Serve warm.

Nutrition Facts: 1 biscuit equals 191 calories, 8 g fat (3 g saturated fat), 36 mg cholesterol, 307 mg sodium, 27 g carbohydrate, 1 g fiber, 4 g protein. **Diabetic Exchanges:** 2 starch, 1 fat.

Makeover Pumpkin Spice Bread **F**

PREP: 20 min. **BAKE:** 45 min. + cooling
YIELD: 2 loaves (16 slices each)

HEIDI FIGIEL • BRIDGEPORT, WEST VIRGINIA

I wanted to indulge in this family favorite without guilt. This lighter version offers all the taste with hardly any fat!

2-1/4	cups sugar
2	cups all-purpose flour
1-1/3	cups cake flour
2	tsp. baking soda
2	tsp. ground cinnamon

MAKEOVER PUMPKIN SPICE BREAD

CRANBERRY GINGERBREAD MUFFINS

1	tsp. salt
1	tsp. baking powder
3/4	tsp. ground cloves
1/2	tsp. ground nutmeg
4	eggs
1	can (15 oz.) solid-pack pumpkin
1	cup buttermilk
1/2	cup unsweetened applesauce
1/3	cup canola oil

1. In a large bowl, combine the first nine ingredients. In another bowl, whisk the eggs, pumpkin, buttermilk, applesauce and oil. Stir into the dry ingredients just until moistened.

2. Transfer to two 9-in. x 5-in. loaf pans coated with cooking spray. Bake at 350° for 45-55 minutes or until golden brown and a toothpick inserted near the center comes out with moist crumbs. Cool for 10 minutes before removing from pans to wire racks.

Nutrition Facts: 1 slice equals 143 calories, 3 g fat (trace saturated fat), 27 mg cholesterol, 183 mg sodium, 27 g carbohydrate, 1 g fiber, 3 g protein. **Diabetic Exchanges:** 2 starch, 1/2 fat.

Makeover Holiday Loaf

PREP: 25 min. **BAKE:** 55 min. + cooling
YIELD: 1 loaf (16 slices)

IRIS COOK • GLASGOW, MONTANA

Christmas wouldn't be the same without fruit cake, but I try to bake with less sugar these days. You can image how happy I was when "Healthy Cooking" revised my recipe.

3/4	cup *each* golden raisins and cherries
3/4	cup chopped walnuts
1/2	cup raisins
1/4	cup shortening

1/4	cup brown sugar blend
2	eggs
1/2	cup molasses
1/4	cup unsweetened applesauce
2	cups all-purpose flour
1-1/2	tsp. ground cinnamon
1-1/4	tsp. baking powder
3/4	tsp. ground nutmeg
3/4	tsp. ground allspice
1/2	tsp. salt
1/2	tsp. baking soda
1/4	tsp. ground cloves
3/4	cup fat-free milk

1. Coat a 9-in. x 5-in. loaf pan with cooking spray. Line the bottom with waxed paper; spray the paper and sprinkle with flour. Set aside.

2. Combine the golden raisins and cherries, walnuts and raisins. Set aside. In a large bowl, beat shortening and brown sugar blend until well blended. Add eggs, one at a time, beating well after each addition. Beat in molasses and applesauce (mixture will appear curdled).

3. Combine the flour, cinnamon, baking powder, nutmeg, allspice, salt, baking soda and cloves; add to shortening mixture alternately with milk. Fold in raisin mixture.

4. Transfer to prepared pan. Bake at 325° for 55-65 minutes or until a toothpick inserted near the center comes out clean. Cool for 10 minutes before removing from pan to a wire rack to cool completely. Store in the refrigerator.

Editor's Note: This recipe was tested with Splenda brown sugar blend.

Nutrition Facts: 1 slice equals 208 calories, 7 g fat (1 g saturated fat), 27 mg cholesterol, 164 mg sodium, 32 g carbohydrate, 2 g fiber, 5 g protein.

Hazelnut Wheat Bread M

PREP: 20 min. **BAKE:** 3 hours
YIELD: 1 loaf (2 pounds, 12 slices)

RUTH FANGER • MONROE, OREGON

I developed this recipe to match the flavors of our favorite store-bought bread, adapting it to a recipe in my bread machine manual. It makes a great-tasting loaf!

1	cup water (70° to 80°)
1	Tbsp. honey
1	Tbsp. butter, softened
3	Tbsp. toasted wheat germ
2	Tbsp. mashed potato flakes
1	Tbsp. nonfat dry milk powder
1	Tbsp. ground flaxseed
1	Tbsp. sesame seeds
1	Tbsp. poppy seeds
1	tsp. salt
1-1/4	cups whole wheat flour
1	cup bread flour
1/4	cup chopped hazelnuts
1-1/2	tsp. active dry yeast

1. In bread machine pan, place all ingredients in order suggested by manufacturer. Choose crust color and loaf size if available.

2. Bake according to bread machine directions (check dough after 5 minutes of mixing; add 1 to 2 Tbsp. of water or flour if needed).

Nutrition Facts: 1 slice equals 127 calories, 4 g fat (1 g saturated fat), 3 mg cholesterol, 213 mg sodium, 21 g carbohydrate, 3 g fiber, 5 g protein. **Diabetic Exchanges:** 1 starch, 1/2 fat.

Asparagus Scones M

PREP: 25 min. **BAKE:** 20 min. + cooling
YIELD: 8 scones

MARY ANN DELL • PHOENIXVILLE, PENNSYLVANIA

Featuring fresh asparagus, these moist scones have a mild peppery bite and go great with soup for a light lunch. I sometimes substitute Parmesan and smoked mozzarella cheese for the cheddar.

1-3/4	cups cut fresh asparagus (1/4-in. pieces)
2	cups all-purpose flour
1	Tbsp. sugar
2	tsp. baking powder
1/2	tsp. salt
1/4	tsp. baking soda
1/4	tsp. pepper
1/4	tsp. cayenne pepper
1/4	cup cold butter
3/4	cup plus 2 Tbsp. buttermilk, *divided*
1/2	cup shredded reduced-fat cheddar cheese

1. In a large saucepan, bring 1/2 in. of water to a boil. Add asparagus; cover and boil for 3 minutes. Drain and immediately place asparagus in ice water. Drain and pat dry; set aside.

2. In a large bowl, combine the flour, sugar, baking powder, salt, baking soda, pepper and cayenne. Cut in butter until mixture resembles coarse crumbs. Stir in 3/4 cup buttermilk just until moistened. Stir in cheese and asparagus.

3. Turn onto a floured surface; knead 10 times. Transfer dough to a baking sheet coated with cooking spray. Pat into a 9-in. circle. Cut into eight wedges, but do not separate.

4. Brush with remaining buttermilk. Bake at 425° for 18-20 minutes or until golden brown. Cool scones on a wire rack.

Nutrition Facts: 1 scone equals 211 calories, 8 g fat (5 g saturated fat), 21 mg cholesterol, 419 mg sodium, 29 g carbohydrate, 2 g fiber, 7 g protein. **Diabetic Exchanges:** 2 starch, 1-1/2 fat.

Pumpkin Oat Bran Muffins

PREP: 15 min. **BAKE:** 20 min. **YIELD:** 9 muffins

IRENE ROBINSON • CINCINNATI, OHIO

The aroma from these muffins is especially wonderful in the fall. They're healthy and yummy and disappear quite quickly. They also freeze well.

1-1/2	cups oat bran
1/2	cup all-purpose flour
1/2	cup packed brown sugar
2	tsp. baking powder
1	tsp. pumpkin pie spice
1/2	tsp. salt
2	egg whites
1	cup canned pumpkin
1/2	cup fat-free milk
2	Tbsp. canola oil

1. In a small bowl, combine the first six ingredients. In another bowl, whisk the egg whites, pumpkin, milk and oil until well blended. Stir into dry ingredients just until moistened.

2. Coat muffin cups with cooking spray; fill half full. Bake at 400° for 20-25 minutes or until a toothpick comes out clean. Cool for 5 minutes before removing from pan to wire rack.

Nutrition Facts: 1 muffin equals 155 calories, 4 g fat (trace saturated fat), trace cholesterol, 246 mg sodium, 30 g carbohydrate, 4 g fiber, 5 g protein. **Diabetic Exchanges:** 2 starch, 1/2 fat.

Yogurt Wheat Bread 🅵 🅼

PREP: 30 min. + rising **BAKE:** 35 min.
YIELD: 1 loaves (16 slices each)

CAROL FORCUM • MARION, ILLINOIS

I make my own yogurt and use it in cooking and baking as well as for snacking. You can use homemade yogurt or store-bought in this healthy wheat bread. It's a great way to keep things light.

1/2	cup plain yogurt
1	pkg. (1/4 oz.) active dry yeast
1	cup warm water (110° to 115°)
1	cup whole wheat flour
1/4	cup toasted wheat germ
1	Tbsp. sugar
1	Tbsp. olive oil
1	tsp. salt
1-2/3	to 2 cups bread flour

1. Let yogurt stand at room temperature for 15 minutes. In a large mixing bowl, dissolve yeast in warm water. Add the whole wheat flour, wheat germ, sugar, oil, salt and yogurt. Stir in enough bread flour to form a firm dough.

2. Turn onto a lightly floured surface; knead until smooth and elastic, about 6-8 minutes. Place in a bowl coated with cooking spray, turning once to coat the top. Cover and let rise in a warm place until doubled, about 1 hour.

3. Punch dough down. Turn onto a lightly floured surface; shape into a loaf. Place in a 9-in. x 5-in. loaf pan coated with cooking spray. Cover and let rise until doubled, about 40 minutes.

4. Bake at 375° for 35-40 minutes or until golden brown. Remove from pan to a wire rack to cool.

Nutrition Facts: 1 slice equals 92 calories, 1 g fat (trace saturated fat), 1 mg cholesterol, 152 mg sodium, 17 g carbohydrate, 2 g fiber, 4 g protein. **Diabetic Exchange:** 1 starch.

YOGURT WHEAT BREAD

PUMPKIN OAT BRAN MUFFINS

Cheese Straws F S C M

PREP/TOTAL TIME: 30 min. **YIELD:** 4 dozen

ANN NACE • PERKASIE, PENNSYLVANIA

You'll have a hard time eating just one of these cheesy, buttery treats. They make a fun appetizer or side for soups or salads. Try twisting the sticks for an extra-fancy look.

1	cup all-purpose flour
1-1/2	tsp. baking powder
1/2	tsp. salt
1/2	cup shredded reduced-fat cheddar cheese
2	Tbsp. plus 1-1/2 tsp. cold butter
1/3	cup fat-free milk
2	tsp. paprika

1. In a small bowl, combine the flour, baking powder and salt; stir in cheese. Cut in butter until mixture resembles coarse crumbs. Gradually add milk, tossing with a fork until dough forms a ball.

2. On a lightly floured surface, roll dough into a 12-in. square. Cut in half lengthwise; cut each half widthwise into 1/2-in. strips. Sprinkle with paprika.

3. Place 1 in. apart on baking sheets coated with cooking spray. Bake at 425° for 6-8 minutes or until golden brown. Serve warm.

Nutrition Facts: 1 cheese straw equals 19 calories, 1 g fat (1 g saturated fat), 2 mg cholesterol, 52 mg sodium, 2 g carbohydrate, trace fiber, 1 g protein.

Southwest Surprise Bread F M

PREP: 30 min. + rising **BAKE:** 40 min. + cooling
YIELD: 2 loaves (16 slices each)

SANDRA LEE HERR • STEVENS, PENNSYLVANIA

Fat-free refried beans are the surprise ingredient in these soft, high-rising loaves with just a hint of heat. Beans increase the bread's protein content and are so good! We serve this instead of garlic bread with Mexican dishes.

2	pkg. (1/4 oz. *each*) active dry yeast
2	cups warm 2% milk (110° to 115°)
1	can (16 oz.) spicy fat-free refried beans
2	Tbsp. sugar
2	Tbsp. butter, melted
2	tsp. salt
5	to 6 cups all-purpose flour

1. In a large mixing bowl, dissolve yeast in warm milk. Add the beans, sugar, butter, salt and 2 cups flour. Beat until smooth. Stir in enough remaining flour to form a firm dough.

2. Turn onto a lightly floured surface; knead until smooth and elastic, about 6-8 minutes. Place in a bowl coated with cooking spray, turning once to coat the top. Cover and let rise in a warm place until doubled, about 1 hour.

3. Punch dough down. Turn onto a lightly floured surface; divide in half. Shape into loaves. Place in two 9-in. x 5-in. loaf pans coated with cooking spray. Cover and let rise until doubled, about 30 minutes. Bake at 350° for 40-45 minutes or until golden brown. Remove from pans to wire racks to cool.

Nutrition Facts: 1 slice equals 104 calories, 1 g fat (1 g saturated fat), 3 mg cholesterol, 219 mg sodium, 19 g carbohydrate, 1 g fiber, 4 g protein. **Diabetic Exchange:** 1 starch.

Apricot-Banana Quick Bread

PREP: 20 min. **BAKE:** 1 hour + cooling
YIELD: 1 loaf (16 slices)

DIXIE TERRY • GOREVILLE, ILLINOIS

Bananas and apricots lend sweet flavor to this bread, while wheat germ gives it a dose of nutrition.

1/4	cup butter, softened
3/4	cup sugar
2	eggs
1	cup mashed ripe bananas
1-2/3	cups all-purpose flour
2/3	cup toasted wheat germ
2	tsp. baking powder
1/4	tsp. salt
1/4	tsp. baking soda
1	cup finely chopped dried apricots
2	tsp. grated lemon peel

CHEESE STRAWS

SOUTHWEST SURPRISE BREAD

MILK-FREE CORN BREAD

1. In a large mixing bowl, beat butter and sugar until crumbly, about 2 minutes. Add eggs, one at a time, beating well after each addition. Beat in bananas. Combine the flour, wheat germ, baking powder, salt and baking soda; gradually beat into the banana mixture. Stir in apricots and lemon peel.

2. Transfer to a 9-in. x 5-in. loaf pan coated with cooking spray.

3. Bake at 350° for 60-70 minutes or until a toothpick inserted near the center comes out clean. Cool for 10 minutes before removing from pan to a wire rack.

Nutrition Facts: 1 slice equals 168 calories, 4 g fat (2 g saturated fat), 34 mg cholesterol, 150 mg sodium, 30 g carbohydrate, 2 g fiber, 4 g protein. **Diabetic Exchanges:** 1-1/2 starch, 1/2 fruit, 1/2 fat.

Honey-Wheat Oatmeal Bread F M

PREP: 10 min. **BAKE:** 3 hours
YIELD: 1 loaf (2 pounds) (20 slices)

WANNETTA EHNES • EAGLE BEND, MINNESOTA

This wholesome bread is great for the bread machine and uses less fat. Serve it with dinner or toasted for breakfast.

1-1/4   cups water (70° to 80°)
  1/2   cup honey
    2   Tbsp. canola oil
1-1/2   tsp. salt
    1   cup quick-cooking oats
1-1/2   cups bread flour
1-1/2   cups whole wheat flour
1 pkg. (1/4 oz.) active dry yeast

1. In bread machine pan, place all ingredients in order suggested by manufacturer. Select basic bread setting. Choose crust color and loaf size if available.

2. Bake according to bread machine directions (check dough after 5 minutes of mixing; add 1 to 2 tablespoons of water or flour if needed).

Nutrition Facts: 1 slice equals 115 calories, 2 g fat (trace saturated fat), 0 cholesterol, 178 mg sodium, 23 g carbohydrate, 2 g fiber, 3 g protein. **Diabetic Exchange:** 1-1/2 starch.

Milk-Free Corn Bread M

PREP/TOTAL TIME: 30 min.   **YIELD:** 9 servings

ANGIE PHILKILL • FORT GRATIOT, MICHIGAN

My children have food allergies, so I always take this bread with me when we're invited to dinner. It goes great with most any meal and my kids absolutely adore its hearty wedges. Best of all, I can whip it up and pull it out of the oven in just half an hour. What a time saver!

    1   cup all-purpose flour
    1   cup cornmeal
  1/4   cup sugar
    2   tsp. baking powder
  1/4   tsp. salt
    1   egg
    1   cup rice drink
    2   Tbsp. canola oil
    2   Tbsp. unsweetened applesauce

1. In a small bowl, combine the first five ingredients. In another bowl, whisk the egg, rice drink, oil and applesauce. Stir into dry ingredients just until moistened. Transfer to a 9-in. square baking pan coated with cooking spray.

2. Bake at 425° for 15-20 minutes or until a toothpick inserted near the center comes out clean. Serve warm.

Nutrition Facts: 1 piece equals 178 calories, 4 g fat (trace saturated fat), 24 mg cholesterol, 173 mg sodium, 31 g carbohydrate, 2 g fiber, 4 g protein. **Diabetic Exchanges:** 2 starch, 1/2 fat.

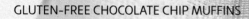

GLUTEN-FREE CHOCOLATE CHIP MUFFINS

Makeover Cranberry Rolls

PREP: 45 min. + chilling
BAKE: 20 min. **YIELD:** 1-1/2 dozen

DONNA TAYLOR • PORTLAND, OREGON

Cutting the butter and sugar from my original recipe really slimmed down these holiday favorites.

2   cups all-purpose flour
2   cups cake flour
1/4   cup sugar
1   pkg. (1/4 oz.) active dry yeast
1   tsp. salt
1-1/4   cups fat-free milk
1/2   cup reduced-fat butter, cubed
2   eggs

CRANBERRY FILLING:
3/4   cup chopped fresh *or* frozen cranberries
3/4   cup frozen unsweetened strawberries, thawed and chopped
1/2   cup sugar
1/2   cup raisins
1/3   cup chopped pecans
2   Tbsp. honey
1-1/2   tsp. grated orange peel

GLAZE:
1   cup confectioners' sugar
1   Tbsp. reduced-fat butter, melted
1   Tbsp. fat-free half-and-half

1. In a large bowl, combine the flours, sugar, yeast and salt. In a small saucepan, heat milk and butter to 120°-130°. Add to dry ingredients; beat just until moistened. Add eggs; beat until smooth (dough will be very sticky). Cover and refrigerate overnight.

2. In a small saucepan, bring the filling ingredients to a boil. Reduce heat; simmer, uncovered, for 5 minutes. Cool.

3. On a lightly floured surface, roll dough into an 18-in. x 12-in. rectangle. Spread filling over dough to within 1/2 in. of edges. Roll up jelly-roll style, starting with a long side; pinch seam to seal. Cut into 18 slices.

4. Place cut side down in two 8-in. square baking dishes coated with cooking spray. Cover and let rise until nearly doubled, about 40 minutes. Bake at 375° for 20-25 minutes or until golden brown.

5. For glaze, in a small bowl, beat the confectioners' sugar, butter and half-and-half until blended. Spread over warm rolls.

Editor's Note: This recipe was tested with Land O'Lakes light stick butter.

Nutrition Facts: 1 roll equals 243 calories, 5 g fat (2 g saturated fat), 31 mg cholesterol, 196 mg sodium, 46 g carbohydrate, 1 g fiber, 5 g protein.

Gluten-Free Chocolate Chip Muffins

PREP: 25 min. **BAKE:** 15 min. **YIELD:** 1 dozen

DONNA LOVESTRAND • SENECA, PENNSYLVANIA

I have a friend with celiac disease, and I didn't want her to miss out on the joy of chocolate and other baked goods, so I started experimenting to make some fun treats for her.

1   cup brown rice flour
1/2   cup soy flour
1/4   cup sugar
1/4   cup packed brown sugar
1/4   cup tapioca flour
1/4   cup buckwheat flour
1/4   cup baking cocoa
3   tsp. baking powder
1/4   tsp. salt
2   eggs
2/3   cup buttermilk
1/3   cup fat-free milk
2   Tbsp. butter, melted
1   tsp. vanilla extract
1/2   cup plus 2 Tbsp. miniature semisweet chocolate chips, *divided*

1. In a large bowl, combine the first nine ingredients. In another bowl, whisk the eggs, buttermilk, milk, butter and vanilla. Stir into dry ingredients just until moistened. Fold in 1/2 cup chocolate chips.

2. Coat muffin cups with cooking spray; fill three-fourths full with batter. Sprinkle with remaining chips. Bake at 350° for 12-16 minutes or until a toothpick comes out clean. Cool for 5 minutes before removing from pan to a wire rack. Serve warm.

Nutrition Facts: 1 muffin equals 184 calories, 6 g fat (3 g saturated fat), 41 mg cholesterol, 194 mg sodium, 30 g carbohydrate, 2 g fiber, 5 g protein. **Diabetic Exchanges:** 2 starch, 1 fat.

Makeover Chocolate Zucchini Bread

PREP: 15 min. **BAKE:** 40 min. + cooling
YIELD: 2 loaves (12 slices each)

JENNIFER SICKELS • GREENFIELD, INDIANA

My original recipe for this loaf had too many eggs and too much oil. With this healthier version, I can enjoy rich slices with a cup of coffee and not one bit of guilt.

1-1/4	cups sugar
3	eggs
2/3	cup unsweetened applesauce
1/3	cup canola oil
3	tsp. vanilla extract
1-1/2	cups all-purpose flour
1	cup cake flour
1/2	cup baking cocoa
1	tsp. salt
1	tsp. baking soda
1	tsp. ground cinnamon
1/4	tsp. baking powder
2	cups shredded peeled zucchini

1. In a large mixing bowl, beat the sugar, eggs, applesauce, oil and vanilla until well blended. Combine the flours, cocoa, salt, baking soda, cinnamon and baking powder; gradually beat into sugar mixture until blended. Stir in the zucchini. Transfer to two 8-in. x 4-in. loaf pans coated with cooking spray.

2. Bake at 350° for 40-45 minutes or until a toothpick inserted near the center comes out clean. Cool for 10 minutes before removing from pans to wire racks to cool completely.

Nutrition Facts: 1 slice equals 137 calories, 4 g fat (trace saturated fat), 26 mg cholesterol, 165 mg sodium, 23 g carbohydrate, 1 g fiber, 3 g protein. **Diabetic Exchanges:** 1-1/2 starch, 1/2 fat.

Chocolate Pistachio Biscotti ▣

PREP: 30 min. **BAKE:** 30 min. + cooling
YIELD: 40 cookies

GILDA LESTER • WILMINGTON, NORTH CAROLINA

Chocolate, pistachios and cranberries are great together. Adding the cranberries to this recipe made it not only sweeter, but healthier, too.

1/3	cup butter, softened
1	cup plus 1 Tbsp. sugar, *divided*
3	eggs
2	tsp. vanilla extract
2-3/4	cups all-purpose flour
1/3	cup baking cocoa
2-1/2	tsp. baking powder
1/2	tsp. ground cinnamon
1	cup (6 oz.) semisweet chocolate chips
1/2	cup pistachios
1/2	cup dried cranberries

1. In a large bowl, cream butter and 1 cup sugar until light and fluffy. Add eggs, one at a time, beating well after each addition. Beat in vanilla. Combine the flour, cocoa, baking powder and cinnamon; add to the creamed mixture and mix well (dough will be sticky). Stir in the chips, pistachios and cranberries.

2. Divide dough into four portions. On ungreased baking sheets, shape portions into 10-in. x 2-1/2-in. rectangles. Sprinkle with remaining sugar. Bake at 350° for 20-25 minutes or until set. Carefully remove to wire racks; cool for 5 minutes.

3. Transfer to a cutting board; cut each rectangle into 10 slices. Place cut side down on ungreased baking sheets. Bake for 5-8 minutes on each side or until lightly browned. Remove to wire racks to cool. Store in an airtight container.

Nutrition Facts: 1 cookie equals 107 calories, 4 g fat (2 g saturated fat), 20 mg cholesterol, 48 mg sodium, 17 g carbohydrate, 1 g fiber, 2 g protein. **Diabetic Exchanges:** 1 starch, 1 fat.

CHOCOLATE PISTACHIO BISCOTTI

MAKEOVER YUMMY CAKE

BOSTON CREAM PIE

MAKEOVER SWEET POTATO PECAN PIE

Cakes & Pies

You couldn't create a list of comfort foods without including a few cakes and pies. With the tooth-tingling recipes found in this chapter, you'll see that eating right doesn't mean giving up all of those sweet treats everyone simply adores.

Boston Cream Pie

PREP: 35 min. **BAKE:** 15 min. + cooling **YIELD:** 12 servings

NANCY ZIMMERMAN • CAPE MAY COURT HOUSE, NEW JERSEY

This is my lighter version of a Boston cream pie cake. You'll be pleased to serve it during special occasions.

1/3	cup butter, softened
3/4	cup sugar
2	eggs, lightly beaten
1/3	cup unsweetened applesauce
1-1/2	tsp. vanilla extract
2-1/4	cups cake flour
2	tsp. baking powder
1/2	tsp. salt
1/2	cup fat-free milk

FILLING:

1-1/4	cups cold fat-free milk
1	pkg. (1 oz.) sugar-free instant vanilla pudding mix

GLAZE:

1-1/4	cups confectioners' sugar
2	Tbsp. baking cocoa
1/2	tsp. vanilla extract
1	to 2 Tbsp. fat-free milk

1. In a large mixing bowl, beat butter and sugar until crumbly, about 2 minutes. Add eggs; mix well. Beat in applesauce and vanilla. Combine the flour, baking powder and salt; add to butter mixture alternately with milk until blended.

2. Coat two 9-in. round baking pans with cooking spray and sprinkle with flour; add batter. Bake at 350° for 12-15 minutes or until a toothpick inserted near the center comes out clean. Cool for 10 minutes before removing from pans to wire racks to cool completely.

3. For filling, in a small bowl, whisk milk and pudding mix for 2 minutes. Let stand for 2 minutes or until soft-set. Place one cake layer on a serving plate; top with filling and remaining cake layer.

4. For glaze, in a small bowl, combine the confectioners' sugar, cocoa and vanilla. Add enough milk to achieve desired consistency. Spread over top of cake, allowing some glaze to drape down the sides.

Nutrition Facts: 1 slice equals 275 calories, 6 g fat (3 g saturated fat), 50 mg cholesterol, 345 mg sodium, 50 g carbohydrate, 1 g fiber, 5 g protein.

Makeover Sweet Potato Pecan Pie

PREP: 25 min. **BAKE:** 45 min. + chilling
YIELD: 8 servings

MARGE WILLIAMS • JULIET, TENNESSEE

My original recipe for this treat was wonderful, but this lighter version means I can enjoy it without a bit of guilt!

1	sheet refrigerated pie pastry
1-1/2	cups mashed sweet potatoes
1/3	cup 2% milk
1/4	cup packed dark brown sugar
1	Tbsp. reduced-fat butter, melted
1/2	tsp. vanilla extract
1/4	tsp. salt
1/2	tsp. ground cinnamon
1/4	tsp. ground allspice
1/4	tsp. ground nutmeg

PECAN LAYER:

1	egg
1/3	cup packed dark brown sugar
1/3	cup corn syrup
1	Tbsp. reduced-fat butter, melted
1/4	tsp. vanilla extract
2/3	cup chopped pecans

1. On a lightly floured surface, unroll pastry. Transfer to a 9-in. pie plate. Trim pastry to 1/2 in. beyond edge of plate; flute edges.

2. In a small bowl, combine the next nine ingredients. Carefully spread into the pastry shell.

3. For pecan layer, in another small bowl, whisk egg and brown sugar until blended. Add the corn syrup, butter and vanilla; mix well. Stir in pecans. Pour over sweet potato mixture.

4. Bake at 350° for 45-55 minutes or until a knife inserted near the center comes out clean. Cool completely on a wire rack. Refrigerate for at least 3 hours before serving.

Editor's Note: This recipe was tested with Land O'Lakes light stick butter.

Nutrition Facts: 1 piece equals 363 calories, 17 g fat (5 g saturated fat), 36 mg cholesterol, 255 mg sodium, 53 g carbohydrate, 3 g fiber, 4 g protein.

Flourless Dark Chocolate Cake ⑤

PREP: 25 min. **BAKE:** 30 min. + cooling
YIELD: 12 servings

HEALTHY COOKING TEST KITCHEN

This lovely cake from our Test Kitchen is rich and over-the-top chocolaty. Garnishing it with confectioners' sugar makes for a very pretty presentation when you want to impress.

4	eggs, *separated*
1	pkg. (8 oz.) 53% cacao dark baking chocolate, coarsely chopped
3	Tbsp. butter, cubed
1/3	cup plus 1/4 cup sugar, *divided*
1-1/2	tsp. vanilla extract
1	container (2-1/2 oz.) prune baby food
1	tsp. dark baking cocoa *or* baking cocoa
1/2	tsp. confectioners' sugar

1. Place egg whites in a small mixing bowl; let stand at room temperature for 30 minutes. Meanwhile, in a small saucepan, melt chocolate and butter over low heat, stirring constantly. Remove from the heat; cool slightly. Coat a 9-in. springform pan with cooking spray. Place pan on a baking sheet; set aside.

2. In a large mixing bowl, beat the egg yolks on high speed for 3 minutes or until light and fluffy. Gradually add 1/3 cup sugar and vanilla, beating until thick and lemon-colored. Beat in baby food and chocolate mixture.

3. Beat the egg whites on medium speed until soft peaks form. Gradually beat in the remaining sugar, 1 tablespoon at a time, on high until stiff glossy peaks form; fold into the batter.

4. Pour into a prepared pan. Bake at 350° for 30-35 minutes or until a toothpick inserted near the center comes out with moist crumbs. Cool on a wire rack for 20 minutes. Carefully run a knife around edge of pan to loosen; remove sides from pan. Cool completely.

5. Sprinkle with cocoa and confectioners' sugar. Refrigerate leftovers.

Nutrition Facts: 1 slice equals 188 calories, 11 g fat (6 g saturated fat), 78 mg cholesterol, 50 mg sodium, 22 g carbohydrate, 2 g fiber, 4 g protein.

Gluten-Free Spice Cake

PREP: 25 min. **BAKE:** 30 min. + cooling **YIELD:** 9 servings

LAURA FALL-SUTTON • BUHL, IDAHO

A mix of seasonal spices fills this cake with mouth-watering flavor. Enjoy it with coffee.

1	cup unsweetened applesauce
1/2	cup honey
2	eggs
2	Tbsp. canola oil
1	tsp. vanilla extract
1-1/2	cups brown rice flour
1-1/2	tsp. ground ginger
1-1/2	tsp. ground cinnamon
1-1/4	tsp. baking powder
1/2	tsp. salt
1/4	tsp. baking soda
1/4	tsp. ground nutmeg
1/4	tsp. ground allspice
1/8	tsp. ground cloves
1/2	cup finely chopped walnuts
1/4	cup finely chopped dried apricots
1	tsp. grated orange peel
1	tsp. confectioners' sugar

1. In a large mixing bowl, beat the applesauce, honey, eggs, oil and vanilla until well blended. Combine the rice flour, ginger, cinnamon, baking powder, salt, baking soda, nutmeg, allspice and cloves; gradually beat into applesauce mixture until blended. Stir in the walnuts, apricots and orange peel.

2. Transfer to an 8-in. square baking dish coated with cooking spray. Bake at 350° for 28-32 minutes or until a toothpick inserted near the center comes out clean. Cool on a wire rack. Sprinkle with confectioners' sugar.

Nutrition Facts: 1 piece equals 249 calories, 9 g fat (1 g saturated fat), 47 mg cholesterol, 241 mg sodium, 41 g carbohydrate, 3 g fiber, 5 g protein.

FLOURLESS DARK CHOCOLATE CAKE

GLUTEN-FREE SPICE CAKE

MAKEOVER FUDGE CAKE

Makeover Fudge Cake §

PREP: 30 min. **BAKE:** 40 min. + cooling
YIELD: 12 servings

MARY JO KOPECKY • MADISON, WISCONSIN

I asked the "Healthy Cooking" team to lighten up my favorite cake. They used baby food and a few other strategies to cut the fat in half but keep all of the fudgy goodness!

4	egg whites
1-1/2	cups semisweet chocolate chips
1/3	cup butter, cubed
3	egg yolks
1	cup packed brown sugar
1	container (2-1/2 oz.) prune baby food
5	Tbsp. strong brewed coffee
1/4	cup all-purpose flour
1/4	tsp. salt
1/4	tsp. ground cinnamon
1/4	tsp. cream of tartar

FROSTING:

3	Tbsp. butter, softened
1/3	cup baking cocoa
3	Tbsp. fat-free milk
3/4	tsp. vanilla extract
1-1/2	cups confectioners' sugar

1. Place egg whites in a small mixing bowl; let stand at room temperature for 30 minutes. Coat a 9-in. springform pan with cooking spray. Place pan on a baking sheet; set aside. In a small saucepan, melt chocolate chips and butter over low heat, stirring constantly. Remove chocolate mixture from the heat; set aside to cool slightly.

2. In a large mixing bowl, beat egg yolks on high speed for 3 minutes or until thick and lemon-colored. Gradually beat in brown sugar. Beat in the baby food, coffee and reserved chocolate mixture.

3. Combine the flour, salt and cinnamon; gradually beat into the chocolate mixture. With clean beaters, beat egg whites and cream of tartar on high speed until stiff peaks form; fold into batter.

4. Spread evenly into prepared pan. Bake at 350° for 40-50 minutes or until a toothpick inserted near the center comes out with moist crumbs. Cool for 15 minutes before removing sides of pan. Cool completely on a wire rack.

5. For frosting, in a small mixing bowl, beat the butter, cocoa, milk and vanilla until smooth. Gradually beat in confectioners' sugar. Frost top of cake. Refrigerate leftovers.

Nutrition Facts: 1 slice equals 340 calories, 16 g fat (9 g saturated fat), 72 mg cholesterol, 137 mg sodium, 51 g carbohydrate, 2 g fiber, 4 g protein.

Blueberry Shortcake F

PREP: 15 min. **BAKE:** 25 min. **YIELD:** 4 servings

MARY DAMM • EAST PEORIA, ILLINOIS

Blueberries are so good for you. You should try this tender shortcake warm or cold, for dessert or breakfast, or even with extra milk poured over the top.

4	Tbsp. sugar, *divided*
2	tsp. all-purpose flour
1/8	tsp. ground cinnamon
1	cup plus 2 Tbsp. reduced-fat biscuit/baking mix
1/3	cup fat-free milk
1	cup fresh *or* frozen blueberries

1. In a small bowl, combine 2 tablespoons sugar, flour and cinnamon; set aside. In another bowl, combine the biscuit mix, milk and remaining sugar.

2. Spread half of the batter into a 1-qt. baking dish coated with cooking spray; top with half of the blueberries and half of the reserved sugar mixture. Repeat layers.

3. Bake at 350° for 25-30 minutes or until a toothpick inserted near the center comes out clean. Serve warm if desired, or cool on a wire rack.

Nutrition Facts: 1 piece equals 209 calories, 2 g fat (trace saturated fat), trace cholesterol, 403 mg sodium, 44 g carbohydrate, 1 g fiber, 4 g protein.

Makeover Grandma's Strawberry Pie

PREP: 40 min. + chilling **YIELD:** 8 servings

SHANNON CABES • PORTAGE, INDIANA

This was one of the first recipes Grandma taught me to make. With half the calories, this version lets me enjoy it regularly.

1-1/4	cups all-purpose flour
2	Tbsp. sugar
1/4	tsp. salt
3	Tbsp. cold butter
3	Tbsp. canola oil
4	to 5 Tbsp. buttermilk

FILLING:

1/2	cup sugar
2	Tbsp. cornstarch
1	cup cold water
1	pkg. (.3 oz.) sugar-free strawberry gelatin
4	cups sliced fresh strawberries
1/2	cup reduced-fat whipped topping

1. In a large bowl, combine flour, sugar and salt; cut in butter until crumbly. Gradually add oil, then buttermilk, tossing with a fork until dough forms a ball.

2. Between two sheets of lightly floured waxed paper, roll out pastry to fit a 9-in. pie plate. Transfer pastry to pie plate; trim to 1/2 in. beyond edge of plate. Flute edges.

3. Line unpricked pastry shell with a double thickness of heavy-duty foil. Bake at 450° for 8 minutes. Remove foil; bake 5-7 minutes longer or until lightly browned (cover edges with foil during the last few minutes to prevent overbrowning if necessary). Cool on a wire rack.

4. For filling, in a small saucepan, combine sugar and cornstarch. Stir in water until smooth. Bring to a boil, stirring constantly. Cook and stir for 2 minutes or until thickened. Remove from the heat; stir in gelatin until dissolved. Let stand for 15 minutes.

5. Place strawberries in a large bowl. Add gelatin mixture; gently toss to coat. Pour into crust. Refrigerate for 4 hours or until set. Garnish with whipped topping.

Nutrition Facts: 1 piece with 1 tablespoon whipped topping equals 255 calories, 10 g fat (3 g saturated fat), 12 mg cholesterol, 150 mg sodium, 39 g carbohydrate, 2 g fiber, 3 g protein.

Makeover Pineapple Nut Cake

PREP: 20 min. **BAKE:** 35 min. + cooling **YIELD:** 16 servings

ALICE HOFMAN • SUSSEX, WISCONSIN

I've had this no-fuss recipe for years, but I needed it to be lower in fat and calories. Luckily, the "Healthy Cooking" staff jumped in and came up with this healthy take on it.

2	cups all-purpose flour
1/2	cup sugar
1/2	cup sugar blend for baking
2	tsp. baking soda
2	eggs, beaten
1	can (20 oz.) unsweetened crushed pineapple, undrained
1/2	cup chopped pecans *or* walnuts, toasted

FROSTING:

1	pkg. (8 oz.) reduced-fat cream cheese
2	Tbsp. butter, softened
1-1/2	cups confectioners' sugar
1	tsp. vanilla extract

1. In a large bowl, combine the flour, sugar, sugar blend and baking soda. Combine eggs and pineapple; stir into dry ingredients just until moistened. Fold in nuts.

2. Transfer to a 13-in. x 9-in. baking pan coated with cooking spray. Bake at 350° for 32-38 minutes or until a toothpick inserted near the center comes out clean. Cool completely on a wire rack.

3. For frosting, in a large mixing bowl, beat cream cheese and butter until fluffy. Add confectioners' sugar and vanilla; beat until smooth. Frost cake. Store in the refrigerator.

Editor's Note: This recipe was tested with Splenda Sugar Blend for Baking.

Nutrition Facts: 1 piece equals 253 calories, 8 g fat (3 g saturated fat), 40 mg cholesterol, 237 mg sodium, 42 g carbohydrate, 1 g fiber, 4 g protein.

Gluten-Free Carrot Cake

PREP: 35 min. **BAKE:** 40 min. + cooling
YIELD: 20 servings

HEALTHY COOKING TEST KITCHEN

Pineapple makes this cake moist and tender. Your family and friends will never guess that it's wheat- and gluten-free!

- 1-1/2 cups sugar
- 2 cans (8 oz. *each*) unsweetened crushed pineapple, drained
- 4 eggs
- 3/4 cup reduced-fat mayonnaise
- 1-1/2 cups white rice flour
- 1/2 cup potato starch
- 1/2 cup soy flour
- 2 tsp. baking soda
- 2 tsp. ground cinnamon
- 1 tsp. xanthan gum
- 1/2 tsp. ground ginger
- 1/4 tsp. salt
- 3-1/4 cups shredded carrots
- 1 cup flaked coconut

FROSTING:
- 4 oz. reduced-fat cream cheese
- 1/4 cup reduced-fat butter, softened
- 2-1/2 cups confectioners' sugar
- 3/4 tsp. grated orange peel
- 1/4 tsp. vanilla extract

1. In a large mixing bowl, beat the sugar, pineapple, eggs and mayonnaise until well blended. Combine the rice flour, potato starch, soy flour, baking soda, cinnamon, xanthan gum, ginger and salt; gradually beat into sugar mixture until blended. Stir in carrots and coconut.

2. Pour into a 13-in. x 9-in. baking dish coated with cooking spray. Bake at 350° for 40-50 minutes or until a toothpick inserted near the center comes out clean. Cool on a wire rack.

3. For frosting, in a small mixing bowl, beat cream cheese and butter until fluffy. Add the confectioners' sugar, orange peel and vanilla; beat until smooth. Spread over top of cake. Refrigerate leftovers.

Editor's Note: Ingredient formulas and production facilities vary among brands. If you're concerned your brand may contain gluten, contact the company. This recipe was tested with Land O'Lakes light stick butter.

Nutrition Facts: 1 piece equals 287 calories, 9 g fat (4 g saturated fat), 52 mg cholesterol, 311 mg sodium, 51 g carbohydrate, 2 g fiber, 4 g protein.

Makeover Mama Cake

PREP: 25 min. **BAKE:** 40 min. + cooling
YIELD: 16 servings

TONYA PEELE • WAKE FOREST, NORTH CAROLINA

My great-grandmother made this cake on a weekly basis. Now that it's lighter, I can serve it without any guilt.

- 1/3 cup butter, softened
- 1-1/2 cups sugar
- 3 eggs
- 1/2 cup unsweetened applesauce
- 2 Tbsp. canola oil
- 1 can (12 oz.) evaporated milk
- 1/3 cup buttermilk
- 2 tsp. vanilla extract
- 1 tsp. lemon extract
- 1/4 to 1/2 tsp. food coloring, optional
- 2 cups all-purpose flour
- 1-1/2 cups cake flour
- 3 tsp. baking powder
- 1 tsp. salt
- 1/4 tsp. baking soda

1. In a large mixing bowl, beat butter and sugar until crumbly, about 2 minutes. Beat in the eggs, applesauce and oil. In a small bowl, combine the evaporated milk, buttermilk, extracts and food coloring if desired.

2. Combine the flours, baking powder, salt and baking soda; add to the butter mixture alternately with milk mixture, beating well after each addition.

3. Pour into a 10-in. fluted tube pan coated with cooking spray. Bake at 350° for 40-45 minutes or until a toothpick inserted near the center comes out clean. Cool for 10 minutes before removing from pan to a wire rack to cool completely.

Nutrition Facts: 1 slice equals 273 calories, 8 g fat (4 g saturated fat), 57 mg cholesterol, 308 mg sodium, 44 g carbohydrate, 1 g fiber, 5 g protein.

MAKEOVER GRANDMA'S STRAWBERRY PIE

MAKEOVER MAMA CAKE

Delightful Banana Cake

PREP: 35 min. **BAKE:** 40 min. + cooling **YIELD:** 16 servings

VICKI RAATZ • WATERLOO, WISCONSIN

Nuts and chocolate complement the banana flavor in this pretty, crowd-pleasing dessert.

2	eggs, *separated*
1/4	cup plus 1 Tbsp. butter, softened, *divided*
1-1/2	cups sugar, *divided*
1	cup mashed ripe bananas (2 to 3 medium)
1/3	cup reduced-fat sour cream
1/4	cup unsweetened applesauce
1	tsp. vanilla extract
2	cups all-purpose flour
2-1/2	tsp. baking powder
1/2	tsp. salt
1/4	tsp. baking soda
1/2	cup semisweet chocolate chips
1	Tbsp. water
1/2	cup chopped walnuts *or* chopped pecans

DRIZZLE:

2	Tbsp. butter
1	cup confectioners' sugar
1/2	tsp. vanilla extract
1	to 2 Tbsp. fat-free milk

1. Place egg whites in a small bowl; let stand at room temperature for 30 minutes.

2. In a large mixing bowl, beat 1/4 cup butter and 1 cup sugar until crumbly, about 2 minutes. Add egg yolks; mix well. In a small mixing bowl, beat the bananas, sour cream, applesauce and vanilla until blended. Combine the flour, baking powder, salt and baking soda; add to the butter mixture alternately with banana mixture. In a microwave, melt chocolate chips and remaining butter; stir until smooth. Cool slightly; stir in water.

3. Beat egg whites on medium speed until soft peaks form. Gradually beat in remaining sugar, 1 tablespoon at a time, on high until stiff glossy peaks form and sugar is dissolved. Fold into batter. Fold in walnuts.

4. Coat a 10-in. fluted tube pan with cooking spray and sprinkle with flour; add a third of the cake batter. Drizzle with half of the chocolate mixture. Repeat layers; top with remaining batter. Bake at 350° for 40-45 minutes or until a toothpick inserted near the center comes out clean. Cool for 10 minutes before removing from pan to a wire rack to cool completely.

5. For drizzle, in a small heavy saucepan, melt butter until lightly browned. Remove from the heat; stir in the confectioners' sugar, vanilla and enough milk to achieve desired consistency. Drizzle over cake.

Nutrition Facts: 1 slice equals 283 calories, 10 g fat (5 g saturated fat), 42 mg cholesterol, 220 mg sodium, 46 g carbohydrate, 1 g fiber, 4 g protein.

Crumb-Topped Apple & Pumpkin Pie

PREP: 35 min. **BAKE:** 50 min. + cooling **YIELD:** 10 servings

TRISHA FOX • PLAINFIELD, ILLINOIS

This special recipe combines all the warm, delicious flavors of the season and makes a truly unique presentation.

1	sheet refrigerated pie pastry
2	cups thinly sliced peeled tart apples
1/4	cup sugar
2	tsp. all-purpose flour
1	tsp. lemon juice
1/4	tsp. ground cinnamon

PUMPKIN FILLING:

1-1/2	cups canned pumpkin
1	cup fat-free evaporated milk
1/2	cup egg substitute
1/2	cup sugar
3/4	tsp. ground cinnamon
1/4	tsp. salt
1/8	tsp. ground nutmeg

TOPPING:

1/2	cup all-purpose flour
3	Tbsp. sugar
4-1/2	tsp. cold butter
3	Tbsp. chopped walnuts

1. On a lightly floured surface, unroll pastry. Transfer pastry to a 9-in. deep-dish pie plate. Trim pastry to 1/2 in. beyond edge of plate; flute edges. In a large bowl, combine the apples, sugar, flour, lemon juice and cinnamon. Spoon into crust.

2. In another large bowl, whisk the pumpkin filling ingredients. Pour over apple mixture. Bake at 375° for 30 minutes.

3. For topping, combine flour and sugar. Cut in butter until crumbly; stir in walnuts. Sprinkle over pie. Bake 20-25 minutes longer or until a knife inserted into pumpkin layer comes out clean (cover edges with foil during the last 15 minutes to prevent overbrowning if necessary).

4. Cool on a wire rack. Refrigerate leftovers.

DELIGHTFUL BANANA CAKE

CHOCOLATE BLISS MARBLE CAKE

Nutrition Facts: 1 piece equals 342 calories, 11 g fat (5 g saturated fat), 12 mg cholesterol, 259 mg sodium, 55 g carbohydrate, 3 g fiber, 7 g protein.

Chocolate Bliss Marble Cake

PREP: 40 min. **BAKE:** 30 min. + cooling **YIELD:** 16 servings

JOSEPHINE PIRO • EASTON, PENNSYLVANIA

This cake is served at all of our family parties. It's low in fat, but still delicious. I've been making it since 1985, when my late husband had heart surgery and had to watch his diet.

5	egg whites
1/4	cup baking cocoa
1/4	cup hot water
1	cup sugar, *divided*
1	cup fat-free milk
3	Tbsp. canola oil
1	tsp. vanilla extract
3/4	tsp. almond extract
2-1/2	cups all-purpose flour
3	tsp. baking powder
1/2	tsp. salt
1-1/2	cups reduced-fat whipped topping
4	squares (1 oz. *each*) semisweet chocolate, chopped
1-1/2	cups fresh raspberries

1. Let egg whites stand at room temperature for 30 minutes. Dissolve cocoa in water; let stand until cool.

2. In a large bowl, beat 3/4 cup sugar, milk, oil and extracts until well blended. Combine the flour, baking powder and salt; gradually beat into sugar mixture until blended.

3. In another bowl with clean beaters, beat egg whites on medium speed until soft peaks form. Beat in remaining sugar, 1 tablespoon at a time, on high until stiff peaks form. Gradually fold into batter. Remove 2 cups batter; stir in the reserved cocoa mixture.

4. Coat a 10-in. fluted tube pan with cooking spray. Alternately spoon the plain and chocolate batters into pan. Cut through batter with a knife to swirl.

5. Bake at 350° for 30-35 minutes or until a toothpick inserted near the center comes out clean. Cool for 10 minutes before removing from pan to a wire rack to cool completely.

6. For topping, in a microwave-safe bowl, microwave the whipped topping and chocolate until melted; stir until smooth. Place cake on a serving plate. Drizzle with topping. Place raspberries in center of cake.

Nutrition Facts: 1 slice equals 215 calories, 6 g fat (2 g saturated fat), trace cholesterol, 172 mg sodium, 37 g carbohydrate, 2 g fiber, 4 g protein.

Not a big fan of fresh raspberries? Feel free to set a handful or two of fresh strawberries in the center of **Chocolate Bliss Marble Cake** instead.

Makeover Crumb-Topped Chocolate Cake

PREP: 35 min. **BAKE:** 20 min. + cooling **YIELD:** 16 servings

SHARON ANDERSON • LYONS, ILLINOIS

My favorite cake was wonderful on the lips but murder on the thighs. By reducing the sugar, butter and flour, this rich cake offers far less fat and fewer calories than my original recipe.

- 1/4 cup plus 5 Tbsp. butter, softened, *divided*
- 1 cup sugar
- 2 eggs
- 1/4 cup unsweetened applesauce
- 1 tsp. vanilla extract
- 1 cup all-purpose flour
- 1 cup cake flour
- 1/3 cup baking cocoa
- 1 tsp. baking soda
- 1 tsp. salt
- 1-1/4 cups buttermilk
- 1/2 cup graham cracker crumbs
- 1/3 cup chopped walnuts
- 1/3 cup semisweet chocolate chips
- 2 cups reduced-fat whipped topping

1. In a large mixing bowl, beat 1/4 cup butter and sugar until crumbly, about 2 minutes. Add eggs, one at a time, beating well after each addition. Beat in applesauce and vanilla. Combine the flours, cocoa, baking soda and salt; add to butter mixture alternately with buttermilk, beating well after each addition. Transfer to two 9-in. round baking pans coated with cooking spray.

2. Combine the graham cracker crumbs, walnuts, chocolate chips and remaining butter. Break into small pieces; sprinkle evenly over batter.

3. Bake at 375° for 18-22 minutes or until a toothpick inserted near center comes out clean. Cool for 10 minutes before removing from pans to wire racks to cool completely.

4. Spread whipped topping between layers and over sides of cake, leaving the crumb top exposed. Refrigerate leftovers.

Nutrition Facts: 1 slice equals 253 calories, 11 g fat (6 g saturated fat), 45 mg cholesterol, 336 mg sodium, 34 g carbohydrate, 1 g fiber, 4 g protein.

Makeover Chocolate Eggnog Pie [S]

PREP: 45 min. + chilling **YIELD:** 8 servings

BETH MCCREEDY • LAPEER, MICHIGAN

I always made this pie during the holidays, but after vowing to eat healthy one year, I knew it needed a makeover. This pie has all the flavor with one-third fewer calories and half the fat.

- 1/2 cup all-purpose flour
- 1/3 cup ground walnuts
- 3 Tbsp. packed brown sugar
- 1 Tbsp. baking cocoa
- 1/4 cup reduced-fat butter, melted

FILLING:
- 1/2 cup sugar
- 2 Tbsp. cornstarch
- 2 cups eggnog
- 2-1/2 tsp. unflavored gelatin
- 1/2 cup cold water, *divided*
- 2 Tbsp. baking cocoa
- 3/4 teaspoon rum extract
- 2 cups reduced-fat whipped topping

GARNISH:
- 1/2 cup reduced-fat whipped topping

Ground nutmeg, optional

1. In a small bowl, combine the flour, walnuts, brown sugar and cocoa. Stir in butter. Lightly coat hands with cooking spray; press mixture into an ungreased 9-in. pie plate. Bake at 375° for 8-10 minutes or until set. Cool completely on a wire rack.

2. For filling, in a small saucepan, combine sugar and cornstarch. Stir in eggnog until smooth. Bring to a boil; cook and stir for 2 minutes or until thickened and bubbly. Remove from the heat; set aside.

3. Sprinkle gelatin over 1/4 cup cold water; let stand for 1 minute. Microwave on high for 20 seconds. Stir and let stand for 1 minute or until gelatin is completely dissolved. Stir into reserved eggnog mixture.

4. Divide mixture in half. Combine cocoa and remaining water; stir into one portion of eggnog mixture. Stir rum extract into the other portion. Cover and refrigerate mixtures until partially set.

5. Fold whipped topping into rum-flavored filling; spoon into crust. Gently spread chocolate filling over the top. Cover and refrigerate for at least 2 hours before serving. Garnish with whipped topping and nutmeg.

Editor's Note: This recipe was tested with Land O'Lakes light stick butter and commercially prepared eggnog.

Nutrition Facts: 1 piece equals 297 calories, 13 g fat (7 g saturated fat), 45 mg cholesterol, 86 mg sodium, 44 g carbohydrate, 1 g fiber, 5 g protein.

Chocolate Ganache Cake

PREP: 20 min. **BAKE:** 20 min. + cooling
YIELD: 12 servings

HEALTHY COOKING TEST KITCHEN

This mouth-watering cake looks very elegant, but it's really simple. As one of our Test Kitchen pros put it, "It's the easiest cake you could ever make." Need we say more?

- 2 oz. 53% cacao dark baking chocolate, coarsely chopped
- 2 Tbsp. butter
- 3/4 cup boiling water
- 3/4 cup sugar
- 1/4 cup buttermilk
- 1 egg
- 1 tsp. vanilla extract
- 1/2 tsp. orange extract
- 1 cup all-purpose flour
- 1 tsp. baking soda
- 1/2 tsp. salt

GANACHE:
- 1/4 cup half-and-half cream
- 3 oz. 53% cacao dark baking chocolate, coarsely chopped

1. Place chocolate and butter in a large mixing bowl; add boiling water and stir until smooth. Stir in the sugar, buttermilk, egg and extracts. Combine the flour, baking soda and salt; beat into chocolate mixture just until blended.

2. Transfer to a 9-in. round baking pan coated with cooking spray. Bake at 350° for 18-22 minutes or until a toothpick inserted near the center comes out clean. Cool for 10 minutes before removing from pan to a wire rack to cool completely.

3. In a small heavy saucepan, combine the ganache ingredients. Cook and stir over low heat until smooth. Transfer to a small bowl; cool 10 minutes or until slightly thickened.

4. Place cake on a serving plate. Slowly pour ganache over cake, allowing some ganache to drape over the sides. Refrigerate until serving.

Nutrition Facts: 1 slice equals 179 calories, 7 g fat (4 g saturated fat), 26 mg cholesterol, 236 mg sodium, 28 g carbohydrate, 1 g fiber, 3 g protein. **Diabetic Exchanges:** 2 starch, 1 fat.

Pineapple Pudding Cake **F**

PREP: 25 min. **BAKE:** 15 min. + chilling **YIELD:** 20 servings

KATHLEEN WORDEN • NORTH ANDOVER, MASSACHUSETTS

My mother used to love making this dessert in the summertime. It's so cool and refreshing that it never lasts very long!

- 1 pkg. (9 oz.) yellow cake mix
- 1-1/2 cups cold fat-free milk
- 1 pkg. (1 oz.) sugar-free instant vanilla pudding mix
- 1 pkg. (8 oz.) fat-free cream cheese
- 1 can (20 oz.) unsweetened crushed pineapple, well drained
- 1 carton (8 oz.) frozen fat-free whipped topping, thawed
- 1/4 cup chopped walnuts, toasted
- 20 maraschino cherries, well drained

1. Prepare cake mix batter according to package directions; pour into a 13-in. x 9-in. baking pan coated with cooking spray. Bake at 350° for 15-20 minutes or until a toothpick inserted near the center comes out clean. Cool completely on a wire rack.

2. In a bowl, whisk milk and pudding mix for 2 minutes. Let stand for 2 minutes or until soft-set. In a small mixing bowl, beat cream cheese until smooth. Beat in pudding mixture until blended. Spread evenly over cake. Sprinkle with pineapple; spread with whipped topping. Sprinkle with walnuts and garnish with cherries. Refrigerate until serving.

Nutrition Facts: 1 piece equals 131 calories, 2 g fat (1 g saturated fat), 1 mg cholesterol, 217 mg sodium, 24 g carbohydrate, 1 g fiber, 3 g protein. **Diabetic Exchange:** 1-1/2 starch.

PINEAPPLE PUDDING CAKE

Chocolate-Raspberry Mousse Pie

PREP: 35 min. + chilling **YIELD:** 8 servings

VIRGINIA ANTHONY • JACKSONVILLE, FLORIDA

Many years ago, I found a recipe for a raspberry mousse and played with it for a lighter pie. I just love the combination of raspberry and chocolate.

10	whole reduced-fat graham crackers
1	egg white
2	Tbsp. butter, melted
1/2	cup semisweet chocolate chips
1	envelope unflavored gelatin
1/2	cup cold water
2-1/2	cups fresh raspberries
4	oz. reduced-fat cream cheese, cubed
1/2	cup sugar
1/2	cup nonfat dry milk powder
1/2	cup ice-cold water
2	Tbsp. lemon juice

1. Place graham crackers in a food processor; cover and process until fine crumbs form. Add egg white and butter; cover and process until blended. Pat onto the bottom and up the sides of a 9-in. pie plate coated with cooking spray.

2. Bake at 350° for 8-10 minutes or until set. Sprinkle with chocolate chips; let stand for 1-2 minutes. Spread melted chips over crust. Cool on a wire rack.

3. In a saucepan, sprinkle gelatin over cold water; let stand for 1 minute. Heat over low heat, stirring until the gelatin is completely dissolved. Remove from heat; set aside.

4. Puree raspberries in a food processor; strain, discarding seeds. Return puree to food processor. Add cream cheese and sugar; cover and process until smooth. Add gelatin mixture; cover and process until blended. Transfer to a bowl; cover and refrigerate for 40 minutes or until partially set.

5. In a small mixing bowl, beat milk powder and ice-cold water on high speed until soft peaks form, about 7 minutes. Beat in lemon juice. Stir a third of the mixture into the raspberry mixture; fold in remaining

EGG-FREE CHOCOLATE CARAMEL CAKE

milk mixture. Spread evenly into crust. Cover and refrigerate for at least 3 hours.

Nutrition Facts: 1 piece equals 231 calories, 10 g fat (6 g saturated fat), 19 mg cholesterol, 170 mg sodium, 33 g carbohydrate, 4 g fiber, 7 g protein.

Egg-Free Chocolate Caramel Cake

PREP: 25 min. **BAKE:** 30 min. + cooling **YIELD:** 20 servings

HEALTHY COOKING TEST KITCHEN

Chocolaty cake only gets better when topped with caramel frosting. Kids and adults will devour this and never miss the eggs.

2	cups water
1-1/2	cups sugar
1/3	cup canola oil
1/3	cup unsweetened applesauce
2	tsp. cider vinegar
2	tsp. vanilla extract
3	cups all-purpose flour
1/3	cup baking cocoa
2	tsp. baking soda
1	tsp. salt

FROSTING:

2-2/3	cups confectioners' sugar
1/3	cup caramel ice cream topping
3	Tbsp. butter, softened
1-1/2	tsp. vanilla extract
3	to 6 Tbsp. fat-free milk

1. In a large mixing bowl, beat the first six ingredients until well blended. Combine the flour, cocoa, baking soda and salt; gradually beat into sugar mixture until blended.

2. Pour into a 13-in. x 9-in. baking pan coated with cooking spray. Bake at 350° for 28-32 minutes or until a toothpick inserted near the center comes out clean. Cool completely on a wire rack.

3. For frosting, in a small mixing bowl, combine the confectioners' sugar, caramel topping, butter, vanilla and enough milk to achieve a spreading consistency. Frost cake. Store in the refrigerator.

Nutrition Facts: 1 piece equals 259 calories, 6 g fat (1 g saturated fat), 5 mg cholesterol, 277 mg sodium, 50 g carbohydrate, 1 g fiber, 2 g protein.

Cranberry Date Upside-Down Cake

PREP: 30 min. **BAKE:** 40 min. + cooling **YIELD:** 12 servings

PRISCILLA GILBERT • INDIAN HARBOUR BEACH, FLORIDA

Cranberries and orange peel punch up the slightly tart taste in this cake that's tamed to perfection by a sweet glaze.

1/2	cup reduced-fat margarine, softened, *divided*
1/2	cup packed brown sugar
2	Tbsp. orange juice
1/4	tsp. ground cinnamon
1	cup fresh or frozen cranberries
2/3	cup chopped dates
1/4	cup chopped walnuts
1	tsp. grated orange peel

1 cup sugar
1 egg
1 tsp. vanilla extract
1-1/2 cups all-purpose flour
1 tsp. baking powder
1/2 tsp. salt
1/2 cup buttermilk

DRIZZLE:
1/2 cup confectioners' sugar
1 Tbsp. orange juice
1/2 tsp. reduced-fat margarine, melted
1/4 tsp. grated orange peel

1. In a small saucepan, melt 2 tablespoons margarine. Stir in the brown sugar, orange juice and cinnamon until blended. Pour into an 8-in. square baking dish coated with cooking spray. Combine the cranberries, dates, walnuts and orange peel; sprinkle over brown sugar mixture.

2. In a large mixing bowl, beat sugar and remaining margarine until crumbly, about 2 minutes. Add egg and vanilla; mix well. Combine the flour, baking powder and salt; add to the sugar mixture alternately with buttermilk, beating well after each addition. Spread over cranberry mixture.

3. Bake at 350° for 40-50 minutes or until a toothpick inserted near the center comes out clean. Cool for 10 minutes before inverting onto a serving plate.

4. Combine the drizzle ingredients; drizzle over cake.

Editor's Note: This recipe was tested with Parkay Light stick margarine.

Nutrition Facts: 1 piece equals 270 calories, 6 g fat (1 g saturated fat), 18 mg cholesterol, 204 mg sodium, 52 g carbohydrate, 2 g fiber, 3 g protein.

Makeover Yummy Cake

PREP: 25 min. **BAKE:** 30 min. + cooling **YIELD:** 16 servings

DEBBIE KNOLL • OTTAWA, ILLINOIS

The original recipe for this treat came from my husband's family. I love it, but with 25 percent of a day's worth of calories, I thought it could use a healthy makeover. By decreasing the amounts of some ingredients and using low-fat substitutions for others, this mouth-watering treat can still be considered a family favorite.

1 pkg. (18-1/4 oz.) yellow cake mix
1 cup fat-free milk
3 eggs
1/2 cup unsweetened applesauce
3/4 cup flaked coconut, toasted
3/4 cup chopped pecans, toasted
1 can (15 oz.) coconut-pecan frosting
1 carton (12 oz.) frozen reduced-fat whipped topping, thawed

1. In a large mixing bowl, combine the cake mix, milk, eggs and applesauce; beat on low speed for 30 seconds. Beat on medium for 2 minutes. Fold in coconut and pecans. Pour into two 9-in. round baking pans coated with cooking spray.

2. Bake at 350° for 28-32 minutes or until a toothpick inserted near the center comes out clean. Cool for 10 minutes before removing from pans to wire racks to cool completely.

3. Place frosting in a large bowl; fold in whipped topping. Spread mixture between layers and over the top and sides of cake. Refrigerate leftovers.

Nutrition Facts: 1 slice equals 365 calories, 17 g fat (8 g saturated fat), 40 mg cholesterol, 283 mg sodium, 51 g carbohydrate, 1 g fiber, 4 g protein.

STRAWBERRY MERINGUE TART

MAKEOVER CHEESECAKE BARS

CHOCOLATE CREPES WITH RASPBERRY SAUCE

There's more to dessert than cakes and pies...not that there's anything wrong with those goodies. Sometimes, however, you want something different. That's when you should see this chapter's collection of crepes, crisps and frozen delights.

Chocolate Crepes With Raspberry Sauce F

PREP: 25 min. + chilling **COOK:** 20 min. **YIELD:** 8 servings

REBECCA BAIRD • SALT LAKE CITY, UTAH

Everyone at the table will feel special eating this scrumptious treat. They're even great for brunch.

1	cup fat-free milk
1/2	cup fat-free evaporated milk
2	egg whites
1	egg
1	cup all-purpose flour
1/4	cup plus 1/3 cup sugar, *divided*
1/4	cup baking cocoa
1/2	tsp. salt
4-1/2	tsp. cornstarch
1	cup water
4-1/2	cups fresh *or* frozen raspberries, thawed, *divided*

Reduced-fat whipped cream in a can

| 1 | tsp. confectioners' sugar |

1. In a small mixing bowl, combine the milk, evaporated milk, egg whites and egg. Combine the flour, 1/4 cup sugar, cocoa and salt; add to milk mixture and mix well. Cover and refrigerate for 1 hour.

2. In a small saucepan, combine cornstarch and remaining sugar; set aside. Place water and 3-1/2 cups raspberries in a blender; cover and process for 2-3 minutes or until pureed.

3. Strain puree into cornstarch mixture and discard seeds. Bring to a boil; cook and stir for 2 minutes or until thickened. Transfer to a small bowl; refrigerate until chilled.

4. Coat an 8-in. nonstick skillet with cooking spray; heat over medium heat. Stir crepe batter; pour a scant 3 tablespoons into center of skillet. Lift and tilt pan to coat bottom evenly. Cook until top appears dry; turn and cook 15-20 seconds longer. Remove to a wire rack.

5. Repeat with remaining batter, coating skillet with cooking spray as needed. When cool, stack crepes with waxed paper or paper towels in between.

6. To serve, spoon a scant 3 tablespoons sauce over each crepe; roll up. Top each with 1 tablespoon whipped cream. Garnish with remaining raspberries and sprinkle with confectioners' sugar.

Nutrition Facts: 2 filled crepes equals 203 calories, 2 g fat (1 g saturated fat), 30 mg cholesterol, 202 mg sodium, 42 g carbohydrate, 6 g fiber, 7 g protein.

Makeover Cheesecake Bars

PREP: 25 min. **BAKE:** 15 min. + chilling **YIELD:** 9 servings

BECKY STONE • MENOMONEE FALLS, WISCONSIN

With only a few changes, this recipe cut more than 16 grams of fat from my favorite potluck contribution.

1	cup all-purpose flour
1/2	cup ground walnuts
3	Tbsp. brown sugar blend for baking
1/4	cup cold butter

FILLING:

4	oz. reduced-fat cream cheese
4	oz. fat-free cream cheese
1/3	cup sugar
2	tsp. all-purpose flour
1/4	cup egg substitute
2	Tbsp. fat-free milk
1	Tbsp. lemon juice
1/2	tsp. vanilla extract

1. In a small bowl, combine the flour, walnuts and brown sugar blend; cut in butter until crumbly. Set aside 2/3 cup for topping; press remaining crumb mixture into an 8-in. square baking dish coated with cooking spray. Bake at 350° for 9-11 minutes or until lightly browned.

2. Meanwhile, in a small mixing bowl, beat the cream cheeses, sugar and flour until light and fluffy. Beat in the egg substitute, milk, lemon juice and vanilla just until blended. Pour over crust; sprinkle with reserved crumb mixture.

3. Bake for 12-15 minutes or until filling is set. Cool on a wire rack for 1 hour. Refrigerate for at least 2 hours. Cut into bars. Refrigerate leftovers.

Editor's Note: This recipe was tested with Splenda Brown Sugar Blend for Baking.

Nutrition Facts: 1 bar equals 219 calories, 11 g fat (5 g saturated fat), 24 mg cholesterol, 191 mg sodium, 25 g carbohydrate, 1 g fiber, 6 g protein.

Chocolate Cherry Cake Roll

PREP: 45 min. **BAKE:** 10 min. + cooling
YIELD: 12 servings

JANE SHAPTON • TUSTIN, CALIFORNIA

Serve up a little luxury with an elegant dessert that's easy to make. Cherries and chocolate are the perfect partners for this moist yellow cake.

4	eggs
3/4	cup sugar
3/4	cup cake flour
1	tsp. baking powder
1/2	tsp. salt

Confectioners' sugar

FILLING:

1-1/4	cups reduced-fat whipped topping
3	Tbsp. chocolate syrup
3	cups fresh or frozen pitted sweet cherries, thawed, chopped and drained

FROSTING:

| 1 | cup reduced-fat whipped topping |
| 2 | Tbsp. chocolate syrup |

Additional fresh sweet cherries, optional

1. Line a 15-in. x 10-in. x 1-in. baking pan with waxed paper; coat the paper with cooking spray and set aside. In a large mixing bowl, beat eggs for 3 minutes. Gradually beat in sugar; beat for 2 minutes or until thick and lemon-colored. Combine the flour, baking powder and salt; gradually add to egg mixture and mix well.

2. Spread evenly into prepared pan. Bake at 400° for 8-10 minutes or until cake springs back when lightly touched. Cool for 5 minutes. Invert onto a kitchen towel dusted with confectioners' sugar. Gently peel off waxed paper. Roll up cake in the towel jelly-roll style, starting with a short side. Cool completely on a wire rack.

3. For filling, combine whipped topping and chocolate syrup; fold in cherries. Unroll cake; spread filling evenly over cake to within 1/2 in. of edges. Roll up again. Place seam side down on a serving platter.

4. For frosting, combine whipped topping and chocolate syrup. Frost cake; garnish with cherries if desired. Refrigerate until serving.

Nutrition Facts: 1 slice equals 189 calories, 4 g fat (2 g saturated fat), 71 mg cholesterol, 157 mg sodium, 35 g carbohydrate, 1 g fiber, 3 g protein. **Diabetic Exchanges:** 2 starch, 1/2 fruit, 1/2 fat.

Blueberry Cobbler

PREP: 20 min. **BAKE:** 30 min. **YIELD:** 8 servings

MARY RELYEA • CANASTOTA, NEW YORK

With a crisp biscuit topping and warm blueberry filling, my home-style cobbler sure doesn't taste light—but it is!

4	cups fresh or frozen blueberries, thawed
3/4	cup sugar, *divided*
3	Tbsp. cornstarch
2	Tbsp. lemon juice
1/4	tsp. ground cinnamon
1/8	tsp. ground nutmeg
1	cup all-purpose flour
2	tsp. grated lemon peel
3/4	tsp. baking powder
1/4	tsp. salt
1/4	tsp. baking soda
3	Tbsp. cold butter
3/4	cup buttermilk

1. In a large bowl, combine the blueberries, 1/2 cup sugar, cornstarch, lemon juice, cinnamon and nutmeg. Transfer to a 2-qt. baking dish coated with cooking spray.

2. In a small bowl, combine the flour, lemon peel, baking powder, salt, baking soda and remaining sugar; cut in butter until mixture resembles coarse crumbs. Stir in buttermilk just until moistened. Drop by tablespoonfuls onto blueberry mixture. Bake, uncovered, at 375° for 30-35 minutes or until golden brown. Serve warm.

Nutrition Facts: 1 serving equals 231 calories, 5 g fat (3 g saturated fat), 12 mg cholesterol, 220 mg sodium, 45 g carbohydrate, 2 g fiber, 3 g protein. **Diabetic Exchanges:** 2 starch, 1 fruit, 1 fat.

CHOCOLATE CHERRY CAKE ROLL

BLUEBERRY COBBLER

Raspberry Crumb Coffee Cake

PREP: 35 min. **BAKE:** 30 min. + cooling
YIELD: 20 servings

PAULA ERICKSEN • PALM HARBOR, FLORIDA

I lightened up an original recipe by replacing some of the sugar with sugar substitute, some white flour with whole wheat, and I went from using whole milk to skim. The result is delicious.

1/4	cup sugar

Sugar substitute equivalent to 1/4 cup sugar

1/4	cup cornstarch
3/4	cup cold water
2	cups fresh *or* frozen raspberries
1	Tbsp. lemon juice

BATTER:

1-1/2	cups all-purpose flour
3/4	cup whole wheat flour
1/2	cup sugar

Sugar substitute equivalent to 1/4 cup sugar

2-1/4	tsp. baking powder
3/4	tsp. salt
3/4	tsp. ground cinnamon
1/8	tsp. ground nutmeg
1/2	cup cold butter
1/4	cup cold reduced-fat butter
2	eggs, lightly beaten
1/2	cup fat-free milk
1	tsp. vanilla extract

TOPPING:

1/2	cup all-purpose flour

Sugar substitute equivalent to 1/2 cup sugar

1/4	cup cold butter
1/4	cup slivered almonds

1. In a small saucepan, combine the sugar, sugar substitute and cornstarch. Stir in water until smooth. Add raspberries. Bring to a boil over medium heat; cook and stir for 2 minutes or until thickened. Remove from the heat; stir in lemon juice.

2. In a large bowl, combine the first eight batter ingredients. Cut in butter and reduced-fat butter until crumbly.

3. Combine the eggs, milk and vanilla; stir into crumb mixture (batter will be thick).

4. Spread half of the batter into a 13-in. x 9-in. baking dish coated with cooking spray. Spread evenly with raspberry filling. Drop remaining batter by tablespoonfuls over filling.

5. For topping, combine flour and sugar substitute in a small bowl; cut in butter until crumbly. Stir in almonds. Sprinkle over batter.

6. Bake at 350° for 30-35 minutes or until lightly browned. Cool on a wire rack.

Editor's Note: This recipe was tested with Splenda No Calorie Sweetener and Land O'Lakes light stick butter.

Nutrition Facts: 1 piece equals 195 calories, 9 g fat (5 g saturated fat), 44 mg cholesterol, 227 mg sodium, 25 g carbohydrate, 2 g fiber, 3 g protein.

Strawberry Meringue Tart [S]

PREP: 25 min. **BAKE:** 55 min. + standing
YIELD: 8 servings

KAREN GRANT • TULARE, CALIFORNIA

I got this recipe from a girlfriend and made a few minor changes so it's less fattening. It's a beautiful, delicious dessert that will charm your guests!

3	egg whites
1/8	tsp. cream of tartar
3/4	cup sugar

FILLING:

1	pkg. (8 oz.) reduced-fat cream cheese
1/3	cup confectioners' sugar
1/2	cup marshmallow creme
1	cup reduced-fat whipped topping
5	cups fresh strawberries, halved
1/4	cup strawberry glaze

1. Line a large pizza pan with parchment paper; set aside. In a large mixing bowl, beat egg whites and cream of tartar on medium speed until soft peaks form. Gradually add sugar, 1 tablespoon at a time, beating on high until stiff glossy peaks form and sugar is dissolved.

2. Spread into a 10-in. circle on prepared pan, forming a shallow well in the center. Bake at 225° for 45-55 minutes or until set and lightly browned. Turn oven off; leave meringue in oven for 1 to 1-1/4 hours.

3. For filling, in a large mixing bowl, beat cream cheese and confectioners' sugar until smooth. Beat in marshmallow creme. Fold in whipped topping. Cover and refrigerate for at least 1 hour. Just before serving, spread filling into meringue shell. Top with strawberries. Drizzle with glaze.

Nutrition Facts: 1 slice equals 196 calories, 6 g fat (4 g saturated fat), 16 mg cholesterol, 123 mg sodium, 32 g carbohydrate, 2 g fiber, 4 g protein. **Diabetic Exchanges:** 1-1/2 starch, 1 fat, 1/2 fruit.

Chocolate Sour Cream Torte

PREP: 40 min. **BAKE:** 20 min. + cooling
YIELD: 16 servings

KAREN RAMES • HICKORY HILLS, ILLINOIS

This elegant cake is sure to evoke stunned "wows" from friends. Create toppings to fit the occasion; it lends itself perfectly to any garnish at all.

1/4	cup shortening
1-1/4	cups sugar
2	eggs
2	squares (1 oz. *each*) bittersweet chocolate, melted and cooled
1-1/2	tsp. vanilla extract
1-1/2	cups all-purpose flour

1/3	cup baking cocoa
1	tsp. baking powder
1/2	tsp. baking soda
1/2	tsp. salt
1	cup (8 oz.) reduced-fat sour cream
1	cup fat-free milk
1/4	cup plain yogurt

FROSTING:

1	cup (8 oz.) reduced-fat sour cream
2/3	cup sugar
1	carton (12 oz.) frozen reduced-fat whipped topping, thawed

1. In a large bowl, beat shortening and sugar until crumbly, about 2 minutes. Add eggs, one at a time, beating well after each addition. Beat in chocolate and vanilla.

2. Combine the flour, cocoa, baking powder, baking soda and salt. Combine the sour cream, milk and yogurt; add to the shortening mixture alternately with dry ingredients, beating well after each addition.

3. Line two 9-in. round baking pans with waxed paper; coat the pans with cooking spray and sprinkle with flour. Add the batter.

4. Bake at 350° for 18-22 minutes or until a toothpick inserted near the center comes out clean. Cool for 10 minutes before removing from pans to wire racks to cool completely.

5. For frosting, in a large bowl, combine sour cream and sugar. Fold in whipped topping. Place bottom layer on a serving plate; top with a third of the frosting. Top with remaining cake layer. Frost top and sides of cake. Refrigerate until serving.

Nutrition Facts: 1 slice equals 290 calories, 10 g fat (6 g saturated fat), 37 mg cholesterol, 175 mg sodium, 46 g carbohydrate, 1 g fiber, 5 g protein.

Raspberry Swirl Frozen Dessert

PREP: 45 min. **COOK:** 20 min. + freezing
YIELD: 12 servings

KAREN SUDERMAN • SUGAR LAND, TEXAS

Rich, creamy and delectable! That's how our tasting panel described this outstanding raspberry treat.

2/3	cup graham cracker crumbs
2	Tbsp. butter, melted
5	tsp. sugar

FILLING:

3	eggs, *separated*
1/4	cup plus 1 Tbsp. water, *divided*
1	cup sugar, *divided*
1/8	tsp. salt
1/8	tsp. cream of tartar
1	pkg. (8 oz.) reduced-fat cream cheese
1-1/2	cups reduced-fat whipped topping
1	pkg. (10 oz.) frozen sweetened raspberries, thawed

1. In a small bowl, combine the cracker crumbs, butter and sugar. Press onto the bottom of an 11-in. x 7-in.

dish coated with cooking spray. Cover and refrigerate for at least 15 minutes.

2. Meanwhile, for filling, in a small heavy saucepan, combine the egg yolks, 1/4 cup water, 1/2 cup sugar and salt. Cook and stir over low heat until mixture reaches 160° or is thick enough to coat the back of a metal spoon. Cool quickly by placing pan in a bowl of ice water; stir for 2 minutes. Set aside.

3. In a small heavy saucepan over low heat, combine egg whites, cream of tartar and remaining water and sugar. With a portable mixer, beat on low speed until mixture reaches 160°. Transfer to a small mixing bowl; beat on high until soft peaks form.

4. In a large mixing bowl, beat cream cheese until smooth. Gradually beat in egg yolk mixture. Fold in whipped topping, then egg white mixture. Drain raspberries, reserving 3 tablespoons juice. In a small bowl, crush half of berries with 1 tablespoon juice. Set remaining berries and juice aside.

5. Spread a third of cream cheese mixture over crust; spoon half of crushed berry mixture over the top. Repeat layers. Cut through with a knife to swirl raspberries.

6. Top with remaining cream cheese mixture. Sprinkle with reserved berries and drizzle with remaining juice. Cover and freeze for 5 hours or until firm. Remove from the freezer 15 minutes before cutting.

Nutrition Facts: 1 piece equals 217 calories, 9 g fat (5 g saturated fat), 71 mg cholesterol, 164 mg sodium, 32 g carbohydrate, 1 g fiber, 4 g protein. **Diabetic Exchanges:** 2 starch, 1-1/2 fat.

When preparing the egg whites for **Raspberry Swirl Frozen Dessert,** avoid using an aluminum saucepan as this can turn the mixture gray.

RASPBERRY SWIRL FROZEN DESSERT

Grapefruit Meringue Shells

F **S**

PREP: 25 min. **BAKE:** 1 hour + standing **YIELD:** 8 servings

PATRICIA POLEWSKI • MCALLEN, TEXAS

This citrus dessert is refreshing, simple and elegant. It's popular at our house after a meal or with afternoon tea.

- 3 egg whites
- 1/8 tsp. cream of tartar
- 3/4 cup sugar

FILLING:
- 1 pkg. (.8 oz.) sugar-free cook-and-serve vanilla pudding mix
- 1 cup red grapefruit juice
- 1 cup 2% milk
- 1 medium red grapefruit, peeled and sectioned
- 1 cup reduced-fat whipped topping

1. Place egg whites in a small mixing bowl; let stand at room temperature for 30 minutes. Add cream of tartar; beat on medium speed until soft peaks form. Gradually beat in sugar, 1 tablespoon at a time, on high until stiff glossy peaks form and sugar is dissolved.

2. Drop eight mounds onto a parchment paper-lined baking sheet. Shape into 3-in. cups with the back of a spoon. Bake at 225° for 1 to 1-1/2 hours or until set and dry. Turn oven off; leave meringues in oven for 1 hour. Cool on wire racks.

3. For filling, combine the pudding mix, grapefruit juice and milk in a small saucepan. Cook and stir over medium heat until mixture comes to a boil. Cook and stir 1-2 minutes longer or until thickened. Transfer to a bowl. Cover surface with waxed paper; refrigerate until chilled.

4. Just before serving, spoon pudding into meringue shells. Garnish with grapefruit and whipped topping.

Nutrition Facts: 1 serving equals 147 calories, 2 g fat (1 g saturated fat), 2 mg cholesterol, 89 mg sodium, 30 g carbohydrate, trace fiber, 3 g protein. **Diabetic Exchange:** 2 starch.

GRAPEFRUIT MERINGUE SHELLS

Peachy Phyllo Packets **F** **S**

PREP: 30 min. + standing
BAKE: 15 min. **YIELD:** 6 servings

AGNES WARD • STRATFORD, ONTARIO

These are so good and so quick to make! Flaky layers of pastry surround a warm, spiced filling of fresh peaches and raisins.

- 2 cups chopped peeled fresh peaches
- 2 Tbsp. raisins
- 1 Tbsp. lemon juice
- 3 Tbsp. plus 1-1/2 tsp. brown sugar, *divided*
- 2 tsp. quick-cooking tapioca
- 1/2 tsp. ground cinnamon, *divided*
- 1/8 tsp. ground ginger
- 2 Tbsp. dry bread crumbs
- 12 sheets phyllo dough (14 in. x 9 in.)

Butter-flavored cooking spray

CINNAMON-SUGAR:
- 1 tsp. sugar

Dash ground cinnamon

1. In a bowl, combine the peaches, raisins, lemon juice, 3 tablespoons brown sugar, tapioca, 1/4 teaspoon cinnamon and ginger; let stand for 10 minutes. In another small bowl, combine bread crumbs with the remaining brown sugar and cinnamon.

2. Spray one sheet of phyllo dough with butter-flavored spray. Sprinkle with 1-1/4 teaspoons bread crumb mixture. Cover with a second sheet of phyllo. (Keep remaining phyllo covered with plastic wrap and a damp towel to prevent it from drying out.)

3. Fold stack in half widthwise; spray with butter-flavored spray. Spoon 1/3 cup filling onto phyllo about 2 in. from the bottom edge. Fold sides and bottom edge over filling and roll up. Place seam side down on a baking sheet coated with cooking spray. Repeat.

4. Spray packets with butter-flavored spray. Combine sugar and cinnamon; sprinkle over the top. Bake at 375° for 12-15 minutes or until golden brown.

Nutrition Facts: 1 packet equals 141 calories, 1 g fat (trace saturated fat), 0 cholesterol, 113 mg sodium, 33 g carbohydrate, 2 g fiber, 3 g protein. **Diabetic Exchanges:** 1-1/2 starch, 1/2 fruit.

Tropical Crisp **S**

PREP: 20 min. **BAKE:** 30 min. **YIELD:** 9 servings

HEALTHY COOKING TEST KITCHEN

One bite of this sweet, juicy, crunchy crisp, and you'll be sure you hear the crash of the ocean and feel warm sand under your toes!

- 1 fresh pineapple, peeled and cubed
- 4 medium bananas, sliced
- 1/4 cup packed brown sugar
- 2 Tbsp. all-purpose flour

TOPPING:
- 1/3 cup old-fashioned oats
- 1/4 cup all-purpose flour
- 2 Tbsp. flaked coconut, toasted
- 2 Tbsp. brown sugar
- 1/4 tsp. ground nutmeg
- 1/4 cup cold butter

TROPICAL CRISP

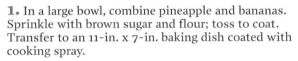

1. In a large bowl, combine pineapple and bananas. Sprinkle with brown sugar and flour; toss to coat. Transfer to an 11-in. x 7-in. baking dish coated with cooking spray.

2. In a small bowl, combine the oats, flour, coconut, brown sugar and nutmeg. Cut in butter until crumbly. Sprinkle over pineapple mixture.

3. Bake at 350° for 30-35 minutes or until filling is bubbly and topping is golden brown. Serve warm or at room temperature.

Nutrition Facts: 1 serving equals 188 calories, 6 g fat (4 g saturated fat), 13 mg cholesterol, 44 mg sodium, 34 g carbohydrate, 3 g fiber, 2 g protein. **Diabetic Exchanges:** 1 starch, 1 fruit, 1 fat.

Chewy Chocolate Brownies ⬛S

PREP: 15 min. **BAKE:** 15 min. + cooling
YIELD: 1-1/2 dozen

MICHELE DOUCETTE • STEPHENVILLE, NEWFOUNDLAND

Cap off lunch with a sweet treat. These chewy, fudgy brownies are so yummy, it's hard to believe they're just 124 calories each!

3	squares (1 oz. *each*) semisweet chocolate, chopped
1	cup packed brown sugar
3	Tbsp. unsweetened applesauce
1	egg
1	egg white
2	Tbsp. canola oil
4-1/2	tsp. light corn syrup
2	tsp. vanilla extract
1	cup all-purpose flour
1/4	cup baking cocoa
1/2	tsp. baking soda
1/8	tsp. salt

1. In a microwave, melt chocolate; stir until smooth. Cool slightly. Meanwhile, in a large mixing bowl, beat the brown sugar, applesauce, egg, egg white, oil, corn syrup and vanilla. Beat in chocolate until blended. Combine the flour, cocoa, baking soda and salt; beat into brown sugar mixture just until blended.

2. Pour into a 13-in. x 9-in. baking pan coated with cooking spray. Bake at 350° for 15-18 minutes or until a toothpick inserted near the center comes out clean. Cool on a wire rack. Cut into bars.

Nutrition Facts: 1 brownie equals 124 calories, 4 g fat (1 g saturated fat), 12 mg cholesterol, 65 mg sodium, 22 g carbohydrate, 1 g fiber, 2 g protein. **Diabetic Exchanges:** 1-1/2 starch, 1/2 fat.

Fat and calories stay at bay because **Chewy Chocolate Brownies** aren't frosted. If you'd like a special touch, however, dust them with confectioners' sugar.

Black Forest Crepes

PREP/TOTAL TIME: 20 min. **YIELD:** 8 servings

MARY RELYEA • CANASTOTA, NEW YORK

Cherries and chocolate just naturally taste great together, but the combination is even better when enhanced by tender crepes and a creamy filling.

- 1 pkg. (8 oz.) reduced-fat cream cheese, softened
- 1/2 cup reduced-fat sour cream
- 1/2 tsp. vanilla extract
- 2/3 cup confectioners' sugar
- 8 prepared crepes (9 in.)
- 1 can (20 oz.) reduced-sugar cherry pie filling, warmed
- 1/4 cup chocolate syrup

1. In a small mixing bowl, beat the cream cheese, sour cream and vanilla until smooth. Gradually beat in confectioners' sugar. Spread about 3 tablespoons over each crepe to within 1/2 in. of edges and roll up.

2. Arrange in an ungreased 13-in. x 9-in. baking dish. Bake, uncovered, at 350° for 5-7 minutes or until warm. To serve, top each crepe with 1/4 cup pie filling and drizzle with 1-1/2 teaspoons chocolate syrup.

Nutrition Facts: 1 filled crepe equals 256 calories, 9 g fat (6 g saturated fat), 31 mg cholesterol, 222 mg sodium, 39 g carbohydrate, 1 g fiber, 6 g protein. **Diabetic Exchanges:** 2-1/2 starch, 1-1/2 fat.

Guilt-Free Berry Trifle **F**

PREP: 40 min. + chilling **YIELD:** 16 servings

ELAINE ALEVER • SAGINAW, MICHIGAN

I am always cutting fat from recipes. When I was invited to a party where the hostess was diabetic, I wanted to take this trifle—a dessert she could enjoy.

Sugar substitute equivalent to 1/2 cup sugar, *divided*
- 9 tsp. cornstarch, *divided*
- 3/4 cup cold water, *divided*
- 1 quart fresh strawberries, chopped
- 4 Tbsp. lemon juice, *divided*
- 3 cups fresh blueberries
- 1 pkg. (1 oz.) sugar-free instant vanilla pudding mix
- 2 cups fat-free milk
- 2 loaves (10-1/2 oz. *each*) angel food cake, cubed
- 1 carton (8 oz.) frozen reduced-fat whipped topping, thawed

1. In a small heavy saucepan, combine 1/4 cup sugar substitute, 4-1/2 teaspoons cornstarch and 1/4 cup water until smooth. Bring to a boil over medium heat, stirring constantly. Add strawberries; cook and stir for 2 minutes or until thickened and bubbly. Remove from the heat; stir in 2 tablespoons lemon juice. Cool to room temperature without stirring.

2. In another heavy saucepan, combine the remaining sugar substitute, cornstarch and water until smooth. Bring to a boil over medium heat, stirring constantly. Add blueberries; cook and stir for 2 minutes or until thickened and bubbly. Remove from the heat; stir in remaining lemon juice. Cool to room temperature without stirring.

3. Prepare pudding according to package directions, using fat-free milk. Let stand for 2 minutes or until soft-set.

4. Place half of the cake cubes in a 4-qt. trifle bowl. Layer with strawberry mixture, half of the pudding, remaining cake cubes, blueberry mixture and remaining pudding. Top with whipped topping. Cover and refrigerate for at least 1 hour.

Nutrition Facts: 1 cup equals 180 calories, 2 g fat (2 g saturated fat), 1 mg cholesterol, 369 mg sodium, 36 g carbohydrate, 2 g fiber, 4 g protein. **Diabetic Exchanges:** 2 starch, 1/2 fruit.

Skinny Mint-Chip Ice Cream

PREP: 15 min. + freezing **YIELD:** 1-1/2 quarts

NANCY QUELLE • CEDAR RAPIDS, IOWA

No one will ever guess that this smooth and creamy mint treat is light at all. For the Christmas holidays, it's fun to substitute 2 cups of crushed peppermint candy canes for the semisweeet chocolate chunks.

- 4 cups fat-free half-and-half
- 1 pkg. (3.4 oz.) instant vanilla pudding mix
- 1 can (14 oz.) fat-free sweetened condensed milk
- 2 tsp. mint extract
- 3 to 4 drops green food coloring, optional
- 1-1/2 cups semisweet chocolate chunks

1. In a large mixing bowl, beat half-and-half and pudding mix on low speed for 2 minutes. Beat in the condensed milk, extract and food coloring if desired.

2. Fill cylinder of ice cream freezer; freeze according to manufacturer's directions. Coarsely chop chocolate chunks if desired; stir into ice cream. Transfer to freezer containers. Freeze for 2-4 hours before serving.

Nutrition Facts: 1/2 cup equals 289 calories, 7 g fat (4 g saturated fat), 4 mg cholesterol, 216 mg sodium, 50 g carbohydrate, 1 g fiber, 6 g protein.

Summer Fruit Crisp S

PREP: 30 min. **BAKE:** 20 min. **YIELD:** 10 servings

BETH GARVIN • CISCO, TEXAS

What says summer more than this sweet dessert simply packed with fresh cherries and juicy peaches? To beat the heat, dollop servings with scoops of low-fat frozen yogurt or ice cream.

- 4 cups fresh dark sweet cherries (about 1-1/4 lbs.), pitted
- 4 cups sliced peeled peaches
- 1/3 cup sugar
- 2 Tbsp. all-purpose flour
- 1/8 tsp. salt

TOPPING:
- 1/2 cup old-fashioned oats
- 1/2 cup packed brown sugar
- 1/3 cup all-purpose flour
- 1/4 cup chopped pecans
- 1/4 tsp. salt
- 1/4 tsp. ground cinnamon
- 3 Tbsp. cold butter

1. In a large bowl, combine the cherries, peaches, sugar, flour and salt. Transfer to a 13-in. x 9-in. baking dish coated with cooking spray.

2. For topping, in a small bowl, combine the oats, brown sugar, flour, pecans, salt and cinnamon. Cut in butter until crumbly. Sprinkle over fruit mixture.

3. Bake at 400° for 20-25 minutes or until filling is bubbly and topping is golden brown. Serve warm.

Nutrition Facts: 1 serving equals 234 calories, 6 g fat (2 g saturated fat), 9 mg cholesterol, 128 mg sodium, 45 g carbohydrate, 3 g fiber, 3 g protein.

When whipping up **Summer Fruit Crisp,** consider using plums instead of the peaches. You can also swap out the pecans for walnuts if you'd like, or leave out the nuts in the topping altogether and cut even more calories. Add a dash of nutmeg along with the cinnamon.

SUMMER FRUIT CRISP

SKINNY MINT-CHIP ICE CREAM

Pumpkin Cake Roll

PREP: 25 min. **BAKE:** 10 min. + chilling **YIELD:** 12 servings

HEIDI REINHARD • MONTPELIER, INDIANA

If you'd like, you could substitute lemon juice for the almond extract. For a frozen dessert, replace the filling with reduced-fat vanilla ice cream.

3	eggs
3/4	cup sugar
2/3	cup canned pumpkin
1/2	tsp. almond extract
3/4	cup all-purpose flour
2	tsp. ground cinnamon
1	tsp. baking powder
1	tsp. ground ginger
1/2	tsp. salt
1	Tbsp. plus 1 cup confectioners' sugar, *divided*
6	oz. reduced-fat cream cheese, cubed
1	tsp. butter
1/2	tsp. vanilla extract

1. Line a 15-in. x 10-in. x 1-in. baking pan with waxed paper. Coat the paper with cooking spray; set aside. In a large mixing bowl, beat eggs for 3 minutes. Gradually add sugar; beat for 2 minutes or until mixture becomes thick and lemon-colored. Beat in pumpkin and extract. Combine the flour, cinnamon, baking powder, ginger and salt; fold into pumpkin mixture. Spread batter evenly into prepared pan.

2. Bake at 375° for 10-15 minutes or until cake springs back when lightly touched (do not overbake). Cool for 5 minutes. Invert onto a kitchen towel dusted with 1 tablespoon confectioners' sugar. Gently peel off waxed paper. Roll up cake in the towel jelly-roll style, starting with a short side. Cool completely on a wire rack.

3. For filling, in a small mixing bowl, beat the cream cheese, butter, vanilla and remaining confectioners' sugar until fluffy.

4. Unroll cake; spread filling evenly over cake to within 1/2 in. of edges. Roll up again. Cover and refrigerate for 1 hour before serving.

Nutrition Facts: 1 slice equals 182 calories, 5 g fat (3 g saturated fat), 64 mg cholesterol, 212 mg sodium, 31 g carbohydrate, 1 g fiber, 4 g protein. **Diabetic Exchanges:** 2 starch, 1/2 fat.

Berry-Licious Crisp ⑤

PREP: 15 min. **BAKE:** 20 min. **YIELD:** 9 servings

EDNA WOODARD • FREDERICKSBURG, TEXAS

I lightened up one of my favorite recipes, and this is the delicious result. I like to serve it with low-fat vanilla ice cream or frozen yogurt.

1	cup *each* fresh blackberries, blueberries and raspberries
1	cup fresh *or* frozen cranberries, thawed
1	medium tart apple, peeled and diced
3/4	cup sugar
3	Tbsp. cornstarch
1/2	cup all-purpose flour
1/2	cup packed brown sugar
1/4	cup cold butter

1. In a large bowl, combine the berries and apple. Combine sugar and cornstarch; sprinkle over fruit and gently toss to coat.

2. Transfer to an 8-in. square baking dish coated with cooking spray. In a small bowl, combine flour and brown sugar; cut in butter until crumbly. Sprinkle over fruit mixture.

3. Bake at 400° for 20-25 minutes or until filling is bubbly and topping is golden brown. Serve warm.

Nutrition Facts: 1 serving equals 228 calories, 5 g fat (3 g saturated fat), 14 mg cholesterol, 57 mg sodium, 45 g carbohydrate, 3 g fiber, 1 g protein.

Gluten-Free Crumb Crust ⑤

PREP/TOTAL TIME: 20 min. **YIELD:** 1 crust

CHRISTA HAGEMAN • TELFORD, PENNSYLVANIA

I use this recipe to replace graham cracker crusts because my father can't have the hydrogenated fats and sugars in them. It's so fast!

1	cup brown rice flour
1/2	cup ground walnuts
3	Tbsp. apple juice concentrate
2	Tbsp. olive oil

1. In a small bowl, combine all ingredients. Press onto the bottom and up the sides of a 9-in. pie plate coated with cooking spray. Bake at 375° for 10-14 minutes or until set. Cool on a wire rack.

2. Fill as desired. If baking the filling, shield edges of crust with foil to prevent overbrowning.

Nutrition Facts: 1/8 of crust equals 133 calories, 7 g fat (1 g saturated fat), 0 cholesterol, 2 mg sodium, 17 g carbohydrate, 1 g fiber, 2 g protein. **Diabetic Exchanges:** 1-1/2 fat, 1 starch.

PUMPKIN CAKE ROLL

MAKEOVER CHOCOLATE LAYER BARS

Makeover Chocolate Layer Bars S

PREP: 35 min. **BAKE:** 15 min. + cooling **YIELD:** 40 bars

ANITA NICKLESS • PLATTE CITY, MISSOURI

Relatives often ask for these bars at get-togethers and people don't want to stop at just one...I don't blame them! With this pared-down version, we can all enjoy them guilt-free.

  1/2 cup butter, softened
1-1/2 cups sugar
    2 eggs
  1/2 cup unsweetened applesauce
    1 tsp. vanilla extract
    2 cups all-purpose flour
    3 Tbsp. baking cocoa
    1 tsp. baking soda
    1 cup buttermilk

CREAMY LAYER:
  1/3 cup butter, softened
  1/3 cup reduced-fat butter, softened
    2 cups confectioners' sugar
    3 Tbsp. fat-free milk
    1 tsp. vanilla extract

FROSTING:
    1 cup sugar
  1/3 cup butter, cubed
  1/3 cup fat-free milk
  1/4 cup baking cocoa
  3/4 cup semisweet chocolate chips

1. In a large mixing bowl, cream butter and sugar until light and fluffy. Beat in the eggs, applesauce and vanilla until well blended. Combine the flour, cocoa and baking soda; add to the creamed mixture alternately with buttermilk, beating well after each addition.

2. Pour into a 15-in. x 10-in. x 1-in. baking pan coated with cooking spray. Bake at 350° for 15-20 minutes or until a toothpick inserted near the center comes out clean. Cool completely on a wire rack.

3. For creamy layer, in a small mixing bowl, beat the butters, confectioners' sugar, milk and vanilla until fluffy, about 4 minutes. Spread over top of cake.

4. For frosting, in a small heavy saucepan, combine the sugar, butter, milk and cocoa. Bring to a boil over medium heat, stirring frequently; cook and stir 2 minutes longer. Remove from the heat; stir in chocolate chips until melted.

5. With a hand mixer, beat frosting for 2-4 minutes or until thickened. Gently spread over the top. Store in the refrigerator.

Editor's Note: This recipe was tested with Land O'Lakes light stick butter.

Nutrition Facts: 1 bar equals 175 calories, 8 g fat (5 g saturated fat), 27 mg cholesterol, 94 mg sodium, 27 g carbohydrate, 1 g fiber, 2 g protein. **Diabetic Exchanges:** 1-1/2 starch, 1-1/2 fat.

By replacing the oil Anita's recipe originally called for with unsweetened applesauce, and by combining full- and reduced-fat butter to use instead of shortening, the *Healthy Cooking* team skimmed **Chocolate Layer Bars** of 75 calories.

Makeover Oatmeal Brownie Bars S

PREP: 25 min. **BAKE:** 20 min. + cooling **YIELD:** 2 dozen

LYNETTE RENS • MAYNARD, MINNESOTA

This revamp of my recipe cut more than 100 calories from the original. For extra nutrition, replace 1/2 cup of all-purpose flour with the whole wheat variety.

1/3	cup butter, softened
3/4	cup sugar
1/3	cup sugar blend for baking
2	eggs
1	cup buttermilk
1/2	cup unsweetened applesauce
2	tsp. vanilla extract
1	cup all-purpose flour
1	cup quick-cooking oats
1/4	cup baking cocoa
1/2	tsp. baking powder
1/2	tsp. salt
1/2	cup chopped walnuts

FROSTING:

1/3	cup butter, cubed
1/4	cup baking cocoa
1/4	cup fat-free milk
2	cups confectioners' sugar

1. In a large mixing bowl, beat the butter, sugar and sugar blend until well blended. Beat in the eggs, buttermilk, applesauce and vanilla. Combine the flour, oats, cocoa, baking powder and salt; gradually add to butter mixture and mix well. Beat in walnuts.

2. Spread batter into a 15-in. x 10-in. x 1-in. baking pan coated with cooking spray. Bake at 350° for 20-25 minutes or until a toothpick inserted near the center comes out clean. Cool completely on a wire rack.

3. For frosting, in a small saucepan, melt butter. Whisk in cocoa and milk until blended. Bring to a boil. Remove from the heat; whisk in confectioners' sugar until smooth. Immediately spread over bars. Let stand until frosting is set. Cut into squares.

Editor's Note: This recipe was tested with Splenda Sugar Blend for Baking.

Nutrition Facts: 1 bar equals 185 calories, 7 g fat (3 g saturated fat), 32 mg cholesterol, 127 mg sodium, 28 g carbohydrate, 1 g fiber, 3 g protein.

Spiced Cranberry Oatmeal Cookies F S C

PREP: 30 min. **BAKE:** 10 min./batch **YIELD:** 5-1/2 dozen

KARIE SAXTON • SOUTH BOARDMAN, MICHIGAN

Every bite of these delicious cookies is packed with flavor! You'll love the tasty combination of pecans, dried cranberries and chocolate chips.

1/2 cup butter, softened
3/4 cup packed brown sugar
1/4 cup sugar blend
3/4 cup unsweetened applesauce
1 egg
1 tsp. vanilla extract
3 cups old-fashioned oats
1-3/4 cups all-purpose flour
1-1/2 tsp. ground cinnamon
1 tsp. baking powder
1/2 tsp. salt
1/2 tsp. ground nutmeg
1 cup dried cranberries
1/2 cup miniature semisweet chocolate chips
1/2 cup chopped pecans

1. In a large mixing bowl, beat the butter, brown sugar and sugar blend until well blended. Beat in the applesauce, egg and vanilla (mixture will appear curdled). Combine the oats, flour, cinnamon, baking powder, salt and nutmeg; gradually add to the butter mixture and mix well. Stir in the cranberries, chocolate chips and pecans.

2. Drop by tablespoonfuls 2 in. apart onto ungreased baking sheets; flatten slightly. Bake at 350° for 10-12 minutes or until edges are lightly browned. Remove to wire racks.

Editor's Note: This recipe was tested with Splenda sugar blend.

Nutrition Facts: 1 cookie equals 71 calories, 3 g fat (1 g saturated fat), 7 mg cholesterol, 36 mg sodium, 11 g carbohydrate, 1 g fiber, 1 g protein. **Diabetic Exchanges:** 1 starch, 1/2 fat.

Ginger Cream Cookies F S C

PREP: 25 min. **BAKE:** 10 min./batch **YIELD:** 3 dozen

SUVILLA JORDAN • KERSEY, PENNSYLVANIA

Cookies can be difficult to lighten up, but this great-tasting ginger cookie perfectly captures the holiday season if you ask me. A sugar blend makes them a bit healthier than other cookies without affecting the flavor or texture.

1/2 cup molasses
1/4 cup sugar blend
1/4 cup canola oil
1 egg
1 tsp. vanilla extract
2 cups all-purpose flour
1-1/2 tsp. ground cinnamon
1 tsp. baking soda
1 tsp. ground ginger
3/4 tsp. ground cloves
3/4 tsp. ground nutmeg

1. In a large mixing bowl, beat the molasses, sugar blend, oil, egg and vanilla until well blended. Combine the remaining ingredients; gradually add to molasses mixture and mix well.

2. Drop by rounded teaspoonfuls 2 in. apart onto baking sheets lightly coated with cooking spray. Bake at 350° for 8-10 minutes or until edges are lightly browned. Remove to wire racks.

Editor's Note: This recipe was tested with Splenda Sugar Blend for Baking.

Nutrition Facts: 1 cookie equals 60 calories, 2 g fat (trace saturated fat), 6 mg cholesterol, 39 mg sodium, 10 g carbohydrate, trace fiber, 1 g protein. **Diabetic Exchanges:** 1/2 starch, 1/2 fat.

When lightening your **cookie recipes** you may need to undergo some trial and error. Decrease the mix-ins and replace some of the butter with canola oil to start.

SPICED CRANBERRY OATMEAL COOKIES

GINGER CREAM COOKIES

Chocolate Peanut Butter Parfaits

PREP: 20 min. + chilling **YIELD:** 6 servings

PAT SOLOMAN • CASPER, WYOMING

When a friend gave me this recipe, I knew it was a keeper. It meets all requirements: It's easy, low-calorie and low-fat, and it's pretty to boot!

- 2 Tbsp. reduced-fat chunky peanut butter
- 2 Tbsp. plus 2 cups cold fat-free milk, *divided*
- 1 cup plus 6 Tbsp. reduced-fat whipped topping, *divided*
- 1 pkg. (1.4 oz.) sugar-free instant chocolate fudge pudding mix
- 3 Tbsp. finely chopped salted peanuts

1. In a small bowl, combine peanut butter and 2 tablespoons milk. Fold in 1 cup whipped topping; set aside. In another small bowl, whisk remaining milk with the pudding mix for 2 minutes. Let stand for 2 minutes or until soft-set.

2. Spoon half of the pudding into six parfait glasses or dessert dishes. Layer with reserved peanut butter mixture and remaining pudding. Refrigerate for at least 1 hour. Refrigerate remaining whipped topping.

3. Just before serving, garnish each parfait with 1 tablespoon whipped topping and 1-1/2 teaspoons peanuts.

Nutrition Facts: 1 parfait equals 146 calories, 6 g fat (3 g saturated fat), 2 mg cholesterol, 300 mg sodium, 16 g carbohydrate, 1 g fiber, 6 g protein. **Diabetic Exchanges:** 1 fat, 1/2 starch, 1/2 fat-free milk.

Frozen Chocolate Mint Dessert

PREP: 30 min. + freezing **YIELD:** 24 servings

SARAH NEWMAN • BROOKLYN CENTER, MINNESOTA

This is adapted from my great-aunt's recipe for grasshopper pie. My last version was a fluke, as I put in too much mint extract. I needed to cut the mint taste with something gooey and chocolaty, so I ended up flipping the whole thing upside down on top of a brownie crust!

- 1 pkg. fudge brownie mix (13-in. x 9-in. pan size)
- 2 egg whites
- 1/4 cup unsweetened applesauce
- 2 tsp. vanilla extract
- 1/2 cup baking cocoa
- 1-1/2 cups fat-free milk
- 2 pkg. (16 oz. *each*) large marshmallows
- 1/2 tsp. mint extract
- 1 carton (16 oz.) frozen reduced-fat whipped topping, thawed
- 2/3 cup cream-filled chocolate sandwich cookie crumbs

1. In a large bowl, combine the brownie mix, egg whites, applesauce and vanilla. Spread into a 13-in. x 9-in. baking dish coated with cooking spray. Bake at 350° for 18-22 minutes or until a toothpick inserted near the center comes out clean. Cool on a wire rack.

2. In a Dutch oven, combine cocoa and milk. Cook and stir over medium heat until cocoa is dissolved. Stir in marshmallows until melted. Remove from the heat; stir in extract. Cool completely.

3. Fold in whipped topping. Spread over brownies. Sprinkle with cookie crumbs. Cover and freeze for at least 8 hours. Remove from the freezer 10 minutes before serving.

Nutrition Facts: 1 piece equals 293 calories, 6 g fat (3 g saturated fat), 1 mg cholesterol, 141 mg sodium, 60 g carbohydrate, 1 g fiber, 3 g protein.

CHOCOLATE PEANUT BUTTER PARFAITS

FROZEN CHOCOLATE MINT DESSERT

Frozen Pistachio Dessert With Raspberry Sauce

PREP: 35 min. + freezing **YIELD:** 12 servings

SUZETTE JURY • KEENE, CALIFORNIA

Raspberry sauce adds pretty holiday color to this cool and creamy treat, while pistachios provide a savory hint.

1-1/2	cups crushed vanilla wafers (about 45 wafers)
1/4	cup finely chopped pistachios
1/4	cup reduced-fat butter, melted
1-1/4	cups fat-free milk
1	pkg. (1 oz.) sugar-free instant pistachio pudding mix
6	oz. reduced-fat cream cheese
1	carton (8 oz.) frozen fat-free whipped topping, thawed, *divided*
1	pkg. (12 oz.) frozen unsweetened raspberries, thawed
2	Tbsp. sugar
2	Tbsp. orange liqueur *or* orange juice
2	Tbsp. chopped pistachios

1. In a small bowl, combine the wafers, finely chopped pistachios and butter. Press onto the bottom of a 9-in. springform pan coated with cooking spray. Place pan on a baking sheet. Bake at 350° for 10 minutes or until lightly browned. Cool on a wire rack.

2. Meanwhile, in a small bowl, whisk milk and pudding mix for 2 minutes. Let stand for 2 minutes or until soft-set. In a large mixing bowl, beat cream cheese until smooth. Beat in the pudding.

3. Set aside 3/4 cup whipped topping for garnish; fold remaining whipped topping into cream cheese mixture. Pour filling over crust. Freeze for 5 hours or overnight. Cover and refrigerate remaining whipped topping.

4. For sauce, place the raspberries, sugar and liqueur in a food processor. Cover and process for 1-2 minutes or until smooth. Strain and discard seeds and pulp. Refrigerate until serving.

5. Remove dessert from the freezer 15 minutes before serving. Remove sides of pan. Garnish with chopped pistachios and remaining whipped topping. Serve with sauce.

Editor's Note: This recipe was tested with Land O'Lakes light stick butter.

Nutrition Facts: 1 slice with 4 teaspoons sauce equals 214 calories, 9 g fat (4 g saturated fat), 18 mg cholesterol, 268 mg sodium, 28 g carbohydrate, 2 g fiber, 4 g protein. **Diabetic Exchanges:** 2 starch, 2 fat.

Consider using the **raspberry sauce** from the frosty pistachio dessert as a simple way to jazz up slices of store-bought pound cake or even vanilla ice cream.

Hot Fudge Pudding Cake F

PREP: 15 min. **BAKE:** 30 min. **YIELD:** 9 servings

JACKIE TERMONT • ELKHART, INDIANA

My mom used to make a recipe like this when I was younger. I decided to make some healthy changes, and this version is as good as, if not better than, the original. Being a dietitian, I love to come up with ways to lighten recipes. I would bake all the time if I could!

1	cup all-purpose flour
1	cup sugar, *divided*
3	Tbsp. plus 1/4 cup baking cocoa, *divided*
2	tsp. baking powder
1/4	tsp. salt
1/2	cup fat-free milk
1/3	cup prune baby food
1-1/2	tsp. vanilla extract
1/4	cup plus 2 Tbsp. packed brown sugar
1-1/4	cups boiling water

1. In a large bowl, combine the flour, 3/4 cup sugar, 3 tablespoons cocoa, baking powder and salt. In another bowl, combine the milk, baby food and vanilla. Stir into dry ingredients just until moistened. Spread into an 8-in. square baking dish coated with cooking spray.

2. Combine brown sugar with remaining sugar and cocoa; sprinkle over the batter. Carefully pour water over the top (do not stir). Bake, uncovered, at 350° for 28-32 minutes or until top is set and edges pull away from sides of dish. Serve warm.

Nutrition Facts: 1 serving equals 196 calories, 1 g fat (trace saturated fat), trace cholesterol, 164 mg sodium, 46 g carbohydrate, 1 g fiber, 3 g protein.

Warm Chocolate Melting Cups F S

PREP: 20 min. **BAKE:** 20 min. **YIELD:** 10 servings

KISSA VAUGHN • TROY, TEXAS

These have become a favorite of our guests. They're always so surprised that these little desserts are so light and healthy.

1-1/4	cups sugar, *divided*
1/2	cup baking cocoa
2	Tbsp. all-purpose flour
1/8	tsp. salt
3/4	cup water
3/4	cup plus 1 Tbsp. semisweet chocolate chips
1	Tbsp. brewed coffee
1	tsp. vanilla extract
2	eggs
1	egg white

1. In a small saucepan, combine 3/4 cup sugar, cocoa, flour and salt. Gradually stir in water. Bring to a boil; cook and stir for 2 minutes or until thickened. Remove from the heat; stir in the chocolate chips, coffee and vanilla until smooth. Transfer to a large bowl.

2. In another bowl, beat eggs and egg white until slightly thickened. Gradually add remaining sugar, beating until thick and lemon-colored. Fold into chocolate mixture.

3. Transfer to ten 4-oz. ramekins coated with cooking spray. Place ramekins in a baking pan; add 1 in. of boiling water to pan. Bake, uncovered, at 350° for 20-25 minutes or just until centers are set. Serve desserts immediately.

Turtle Bread Pudding

PREP: 25 min. **BAKE:** 35 min. + standing
YIELD: 10 servings

GLORIA BRADLEY • NAPERVILLE, ILLINOIS

This yummy, gooey, oh-so-chocolaty bread pudding will put your taste buds in overload. With only 3 grams of saturated fat and less than 300 calories per serving, what's not to love?

7	cups cubed day-old French bread (1-in. cubes)
1/3	cup semisweet chocolate chips
4	Tbsp. chopped pecans, *divided*
3	cups fat-free milk, *divided*
1/2	cup packed brown sugar
1/4	cup baking cocoa
8	caramels
2	tsp. butter
1/4	tsp. chili powder
3	eggs, beaten
1	tsp. vanilla extract
1/4	cup caramel ice cream topping
1/4	cup milk chocolate chips

1. Place bread cubes in an 11-in. x 7-in. baking dish coated with cooking spray. Sprinkle with semisweet chips and 2 tablespoons pecans. In a large saucepan, combine 1 cup milk, brown sugar, cocoa, caramels, butter and chili powder. Cook and stir over medium-low heat until caramels are melted. Add remaining milk; heat through.

2. Stir a small amount of mixture into eggs; return all to the pan, stirring constantly. Stir in vanilla. Pour mixture over bread cubes; let stand for 10 minutes or until bread is softened.

3. Bake, uncovered, at 350° for 35-40 minutes or until a knife inserted near the center comes out clean. Drizzle with caramel topping and sprinkle with remaining pecans; bake 2-3 minutes longer or until caramel topping is heated through. Let stand for 10 minutes.

4. In a microwave, melt milk chocolate chips; stir until smooth. Drizzle over bread pudding. Refrigerate leftovers.

Nutrition Facts: 1 serving equals 288 calories, 9 g fat (3 g saturated fat), 69 mg cholesterol, 281 mg sodium, 46 g carbohydrate, 2 g fiber, 8 g protein.

Green Tea Tiramisu Ⓢ

PREP/TOTAL TIME: 20 min. **YIELD:** 8 servings

HEALTHY COOKING TEST KITCHEN

Put a creative spin on a classic dessert! Green tea and orange peel add a special taste to this light treat that is perfect for weekend entertaining.

3/4	cup Mascarpone cheese
2	Tbsp. sugar
2	tsp. grated orange peel
2	cups fat-free whipped topping
1/4	cup strong brewed green tea
1	Tbsp. orange juice
1	pkg. (3 oz.) ladyfingers, split

Mint sprigs and orange peel strips, optional

1. In a small bowl, combine the Mascarpone cheese, sugar and orange peel. Fold in whipped topping; set aside. In another small bowl, combine tea and orange juice.

2. Arrange six ladyfinger halves, split side up, in an ungreased 8-in. x 4-in. loaf pan. Brush with a fourth of the tea mixture. Spread 1/2 cup of the cheese mixture just over the top of ladyfingers. Repeat layers three times.

3. Cover and refrigerate until serving. Cut into slices; garnish with mint and orange peel strips if desired.

Nutrition Facts: 1 slice equals 200 calories, 11 g fat (6 g saturated fat), 88 mg cholesterol, 47 mg sodium, 20 g carbohydrate, trace fiber, 3 g protein.

WARM CHOCOLATE MELTING CUPS

TURTLE BREAD PUDDING

Blueberry Torte Squares

PREP: 30 min. + chilling **YIELD:** 2 dozen

MICHELE RAINES • LYNDONVILLE, NEW YORK

Super-healthy blueberries star in this soon-to-be family favorite. Can't find fresh blueberries? Frozen work just as well.

- 2/3 cup butter, softened
- 3 Tbsp. plus 1/2 cup sugar, *divided*
- 1-1/4 cups all-purpose flour
- 1 pkg. (8 oz.) reduced-fat cream cheese
- 1 cup confectioners' sugar
- 1 carton (12 oz.) frozen reduced-fat whipped topping, thawed
- 2 Tbsp. cornstarch
- 3/4 cup cold water
- 3 cups fresh blueberries

1. In a small mixing bowl, cream butter and 2 tablespoons sugar. Gradually add flour and mix well. Press onto the bottom of a 13-in. x 9-in. baking dish coated with cooking spray. Bake at 350° for 12-14 minutes or until set and edges are lightly browned. Cool on a wire rack.

2. In a large mixing bowl, beat cream cheese and confectioners' sugar until smooth. Fold in whipped topping; spread mixture over crust. Refrigerate for 20 minutes.

3. Meanwhile, in a large saucepan, combine cornstarch and water until smooth. Stir in blueberries and remaining sugar. Bring to a boil; cook and stir for 2 minutes or until thickened. Cool to room temperature.

4. Spoon topping over cream cheese layer. Cover and refrigerate for at least 4 hours. Cut into squares.

Nutrition Facts: 1 square equals 178 calories, 9 g fat (6 g saturated fat), 20 mg cholesterol, 76 mg sodium, 24 g carbohydrate, 1 g fiber, 2 g protein. **Diabetic Exchanges:** 1-1/2 starch, 1-1/2 fat.

BLUEBERRY TORTE SQUARES

Raspberry Gelatin Dessert **F S C**

PREP: 20 min. + chilling **YIELD:** 8 servings

BONNIE OSTHIMER • SOUTH BEND, INDIANA

My friends and family often finish the whole pan because this colorful dessert is very low-cal. If you're cooking for a crowd, this easily doubles to fit in a 13-in. x 9-in. baking dish.

- 1 pkg. (.3 oz.) sugar-free raspberry gelatin
- 1 cup boiling water
- 1 pkg. (.8 oz.) sugar-free cook-and-serve vanilla pudding mix
- 1 cup cold water
- 1 pkg. (12 oz.) frozen unsweetened raspberries, thawed

1. In a large bowl, dissolve gelatin in boiling water; set aside. In a small saucepan, combine the pudding mix, water and raspberries. Bring to a boil over medium heat, stirring constantly. Cook and stir 1-2 minutes longer or until thickened.

2. Remove from the heat; stir in reserved gelatin mixture. Pour into an 8-in. square dish coated with cooking spray. Cover and refrigerate for 8 hours or overnight.

Nutrition Facts: 1 serving equals 33 calories, trace fat (trace saturated fat), 0 cholesterol, 78 mg sodium, 6 g carbohydrate, 1 g fiber, 1 g protein. **Diabetic Exchange:** 1/2 fruit.

Gluten-Free Sugar Cookies **S**

PREP: 25 min. **BAKE:** 10 min./batch **YIELD:** 3 dozen

HEALTHY COOKING TEST KITCHEN

These cake-like cookies will be a welcome snack with a cold glass of milk. Feel free to use this recipe as a base and mix in dried cranberries or cherries, nuts or other extracts. It's a must-have recipe for those on gluten-free diets.

- 2/3 cup butter, softened
- 1 cup sugar
- 2 eggs
- 1/4 cup unsweetened applesauce
- 4 tsp. grated lemon peel
- 1 tsp. almond extract
- 1-1/3 cups potato starch
- 1-1/3 cups gluten-free garbanzo and fava flour
- 1 cup tapioca flour
- 1 tsp. salt
- 1 tsp. xanthan gum
- 1/2 tsp. baking soda
- 1/3 cup coarse sugar

1. In a large mixing bowl, cream butter and sugar until light and fluffy. Beat in the eggs, applesauce, lemon peel and extract. Combine the potato starch, garbanzo and fava flour, tapioca flour, salt, xanthan gum and baking soda; gradually add to the creamed mixture and mix well.

2. Shape into 1-1/2-in. balls and roll in coarse sugar. Place 2 in. apart on baking sheets coated with cooking spray. Bake at 350° for 7-9 minutes or until lightly browned. Remove from pans to wire racks.

Nutrition Facts: 1 cookie equals 110 calories, 4 g fat (2 g saturated fat), 21 mg cholesterol, 116 mg sodium, 18 g carbohydrate, 1 g fiber, 1 g protein. **Diabetic Exchanges:** 1 starch, 1/2 fat.

Breezy Lemon-Berry Dessert ⑤

PREP: 30 min. + chilling   **YIELD:** 12 servings

ANNA GINSBERG • AUSTIN, TEXAS

I love the combination of berries and lemon, and wanted to come up with a light, refreshing and tasty dessert that used them both.

2	envelopes unflavored gelatin
1/2	cup cold water
1	pkg. (3 oz.) ladyfingers, split
1-1/2	cups fat-free milk
1/2	cup refrigerated French vanilla nondairy creamer
1	pkg. (3.4 oz.) instant lemon pudding mix
1	carton (12 oz.) frozen reduced-fat whipped topping, thawed, *divided*
3	cups mixed fresh berries
2	cups sliced fresh strawberries

1. In a small saucepan, sprinkle gelatin over cold water; let stand for 1 minute. Heat over low heat, stirring until gelatin is completely dissolved. Remove from the heat and set aside.

2. Cut ladyfingers in half widthwise; arrange cut side down around the sides of an ungreased 9-in. springform pan. Place remaining ladyfingers in the bottom of the pan (bottom will not be completely covered).

3. In a large bowl, whisk the milk, creamer and pudding mix for 2 minutes. Let stand for 2 minutes or until soft-set. Stir in gelatin mixture. Fold in 3 cups whipped topping.

4. Spread 2 cups of the filling evenly into prepared pan; top with the mixed berries. Spread with remaining filling (filling will be higher than ladyfinger border).

5. Cover and refrigerate for 5 hours or until set. Garnish with the remaining whipped topping and the strawberries.

Nutrition Facts: 1 slice equals 183 calories, 5 g fat (3 g saturated fat), 26 mg cholesterol, 129 mg sodium, 29 g carbohydrate, 2 g fiber, 3 g protein. **Diabetic Exchanges:** 2 starch, 1 fat.

Makeover Cherry-Topped Cheesecake

PREP: 35 min. + cooling **BAKE:** 45 min. + chilling
YIELD: 16 servings

KATHI MULCHIN • WEST VALLEY CITY, UTAH

My cheesecake recipe was so high in fat and calories that I only made it a few times per year. With this lighter spinoff, I plan to serve it far more often.

- 3/4 cup graham cracker crumbs
- 1/3 cup crushed gingersnap cookies (about 8 cookies)
- 2 Tbsp. sugar
- 2 Tbsp. butter, melted

FILLING:
- 2 pkg. (8 oz. *each*) reduced-fat cream cheese
- 1/2 cup sugar
- 2 Tbsp. all-purpose flour
- 1/2 tsp. salt
- 1 cup half-and-half cream
- 3 Tbsp. lemon juice
- 3 Tbsp. orange juice
- 2 eggs, lightly beaten

TOPPING:
- 1 can (20 oz.) reduced-sugar cherry pie filling
- 1 cup (8 oz.) reduced-fat sour cream
- 2 Tbsp. sugar
- 1/2 tsp. vanilla extract

1. In a small bowl, combine the cracker crumbs, crushed cookies, sugar and butter. Press onto the bottom of a 9-in. springform pan coated with cooking spray. Place pan on a baking sheet. Bake at 350° for 10 minutes. Cool on a wire rack.

2. In a large bowl, beat the cream cheese, sugar, flour and salt until smooth. Beat in the cream and juices until blended. Add eggs; beat on low speed just until combined. Pour over crust.

3. Return pan to baking sheet. Bake for 35-45 minutes or until center is almost set. Meanwhile, combine topping ingredients. Gently spread over cheesecake; bake 10 minutes longer.

4. Cool on a wire rack for 10 minutes. Carefully run a knife around edge of pan to loosen; cool 1 hour longer.

5. Refrigerate overnight. Remove sides of pan.

Nutrition Facts: 1 slice equals 222 calories, 12 g fat (7 g saturated fat), 63 mg cholesterol, 281 mg sodium, 23 g carbohydrate, 1 g fiber, 6 g protein.

Dreamy Orange Lactose-Free Cupcakes

PREP: 25 min. **BAKE:** 20 min. + cooling **YIELD:** 2 dozen

HEALTHY COOKING TEST KITCHEN

The classic vanilla-orange flavor combination comes through in these yummy cupcakes made for the lactose-intolerant. Sprinkles add a touch of fun to these travel-ready treats.

- 6 egg whites
- 3 eggs
- 1 cup sugar
- 3/4 cup vanilla soy milk
- 1/3 cup canola oil

1/3	cup unsweetened applesauce
1/3	cup plus 1/4 cup orange juice concentrate, *divided*
3	cups all-purpose flour
1	Tbsp. plus 1-1/2 tsp. baking powder
1-1/2	tsp. salt
1-1/2	cups confectioners' sugar

Assorted sprinkles, optional

1. In a large mixing bowl, beat the egg whites, eggs, sugar, soy milk, oil, applesauce and 1/3 cup orange juice concentrate until well blended. Combine the flour, baking powder and salt; gradually beat into egg mixture until blended.

2. Fill paper-lined muffin cups two-thirds full. Bake at 350° for 18-22 minutes or until a toothpick comes out clean. Cool for 10 minutes before removing from pans to wire racks to cool completely.

3. For glaze, in a small bowl, combine confectioners' sugar and remaining orange juice concentrate. Dip cupcakes into glaze; decorate with sprinkles if desired. Let stand until set.

Nutrition Facts: 1 cupcake (calculated without sprinkles) equals 164 calories, 4 g fat (trace saturated fat), 26 mg cholesterol, 249 mg sodium, 29 g carbohydrate, trace fiber, 4 g protein. **Diabetic Exchanges:** 2 starch, 1 fat.

Makeover White Christmas Cake

PREP: 30 min. + cooling **BAKE:** 25 min. + chilling
YIELD: 16 servings

ANNA KNAUER • ROBESONIA, PENNSYLVANIA

This was a regular dessert at Christmas, but it was so heavy that I asked "Healthy Cooking" to trim it down. This version offers half the cholesterol and 28 grams less fat.

1/2	cup water
2	squares (1 oz. *each*) white baking chocolate, chopped
1/4	cup butter, softened
1	cup sugar
2	eggs
1/2	cup unsweetened applesauce
1/8	tsp. rum extract
1-1/3	cups all-purpose flour

1	cup cake flour
3/4	tsp. baking powder
3/4	tsp. baking soda
1	cup buttermilk
1/3	cup chopped pecans, toasted
1/4	cup flaked coconut

FROSTING:
1	pkg. (8 oz.) reduced-fat cream cheese
1/3	cup butter, softened
2	squares (1 oz. *each*) white baking chocolate, melted
3-1/2	cups confectioners' sugar

1. In a small saucepan, bring water to a boil. Remove from the heat; stir in chocolate until melted. Cool for 20 minutes. Line two 9-in. round baking pans with waxed paper and coat the paper with cooking spray; set aside.

2. Meanwhile, in a large mixing bowl, beat butter and sugar until crumbly, about 2 minutes. Add eggs, one at a time, beating well after each addition. Beat in the applesauce, extract and reserved chocolate mixture (batter will appear curdled). Combine the flours, baking powder and baking soda; add to butter mixture alternately with buttermilk, beating well after each addition. Stir in pecans and coconut.

3. Transfer to prepared pans. Bake at 350° for 22-27 minutes or until a toothpick inserted near the center comes out clean. Cool for 10 minutes before removing from pans to wire racks to cool completely.

4. For frosting, in a large mixing bowl, beat the cream cheese, butter and chocolate until blended. Add confectioners' sugar; beat until smooth. Spread frosting between layers and over top and sides of cake. Refrigerate for at least 2 hours. Remove from the refrigerator 15 minutes before serving.

Nutrition Facts: 1 slice equals 396 calories, 15 g fat (9 g saturated fat), 56 mg cholesterol, 222 mg sodium, 60 g carbohydrate, 1 g fiber, 5 g protein.

DREAMY ORANGE LACTOSE-FREE CUPCAKES

MAKEOVER WHITE CHRISTMAS CAKE

Egg-Free Toffee Chip Cookies §C

PREP: 20 min. **BAKE:** 10 min./batch **YIELD:** 4 dozen

HEALTHY COOKING TEST KITCHEN

Toffee and chocolate chips make these crisp, lower-calorie cookies taste anything but light. Best of all, you can have a batch ready in just 30 minutes!

1/2	cup butter, softened
1/2	cup sugar
1/2	cup packed brown sugar
1/4	cup water
1/4	cup canola oil
1	tsp. vanilla extract
2-1/2	cups all-purpose flour
2	tsp. baking powder
1	tsp. baking soda
1/2	tsp. salt
1/2	cup miniature semisweet chocolate chips
1/2	cup milk chocolate English toffee bits

1. In a large bowl, cream butter and sugars. Beat in the water, oil and vanilla. Combine the flour, baking powder, baking soda and salt; gradually add to creamed mixture and mix well. Stir in the chocolate chips and toffee bits.

2. Drop by rounded tablespoonfuls 2 in. apart onto ungreased baking sheets; flatten with the bottom of a small glass. Bake at 350° for 10-12 minutes or until edges begin to brown. Remove to wire racks.

Nutrition Facts: 1 cookie equals 88 calories, 4 g fat (2 g saturated fat), 7 mg cholesterol, 92 mg sodium, 12 g carbohydrate, trace fiber, 1 g protein. **Diabetic Exchanges:** 1 starch, 1 fat.

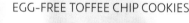

EGG-FREE TOFFEE CHIP COOKIES

Bedtime Brownies

PREP: 15 min. **BAKE:** 20 min. + cooling
YIELD: 9 brownies

DONNA BROCKETT • KINGFISHER, OKLAHOMA

Here's a recipe for brownies that are so super-chewy, fudgy and delightful, no one believes they're light!

1	tsp. instant espresso or other coffee granules
1	tsp. boiling water
1	egg
3/4	cup sugar
1/4	cup dark corn syrup
3	Tbsp. butter, melted
1-1/2	tsp. vanilla extract
3/4	cup all-purpose flour
1/2	cup dark baking cocoa
1/2	tsp. baking powder
1/4	tsp. salt
1	tsp. confectioners' sugar

1. In a small bowl, dissolve the espresso granules in boiling water. Stir in the egg, sugar, corn syrup, butter and vanilla until blended. Combine the flour, cocoa, baking powder and salt; stir into the sugar mixture until blended.

2. Transfer to an 8-in. square baking dish coated with cooking spray. Bake at 350° for 20-25 minutes or until a toothpick inserted near the center comes out clean and brownies begin to pull away from sides of dish. Cool on a wire rack.

3. Sprinkle with confectioners' sugar. Cut into squares.

Nutrition Facts: 1 brownie equals 186 calories, 5 g fat (3 g saturated fat), 34 mg cholesterol, 148 mg sodium, 35 g carbohydrate, 1 g fiber, 3 g protein. **Diabetic Exchanges:** 2 starch, 1/2 fat.

Almond Pear-Apple Crumble §

PREP: 20 min. **BAKE:** 35 min. **YIELD:** 6 servings

TRISHA KRUSE • EAGLE, IDAHO

The delicate flavors of pears and apples are nicely accented with almond extract and crunchy almonds sprinkled on top.

3	medium pears, peeled and sliced
2	medium apples, peeled and sliced
1	Tbsp. cornstarch
1/3	cup pear nectar
1/2	tsp. almond extract
1/3	cup packed brown sugar

TOPPING:
1/4	cup all-purpose flour
1/4	cup old-fashioned oats
1/4	cup packed brown sugar
1/8	tsp. salt
2	Tbsp. cold butter
3	Tbsp. sliced almonds

1. In a large bowl, combine pears and apples. In a small bowl, combine the cornstarch, pear nectar and extract; stir until smooth. Stir in brown sugar until blended. Drizzle over pear mixture and stir gently to

CARAMEL TOFFEE ICE CREAM PIE

coat. Transfer to an 11-in. x 7-in. baking dish coated with cooking spray.

2. For topping, in a small bowl, combine the flour, oats, brown sugar and salt. Cut in butter until crumbly; stir in almonds. Sprinkle over fruit mixture.

3. Bake, uncovered, at 350° for 35-40 minutes or until fruit is tender. Serve warm or at room temperature.

Nutrition Facts: 1 serving equals 247 calories, 6 g fat (3 g saturated fat), 10 mg cholesterol, 86 mg sodium, 49 g carbohydrate, 4 g fiber, 2 g protein.

Caramel Toffee Ice Cream Pie

PREP: 25 min. + freezing **YIELD:** 8 servings

DIANE LOMBARDO • NEW CASTLE, PENNSYLVANIA

Not only does this dessert come together in no time, but you can make it in advance, it's ideal for entertaining and it comes in at only 8 grams of fat per slice!

1-1/2	cups chocolate graham cracker crumbs (about 8 whole crackers)
2	Tbsp. sugar
1	egg white, beaten
2	Tbsp. butter, melted
4	cups fat-free vanilla frozen yogurt, softened
2	English toffee candy bars (1.4 oz. *each*), coarsely chopped
1/2	cup caramel ice cream topping

1. In a small bowl, combine cracker crumbs and sugar; stir in egg white and butter. Press onto the bottom and up the sides of a 9-in. pie plate coated with cooking spray. Bake at 375° for 6-8 minutes or until set. Cool completely on a wire rack.

2. Spread 2-2/3 cups of frozen yogurt into the crust. Sprinkle with half of the toffee bits; drizzle with half of caramel. Repeat with remaining yogurt, toffee and caramel. Cover and freeze for 8 hours or overnight. Remove from the freezer 15 minutes before serving.

Nutrition Facts: 1 piece equals 304 calories, 8 g fat (4 g saturated fat), 15 mg cholesterol, 289 mg sodium, 54 g carbohydrate, 1 g fiber, 7 g protein.

For surefire success, keep a few tips in mind when preparing **Caramel Toffee Ice Cream Pie.** Crush the graham crackers by placing them in a sealed plastic bag first, then roll them with a rolling pin. In addition, remember that the vanilla frozen yogurt will spread easily if you let it soften slightly. Transfer it to the refrigerator 10 to 20 minutes before you're ready to fill the pie.

Makeover Lemon Custard Ice Cream **F** **S**

PREP: 25 min. + chilling **FREEZE:** 2 hours **YIELD:** 2 quarts

LINDA TIPTON • ROANOKE RAPIDS, NORTH CAROLINA

I found this wonderful recipe in a magazine, but I knew I'd make it more if it were lighter. This version cuts the fat and calories without skimping on the flavor.

1-3/4	cups sugar
1/3	cup all-purpose flour
1/4	tsp. salt
3	cups milk
2	eggs, lightly beaten
2	Tbsp. apple jelly
3	cups fat-free half-and-half
1	cup (8 oz.) fat-free sour cream
1	cup lemon juice

1. In a large saucepan, combine the sugar, flour and salt. Gradually add milk. Bring to a boil over medium heat; cook and stir for 2 minutes or until thickened. Remove from the heat; cool slightly.

2. Whisk a small amount of hot milk mixture into the eggs. Return all to the pan, whisking constantly. Cook and stir until mixture reaches 160° and coats the back of a metal spoon.

3. Remove from the heat; stir in jelly until melted. Stir in the half-and-half, sour cream and lemon juice. Cool quickly by placing pan in a bowl of ice water; stir for 2 minutes. Press waxed paper onto surface of custard. Refrigerate for several hours or overnight.

4. Fill cylinder of ice cream freezer two-thirds full; freeze according to manufacturer's directions. Refrigerate remaining mixture until ready to freeze. When ice cream is frozen, transfer to a freezer container; freeze for 2-4 hours before serving.

Nutrition Facts: 1/2 cup equals 189 calories, 2 g fat (1 g saturated fat), 35 mg cholesterol, 118 mg sodium, 36 g carbohydrate, trace fiber, 5 g protein.

> Our home economists were pleased that Makeover Lemon Custard Ice Cream was their best revision. They cut 90 percent of the fat by using low-fat products and by replacing some of the sugar with apple jelly.

Toffee Meringue Torte **S**

PREP: 20 min. **BAKE:** 50 min. + standing **YIELD:** 12 servings

KAREN NEMETH • CALGARY, ALBERTA

This is one of those "Where did you get this recipe?"creations! Simple to make ahead, it's perfect to have on hand for a large gathering.

6 egg whites
2 tsp. vanilla extract
1/2 tsp. cream of tartar
1-1/2 cups sugar
1 carton (8 oz.) frozen whipped topping, thawed
4 Butterfinger candy bars (2.1 oz. *each*), coarsely crushed, *divided*

1. Place egg whites in a large mixing bowl; let stand at room temperature for 30 minutes. Using a pencil, draw a 10-in. circle on each of two sheets of parchment paper. Place each sheet, pencil mark down, on a baking sheet or pizza pan; set aside.

2. Add vanilla and cream of tartar to egg whites; beat on medium speed until soft peaks form. Gradually beat in sugar, 1 tablespoon at a time, on high until stiff peaks form.

3. Spread into 10-in. circles on prepared pans. Bake at 225° for 50-60 minutes or until set and lightly browned. Turn oven off; leave meringues in oven for 1 to 1-1/4 hours.

4. Just before serving, place whipped topping in a large bowl; fold in three candy bars. Place one meringue layer on a serving plate; top with half of topping mixture. Repeat layers. Sprinkle with remaining candy bar.

Nutrition Facts: 1 slice equals 251 calories, 7 g fat (5 g saturated fat), 0 cholesterol, 73 mg sodium, 44 g carbohydrate, trace fiber, 3 g protein.

Caramel Apple Pizza

PREP: 40 min. + cooling **YIELD:** 12 slices

TARI AMBLER • SHOREWOOD, ILLINOIS

I made a favorite recipe lighter by making my own cookie crust and using a combination of lower-fat ingredients. It tastes so great, my family hasn't noticed the difference.

1/4 cup butter, softened
1/4 cup sugar
1/4 cup packed brown sugar
1 egg

2 Tbsp. canola oil
1 Tbsp. light corn syrup
1 tsp. vanilla extract
1 cup whole wheat pastry flour
3/4 cup all-purpose flour
1/2 tsp. baking powder
1/4 tsp. salt
1/4 tsp. ground cinnamon

TOPPING:
1 pkg. (8 oz.) fat-free cream cheese
1/4 cup packed brown sugar
1/2 tsp. ground cinnamon
1/2 tsp. vanilla extract
3 medium Granny Smith apples, thinly sliced
1/4 cup fat-free caramel ice cream topping
1/4 cup chopped unsalted dry roasted peanuts

1. In a large mixing bowl, cream butter and sugars. Beat in the egg, oil, corn syrup and vanilla. Combine the flours, baking powder, salt and cinnamon; gradually add to creamed mixture and mix well.

2. Press dough onto a 14-in. pizza pan coated with cooking spray. Bake at 350° for 12-15 minutes or until lightly browned. Cool on a wire rack.

3. In a small mixing bowl, beat the cream cheese, brown sugar, cinnamon and vanilla until smooth. Spread over crust. Arrange apples over the top. Drizzle with caramel topping; sprinkle with peanuts. Serve immediately.

Nutrition Facts: 1 slice equals 238 calories, 9 g fat (3 g saturated fat), 29 mg cholesterol, 228 mg sodium, 36 g carbohydrate, 2 g fiber, 6 g protein.

CARAMEL APPLE PIZZA

TOFFEE MERINGUE TORTE

CHICKEN KIEV WITH ROSEMARY RICE

SUMMER GARDEN OMELET

BEEF STRIP SALAD

Table for Two

Thanks to these must-try recipes, you won't have to deal with a fridge full of leftovers. That's because each dish is sized right for two. So whether you're an empty nester or a newlywed, a perfectly sized meal is always at your fingertips.

Cherry-Berry Soy Smoothies F S

PREP/TOTAL TIME: 10 min. **YIELD:** 3 servings

HEALTHY COOKING TEST KITCHEN

Enjoy a thick and creamy smoothie without any dairy products. Cherries and blueberries pair perfectly with the sweet flavor of vanilla in this delight.

   1   cup vanilla soy milk
   1/2   cup vanilla soy yogurt
   2   tsp. honey
   1   cup fresh or frozen pitted dark sweet cherries
   1/2   cup fresh or frozen blueberries
   1/2   cup crushed ice

1. In a blender, combine all ingredients; cover and process for 30-45 seconds or until smooth. Stir if necessary.

2. Pour into chilled glasses; serve immediately.

Nutrition Facts: 3/4 cup equals 130 calories, 2 g fat (trace saturated fat), 0 cholesterol, 41 mg sodium, 24 g carbohydrate, 3 g fiber, 4 g protein. **Diabetic Exchanges:** 1 fruit, 1/2 starch, 1/2 fat.

Beef Strip Salad C

PREP: 20 min. + chilling **YIELD:** 2 servings

BETTY GREGOIRE • AUSTIN, TEXAS

For a refreshing light meal in minutes, I like to add beef tenderloin to a tasty green salad with a tangy homemade dressing.

   1/2   lb. beef tenderloin
   1   small red onion, thinly sliced and separated into rings
   1/4   tsp. salt
Dash coarsely ground pepper
   1   cup torn leaf lettuce
   1/4   cup chopped green pepper
   2   Tbsp. sliced pimientos
   2   Tbsp. sliced ripe olives
   1/4   cup reduced-fat sour cream
4-1/2   tsp. lemon juice

1. In a large nonstick skillet coated with cooking spray, cook beef over medium heat for 5-7 minutes on each side or until meat reaches desired doneness (for medium-rare, a meat thermometer should read 145°; medium, 160°; well-done, 170°). Cool for 10 minutes. Refrigerate until chilled.

2. Thinly slice the beef; place in a small bowl. Add the onion, salt and pepper; toss to combine. Divide lettuce between two salad plates; top with beef mixture, green pepper, pimientos and olives. Combine sour cream and lemon juice; serve with salad.

Nutrition Facts: 1 serving equals 251 calories, 11 g fat (5 g saturated fat), 81 mg cholesterol, 432 mg sodium, 9 g carbohydrate, 2 g fiber, 27 g protein. **Diabetic Exchanges:** 3 lean meat, 1 vegetable, 1/2 starch, 1/2 fat.

Sauteed Mushrooms C

PREP/TOTAL TIME: 15 min. **YIELD:** 2 servings

ELIZABETH LOTT • AMARILLO, TEXAS

This is a special recipe I've used for over 20 years. Everyone I've ever served it to has raved about it.

   1/2   lb. sliced fresh mushrooms
   1   Tbsp. olive oil
   2   Tbsp. dry red wine or reduced-sodium beef broth
   1/2   tsp. reduced-sodium beef bouillon granules
   1/8   tsp. garlic powder
   1/8   tsp. pepper

1. In a skillet, saute mushrooms in oil for 2 minutes.

2. Add wine or broth, bouillon, garlic powder and pepper; saute 5 minutes longer or until mushrooms are tender and liquid is reduced by half.

Nutrition Facts: 1 serving equals 103 calories, 7 g fat (1 g saturated fat), trace cholesterol, 202 mg sodium, 5 g carbohydrate, 1 g fiber, 3 g protein. **Diabetic Exchanges:** 1-1/2 fat,1 vegetable.

> Watching your sodium? Skip the 1/4 teaspoon of salt called for in pretty **Beef Strip Salad,** and you will save 295 milligrams of sodium per serving, making it an ideal low-sodium lunch.

Tomato-Basil Pita Pizzas M

PREP/TOTAL TIME: 20 min. **YIELD:** 2 servings

BARBRA ANNINO • GALENA, ILLINOIS

This is one of my favorite warm-weather recipes. It's so easy and tasty! You can use it as a snack, appetizer or entree and double it to suit your needs.

- 2 pita breads (6 in.)
- 2 plum tomatoes, thinly sliced
- 8 fresh basil leaves, thinly sliced
- 1/4 cup shredded Asiago cheese
- 2 tsp. olive oil

1. Place pita breads on an ungreased baking sheet. Layer with tomatoes, basil and cheese; drizzle with oil.

2. Bake at 350° for 12-14 minutes or until the cheese is melted.

Nutrition Facts: 1 pizza equals 269 calories, 9 g fat (3 g saturated fat), 12 mg cholesterol, 362 mg sodium, 37 g carbohydrate, 2 g fiber, 10 g protein. **Diabetic Exchanges:** 2 starch, 1 lean meat, 1 fat.

Gingered Carrots & Parsnips S M

PREP/TOTAL TIME: 30 min. **YIELD:** 3 servings

MARIE RIZZIO • INTERLOCHEN, MICHIGAN

Ginger adds a marvelous taste to these root vegetables. The quick and fancy side will be a hit on any buffet table.

- 3 medium parsnips, peeled and sliced
- 4 medium carrots, peeled and sliced
- 2 Tbsp. honey
- 1 tsp. butter
- 1/2 tsp. ground ginger
- Dash salt
- 2 Tbsp. chopped pecans, toasted

1. Place 1 in. of water in a small saucepan; add parsnips. Bring to a boil. Reduce heat; cover and simmer for 1 minute. Stir in carrots; cover and simmer 6-8 minutes longer or until vegetables are crisp-tender. Drain and set aside.

2. In the same pan, combine the honey, butter, ginger and salt. Stir in vegetables; heat through. Sprinkle with pecans.

Nutrition Facts: 3/4 cup equals 173 calories, 5 g fat (1 g saturated fat), 3 mg cholesterol, 121 mg sodium, 32 g carbohydrate, 6 g fiber, 2 g protein.

Chilly-Day Chicken Soup

PREP: 10 min. **COOK:** 25 min. **YIELD:** 2 servings

DEBORAH MITCHELL • CLARKSVILLE, INDIANA

You can make this a completely different soup by changing the chicken and chicken broth to beef and beef broth.

- 1/4 lb. boneless skinless chicken breast, cut into small pieces
- 1/4 cup chopped onion
- 2 tsp. butter
- 1 cup diced red potatoes
- 1 medium carrot, grated
- 1 can (14-1/2 oz.) reduced-sodium chicken broth
- 1/2 cup water
- 1/4 tsp. pepper
- 2 Tbsp. uncooked instant rice
- 1/8 tsp. salt

1. In a small nonstick saucepan, saute chicken and onion in butter until chicken is no longer pink. Stir in the potatoes, carrot, broth, water and pepper. Bring to a boil. Reduce heat; cover and simmer for 10-12 minutes or until potatoes are tender.

GINGERED CARROTS & PARSNIPS

TOMATO-BASIL PITA PIZZAS

CHILLY-DAY CHICKEN SOUP

TERIYAKI VEGGIE WRAPS

2. Return to a boil; stir in rice and salt. Remove from the heat. Cover and let stand for 5 minutes or until rice is tender.

Nutrition Facts: 1-1/2 cups equals 205 calories, 5 g fat (3 g saturated fat), 42 mg cholesterol, 772 mg sodium, 23 g carbohydrate, 3 g fiber, 17 g protein. **Diabetic Exchanges:** 2 very lean meat, 1 starch, 1 vegetable, 1/2 fat.

Teriyaki Veggie Wraps M

PREP/TOTAL TIME: 20 min.   **YIELD:** 2 servings

JOAN MAZZEO • PITTSFIELD, MASSACHUSETTS

Asian and Mexican flavors come together in these easy wraps that make a nice snack or light lunch.

1	medium green pepper, thinly sliced
1	small onion, thinly sliced
2	garlic cloves, minced
1	tsp. olive oil
1	cup sliced fresh mushrooms
3	Tbsp. reduced-sodium teriyaki sauce
2	flour tortillas (8 in.), warmed
1/4	cup shredded reduced-fat Mexican cheese blend

1. In a small nonstick skillet coated with cooking spray, saute the green pepper, onion and garlic in oil for 2 minutes. Add mushrooms; cook 3 minutes longer. Stir in teriyaki sauce; cook and stir for 1-2 minutes or until vegetables are tender.

2. Spoon vegetable mixture down the center of each tortilla. Sprinkle with cheese; roll up tightly.

Nutrition Facts: 1 wrap equals 271 calories, 9 g fat (2 g saturated fat), 10 mg cholesterol, 833 mg sodium, 40 g carbohydrate, 2 g fiber, 12 g protein. **Diabetic Exchanges:** 2 starch, 2 vegetable, 1 lean meat, 1/2 fat.

Get creative with **Teriyaki Veggie Wraps.** Adjust the ingredients to fit your taste, clean out your refrigerator or use up last night's leftovers. Joan Mazzeo suggests replacing the Mexican cheese blend with cubes of Swiss cheese, for example.

ROSEMARY RICE

CHICKEN KIEV

Chicken Kiev C

PREP: 25 min. **BAKE:** 20 min. **YIELD:** 2 servings

BETH DAUENHAUER • PUEBLO, COLORADO

This recipe is the one most requested by my husband. I vary the herbs, using what's on hand or using fresh herbs during the summer. I often serve it with roasted potatoes.

1	Tbsp. butter, softened
1/4	tsp. *each* dried thyme, parsley flakes and crushed dried rosemary
1/4	cup all-purpose flour
1/4	tsp. salt
1/4	tsp. pepper
1	egg white
1/2	cup soft bread crumbs
1	Tbsp. grated Parmesan cheese
1/4	tsp. paprika
2	boneless skinless chicken breast halves (4 oz. *each*)

1. Combine the butter, thyme, parsley and rosemary; shape into two cubes. Cover and freeze until firm, about 10 minutes. Meanwhile, in a shallow bowl, combine the flour, salt and pepper. In another shallow bowl, lightly whisk the egg white. In a third bowl, combine the bread crumbs, Parmesan cheese and paprika.

2. Flatten chicken breasts to 1/4-in. thickness. Place a butter cube on the center of each. Roll up and tuck in ends; secure with toothpicks. Coat the chicken with flour mixture; dip in egg white, then roll the chicken in the crumb mixture.

3. Place seam side down in an 8-in. square baking dish coated with cooking spray. Bake, uncovered, at 425° for 20-25 minutes or until a meat thermometer reads 170°. Discard toothpicks before serving.

Nutrition Facts: 1 chicken breast half equals 231 calories, 9 g fat (5 g saturated fat), 80 mg cholesterol, 315 mg sodium, 8 g carbohydrate, 1 g fiber, 27 g protein. **Diabetic Exchanges:** 3 very lean meat, 1-1/2 fat, 1/2 starch.

Rosemary Rice F

PREP/TOTAL TIME: 30 min. **YIELD:** 2 servings

SUZANNE MCKINLEY • LYONS, GEORGIA

This tender, full-flavored rice makes a lovely side for a wide variety of main dishes. It's also an easy recipe to double for company or extra guests.

1	cup water
1/2	cup uncooked long grain rice
1-1/2	tsp. chopped green onions
1	tsp. reduced-sodium beef bouillon granules
1/2	tsp. minced fresh rosemary *or* 1/8 tsp. crushed dried rosemary
1/2	tsp. butter
1/4	tsp. dried marjoram
1/4	tsp. dried thyme
1/8	tsp. salt

1. In a small saucepan, combine all ingredients. Bring to a boil. Reduce heat; cover and simmer for 15-18 minutes or until liquid is absorbed and rice is tender.

2. Remove from the heat; let stand for 5 minutes. Fluff with a fork before serving.

Meatball Casserole

PREP: 40 min. **BAKE:** 20 min. **YIELD:** 2 servings

ANU RILEY • BOISE, IDAHO

The mini meatballs in this dish have lots of flavor and give you plenty per serving. If you're cooking for more than two, simply double the recipe and bake in an 8-in. x 8-in. baking dish. Cook until cheese is nice and melted.

3/4	cup uncooked whole wheat penne pasta
2	Tbsp. seasoned bread crumbs
1/4	cup grated Parmesan cheese, *divided*
2	Tbsp. egg substitute
1/2	tsp. Italian seasoning
1/8	tsp. onion powder

Dash salt

Dash garlic powder

1/4	lb. lean ground turkey
3/4	cup marinara sauce *or* meatless spaghetti sauce
1/4	cup 2% cottage cheese
1/4	cup shredded part-skim mozzarella cheese

1. Cook pasta according to package directions. Meanwhile, in a small bowl, combine the bread crumbs, 2 tablespoons Parmesan cheese, egg substitute, Italian seasoning, onion powder, salt and garlic powder. Crumble the turkey over mixture and mix well.

2. Shape into 1/2-in. balls; place on a baking sheet coated with cooking spray. Bake at 350° for 9-11 minutes or until no longer pink.

3. Drain pasta and meatballs. In a small bowl, combine meatballs with marinara sauce. Spoon half of mixture into a 1-qt. baking dish coated with cooking spray. Top with half of the pasta, cottage cheese and mozzarella; sprinkle with 1 tablespoon Parmesan cheese. Repeat layers.

4. Cover and bake at 350° for 20-25 minutes or until cheese is melted.

Nutrition Facts: 1 serving equals 453 calories, 12 g fat (5 g saturated fat), 66 mg cholesterol, 804 mg sodium, 55 g carbohydrate, 5 g fiber, 30 g protein.

Southwestern Sauteed Corn M

PREP/TOTAL TIME: 20 min. **YIELD:** 3 servings

CHANDY WARD • AUMSVILLE, OREGON

My mother-in-law came up with this side dish one night for dinner. Everyone who tries it absolutely loves it!

1	pkg. (16 oz.) frozen corn, thawed *or* 3-1/3 cups fresh corn
1	Tbsp. butter
1	plum tomato, chopped
1	Tbsp. lime juice
1/2	tsp. salt
1/2	tsp. ground cumin
1/3	cup minced fresh cilantro

1. In a large nonstick skillet, saute corn in butter until tender. Reduce heat to medium-low; add the tomato, lime juice, salt and cumin.

2. Cook and stir for 3-4 minutes or until heated through. Remove from the heat; stir in cilantro.

Nutrition Facts: 3/4 cup equals 174 calories, 5 g fat (3 g saturated fat), 10 mg cholesterol, 427 mg sodium, 33 g carbohydrate, 4 g fiber, 5 g protein. **Diabetic Exchanges:** 2 starch, 1 fat.

The miniature meatballs in **Meatball Casserole** are a fun change of pace, but if you have other things to tend to, make them twice as large and double the baking time.

MEATBALL CASSEROLE

SOUTHWESTERN SAUTEED CORN

Cool Coffee Refresher F S

PREP/TOTAL TIME: 10 min. **YIELD:** 2 servings

HEALTHY COOKING TEST KITCHEN

For a cool and creamy breakfast beverage, try this quick recipe from our home economists. Freeze leftover coffee in an ice cube tray ahead of time for coffee cubes that'll keep your drink chilled without diluting the flavor.

- 1 cup strong brewed coffee, chilled
- 1/4 tsp. vanilla extract
- 1/2 cup reduced-fat vanilla yogurt
- 3 Tbsp. sugar
- 1 to 1-1/2 cups ice cubes

1. In a blender, combine the coffee, vanilla, yogurt and sugar; cover and process until smooth. Add ice; cover and process until blended.

2. Pour into chilled glasses; serve immediately.

Nutrition Facts: 1 cup equals 126 calories, 1 g fat (trace saturated fat), 3 mg cholesterol, 41 mg sodium, 27 g carbohydrate, 0 fiber, 3 g protein. **Diabetic Exchanges:** 1 starch, 1/2 fat-free milk.

Summer Garden Omelet C M

PREP/TOTAL TIME: 25 min. **YIELD:** 2 servings

MARY RELYEA • CANASTOTA, NEW YORK

Chock-full of garden flavor, this hearty omelet is ready in less than half an hour. I enjoy adding chopped red pepper for color and variety.

- 1/2 cup chopped zucchini
- 1/3 cup chopped onion
- 1/4 cup chopped green pepper
- 2 tsp. butter
- 4 egg whites
- 2 eggs
- 1/4 cup fat-free milk
- 1/4 tsp. salt
- 1/4 tsp. pepper
- 2 slices reduced-fat process American cheese product, cut into 1/2-in. strips

1. In a 10-in. nonstick skillet coated with cooking spray, saute the zucchini, onion and green pepper in butter until tender.

2. Meanwhile, in a small bowl, whisk the egg whites, eggs, milk, salt and pepper. Pour into skillet; cook over medium heat.

3. As eggs set, lift edges, letting uncooked portion flow underneath. When the eggs are set, place cheese on one side; fold omelet over cheese. Remove from the heat. Cover and let stand for 1-1/2 minutes or until cheese is melted. Cut in half.

Nutrition Facts: 1/2 omelet equals 206 calories, 10 g fat (4 g saturated fat), 228 mg cholesterol, 693 mg sodium, 9 g carbohydrate, 1 g fiber, 19 g protein. **Diabetic Exchanges:** 3 lean meat, 1 vegetable.

COOL COFFEE REFRESHER

SUMMER GARDEN OMELET

Shrimp Quesadillas

PREP/TOTAL TIME: 30 min. **YIELD:** 2 servings

TIFFANY BRYSON • SAN ANTONIO, TEXAS

Simple enough for any weekday, this dish boasts a refreshing flavor that's special enough for guests. Serve with salsa on the side and a frosty smoothie, if you like.

- 1/4 cup chopped onion
- 1 Tbsp. finely chopped jalapeno pepper
- 1/2 lb. uncooked shrimp, peeled, deveined and chopped
- 1/4 tsp. ground cumin
- 1/8 tsp. pepper
- 1/4 cup chopped tomato
- 4 flour tortillas (6 in.)
- 1/3 cup shredded reduced-fat Mexican cheese blend

1. In a large nonstick skillet coated with cooking spray, cook and stir onion and jalapeno until tender. Add the shrimp, cumin and pepper; cook and stir until shrimp turn pink. Transfer the shrimp mixture to a small bowl; stir in tomato.

2. Coat the same skillet with cooking spray; add one tortilla. Top with half of cheese, half of shrimp mixture and one tortilla. Cook over medium heat for 2-3 minutes on each side or until lightly browned; remove. Repeat with remaining tortillas, cheese and shrimp mixture, spraying pan as needed. Cut into wedges.

Editor's Note: When cutting hot peppers, disposable gloves are recommended. Avoid touching your face.

Nutrition Facts: 1 quesadilla equals 333 calories, 11 g fat (2 g saturated fat), 181 mg cholesterol, 777 mg sodium, 30 g carbohydrate, 1 g fiber, 30 g protein. **Diabetic Exchanges:** 3 lean meat, 2 starch.

Herb-Crusted Red Snapper C

PREP/TOTAL TIME: 25 min. **YIELD:** 2 servings

NELLA PARKER • HERSEY, MICHIGAN

An appetizing blend of herbs complements the mild flavor of these flaky fillets. Red pepper flakes give the entree its zip, but feel free to leave them out if you like.

1	Tbsp. dry bread crumbs
1	tsp. dried basil
1	tsp. paprika
1/2	tsp. salt
1/2	tsp. fennel seeds
1/2	tsp. dried thyme
1/2	tsp. dried oregano
1/4	tsp. pepper
1/4	tsp. crushed red pepper flakes
2	red snapper fillets (5 ounces *each*), skin removed
2	tsp. canola oil

1. In a food processor, combine the first nine ingredients; cover and process until fennel is finely ground. Transfer to a shallow bowl; dip fillets in herb mixture, coating both sides.

2. In a heavy skillet over medium-high heat, cook fillets in oil for 3-4 minutes on each side or until fish flakes easily with a fork.

Nutrition Facts: 1 fillet equals 200 calories, 7 g fat (1 g saturated fat), 50 mg cholesterol, 681 mg sodium, 4 g carbohydrate, 1 g fiber, 29 g protein. **Diabetic Exchanges:** 4 very lean meat, 1 fat.

Lime Fizz F S C

PREP/TOTAL TIME: 5 min. **YIELD:** 1 serving

HEALTHY COOKING TEST KITCHEN

Flavored with lime, this summery beverage hits the spot without packing a sugary punch. Try it with lemon wedges if you'd like, a little bit of pineapple juice or create your own combination of citrus tastes.

1/2	to 3/4 cup ice cubes
3	lime wedges
1	cup club soda, chilled

Sugar substitute equivalent to 1 tsp. sugar

1. Place ice in a highball glass. Squeeze lime wedges over ice; drop limes into the glass.

2. Slowly pour club soda into glass; stir in sugar substitute. Serve immediately.

Editor's Note: This recipe was tested with Splenda No Calorie Sweetener.

Nutrition Facts: 1 cup equals 6 calories, trace fat (trace saturated fat), 0 cholesterol, 51 mg sodium, 2 g carbohydrate, trace fiber, trace protein. **Diabetic Exchange:** Free food.

PORK AND NOODLES

Pork and Noodles

PREP/TOTAL TIME: 30 min. **YIELD:** 2 servings

JANICE KENNEDY • SAYVILLE, NEW YORK

This is a quick stovetop recipe that could easily work with leftover pork loin cooked chops or even last night's chicken. Used as a main dish, you can count on two generous and satisfying servings.

3	oz. uncooked angel hair pasta
1/2	lb. boneless pork loin chops, cut into thin strips
1/4	tsp. salt
1/4	tsp. pepper
1	tsp. canola oil, *divided*
1-1/2	cups cut fresh green beans
2	celery ribs, sliced
4-1/2	tsp. chopped onion
3	Tbsp. water
4	tsp. reduced-sodium soy sauce
1	tsp. butter

1. Cook pasta according to package directions. Meanwhile, sprinkle pork with salt and pepper. In a large nonstick skillet or wok coated with cooking spray, stir-fry pork in 1/2 teaspoon oil until no longer pink. Remove and keep warm.

2. In the same pan, stir-fry the beans, celery and onion in remaining oil until crisp-tender. Add the water, soy sauce and reserved pork; heat through. Drain pasta; stir in butter until melted. Add pork mixture and toss to coat.

Nutrition Facts: 2 cups equals 389 calories, 11 g fat (4 g saturated fat), 60 mg cholesterol, 783 mg sodium, 40 g carbohydrate, 5 g fiber, 30 g protein. **Diabetic Exchanges:** 3 lean meat, 2 starch, 1 vegetable, 1 fat.

Smoked Turkey Vegetable Wraps

PREP: 10 min. + marinating   **YIELD:** 2 servings

HEALTHY COOKING TEST KITCHEN

Crispy carrot, cucumber and green pepper add nutrition and zip to these turkey wraps. They're a great lunch or light supper, and you can forget about leftovers or messy cleanup!

1/2	medium cucumber, peeled, seeded and cut into strips
1/2	medium carrot, cut into strips
1/2	medium green pepper, cut into strips
1/4	cup prepared fat-free Italian salad dressing
1/4	cup reduced-fat spreadable garden vegetable cream cheese
2	flour tortillas (8 in.), room temperature
1/4	lb. thinly sliced deli smoked turkey
1/2	cup chopped fresh spinach

1. In a small resealable plastic bag, combine cucumber, carrot, green pepper and Italian dressing. Seal bag and turn to coat; refrigerate for at least 2 hours.

2. Spread cream cheese over tortillas; top with the turkey and spinach. Drain and discard dressing; place vegetables over spinach. Roll up. Warm wraps in the microwave before serving if desired.

Nutrition Facts: 1 wrap equals 299 calories, 9 g fat (3 g saturated fat), 36 mg cholesterol, 1,024 mg sodium, 32 g carbohydrate, 2 g fiber, 21 g protein.

Chocolate Mint Souffles

PREP: 20 min.   **BAKE:** 20 min.   **YIELD:** 2 servings

RUTH LEE • TROY, ONTARIO

These delectable little desserts are fancy, utterly foolproof and have been a family-favorite recipe for decades. I like to garnish them with fresh strawberries or orange segments.

2	eggs
1	tsp. plus 4 Tbsp. sugar, *divided*
2	Tbsp. baking cocoa
1	tsp. cornstarch
Dash salt	
1/3	cup fat-free milk
2	Tbsp. semisweet chocolate chips
1/8	tsp. mint extract
Confectioners' sugar	

1. Separate eggs. Place whites in a small mixing bowl; let stand at room temperature for 30 minutes. Place yolks in another bowl; set aside.

2. Coat two 10-oz. ramekins or custard cups with cooking spray and lightly sprinkle with 1 teaspoon sugar; place on a baking sheet and set aside.

3. In a small saucepan over medium heat, combine 2 tablespoons sugar, cocoa, cornstarch and salt. Gradually stir in milk. Bring to a boil, stirring constantly. Cook and stir for 1-2 minutes or until thickened.

4. Remove from the heat; stir in chocolate chips and extract until chips are melted. Transfer to a small bowl. Stir a small amount of hot mixture into egg yolks; return all to the bowl, stirring constantly. Cool slightly.

5. Beat egg whites on medium speed until soft peaks form. Gradually beat in remaining sugar, 1 tablespoon at a time, on high until stiff peaks form. With a spatula, fold a fourth of the egg whites into chocolate mixture until no white streaks remain. Fold in remaining egg whites until combined.

6. Transfer to prepared ramekins. Bake at 375° for 18-22 minutes or until tops are puffed and centers are almost set. Sprinkle with confectioners' sugar. Serve souffles immediately.

Nutrition Facts: 1 souffle equals 265 calories, 9 g fat (3 g saturated fat), 213 mg cholesterol, 159 mg sodium, 40 g carbohydrate, 2 g fiber, 9 g protein.

When serving **Chocolate Mint Souffles,** be sure to get them from the oven to the table as quickly as possible. No matter what recipe you follow, souffles begin to fall as soon as they start to cool. In addition, gently fold the egg whites into the chocolate mixture. Over mixing at this stage can cause the souffle to deflate while baking.

CHOCOLATE MINT SOUFFLES

My Healthy Life

With the hustle and bustle of today's busy lifestyles, it can be difficult to set healthy, homemade meals on the table night after night. Here, you'll see how busy family cooks tackle this challenge with mouth-watering menus they rely on most.

For Paula Young, hosting a dinner party doesn't mean straying from healthy-eating goals. Check out the sensational pork menu she shares here, and consider it the next time you find yourself cooking for a crowd.

Paula Young of Tiffin, Ohio is a firm believer that living well and eating healthy foods go hand in hand. For friends and family long used to her delicious, good-for-you meals and recipes, that commitment is easy to swallow.

She learned the importance of a diet rich in lean meats, whole grains, plenty of fruits and vegetables, less sodium and lots of water 5 years ago, when she joined a weight-loss program. Paula credits those good-health guidelines both with the 55-pound weight loss she works to maintain and also with helping to keep husband Bob's cholesterol where it should be.

But even before that, she recalls, they and adult daughter Renee had changed from 2% to skim milk, full-fat to low-fat and fat-free salad dressings and cheese, and vegetable oil to olive and canola oil "for the health of it."

"I've always enjoyed shopping local farm markets for fresh produce," she says. "With the recent emphasis on the eco-friendliness of doing that, I'm likely to only increase my visits! I like using my grill basket after visiting the market," Paula adds. "I slice onions, zucchini, squash, eggplant and bell peppers, sprinkle with olive oil, salt and pepper, and grill alongside meat or fish.

"I also use my food processor to whip up fresh salsa, hummus dips or a lower-fat version of guacamole substituting frozen peas for some of the avocado."

Her work as a sign-language interpreter for the deaf keeps her busy and fulfilled, along with a love for boating, photography and computer games. "But when my clothes become more uncomfortable than forgiving, I move away from the computer and simply move more: long, brisk walks, Pilates and yoga classes offered through my workplace. Accountability and the camaraderie of co-workers is a great motivator!"

Marinated Pork Loin C S

PREP: 20 min. **BAKE:** 1-1/2 hours + standing
YIELD: 12 servings

Friends and family enjoying special occasions at our house can count their blessings—not calories—with my Marinated Pork Loin meal. It's relatively low in fat, but still juicy, flavorful and so tender. People tell me it wouldn't be Christmas without it!

- 1 cup orange juice
- 3/4 cup apricot preserves
- 2 Tbsp. plus 1/4 cup sherry or vegetable broth, *divided*
- 3 Tbsp. lemon juice
- 2 Tbsp. olive oil
- 1 Tbsp. curry powder
- 1 Tbsp. Worcestershire sauce
- 1 tsp. dried thyme
- 1/2 tsp. pepper
- 1 boneless whole pork loin roast (3 lbs.)
- 1 Tbsp. cornstarch

1. In a small bowl, combine the orange juice, preserves, 2 tablespoons sherry, lemon juice, oil, curry, Worcestershire sauce, thyme and pepper. Pour 3/4 cup marinade into a large resealable plastic bag; add the pork. Seal bag and turn to coat; refrigerate overnight, turning occasionally. Set aside 1 cup remaining marinade for sauce; cover and refrigerate. Cover and refrigerate the rest of the marinade for basting.

2. Drain roast and discard marinade; place on a rack in a shallow roasting pan. Bake, uncovered, at 350° for 1-1/2 to 1-3/4 hours or until a meat thermometer reads 160°, basting occasionally with the reserved marinade.

3. Transfer to a serving platter. Let stand for 10 minutes before slicing.

4. Meanwhile, in a small saucepan, combine cornstarch with the remaining sherry and 1 cup marinade. Bring to a boil; cook and stir for 2 minutes or until thickened. Serve with the roast.

Nutrition Facts: 3 ounces cooked pork with 5 teaspoons sauce equals 229 calories, 8 g fat (3 g saturated fat), 55 mg cholesterol, 51 mg sodium, 15 g carbohydrate, trace fiber, 22 g protein. **Diabetic Exchanges:** 3 very lean meat, 1 fruit, 1 fat.

Homemade Noodles M

PREP: 45 min. + standing **COOK:** 15 min.
YIELD: 12 servings

I sometimes mix these cooked noodles with sauteed onions and low-fat cottage cheese for a time-crunched pierogi recipe. Also, the pork loin's sauce is so versatile! It's equally tasty served alongside noodles, rice or couscous.

- 4 cups all-purpose flour
- 1/2 cup whole wheat flour
- 2-1/4 tsp. salt, *divided*
- 4 eggs
- 1/2 cup plus 4 quarts water, *divided*
- 2 Tbsp. olive oil
- 3 Tbsp. butter
- 1/2 tsp. pepper

1. In a large bowl, combine flours and 2 teaspoons salt. Make a well in the center. Whisk the eggs, 1/2 cup water and oil; pour into well. Stir together, forming a dough. Cover and let rest for 10 minutes.

2. Turn dough onto a floured surface; knead 8-10 times. Divide into fourths. Roll each portion into a 14-in. x 12-in. rectangle. Cut widthwise into 1/2-in. strips; cut strips into 6-in. lengths. Let noodles rest on a clean towel for at least 1 hour.

3. In a Dutch oven, bring remaining water to a rapid boil. Add noodles; cook for 8-10 minutes or until tender. Drain. In the same pan, cook the butter over medium heat for 3-4 minutes or until golden brown. Add the noodles, pepper and remaining salt; toss to coat.

Nutrition Facts: 1/2 cup equals 162 calories, 6 g fat (2 g saturated fat), 53 mg cholesterol, 341 mg sodium, 23 g carbohydrate, 1 g fiber, 5 g protein. **Diabetic Exchanges:** 1-1/2 starch, 1 fat.

Roasted Veggies C M

PREP: 20 min. **BAKE:** 15 min. **YIELD:** 12 servings

Quick and easy Roasted Veggies round out my menu with natural, earthy sweetness. Whole grape tomatoes, onions, peppers, green beans, halved brussels sprouts and garlic also make delicious additions to this simple side dish.

2	medium heads cauliflower, broken into florets
6	medium carrots
1/4	cup olive oil
1	tsp. salt
1/2	tsp. pepper

1. Cut cauliflowerets and carrots into 1/4-in. slices. Place in a single layer in two ungreased 15-in. x 10-in. x 1-in. baking pans. Drizzle with oil; sprinkle with salt and pepper.

2. Bake, uncovered, at 400° for 15-20 minutes or until tender, stirring once.

Nutrition Facts: 3/4 cup equals 76 calories, 5 g fat (1 g saturated fat), 0 cholesterol, 247 mg sodium, 8 g carbohydrate, 3 g fiber, 2 g protein. **Diabetic Exchanges:** 1 vegetable, 1 fat.

Whole wheat flour pumps up the nutrition and fiber in Homemade Noodles. Paula sometimes makes extra batches to give to friends as hostess gifts along with a jar of homemade marina sauce.

Fast, Friendly Fare

When it comes to staying fit and eating right, this cook turns to friends and family for support and motivation. Here, Donna Noel shares a 30-minute menu that everyone around her seems to enjoy. Add it to your weekly lineup tonight!

There's no doubt about it, support from friends and family can make leading a healthy lifestyle easier—just ask Donna Noel of Gray, Maine. "I exercise with friends and family, and we all encourage each other," she says. "When you know someone's counting on you, it's a big motivator not to cancel!"

Thanks to where she lives and her love for the outdoors, Donna finds endless ways to stay active. "I have the good fortune of living in Maine, so I mountain climb in the autumn, ski and ice-skate in the winter, hike in the spring and swim in the summer. I feel like I get more exercise outside as opposed to inside."

Although she's always exercised regularly, this paralegal and brand-new grandmother has her friends to thank for her healthy-cooking habits. "I started cooking for friends and family members who had diabetes, so calories, content and food balance became very important. They responded almost too positively to my meals—now I'm always asked to bring a dish to pass," she jokes. "In reality, it's a compliment, and I love doing it!"

In fact, the more she cooked, the easier it got to trim down meals. "As I became more confident and knowledgeable, I became braver, too, and experimented with tweaking traditional favorites, with excellent results," she says. "I now prefer cooking light over heavier fare."

Donna keeps her healthy habits on track by enjoying at least two high-quality meals every day—usually breakfast and dinner—and combining protein from fish, poultry and beef with starches, vegetables and fruits. "I also drink a lot of water," she says.

When hitting the grocery store, Donna is prepared with solid **shopping tips.** "When I visit the fish counter and butcher, for instance, I ask if they have any good ideas," she explains. "You'd be surprised how many people share their recipes with them." Donna also picks up fresh citrus fruits. "Use these items to flavor your sauces and dressings and add visual appeal. Ask for locally grown items...the difference in freshness is amazing."

To keep mealtime interesting, Donna recommends experimenting with two ingredients that aren't usually associated with each other. "For example, fig compote on lean pork or roasted red peppers and apricot sauce on a bed of greens with chicken tenders," she says.

Having delicious meals makes healthful dining more appealing, and Donna follows a simple philosophy to stay motivated. "Just try to enjoy yourself and look forward to the fine meals you're eating."

Oven-Fried Chicken with Cranberry Sauce

PREP/TOTAL TIME: 30 min.
YIELD: 4 servings (1 cup sauce)

My oven-fried chicken and the accompanying cranberry sauce pairs a crisp coating of herbs and bread crumbs with sweet-tart cranberry sauce for a lean and satisfying entree. It's great for weeknight and weekend meals alike.

1/2	cup dry bread crumbs
2	Tbsp. grated Parmesan cheese
2	Tbsp. toasted wheat germ
2	garlic cloves, minced
1/2	tsp. paprika
1/4	tsp. *each* dried oregano, thyme and rosemary, crushed
1/4	tsp. pepper
4	boneless skinless chicken breast halves (4 oz. *each*)

SAUCE:

1	cup jellied cranberry sauce
2	Tbsp. lime juice
1	Tbsp. balsamic vinegar
1-1/2	tsp. Dijon mustard

1. In a large resealable plastic bag, combine the bread crumbs, cheese, wheat germ, garlic and seasonings. Add chicken, one piece at a time, and shake to coat. Place on a baking sheet coated with cooking spray.

2. Bake at 375° for 20-25 minutes or until a meat thermometer reads 170°, turning once.

3. Meanwhile, in a small saucepan, bring cranberry sauce to a boil. Remove from the heat; whisk in the lime juice, vinegar and mustard. Serve with chicken.

Nutrition Facts: 1 chicken breast half with 1/4 cup sauce equals 268 calories, 4 g fat (1 g saturated fat), 64 mg cholesterol, 182 mg sodium, 34 g carbohydrate, 2 g fiber, 25 g protein.
Diabetic Exchanges: 3 very lean meat, 2 starch.

Special Green Beans C M

PREP/TOTAL TIME: 20 min. **YIELD:** 4 servings

This yummy green bean recipe rounds out the menu with bright color and fresh flavor. With only a few minutes of prep time, the side dish is ready before you know it! You could also serve it with turkey or beef.

1	lb. fresh green beans, trimmed
2	green onions, thinly sliced
2	Tbsp. minced fresh parsley
2	Tbsp. olive oil
1	Tbsp. red wine vinegar
1	garlic clove, minced
1	tsp. Dijon mustard
1/4	tsp. salt
1/4	tsp. pepper

1. Place beans in a large saucepan and cover with water. Bring to a boil. Cover and cook for 4-7 minutes or until crisp-tender.

2. Meanwhile, in a small bowl, combine the remaining ingredients. Drain beans; stir in onion mixture and heat through.

Nutrition Facts: 3/4 cup equals 97 calories, 7 g fat (1 g saturated fat), 0 cholesterol, 186 mg sodium, 9 g carbohydrate, 4 g fiber, 2 g protein. **Diabetic Exchanges:** 1 vegetable, 1 fat.

Mashed Potato Casserole M

PREP/TOTAL TIME: 30 min. **YIELD:** 5 servings

Be sure to leave room on the plate for this light and creamy casserole. I dress up the spuds with green onions and melted cheddar cheese, and I found it gives the dish a rich texture if I add reduced-fat sour cream.

4	medium potatoes, peeled and quartered
1/2	cup reduced-fat sour cream
1/2	cup cream-style cottage cheese
1/4	cup fat-free milk
2 to 3	green onions, thinly sliced
1/4	cup shredded reduced-fat cheddar cheese

1. Place potatoes in a large saucepan and cover with water. Bring to a boil. Reduce heat; cover and simmer for 15-20 minutes or until tender. Drain.

2. In a large bowl, mash potatoes with sour cream, cottage cheese and milk; stir in onions.

3. Transfer to an 8-in. square baking dish coated with cooking spray; sprinkle with cheddar cheese.

4. Bake at 375° for 5-10 minutes or until heated through and cheese is melted.

Nutrition Facts: 3/4 cup equals 177 calories, 4 g fat (3 g saturated fat), 16 mg cholesterol, 153 mg sodium, 27 g carbohydrate, 2 g fiber, 8 g protein. **Diabetic Exchanges:** 2 starch, 1 fat.

Easy Italian Dinner

You don't have to visit a pricey restaurant to enjoy fine Italian food. Just ask Mary Bilyeu. She knows how to serve up fantastic meals that are low in fat and calories and high in flavor. Read on to learn a few of her secrets.

With a family history of diabetes, osteoporosis and high cholesterol, Mary Bilyeu strives to keep her health in check. "There's no reason to eat unhealthy foods when it's possible to eat nutritious food that tastes great," she says from her Ann Arbor, Michigan home. "You really don't have to let genetics win if you take an active role in staying healthy."

But this busy mom to 16-year-old son Jeremy and part-time writer, proofreader and administrative assistant assures she's not a "food purist." As she says, "If you eat a low-fat, low-sugar diet with lots of whole grains and fruits and vegetables, you can splurge on birthday cake or other, less-healthy foods when they come your way."

When she's not helping out friends or rooting for her favorite sports teams, Mary enjoys watching *Jeopardy!* (she was even invited to be a contestant on the show) and entering cooking contests. "I'm constantly trying to devise new, delicious recipes," she writes.

She also stays fit with long walks and weight-bearing exercises to strengthen her bones. "I exercise for my health, not because I enjoy it!" she says with a laugh. "I'd rather cook than break out in a sweat." And she's willing to share her healthy-cooking secrets—with a lighter dessert, main dish and side.

"I cook the main course, Ragu Bolognese, very slowly. Doing so creates a rich, delicious sauce. The veggies add fiber, and skim milk and turkey sausage keep it so much lighter than other meat sauces I have found over the years," Mary says.

With garlic, red pepper and balsamic vinegar, Mary's good-for-you Steamed Kale is not only packed with vitamins but flavor, too. If you've never prepared kale for your family before, considering introducing the vegetable with this healthy recipe.

Mary's variation of Chocolate Cannoli Cake was a finalist in a "Best Cake in Michigan" contest. "You'll be shocked that something so delectable has just 8 grams of fat per serving," she shares. "I truly hope you try it and that it becomes just as big of a hit with your family as it is with mine."

Ragu Bolognese

PREP: 30 min. **COOK:** 1-1/4 hours **YIELD:** 4 servings

Whole wheat spiral pasta adds a tasty change from the expected to this entree...as well as lots of healthy benefits. Feel free to use whatever pasta you have on hand however. You could even enjoy the dish with tortellini.

- 1/2 lb. Italian turkey sausage links, casings removed
- 1 large carrot, finely chopped
- 1 celery rib, finely chopped
- 1 small onion, finely chopped
- 1 can (15 oz.) crushed tomatoes
- 1/2 cup reduced-sodium chicken broth
- 2 Tbsp. balsamic vinegar
- 1/4 tsp. crushed red pepper flakes
- 3/4 cup fat-free milk
- 8 oz. uncooked whole wheat spiral pasta
- 2 Tbsp. prepared pesto
- 1 Tbsp. chopped ripe olives

1. Crumble sausage into a nonstick Dutch oven. Add the carrot, celery and onion; cook and stir over medium heat until meat is no longer pink. Drain.

2. Stir in the tomatoes, broth, vinegar and pepper flakes. Bring to a boil. Stir in the milk. Reduce heat; simmer, uncovered, for 1 to 1-1/4 hours or until thickened, stirring occasionally.

3. Cook pasta according to package directions. Stir pesto and olives into meat sauce. Drain pasta; serve with meat sauce.

Nutrition Facts: 1 cup pasta with 2/3 cup meat sauce equals 413 calories, 11 g fat (2 g saturated fat), 38 mg cholesterol, 674 mg sodium, 58 g carbohydrate, 6 g fiber, 21 g protein.

Steamed Kale C M

PREP: 15 min. **COOK:** 25 min. **YIELD:** 4 servings

Can't get your gang to eat cabbage? Try serving them kale. It's high in vitamins, calcium and antioxidants. Here, kale gets a tasty treatment from garlic and balsamic vinegar.

- 1 lb. fresh kale
- 3 garlic cloves, minced
- 1 Tbsp. olive oil
- 2/3 cup water
- 1/4 tsp. salt
- 1/8 tsp. crushed red pepper flakes
- 1 Tbsp. balsamic vinegar

1. Trim kale, discarding the thick ribs and stems. Chop leaves. In a Dutch oven, saute the kale leaves and garlic in oil until the kale is wilted.

2. Stir in the water, salt and pepper flakes. Bring to a boil. Reduce heat; cover and simmer for 20-25 minutes or until the kale is tender. Remove from the heat; stir in the vinegar.

Nutrition Facts: 3/4 cup equals 93 calories, 4 g fat (1 g saturated fat), 0 cholesterol, 198 mg sodium, 13 g carbohydrate, 2 g fiber, 4 g protein. **Diabetic Exchanges:** 2 vegetable, 1/2 fat.

Chocolate Cannoli Cake

PREP: 25 min. **BAKE:** 25 min. + cooling
YIELD: 15 servings

Who doesn't like chocolate? This recipe lets you enjoy chocolate cake without any guilt! I lightened up a wonderful recipe, and this dessert was the satisfying outcome.

    1   egg white, lightly beaten
    1   cup reduced-fat ricotta cheese
  1/4   cup sugar
    1   Tbsp. cold brewed coffee
    2   tsp. grated orange peel
  1/2   cup miniature semisweet chocolate chips

BATTER:
    1   cup sugar
  1/2   cup cold brewed coffee
  1/3   cup canola oil
  1/3   cup orange juice
    1   egg
    1   egg white
    1   Tbsp. cider vinegar
    1   Tbsp. vanilla extract
    1   cup all-purpose flour
  1/2   cup whole wheat flour
  1/3   cup baking cocoa
    2   tsp. baking powder
  1/2   tsp. salt

1. In a small bowl, combine the egg white, ricotta cheese, sugar, coffee and orange peel. Stir in chocolate chips; set aside.

2. In a large mixing bowl, combine the first eight batter ingredients; beat until well blended. Combine the flours, cocoa, baking powder and salt; gradually beat into sugar mixture until blended.

3. Transfer to a 13-in. x 9-in. baking dish coated with cooking spray. Top with heaping tablespoons of ricotta mixture; cut through batter with a knife to swirl.

4. Bake at 350° for 25-30 minutes or until a toothpick inserted near the center comes out clean. Cool on a wire rack. Refrigerate any leftovers.

Nutrition Facts: 1 piece equals 213 calories, 8 g fat (2 g saturated fat), 18 mg cholesterol, 160 mg sodium, 32 g carbohydrate, 1 g fiber, 4 g protein. **Diabetic Exchanges:** 2 starch, 1-1/2 fat.

When serving squares of Chocolate Cannoli Cake, consider taking advantage of garishes such as fresh raspberries or strawberries. If time allows, you could even twist a strip of orange peel for added flair.

Light & Lively Supper

Here's a no-fuss dinner that's sure to be a smash during warm-weather menu planning. Not only does it take advantage of fresh vegetables and herbs, but it ends with a frosty specialty that promises to earn rave reviews.

For Dawn Bryant's family, in Thedford, Nebraska, eating a balanced diet doesn't always come easily. "My son, Aidan, who's a toddler, loves fruit and vegetables so much we call him 'fruit fly,'" Dawn says jokingly. "But my husband, Ross, and our 5-year-old daughter, Ariel, struggle with my meal plans. They're what I call 'starchies'. They love anything starchy, full of carbohydrates and light-colored."

That doesn't stop this stay-at-home mother and freelance journalist/artist from whipping up nutritious meals—it's too important to her. "I was slender until I hit 30 and my metabolism bottomed out. Then I met my husband, who's always struggled with his weight," she says. "I tried to cook lower-fat meals, but once the children were born, I really began a healthy-eating kick."

To keep the kids from "becoming lumps in front of the television," Dawn and her family try to stay active. They enjoy fishing, boating and camping.

Dawn's also employed a variety of techniques for making menus healthy. "I grate vegetables and hide them in foods my family likes, and I've cut down on cheese, cream and butter. I've also used more herbs and garlic as their palates adjust to the flavors," she says. The menu she shares here showcases her skills in lightening dishes while keeping great taste.

Chicken Provolone **C**

PREP/TOTAL TIME: 25 min. **YIELD:** 4 servings

Chicken Provolone, though one of my simplest recipes, is also one of my husband's favorites. It looks elegant served on a dark plate with a garnish of fresh parsley or basil.

- 4 boneless skinless chicken breast halves (4 oz. *each*)
- 1/4 tsp. pepper
- Butter-flavored cooking spray
- 8 fresh basil leaves
- 4 thin slices prosciutto *or* deli ham
- 4 slices provolone cheese

1. Sprinkle chicken with pepper. In a large nonstick skillet coated with butter-flavored cooking spray, cook chicken over medium heat for 4-5 minutes on each side or until juices run clear.

2. Transfer to an ungreased baking sheet; top with basil, prosciutto and cheese. Broil 6-8 in. from the heat for 1-2 minutes or until cheese is melted.

Nutrition Facts: 1 chicken breast half equals 236 calories, 11 g fat (6 g saturated fat), 89 mg cholesterol, 435 mg sodium, 1 g carbohydrate, trace fiber, 33 g protein. **Diabetic Exchange:** 4 lean meat.

Common Cutting and Chopping Techniques

Making Bias/Diagonal Cuts
Holding a chef's knife at an angle to the length of the food, carefully slice the items as thick or thin as desired. This technique is often used when adding vegetables to stir-fries, soups and casserole recipes.

Chopping an Onion
To quickly chop an onion, peel and cut in half from the root to the top. Leaving root attached, place flat side down on work surface. Cut vertically through the onion, leaving the root end uncut. Cut across the onion, discarding root end. The closer the cuts, the finer the onion will be chopped.

Peeling and Mincing Fresh Garlic
Using the blade of a chef's knife, crush the garlic clove. Peel away skin. Holding the handle of a knife with one hand, rest the fingers of your other hand on the top of the blade near the tip. Move the knife in an arc across the food with a rocking motion until pieces are the desired size.

Mediterranean Summer Squash C M

PREP/TOTAL TIME: 25 min. **YIELD:** 4 servings

I created the recipe when my garden was producing like crazy and I had lots of fresh zucchini, yellow squash and tomatoes. I combined the three, added some seasonings, garlic and feta and came up with a colorful dish that I really love. My son just eats it up whenever I serve it.

1/4	cup chopped onion
1	Tbsp. olive oil
1	small yellow summer squash, thinly sliced
1	small zucchini, thinly sliced
1	garlic clove, minced
1	plum tomato, seeded and chopped
1/2	tsp. dried oregano
1/4	cup crumbled feta cheese
1/4	tsp. salt
1/4	tsp. pepper

1. In a large skillet, saute onion in oil until tender. Add the squash, zucchini and garlic; saute 6-8 minutes longer or until tender.

2. Stir in the remaining ingredients; heat through.

Nutrition Facts: 2/3 cup equals 69 calories, 5 g fat (1 g saturated fat), 4 mg cholesterol, 220 mg sodium, 5 g carbohydrate, 2 g fiber, 3 g protein. **Diabetic Exchanges:** 1 vegetable, 1 fat.

Fruit Cup with Honey-Lime Syrup F S

PREP: 15 min. + cooling **YIELD:** 4 servings

Fruit Cup with Honey-Lime Syrup is a refreshing way to end the meal. I often experiment with fresh fruit for desserts. This is a nice, cool surprise after dinner, but it also makes a great treat when unexpected guests stop by on summer afternoons. Serve it for a ladies' luncheon and you're bound to receive requests for the recipe.

1/3	cup white wine
2	Tbsp. lime juice
2	Tbsp. honey
2	cups cubed cantaloupe
1	cup green grapes, halved
1	cup red grapes, halved

1. In a small saucepan over medium heat, bring the wine, lime juice and honey to a boil. Reduce heat; simmer, uncovered, until liquid is syrupy and reduced to about 1/4 cup.

2. Remove from the heat; cool completely.

3. In a large bowl, combine fruit. Drizzle with syrup and gently toss to coat.

Nutrition Facts: 1 cup equals 135 calories, 1 g fat (trace saturated fat), 0 cholesterol, 10 mg sodium, 31 g carbohydrate, 1 g fiber, 1 g protein. **Diabetic Exchanges:** 1-1/2 fruit, 1/2 starch.

Bring on the Flavor

Healthy meals don't have to mean flavorless feasts. Check out the menu here. From Pennsylvania, this busy mom shares one of her family's favorite meals that gets plenty of taste from Southwestern ingredients and seasonings.

For some, the decision to lead a healthier lifestyle starts early. "It happened for me when I was a 19-year-old college student," says Heather Byers, Pittsburgh, Pennsylvania. "I realized the habits I set then would impact me for the rest of my life. I was not exactly on the right path, so I began eating better. It's been a lifelong journey."

Years later, this college instructor turned stay-at-home mom continues to practice healthy habits. "My husband, Steve, likes my cooking, which is a great compliment," she says. "I experiment fairly often with recipes, and we have fun with it...usually...some of the experiments have been pretty heinous!

"Our 2-year-old daughter, Arianna, knows no difference," Heather says. "She's less picky than other kids, but whether that's from being introduced to a variety of foods or just her personality is debatable."

For exercise, Heather walks 3 to 4 miles nearly every day. She keeps meals on track by using fresh ingredients. "I try to do the majority of my shopping at local farm markets, which gives us a variety of produce," she says. "Around August, it starts to feel like we've been eating zucchini all year!"

Heather's "fresh perspective" follows her to the grocery store, too. There, she skips 90 percent of the aisles in favor of whole fruits and veggies. She also brings home plenty of lean meats and grains, including whole wheat bread, cereals and rice. "This saves money and cuts out many processed foods, chemicals, preservatives and calories," she says.

Fiesta Salad

PREP/TOTAL TIME: 10 min. **YIELD:** 4 servings

For this salad, I was making a Mexican-themed dinner one night and created a side dish with the fresh produce I had. I threw in anything that reminded me of Mexican food! Thankfully, it turned out, and we use the combination of salsa and ranch dressing on sandwiches, burgers and more.

2	cups torn romaine
3/4	cup frozen corn, thawed
1/3	cup canned black beans, rinsed and drained
1	medium tomato, chopped
1	celery rib, chopped
1	medium carrot, thinly sliced
1/4	cup torn curly endive
1/3	cup salsa
2	Tbsp. reduced-fat sour cream
2	Tbsp. prepared reduced-fat ranch salad dressing

1. In a salad bowl, combine the first seven ingredients. In a small bowl, combine the salsa, sour cream and ranch dressing.

2. Drizzle over salad and toss to coat. Serve immediately.

Nutrition Facts: 3/4 cup equals 100 calories, 3 g fat (1 g saturated fat), 5 mg cholesterol, 235 mg sodium, 16 g carbohydrate, 4 g fiber, 4 g protein. **Diabetic Exchanges:** 1 vegetable, 1/2 starch, 1/2 fat.

Oven Fries **M**

PREP: 10 min. **BAKE:** 40 min. **YIELD:** 4 servings

Jazzed up with paprika and garlic powder, my Oven Fries make a great side. Everyone loves them.

4	medium potatoes
1	Tbsp. olive oil
2-1/2	tsp. paprika
3/4	tsp. salt
3/4	tsp. garlic powder

1. Cut each potato into 12 wedges. In a large bowl, combine oil, paprika, salt and garlic powder. Add potatoes; toss to coat.

2. Transfer to a 15-in. x 10-in. x 1-in. baking pan coated with cooking spray. Bake at 400° for 40-45 minutes or until tender, turning once.

Nutrition Facts: 12 potato wedges equals 204 calories, 4 g fat (1 g saturated fat), 0 cholesterol, 456 mg sodium, 39 g carbohydrate, 4 g fiber, 5 g protein.

Mexican-Inspired Turkey Burgers

PREP/TOTAL TIME: 25 min. **YIELD:** 4 servings

To create these burgers, I used a spice combination from a taco recipe and tinkered with the cheeses and toppings. I hope you like the outcome as much as my family does.

1/2	cup salsa, *divided*
1/4	cup shredded reduced-fat cheddar cheese
3	tsp. paprika
1	tsp. dried oregano
1	tsp. ground cumin
3/4	tsp. sugar
3/4	tsp. garlic powder
1/2	tsp. dried thyme
1/4	tsp. salt
1/4	tsp. cayenne pepper
1	lb. extra-lean ground turkey
1/4	cup reduced-fat sour cream
4	hamburger buns, split
1/2	cup torn curly endive
1	medium tomato, chopped

1. In a large bowl, combine 1/4 cup salsa, cheese, paprika, oregano, cumin, sugar, garlic powder, thyme, salt and cayenne. Crumble turkey over mixture and mix well. Shape into four burgers.

2. If grilling the burgers, coat grill rack with cooking spray before starting the grill. Grill, covered, over medium heat or broil 4 in. from the heat for 5-7 minutes on each side or until a meat thermometer reads 165° and juices run clear.

3. In a small bowl, combine sour cream and remaining salsa. Place burgers on buns; top with endive, tomato and sour cream mixture.

Nutrition Facts: 1 burger equals 312 calories, 7 g fat (2 g saturated fat), 55 mg cholesterol, 599 mg sodium, 29 g carbohydrate, 3 g fiber, 36 g protein. **Diabetic Exchanges:** 4 very lean meat, 2 starch.

Heather's **turkey burgers** get a seasoning boost with help from garlic powder. "We're very big garlic fans," she says. "I always have a bottle of minced garlic, a head of fresh garlic and a container of garlic powder on hand." And while she likes seasonings, she stays clear of butter and oil. "Cooking in nonstick pans means I can almost eliminate butter and oil from our menus," she adds.

Lighthearted Lunch

Making her food fresh, colorful and fun is one way Fay Strait keeps her little ones on the healthy-eating path. The next time you're looking for a change-of-pace to surprise your gang with, give this casual menu a try.

When it comes to keeping her family healthy, Fay Strait from Waukee, Iowa has it figured out...and she's sharing her secrets!

"I thought we ate pretty healthy," writes Fay, a stay-at-home mom. But a trip to the doctor's office made her think twice. "Unfortunately, I have a family history of high cholesterol. Mine was tested last year, and it was elevated. That's when I became concerned about what we ate.

"Now I read labels on everything and love shopping at farmers markets. I also try to limit the sugar in my kids' snacks to 10 grams or less per serving. I always have pretzels and graham crackers in the pantry for Jack, who is 8, and Cort, who's 4."

Besides watching sugar intake, Fay and her family get plenty of exercise. "I go to the gym three to five times a week, and I vary my routine to keep from getting bored," she writes. "But I have the most fun playing with my kids outside. We bike, go on nature walks, go swimming and play tag."

As for keeping mealtime nutritious, Fay has a straightforward philosophy. "If you want your kids to eat healthfully, you need to eat healthily," she says. "I made changes that my husband, Jim, and our sons didn't even notice."

Fay also tries to add some fun to eating. "Mealtime doesn't have to be serious. For kids, it's all about presentation. Arrange food into shapes, like green beans into a star and corn into smiley faces. If all else fails, give your meals or dishes silly, crazy kid names," she says. Try out Fay's deliciously fun menu tonight!

Fresh and Fruity Coleslaw F S C M

PREP: 15 min. + chilling **YIELD:** 10 servings

Full of fruity flavor, this tangy coleslaw comes together easily with a bag of coleslaw mix. Take it to backyard barbecues or try it for a fun after-school snack.

- 1 pkg. (16 oz.) coleslaw mix
- 2 celery ribs, chopped
- 1 cup seedless grapes, halved
- 1 medium tart apple, chopped
- 1/3 cup plain yogurt
- 1/3 cup orange juice
- 2 Tbsp. fat-free mayonnaise
- 1 Tbsp. sugar
- 1 Tbsp. lemon juice

1. In a large bowl, combine the coleslaw mix, celery, grapes and apple. Combine the remaining ingredients; pour over the top. Toss to coat.

2. Cover and refrigerate for at least 2 hours before serving.

Nutrition Facts: 3/4 cup equals 50 calories, trace fat (trace saturated fat), 1 mg cholesterol, 51 mg sodium, 11 g carbohydrate, 2 g fiber, 1 g protein. **Diabetic Exchanges:** 1 vegetable, 1/2 starch.

Super Flatbread Wraps

PREP: 40 min. + rising **GRILL:** 15 min.
YIELD: 4 servings

For a change, you can also fill these wraps with lettuce, grilled chicken and a sauce made from one chopped tomato with 2 tablespoons of light mayonnaise. Or try lettuce, grilled chicken, salsa, fat-free sour cream and cheddar cheese.

- 1/2 tsp. active dry yeast
- 1/2 cup warm water (110° to 115°)
- 1 tsp. olive oil
- 1/2 tsp. salt
- 1/3 cup whole wheat flour
- 1 cup all-purpose flour

FILLING:
- 1 beef flank steak (1 lb.)
- 1/2 tsp. salt
- 1/4 tsp. pepper
- 1 cup shredded lettuce
- 1/4 cup sliced ripe olives
- 2 Tbsp. crumbled feta cheese

1. In a small mixing bowl, dissolve yeast in warm water. Add the oil, salt, whole wheat flour and 3/4 cup all-purpose flour; beat on medium speed for 3 minutes. Stir in enough remaining flour to form a firm dough.

2. Turn onto a lightly floured surface; knead until smooth and elastic, about 6-8 minutes.

3. Place in a bowl coated with cooking spray, turning once to coat the top. Cover and let rise in a warm place until doubled, about 45 minutes.

4. Punch dough down. Turn onto a lightly floured surface; divide into four portions. Roll each into an 8-in. circle.

5. Heat a large nonstick skillet coated with cooking spray over medium heat; add a portion of dough. Cook for 30-60 seconds or until bubbles form on top. Turn and cook until the second side is golden brown.

Remove and keep warm. Repeat with remaining dough, adding cooking spray as needed.

6. Coat grill rack with cooking spray before starting the grill. Sprinkle steak with salt and pepper.

7. Grill, covered, over medium-high heat for 6-8 minutes on each side or until meat reaches desired doneness (for medium-rare, a meat thermometer should read 145°; medium, 160°; well-done, 170°).

8. Let stand for 5 minutes before cutting steak thinly across the grain.

9. Serve on warm flatbreads with lettuce, olives and cheese.

Nutrition Facts: 1 wrap equals 348 calories, 11 g fat (4 g saturated fat), 56 mg cholesterol, 770 mg sodium, 32 g carbohydrate, 3 g fiber, 28 g protein. **Diabetic Exchanges:** 3 lean meat, 2 starch, 1/2 fat.

Monkey Shakes F S

PREP/TOTAL TIME: 10 min. **YIELD:** 4 servings

If the fresh flavors found in this silly shake don't get your kids excited about healthy eating, than the name of this cool concoction should do the trick!

  1 cup fat-free milk
  2 medium ripe bananas
  1 cup halved fresh strawberries
  1 cup rainbow sherbet

1. In a blender, combine all ingredients; cover and process for 1-2 minutes or until smooth.

2. Stir if necessary. Pour into chilled glasses; serve immediately.

Nutrition Facts: 1 cup equals 139 calories, 1 g fat (1 g saturated fat), 1 mg cholesterol, 44 mg sodium, 31 g carbohydrate, 4 g fiber, 3 g protein.

Homemade Flatbread in Just Three Steps!

1. After letting the dough for the flatbread wraps rise until doubled, use your fist to punch it down.

2. Next, turn the dough onto a lightly floured surface; divide into four portions. Roll each into an 8-in. circle.

3. Cook each portion in a large nonstick skillet coated with cooking spray for 30-60 seconds or until bubbles form on top. Turn and cook until the second side is golden brown.

Celebrate!

Where there's a party, there's sure to be plenty of foods, tempting your taste buds to stray from your healthy–eating goals. With this colorful collection of menus, however, you can be the "hostess with the most–ess," and still eat right!

Sweetheart Meal

Peppered Beef Tenderloin
Broccoli Blue Cheese Rice
Baby Carrots with Almonds
No–Bake Chai Cheese Pie

Cinco de Mayo

Chicken Tacos with Pineapple Pico de Gallo
Red Pepper Jalapeno Muffins
Rich Mocha Cake

Celebrate Summer

Chutney Turkey Burgers
Glazed Roasted Pineapple
Grilled Veggie Kabobs

Picnic in the Park

Honey–Balsamic Goat Cheese Dip
Amaretto Cheese-Filled Apricots
Mediterranean Chicken Salad

Giving Thanks

Holiday Lettuce Salad
Cranberry-Orange Roasted Turkey
Traditional Holiday Stuffing

Merry & Light

Cranberry-Glazed Ham
Holiday Green Beans
Herbed Monkey Bread

Sweetheart Meal

It doesn't have to be Valentine's Day to treat friends and family to fabulous foods that are full-flavored and that fit into healthy lifestyles. Make a lasting impression with this sweetheart of a dinner that's sure to please.

No-Bake Chai Cheese Pie

PREP: 25 min. + chilling **YIELD:** 8 servings

HEALTHY COOKING TEST KITCHEN

For make-ahead convenience, you can't beat this simple no-bake pie from our home economists. It boasts a lighter-than-air texture and a sweet touch of spicy sophistication that adults will love!

1	individual tea bag
1/2	cup boiling water
1	envelope unflavored gelatin
1	pkg. (8 oz.) reduced-fat cream cheese
1	pkg. (8 oz.) fat-free cream cheese
1/3	cup sugar
1/2	cup refrigerated fat-free French vanilla nondairy creamer
1/2	tsp. ground cinnamon, *divided*
1/4	tsp. ground ginger
1/8	tsp. *each* ground cardamom, allspice and cloves
1	reduced-fat graham cracker crust (8 in.)
1/2	cup reduced-fat whipped topping

1. Place tea bag in a small bowl; add boiling water. Cover and steep for 5 minutes. Discard tea bag. Refrigerate tea for 30 minutes or until chilled.

2. Sprinkle gelatin over tea; let stand for 1 minute. Microwave on high for 30 seconds; stir. Let stand for 1 minute or until gelatin is completely dissolved.

3. In a large mixing bowl, beat cream cheeses and sugar until smooth. Gradually beat in the creamer, gelatin mixture, 1/4 teaspoon cinnamon, ginger, cardamom, allspice and cloves until blended.

4. Pour into crust. Refrigerate for 3 hours or until set. Garnish with whipped topping and remaining cinnamon.

Nutrition Facts: 1 piece equals 273 calories, 10 g fat (6 g saturated fat), 22 mg cholesterol, 376 mg sodium, 35 g carbohydrate, trace fiber, 9 g protein.

Baby Carrots with Almonds C

PREP/TOTAL TIME: 10 min. **YIELD:** 4 servings

JANE KITTLE • COLUMBIA CROSS ROADS, PENNSYLVANIA

These not-so-candied carrots are a treat for my diabetic husband, but they are actually something we all enjoy.

1	pkg. (16 oz.) fresh baby carrots
2	Tbsp. water
2	Tbsp. slivered almonds, toasted
1	Tbsp. sugar
1	Tbsp. butter
1/8	tsp. salt

1. Place carrots and water in a microwave-safe bowl.

2. Cover and microwave on high for 4-6 minutes or until tender; drain. Stir in the remaining ingredients.

Editor's Note: This recipe was tested in a 1,100-watt microwave.

Nutrition Facts: 3/4 cup equals 96 calories, 5 g fat (2 g saturated fat), 8 mg cholesterol, 191 mg sodium, 13 g carbohydrate, 2 g fiber, 1 g protein. **Diabetic Exchanges:** 2 vegetable, 1 fat.

Broccoli Blue Cheese Rice M

PREP/TOTAL TIME: 30 min. **YIELD:** 4 servings

HEALTHY COOKING TEST KITCHEN

This colorful veggie side will go nicely with a variety of entrees. With a hint of lemon, it's certain to add a fresh touch to the conclusion of any meal.

1-1/3	cups plus 2 Tbsp. water, *divided*
2/3	cup uncooked long grain rice
1-1/2	tsp. grated lemon peel
1/2	tsp. salt
1/8	tsp. white pepper
3	cups fresh broccoli florets
1/2	cup crumbled blue cheese

NO-BAKE CHAI CHEESE PIE

BROCCOLI BLUE CHEESE RICE   PEPPERED BEEF TENDERLOIN

1. In a small saucepan, combine 1-1/3 cups water, rice, lemon peel, salt and pepper; bring to a boil. Reduce heat; cover and simmer for 15-18 minutes or until liquid is absorbed and rice is tender.

2. Place broccoli and remaining water in a small microwave-safe dish. Cover and microwave on high for 2-3 minutes or until crisp-tender; drain. Toss with rice. Sprinkle with blue cheese.

Editor's Note: This recipe was tested in a 1,100-watt microwave.

Nutrition Facts: 1 cup equals 178 calories, 4 g fat (3 g saturated fat), 11 mg cholesterol, 509 mg sodium, 28 g carbohydrate, 2 g fiber, 7 g protein. **Diabetic Exchanges:** 1-1/2 starch, 1 vegetable, 1 fat.

Peppered Beef Tenderloin c

PREP: 10 min. **COOK:** 35 min. **YIELD:** 4 servings

KARIN WOODBURY • OCALA, FLORIDA

I found this recipe at the time I was getting brave about using herbs and rubs to flavor meats. It's been a favorite ever since.

2	tsp. olive oil, *divided*
2	large red onions, cut into 1/2-in. slices
1	tsp. salt, *divided*
2	Tbsp. balsamic vinegar
1/2	tsp. sugar
2	tsp. coarsely ground pepper
1-1/2	tsp. dried thyme
4	beef tenderloin steaks (4 oz. *each*)

1. Heat 1 teaspoon oil in a large nonstick skillet coated with cooking spray; add the onions. Cook and stir over medium heat for 25-30 minutes or until tender and browned. Stir in 1/2 teaspoon salt, vinegar and sugar. Remove and keep warm.

2. Combine the pepper, thyme and remaining salt; rub over steaks. In the same skillet, cook steaks for 4-7 minutes on each side or until meat reaches desired doneness (for medium-rare, a meat thermometer should read 145°; medium, 160°; well-done, 170°). Serve with onions.

Nutrition Facts: 1 steak with 1/2 cup onions equals 259 calories, 14 g fat (5 g saturated fat), 72 mg cholesterol, 647 mg sodium, 9 g carbohydrate, 2 g fiber, 24 g protein. **Diabetic Exchanges:** 3 lean meat, 1 fat, 1/2 starch.

Have any **Peppered Beef Tenderloin** left over? Cut it into small cubes and brown it in canola oil for a bit. Add some sliced carrots, frozen peas, chopped onion and cubed potatoes to the skillet. Stir in a few cups of reduced-sodium beef broth and simmer until the vegetables are tender, stirring occasionally. You'll have a low-fat beef soup in no time, and you'll save money, too!

Cinco de Mayo

This holiday, often mistaken for Mexico's independence day, commemorates an 1862 battle in Pueblo. Celebrate with a sunny spread that's fresh, healthy and fun.

Red Pepper Jalapeno Muffins

F M

PREP: 20 min. **BAKE:** 20 min. **YIELD:** 1 dozen

AGNES WARD • STRATFORD, ONTARIO

These moist, spicy muffins boast as much flavor as color. Substitute a can of chopped green chilies for the jalapenos if you want a bit less heat.

1-1/2	cups all-purpose flour
1/2	cup yellow cornmeal
2	Tbsp. sugar
1	Tbsp. baking powder
1/4	tsp. salt
1/4	tsp. ground cumin
1	egg
1/2	cup fat-free milk
1/4	cup reduced-fat sour cream
2/3	cup shredded reduced-fat Mexican cheese blend
2/3	cup chopped roasted sweet red peppers, patted dry
1	can (4 oz.) diced jalapeno peppers, drained

1. In a large bowl, combine the first six ingredients. In a small bowl, whisk the egg, milk and sour cream. Stir into dry ingredients just until moistened. Fold in the cheese, red peppers and jalapenos.

2. Coat muffin cups with cooking spray; fill three-fourths full with batter. Bake at 375° for 18-22 minutes or until a toothpick comes out clean. Cool for 5 minutes before removing from pan to a wire rack. Serve warm.

Nutrition Facts: 1 muffin equals 126 calories, 2 g fat (1 g saturated fat), 24 mg cholesterol, 281 mg sodium, 20 g carbohydrate, 1 g fiber, 5 g protein. **Diabetic Exchanges:** 1-1/2 starch, 1/2 fat.

Rich Mocha Cake

PREP: 25 min. + cooling **BAKE:** 40 min. **YIELD:** 16 servings

HEALTHY COOKING TEST KITCHEN

Here's a decadent chocolate cake flavored with cinnamon, coffee and Kahlua, then topped with a rich, fudgy frosting.

3	Tbsp. instant coffee granules
2	Tbsp. boiling water
4	eggs
3/4	cup buttermilk
1/2	cup plus 2 Tbsp. Kahlua, *divided*
3	Tbsp. canola oil
2	tsp. vanilla extract
1-1/2	cups all-purpose flour
3/4	cup sugar
2/3	cup baking cocoa
1/2	cup packed brown sugar
1	tsp. salt
1	tsp. baking powder
1	tsp. baking soda
1/4	tsp. ground cinnamon

RED PEPPER JALAPENO MUFFINS

RICH MOCHA CAKE

CHICKEN TACOS WITH PINEAPPLE PICO DE GALLO

ICING:

- 2 squares (1 oz. *each*) semisweet chocolate, chopped
- 2 Tbsp. sweetened condensed milk
- 3 to 4 tsp. Kahlua

1. In a small bowl, dissolve coffee granules in boiling water. In a large mixing bowl, beat the eggs, buttermilk, 1/2 cup Kahlua, oil, vanilla and coffee mixture until well blended. Combine the dry ingredients; gradually beat into egg mixture until blended.

2. Coat a 10-in. fluted tube pan with cooking spray and sprinkle with flour; add batter. Bake at 325° for 40-48 minutes or until a toothpick inserted near the center comes out clean. Cool for 10 minutes before removing from pan to a wire rack. Cool 15 minutes longer; brush with remaining Kahlua. Cool completely.

3. In a small microwave-safe bowl, melt chocolate with milk; stir until smooth. Stir in enough Kahlua to achieve a spreading consistency. Spread over top of cake.

Nutrition Facts: 1 slice equals 224 calories, 6 g fat (1 g saturated fat), 54 mg cholesterol, 286 mg sodium, 36 g carbohydrate, 1 g fiber, 4 g protein.

Chicken Tacos with Pineapple Pico de Gallo

PREP/TOTAL TIME: 30 min. **YIELD:** 4 servings

JENNY FLAKE • GILBERT, ARIZONA

This recipe is not only light and tasty, but also absolutely delicious. The pineapple and mango add great taste to these zesty chicken tacos.

- 1 cup chopped fresh pineapple
- 1/2 cup chopped peeled mango
- 2 Tbsp. minced fresh cilantro
- 1 Tbsp. finely chopped red onion
- 1 Tbsp. lime juice
- 3/4 tsp. salt, *divided*
- 2 cups cubed cooked chicken breast
- 1/2 tsp. ground cumin
- 1/4 tsp. salt-free garlic seasoning blend
- 8 corn tortillas (6 in.), warmed

1. For pico de gallo, in a small bowl, combine the pineapple, mango, cilantro, onion, lime juice and 1/4 teaspoon salt. Set aside.

2. In a large nonstick skillet coated with cooking spray, cook and stir the chicken, cumin, seasoning blend and remaining salt until heated through. Spoon 1/4 cup onto each tortilla. Serve with pico de gallo.

Nutrition Facts: 2 tacos with 1/3 cup pico de gallo equals 257 calories, 4 g fat (1 g saturated fat), 54 mg cholesterol, 572 mg sodium, 33 g carbohydrate, 4 g fiber, 24 g protein. **Diabetic Exchanges:** 3 very lean meat, 1-1/2 starch, 1/2 fruit.

Celebrating **Cinco de Mayo?** Decorate your table with bright tissue-paper flowers and hollowed-out yellow, orange, red and green bell peppers with tea-light candles inside. Don't forget to crank up the mariachi music.

Celebrate Summer

Fire up the grill, grab a cold beverage and enjoy a backyard barbecue that's full of the flavors you've craved all winter. Mouth-watering burgers, colorful kabobs and a refreshing slaw are a few of the specialities you'll find here.

Glazed Roasted Pineapple S

PREP: 15 min. **BAKE:** 35 min. **YIELD:** 6 servings

AGNES WARD • STRATFORD, ONTARIO

These delightful pineapple slices have a wonderful aroma. Raspberry sorbet is an ideal accompaniment, but you could serve the pineapple with other sorbet flavors, too.

1	fresh pineapple
2	Tbsp. butter, melted
1/4	cup packed brown sugar
2	Tbsp. honey
1/2	tsp. pumpkin pie spice *or* ground cinnamon
1/4	tsp. rum extract
3/4	cup raspberry sorbet

1. Peel pineapple; cut into six wedges. Cut wedges lengthwise to remove the core; cut each widthwise into four pieces. Pour butter into a 2-qt. baking dish; top with pineapple. Combine the brown sugar, honey, pie spice and extract; spoon over the pineapple.

2. Bake, uncovered, at 400° for 35-40 minutes or until golden brown. Spoon cooking juices over the top. Serve warm with sorbet.

Nutrition Facts: 4 pineapple pieces with 2 tablespoons sorbet equals 159 calories, 4 g fat (2 g saturated fat), 10 mg cholesterol, 43 mg sodium, 32 g carbohydrate, 1 g fiber, trace protein. **Diabetic Exchanges:** 1 starch, 1 fruit, 1 fat.

GLAZED ROASTED PINEAPPLE

Grilled Veggie Kabobs M

PREP/TOTAL TIME: 30 min. **YIELD:** 4 kabobs

KATHY FRANKLIN • ANTIOCH, TENNESSEE

Serve this colorful side dish with any meal this summer! Simple, fresh and fast, it'll perk up any dinner plate in no time. Add large, whole mushrooms if you'd like.

2	medium ears sweet corn, husked and cut into 1-in. pieces
1	large sweet onion, cut into 16 wedges
1	*each* medium green, sweet red and yellow peppers, cut into 1-in. pieces
1	Tbsp. olive oil
1	tsp. chili powder
3/4	tsp. seasoned salt
1/2	tsp. sugar

1. Coat grill rack with cooking spray before starting the grill. On four metal or soaked wooden skewers, alternately thread the corn, onion and peppers. Brush kabobs with oil. Combine the chili powder, salt and sugar; sprinkle over kabobs.

2. Grill, covered, over medium heat for 10-12 minutes or until crisp-tender, turning occasionally.

Nutrition Facts: 1 kabob equals 122 calories, 4 g fat (1 g saturated fat), 0 cholesterol, 302 mg sodium, 21 g carbohydrate, 4 g fiber, 3 g protein. **Diabetic Exchanges:** 2 vegetable, 1 fat, 1/2 starch.

Orange Fruit Slaw F S

PREP/TOTAL TIME: 20 min. **YIELD:** 6 servings

CYNTHIA FRANCE • MURRAY, UTAH

I love this fruity coleslaw. My neighbor shared it with our women's church group a few years ago, and it's been a favorite in my recipe box ever since. If you want to get creative, try it with different flavors of low-fat yogurt.

3	cups shredded cabbage
1	medium navel orange, peeled and sectioned
1	cup seedless red grapes, halved
1	medium apple, chopped
1/2	cup finely chopped celery
1	carton (6 oz.) reduced-fat orange yogurt
1/4	tsp. salt
1/8	tsp. pepper
1/4	cup slivered almonds, toasted

1. In a large bowl, combine the cabbage, orange, grapes, apple and celery.

CHUTNEY TURKEY BURGERS

GRILLED VEGGIE KABOBS

2. Stir in the yogurt, salt and pepper; toss until well coated. Cover and refrigerate until serving. Sprinkle with almonds just before serving.

Nutrition Facts: 3/4 cup equals 104 calories, 3 g fat (trace saturated fat), 1 mg cholesterol, 133 mg sodium, 18 g carbohydrate, 3 g fiber, 3 g protein. **Diabetic Exchanges:** 1 starch, 1/2 fat.

Chutney Turkey Burgers

PREP/TOTAL TIME: 20 min. **YIELD:** 4 servings

JEANNE LUEDERS • WATERLOO, IOWA

The secret to these burgers is the tangy mango chutney I use, but the arugula adds a special "wow" to the plate. I get lots of compliments when I serve these at summer and fall cookouts.

- 1/2 cup chutney, *divided*
- 1 Tbsp. Dijon mustard
- 2 tsp. lime juice
- 1/4 cup minced fresh parsley
- 2 green onions, chopped
- 1/2 tsp. salt
- 1/4 tsp. pepper
- 1 lb. lean ground turkey
- 4 hamburger buns, split
- 16 fresh arugula *or* baby spinach leaves
- 4 slices red onion

1. Combine 1/4 cup chutney, mustard and lime juice; set aside. In a large bowl, combine the parsley, onions, salt, pepper and remaining chutney. Crumble turkey over mixture and mix well. Shape into four patties.

2. Coat grill rack with cooking spray before starting the grill. Grill burgers, covered, over medium heat for 5-7 minutes on each side or until a meat thermometer reads 165° and juices run clear. Serve on buns with arugula, onion and reserved chutney mixture.

Nutrition Facts: 1 burger equals 359 calories, 12 g fat (3 g saturated fat), 90 mg cholesterol, 749 mg sodium, 38 g carbohydrate, 3 g fiber, 25 g protein. **Diabetic Exchanges:** 3 lean meat, 2-1/2 starch.

Get the blanket and a basket, and claim a spot in the sun. These recipes feature "travel-ability" while keeping flavor at the forefront. Whether you pair this menu with wine or iced tea, it will make any meal feel like a special occasion.

Honey-Balsamic Goat Cheese Dip C M

PREP/TOTAL TIME: 10 min.
YIELD: 8 servings (3/4 cup dip)

JONI HILTON • ROCKLIN, CALIFORNIA

This is so easy and delicious, you can't stop eating it. And at just 5 grams of fat per serving, you don't have to feel guilty.

- 4 oz. goat cheese, crumbled
- 1/3 cup fat-free mayonnaise
- 2 Tbsp. honey
- 1 Tbsp. balsamic vinegar
- 1 medium apple, cut into 16 slices
- 8 slices French bread (1/4 in. thick)

1. In a small mixing bowl, beat the goat cheese, mayonnaise, honey and vinegar until smooth. Serve with apple and bread slices.

Nutrition Facts: 4-1/2 teaspoons dip with 2 apple slices and 1 slice bread equals 101 calories, 5 g fat (3 g saturated fat), 12 mg cholesterol, 189 mg sodium, 12 g carbohydrate, 1 g fiber, 4 g protein. **Diabetic Exchanges:** 1 starch, 1 fat.

HONEY-BALSAMIC GOAT CHEESE DIP

Chocolate Chip Cookies

PREP: 15 min. **BAKE:** 10 min./batch **YIELD:** 4 dozen

BETHANY THAYER • TROUTVILLE, VIRGINIA

I came up with this recipe after trying several low-fat chocolate chip cookies that were puffy and cake-like. Good-for-you walnuts give them a great crunch, too.

- 1/2 cup reduced-fat margarine
- 3/4 cup sugar
- 3/4 cup packed brown sugar
- 2 eggs
- 1/4 cup fat-free plain yogurt
- 2 tsp. vanilla extract
- 2-1/2 cups all-purpose flour
- 1 tsp. baking soda
- 1 tsp. salt
- 1-1/2 cups miniature semisweet chocolate chips
- 1/2 cup chopped walnuts, toasted

1. In a large mixing bowl, lightly cream the margarine and sugars. Add eggs, one at a time, beating well after each addition. Beat in yogurt and vanilla. Combine the flour, baking soda and salt; gradually add to creamed mixture. Stir in chocolate chips and walnuts.

2. Drop by heaping tablespoonfuls 2 in. apart onto baking sheets coated with cooking spray. Bake at 375° for 8-10 minutes or until golden brown. Remove to wire racks.

Editor's Note: This recipe was tested with Parkay Light stick margarine.

Nutrition Facts: 2 cookies equals 190 calories, 7 g fat (2 g saturated fat), 18 mg cholesterol, 187 mg sodium, 30 g carbohydrate, 1 g fiber, 3 g protein. **Diabetic Exchanges:** 2 starch, 1/2 fat.

AMARETTO CHEESE-FILLED APRICOTS

Mediterranean Chicken Salad c

PREP/TOTAL TIME: 25 min. **YIELD:** 6 servings

AMY LEWIS • CARMICHAEL, CALIFORNIA

This is a variation on two different salads I like. My family especially enjoys this when it's warm outside.

3	cups cubed cooked chicken breast
1-1/2	cups chopped tomatoes
1	cup water-packed artichoke hearts, rinsed, drained and quartered
1/2	cup crumbled feta cheese
1/2	cup pitted Greek olives
1/3	cup dried currants
1/4	cup finely chopped red onion

DRESSING:

1/4	cup olive oil
2	Tbsp. tarragon vinegar
1	Tbsp. minced fresh tarragon *or* 1 tsp. dried tarragon
1-1/2	tsp. lemon juice
1-1/2	tsp. Dijon mustard
1/4	tsp. salt
1/8	tsp. pepper

1. In a large bowl, combine the first seven ingredients. In a small bowl, whisk the dressing ingredients.

2. Pour over chicken mixture and toss to coat. Refrigerate until serving.

Nutrition Facts: 1 cup equals 291 calories, 16 g fat (3 g saturated fat), 59 mg cholesterol, 544 mg sodium, 12 g carbohydrate, 2 g fiber, 24 g protein. **Diabetic Exchanges:** 3 lean meat, 2 fat, 1 vegetable, 1/2 fruit.

Amaretto Cheese-Filled Apricots F S C M

PREP/TOTAL TIME: 30 min. **YIELD:** about 2 dozen

YVONNE STARLIN • PORTLAND, TENNESSEE

I had these at a party and thought they were excellent. You get lots of sweet flavor in one little bite!

1	pkg. (6 oz.) dried pitted Mediterranean apricots
4	oz. fat-free cream cheese
1/2	cup finely chopped almonds, toasted, *divided*
1/4	cup dried cherries, finely chopped
2	Tbsp. amaretto *or* 1/2 tsp. almond extract plus 5 tsp. orange juice

1. Gently loosen a long side of each apricot, splitting apricots to resemble clamshells. In a small mixing bowl, beat the cream cheese, 1/4 cup almonds, cherries and amaretto until blended. Spoon 1-1/4 teaspoons filling into each apricot.

2. Place remaining almonds in a small shallow dish; roll exposed cheese portions of apricots in nuts.

Nutrition Facts: 1 filled apricot equals 42 calories, 1 g fat (trace saturated fat), trace cholesterol, 30 mg sodium, 7 g carbohydrate, 1 g fiber, 1 g protein.

Few holidays are marked by such an abundance of decadent food as Thanksgiving.
No one wants to miss out on the classic recipes that make this meal so
special...and with this incredible lineup of traditional tastes, no one has to!

Cranberry-Orange Roasted Turkey

PREP: 30 min. **BAKE:** 3 hours
YIELD: 28 servings (3-1/2 cups sauce)

KARA DE LA VEGA • SANTA ROSA, CALIFORNIA

You'll add an elegant centerpiece to your meal with this tender, juicy turkey. The cranberry sauce makes it so good. It has such a wonderful aroma and flavor.

3	tsp. garlic powder
1/2	tsp. salt
1/2	tsp. pepper
1	turkey (14 lbs.)
1	medium orange
1	can (16 oz.) whole-berry cranberry sauce
3/4	cup reduced-sodium teriyaki sauce
1/2	cup honey
1/2	cup orange marmalade
2	Tbsp. reduced-sodium soy sauce
4	sprigs fresh herbs, such as thyme, rosemary, parsley and sage
2	medium onions, cut into wedges

1. Combine the garlic powder, salt and pepper. With fingers, carefully loosen skin from the turkey breast; spread half of garlic powder mixture under the skin. Sprinkle skin with remaining mixture.

2. Juice the orange, reserving the rind. In a large bowl, combine the cranberry sauce, teriyaki sauce, honey, marmalade, soy sauce and orange juice. Cover and refrigerate 3-1/2 cups mixture for sauce. Rub remaining mixture under the skin. Secure skin to underside of breast with toothpicks. Place herb sprigs and reserved orange rind in turkey cavity.

3. Arrange onions in a shallow roasting pan coated with cooking spray. Place turkey over onions. Bake, uncovered, at 325° for 3 to 3-1/2 hours or until a meat thermometer reads 180°. (Cover loosely with foil if turkey browns too quickly.) Cover and let stand for 15 minutes before carving.

4. Discard herb sprigs and orange before slicing. Place reserved sauce in a large saucepan; heat through. Serve with turkey.

Nutrition Facts: 4 ounces cooked turkey (calculated without skin) with 2 tablespoons sauce equals 257 calories, 6 g fat (2 g saturated fat), 86 mg cholesterol, 308 mg sodium, 17 g carbohydrate, trace fiber, 34 g protein. **Diabetic Exchanges:** 5 very lean meat, 1 starch, 1 fat.

CRANBERRY-ORANGE ROASTED TURKEY

Holiday Lettuce Salad ⬛S ⬛M

PREP/TOTAL TIME: 20 min. **YIELD:** 14 servings

BRYAN BRAACK • ELDRIDGE, IOWA

My family always requests that I make this salad for holiday get-togethers. It's light and very tasty; everyone always goes back for seconds.

10	cups torn romaine
2	medium red apples, cubed
2	medium pears, cubed
1	cup (4 oz.) shredded Swiss cheese
1/2	cup dried cranberries
6	Tbsp. lemon juice
3	Tbsp. canola oil
3	Tbsp. light corn syrup
1-1/2	tsp. grated onion
1-1/2	tsp. Dijon mustard
1/2	tsp. salt
1/2	cup chopped lightly salted cashews

1. In a salad bowl, combine the first five ingredients.

2. For dressing, in a small bowl, whisk the lemon juice, oil, corn syrup, onion, mustard and salt. Pour

TRADITIONAL HOLIDAY STUFFING

over romaine mixture; toss to coat. Sprinkle with cashews. Serve immediately.

Nutrition Facts: 1 cup equals 144 calories, 8 g fat (2 g saturated fat), 7 mg cholesterol, 134 mg sodium, 17 g carbohydrate, 3 g fiber, 4 g protein. **Diabetic Exchanges:** 1-1/2 fat, 1 starch, 1 vegetable.

Traditional Holiday Stuffing

PREP: 35 min. **BAKE:** 45 min. **YIELD:** 24 servings

LORRAINE BRAUCKHOFF • ZOLFO SPRINGS, FLORIDA

Sausage and sage add a gourmet taste to this stuffing. It's perfect for large family gatherings, but no one would complain if you set some away for later.

1	pkg. (12 oz.) reduced-fat bulk pork sausage *or* breakfast turkey sausage links, casings removed
3	celery ribs, chopped
1	large onion, chopped
2	Tbsp. reduced-fat mayonnaise
2	Tbsp. prepared mustard
4	tsp. rubbed sage
1	Tbsp. poultry seasoning
2	loaves (16 oz. *each*) day-old white bread, cubed
1	loaf (16 oz.) day-old whole wheat bread, cubed
3	eggs, lightly beaten
2	cans (14-1/2 oz. *each*) reduced-sodium chicken broth

1. In a large nonstick skillet coated with cooking spray, cook the sausage, celery and onion over medium heat until meat is no longer pink; drain. Remove from the heat; stir in the mayonnaise, mustard, sage and poultry seasoning.

2. Place bread cubes in a large bowl; add sausage mixture. Combine eggs and broth; pour over bread cubes and stir gently to combine. Transfer to two 3-qt. baking dishes coated with cooking spray.

3. Cover and bake at 350° for 30 minutes. Uncover; bake 12-18 minutes longer or until lightly browned and a thermometer reads 160°.

Editor's Note: If using this recipe to stuff poultry, replace the eggs with 3/4 cup egg substitute. Bake until a meat thermometer reads 180° for poultry and 165° for stuffing. Allow 3/4 cup stuffing per pound of turkey. Bake remaining stuffing as the recipe directs.

Nutrition Facts: 3/4 cup equals 202 calories, 6 g fat (2 g saturated fat), 37 mg cholesterol, 572 mg sodium, 28 g carbohydrate, 2 g fiber, 9 g protein. **Diabetic Exchanges:** 2 starch, 1 fat.

With 6 grams of fat per serving Traditional Holiday Stuffing offers 16 grams less than most stuffing recipes.

Merry & Light

At Christmas, everyone craves those time-honored recipes we've come to expect. This year, smarten up your holiday table with sensational delights that pare down calories, fat and sodium a tad. You just may discover a few new additions to your Yuletide lineup.

Holiday Green Beans S C

PREP: 40 min. **BAKE:** 15 min. **YIELD:** 12 servings

LAURA FALL-SUTTON • BUHL, IDAHO

No one will ever know that this holiday staple is low in calories! Try this perked-up green bean casserole this year, and you'll never go back to another version again.

8	cups cut fresh green beans (about 2 lbs.)
1/2	lb. sliced fresh mushrooms
2	Tbsp. butter
2	Tbsp. all-purpose flour
1	tsp. dried minced onion
1/2	tsp. pepper
1/2	cup fat-free milk
1	cup reduced-fat sour cream
1	tsp. Worcestershire sauce
1-1/2	cups (6 oz.) shredded reduced-fat Swiss cheese

TOPPING:
1/3	cup slivered almonds
1/3	cup crushed cornflakes
1	Tbsp. butter, melted

1. Place beans in a Dutch oven and cover with water; bring to a boil. Cover and cook for 3-5 minutes or until crisp-tender; drain and set aside.

2. In a large skillet, saute mushrooms in butter until tender. Stir in the flour, onion and pepper until blended. Gradually stir in milk. Bring to a boil; cook and stir for 1-2 minutes or until thickened. Remove from the heat; stir in sour cream and Worcestershire sauce. Stir in beans and cheese until blended.

3. Transfer to an 11-in. x 7-in. baking dish coated with cooking spray (dish will be full). Combine topping ingredients; sprinkle over the top. Bake, uncovered, at 400° for 12-16 minutes or until bubbly and heated through.

Nutrition Facts: 2/3 cup equals 144 calories, 7 g fat (3 g saturated fat), 20 mg cholesterol, 108 mg sodium, 12 g carbohydrate, 3 g fiber, 9 g protein. **Diabetic Exchanges:** 1 lean meat, 1 vegetable, 1 fat, 1/2 starch.

Cranberry-Glazed Ham

PREP: 10 min. **BAKE:** 1 hour 35 min. **YIELD:** 15 servings

JONI PETERSON • WICHITA, KANSAS

That showstopping entree you've been hoping for is right here, and it takes only five ingredients to prepare. The sweet and tangy cranberry glaze pairs beautifully with ham.

1	can (16 oz.) whole-berry cranberry sauce
1/2	cup maple syrup
1/4	cup cider vinegar
1	to 1-1/2 tsp. ground mustard
1	boneless fully cooked ham (5 lbs.)

HERBED MONKEY BREAD

HOLIDAY GREEN BEANS

CRANBERRY-GLAZED HAM

1. In a small bowl, combine the cranberry sauce, syrup, vinegar and mustard. Set aside 1 cup mixture for sauce.

2. Line a shallow roasting pan with foil. Place ham on a rack in prepared pan. Cover and bake at 325° for 1 hour. Baste with some of the remaining cranberry mixture; bake 35-45 minutes longer or until a meat thermometer reads 140°, basting with additional mixture every 10 minutes. Heat reserved sauce; serve with ham.

Nutrition Facts: 5 ounces cooked ham with about 1 tablespoon sauce equals 233 calories, 6 g fat (2 g saturated fat), 77 mg cholesterol, 1,576 mg sodium, 19 g carbohydrate, trace fiber, 28 g protein.

Herbed Monkey Bread M

PREP: 30 min. + rising **BAKE:** 30 min.
YIELD: 1 loaf (32 pieces)

JOAN HALLFORD • NORTH RICHLAND HILLS, TEXAS

This bread gives your house a wonderful aroma while it bakes. The combination of herbs and seasonings makes it irresistible. In fact, it's my most-requested recipe.

3	to 3-1/2 cups all-purpose flour
2	Tbsp. sugar
1	tsp. salt
1	pkg. (1/4 oz.) active dry yeast
1-1/4	cups fat-free milk
2	Tbsp. canola oil
4	Tbsp. butter, melted, *divided*
1	egg
2	Tbsp. grated Parmesan cheese
1	Tbsp. sesame seeds
1/2	tsp. garlic salt
1/2	tsp. paprika
1/2	tsp. *each* dried parsley flakes, thyme and rosemary, crushed

1. In a large mixing bowl, combine 2 cups flour, sugar, salt and yeast. In a small saucepan, heat the milk, oil and 2 tablespoons butter to 120°-130°. Add to dry ingredients; beat just until moistened. Add egg; beat until smooth. Stir in enough remaining flour to form a soft dough.

2. Turn onto a lightly floured surface and knead until smooth and elastic, about 6-8 minutes. Place in a bowl coated with cooking spray, turning once to coat the top. Cover and let rise in a warm place until doubled, about 1 hour.

3. In a small bowl, combine the cheese, sesame seeds, garlic salt, paprika and herbs. Punch dough down. Divide into 32 pieces; roll each into a ball.

4. Drizzle 2 teaspoons butter into a 10-in. tube pan coated with cooking spray; sprinkle with a third of the cheese mixture. Top with 16 balls. Repeat layers. Drizzle with remaining butter and sprinkle with remaining cheese mixture. Cover and let rise in a warm place until doubled, about 30 minutes.

5. Bake at 350° for 30-35 minutes or until golden brown. Cool for 10 minutes before removing from pan to a wire rack.

Nutrition Facts: 2 pieces equals 150 calories, 6 g fat (2 g saturated fat), 22 mg cholesterol, 260 mg sodium, 21 g carbohydrate, 1 g fiber, 4 g protein. **Diabetic Exchanges:** 1-1/2 starch, 1 fat.

General Recipe Index

This handy index lists every recipe by food category, major ingredient and/or cooking method, so you can easily locate recipes to suit your needs.

•*Table-ready in 30 minutes or less.*

Alphabetical Index

This handy index lists every recipe by food category, major ingredient and/or cooking method, so you can easily locate recipes to suit your needs.
•*Table-ready in 30 minutes or less.*

Reference Index

Use this index to locate the many recipe hints located throughout this book.